# A CORKSCREW IS
# MOST USEFUL

## *The Travellers of Empire*

## NICHOLAS MURRAY

Little, Brown

LITTLE, BROWN

First published in Great Britain in 2008 by Little, Brown

A CIP catalogue record for this book
is available from the British Library.

ISBN 978-0-316-73104-1

Typeset in Garamond by M Rules
Printed and bound in Great Britain by
Clays Ltd, St Ives plc

Little, Brown
An imprint of
Little, Brown Book Group
100 Victoria Embankment
London EC4Y 0DY

An Hachette Livre UK Company

www.littlebrown.co.uk

An irresistible desire to see the great world, to wander through strange countries, and to associate with barbarians who dwell far from the jostling and hurrying of civilization, prompted me to leave my English home at the age of fifteen, and to seek incident in a roving life far from my own kith and kin.

Herbert Ward *Five Years with the Congo Cannibals* (1890)

For S.

# CONTENTS

## PART THREE: THE MIDDLE EAST

## PART FOUR: CHINA AND JAPAN

## PART FIVE: AFRICA

## PART SIX: THE AMERICAS

## PART SEVEN: AUSTRALASIA

## PART EIGHT: THE POLAR REGIONS

## PART NINE: EUROPE, A CODA

# PART ONE
# INDIA

I

*Objects of Attraction: England through Indian Eyes*

On 29 March 1838 the *Buckinghamshire* fluttered its sails and began to glide slowly out of the harbour at Bombay. There were sixty passengers on board, fifteen of them children and most of the adults public servants and employees of the Honourable East India Company, going home to England on furlough, or leave. By the time they reached Gravesend five months later the new queen had been officially crowned at a ceremony in Westminster Abbey on 28 June.

A year earlier, in June 1837, when King William IV died and she realized that she was to be queen, Victoria had written in her private journal: 'Since it has pleased Providence to place me in this station, I shall do my utmost to fulfil my duty towards my country; I am very young, and perhaps in many, though not in all things, inexperienced, but I am sure that very few have more real good will and more real desire to do what is fit and right than I have.'

The authentic note of high moral earnestness had been sounded: the Victorian age was inaugurated.

On board the *Buckinghamshire* spirits were high among the British colonial servants at the prospect of return but there was one exception to the general scene of rejoicing. A small group of three Indian gentlemen of high caste and dressed in Parsee costume did not share the general merriment. They were 'very melancholy' at the thought of leaving their home for a period of three years: 'Every soul on board except ourselves, and some native seamen, were full of joy, with the anticipated pleasure of seeing their native land and the associates of their younger days. Our case indeed was different, we were leaving our birthplace for a strange country, and had exchanged homely comforts for the troubles of a long sea voyage. We gazed on the happy land we had just left till we could see it no longer.'

Jehangeer Nowrojee, Hirjeebhoy Merwanjee, their friend Dorabjee Muncherjee and two servants of their own caste would be away for nearly three years. Distinguished Bombay naval architects, Nowrojee and Merwanjee were son and nephew of Jamjetsee Nowrojee, master builder of the Honourable East India Company's dockyard in the city, which their family had founded in 1735. Five generations of Nowrojees had served the Company for over a century but now times were changing. Aware of the growing challenge of the new steamships, they were coming to England to study the art of steamship building. Failure to keep pace with technical innovation would destroy their business and they knew it.

When their ship finally arrived in mid-August they were fascinated by the mass of shipping entering the River Thames, which is but a stream compared to the Ganges and the Indus, or the still larger rivers of America. We thought it a great wonder that such a small and insignificant a speck as England appears on the map of the world, can thus attract so many of the nations of the world towards her . . . we will tell our countrymen that it is the persevering habits of the English, it is the labour and skill of that people, that is the cause of such attraction . . . it is by the power of knowledge *alone*, and not by the power of arms, that she has so many means of attracting the world to her, and extending the spread of her manufactures.

At Gravesend they stepped on board a steam vessel for the first time in their lives, for the thirty-mile trip to London. 'There were many people on board, and we were the objects of great attraction.' When they reached London Bridge a mob of nearly a thousand curious Londoners gathered to gaze on these strange men in their unusual dress. In the first of a series of neat reversals of the clichés of the English travelogue, Nowrojee and Merwanjee were stared at because of their appearance and overwhelmed, like modern visitors to Calcutta or Delhi, by the dense crowds they saw in the streets. On arriving in central London they were installed at the Portland Hotel and immediately taken off by their host, Sir Charles Forbes, to see the Diorama in Hyde Park and the Zoological Gardens in Regent's Park, where they found they were just as much an object of interest as the animals. 'It was amusing to hear one call us Chinese, they are Turks says another; no they are Spanish vociferates a third; thus they were labouring under mistakes, and taking inhabitants of British India for natives of Europe.'

Their observations, which were recorded in a *Journal of a Residence of Two Years and a Half in Great Britain* (1841), were shrewd. Taken to a reception in that hub of Empire, East India House in Leadenhall Street in the City of London: 'We were very much struck with the appearance of the India House, and we could not help remarking how much of the future happiness or the misery of the countless millions of India depended on the transactions carried on within the walls of this building.' At Madame Tussaud's they saw the fresh display depicting the Queen's coronation but were more interested in radical thinkers such as Wilberforce and Cobbett and the Enlightenment hero Voltaire: 'We looked much at him, thinking he must have had much courage, and have thought himself quite right in his belief to have stood opposed to all the existing religious systems of his native land.'

They were dazzled by the speed of the trains on the Great Western Railway (Paddington to Slough in a mere fifty minutes) and by such sights as the British Museum and the Parks, but they regretted to have to inform their countrymen that 'the majority of the lower orders in England are very rude in their manners and behaviour towards strangers whom they do not like to see in their own country'. They visited scientific institutions, bazaars and markets, even Thomas Flight's fourteen-acre dairy in Islington, where, behind high walls, could be seen four hundred cows that supplied milk for the capital: 'sleek as racehorses, and they are curried with a comb every day'.

The Indian visitors went into the Strangers' Gallery at the House of Commons to hear a great debate on the Irish question at which Daniel O'Connell, Robert Peel and Lord John Russell spoke: 'We consider it the most exciting eight or nine hours that we ever spent.' They visited a criminal court near the Guildhall: 'In a sort of pit below are a number of sallow-looking men, dressed in black gowns with powdered wigs with little tails, and these are called barristers.' At Windsor they were noticed by the Queen, and offered her salaams in return: 'We felt highly honoured in thus being noticed by our gracious sovereign, the greatest in the world.' They were generally amused at the propensity of the English to talk constantly about the weather and at the extraordinary importance they attached to their newspapers: 'We believe to very many, it is the greatest pleasure they have in life to get the newspaper at their breakfast in the morning, and it is laughable to see how immediately readers of a certain class adopt the opinions of the daily paper they take.'

But the real reason for their trip was to study ship-building and, as well as being given the run of the naval dockyard at Chatham, they made a tour of naval arsenals and Britain's principal ports. They were particularly impressed by the fact that the railway tunnel at Lime Street Station in Liverpool seemed to them to go under the town: 'Here then, again, is a remarkable proof of our frequent assertion, that the English are a most wonderful people.'

Much of the amusement of the *Journal of a Residence* naturally comes from witnessing the foreigner write about England in the way the English were to write so copiously about other countries. The 'strangeness' of strange countries, in the end, amounts to no more than the fact that they are not like our own, with the corollary that one person's strangeness is of course another person's normality. On such a slender basis the discreet charm of travel writing rests.

What follows is a book about journeys, and about some of the remarkable men and women who made those journeys, during one of the great ages of British travelling and exploration. Much of what they reported – ethnological, cartographical, geographical, historical – has long been superseded by the advance of specialist knowledge, but what remain vivid and fresh are their accounts of their travels. This is a book about *how* people travelled, about how they expressed their sense of what they saw. The language in which they wrote – and through which they so often unwittingly revealed themselves, frequently telling us more about themselves as Victorian Englishmen and Englishwomen than about the people and countries through which they passed – is at the heart of this book, and I have tried to convey the special flavour of Victorian travel writing by generous quotation from the writers themselves.

The field is vast. In the Topography section in the London Library's basement the shelves of nineteenth-century travelogues stretch seemingly into infinity. I have had to be ruthlessly selective. Certain important guests cannot of course be refused entry to this celebration – Richard Burton, Charles Doughty, Isabella Bird, Mary Kingsley, Charles Darwin, David Livingstone – but I have found room too for the far lesser known, even at the expense of excluding some famous names. I have also been very hard on writers whose primary reputations have been achieved in other literary fields. Trollope in America, Gissing by the Ionian Sea, Thackeray in the East, have been passed over in favour of other travellers in those regions. In the South Seas I have preferred the missionary John Williams to the perhaps more obvious choice of Robert Louis Stevenson. And, while trying to give at least something of a global picture of travel, my bias has been towards those parts of the map that were once shaded red.

Since it has been my aim to reflect the flavour and quiddity of particular journeys, drawing directly on published accounts of travels, I have ignored those travellers who wrote no accounts – though I was mindful of the fact that, as Paul Theroux put it recently, 'some of the most resourceful travellers I've known have never written a word, just kept moving alone across the world'. I have also brazenly elided the terms 'traveller' and 'explorer', my interest being simply in those who moved about countries other than their own and wrote about the experience, whatever the declared purpose. I have confined myself – not through provincialism or complacent xenophobia – to British travellers because it seems to me that British travel writing of this epoch constitutes a phase in the development of the English sensibility, that it reveals as much about the culture of the travellers as it does about the countries they made the object of their narratives.

Undoubtedly many Victorian travellers held views – and expressed them without inhibition – that are offensive now (and would have been offensive to indigenous people at the time). Overall their travels served the needs and reflected the aims and values of a major imperial power at its zenith. Maps were as much the record of acquisition and dominion as of dispassionate geographical knowledge. Ethnographic analysis helped the ruler in the task of ruling. Terms such as 'uncivilized' or 'savage' were universally deployed, even in contexts that were not intended to be derogatory. They show how great a distance stretched between the imperial traveller, however knowledgeable and even well-meaning, and the local peoples he or she encountered. The latter were not equals and they served the needs of a power that saw itself as pursuing a 'civilizing' mission as well as a frankly self-interested one. At its worst – as in Sir Richard Burton's repellent treatise 'On the Negro's Place in Nature' – the tone was plainly racist. But the same man could write elsewhere of the British as 'a nation of strangers, aliens to the country's customs and creed, who, even while resident in India, act the part which absentees do in other lands. Where, in the history of the world, do we read that such foreign dominion ever made itself popular?'

In short, the picture is particular and nuanced. Contradictions show themselves within travellers and even within the pages of a given travel narrative. I have sought, above all, to give some of that particular flavour, that sense of the specificity of travel and the individual traveller's experience, by drawing directly on what they said, in their own idiom, in their time.

Who, then, were the Victorian travellers? Generalizations about such a highly individualistic group of men and women are perilous but at the same time there is no doubt that they had some marked common characteristics. They were the product of their times and of their culture, which determined in large measure the way in which they travelled, the way they expressed themselves about what they saw, the questions they asked themselves and sought to answer. They travelled for many different purposes, spurred on by very different causes. They were not an organized group, though some of the leading explorers – Burton and Speke, Livingstone and Stanley – did collaborate or interact with one another, either in the field or in the meeting rooms of the Royal Geographical Society in London. Then, as now, extended travel was the privilege of those with the means and leisure to pursue it. Victorian travel writing was not a branch of proletarian literature. Although there is an occasional outbreak of sympathy or understanding for the experience of subject peoples, these writers were Victorians at the height of the British Empire and seldom doubted either their right to be where they were or the justice of the imperial 'civilizing mission'.

The travellers in the present book have been selected not for an illusory goal of 'representativeness' but precisely to capture the range and diversity and sheer quirkiness of these men and women. There is, however, no escaping history.

From about 1830 onwards Britain was the world's leading industrial and commercial power and its overseas empire was expanding and consolidating. Travellers and explorers were part of this phenomenon. Britain produced more explorers and exploration than any other leading power in the nineteenth century. Some kinds of exploration, for example the obsession with locating the source of the Nile, had as much to do with national pride as with scientific discovery, and exploration was an important means of consolidating Britain's public image in the world. Later chapters will show how organizations such as the Royal Geographical Society, which gradually took over from the Admiralty as the chief organizer and promoter of journeys of exploration in the Victorian period, masterminded this huge surge of travel.

As well as markets to be created and colonies to be administered, and the radical changes in the very means of travel – railways and steamships – the reasons for leaving England were as many as there were travellers themselves. Some were searching for knowledge, some were searching for themselves, some were driven by a sheer taste for adventure, some liked killing wild animals in large quantities, some were soldiers, sailors, spies, scholars, scientists, some sought physical health for sick bodies ailing in the pallid drawing rooms of stuffy Victorian England, some were interested in acquiring archaeological specimens and ancient works of art, often at bargain prices, some wished to convert the heathen and spread the gospel, some wanted to draw and to paint, some wished simply to do something while spouses discharged the white man's burden under a whirling punkah, some wished for fame, some wished to be the first to discover a tract of land, a lake, a river source, a passage through the ice, an unknown inland sea, and some travelled, as people have always travelled, for no reason at all but sheer enjoyment.

In spite of improvements in the means of travel the journeys explored in the following chapters were often very tough and required great courage. Particularly toxic for Europeans was Equatorial Africa – the notorious White Man's Grave – and tropical diseases made short work of many a venturesome explorer to the region. Children, spouses, friends regularly perished, sometimes with appalling swiftness. And there was the sheer difficulty of moving across difficult terrain, marshalling, for long periods, teams of local bearers and assistants, whose loyalty in all cases to the imperial traveller could not automatically be assured. The leader of an expedition was in a lonely and dangerous position: he or she had to maintain morale (often in profoundly discouraging circumstances), keep the party moving on, even if the next day was uncertain, the future veiled, and negotiate a path through unknown and often hostile country. Even travellers in less dangerous places and climates, in the heart of Europe itself, had to contend with challenges and hardships unknown to the modern traveller in a global playground where modern comforts are taken for granted.

Travellers were not slow to take advantage of changes occurring in Victorian society. Many played to the gallery, like Stanley, dramatizing themselves and their exploits, turning themselves into national heroes and public celebrities, publishing often lucrative, best-selling accounts of their travels. Publishers like John Murray catered to the demand for more and more travel narratives from the Victorian reading public. Journals like the *Edinburgh Quarterly*, *Westminster*, *Macmillan's* and *Athenaeum* published articles and accounts. The *Illustrated London News* brought graphic reports of explorations to a wider public.

A particularly flourishing genre was the missionary account which combined adventure and a high moral tone in pleasing proportions. By the end of the nineteenth century, it has been estimated, ten thousand British missionaries were working outside Europe and many wrote up their experiences. Missionary texts paralleled the imperial imperative (that underlay most secular accounts of travel and exploration in the period) to bring light into darkness, establish the triumph of white over black, civilize the barbarian and tame the savage.

As one historian, Robert Stafford, concluded in *The Oxford History of the British Empire*: 'Exploration thus became an important part of the process of imperialism, for even when it did not lead directly to annexation, it enclosed vast tracts of the periphery, including their inhabitants and resources, within Europe's purview . . . The narratives, as much as the explorations they chronicled, constituted acts of possession that legitimized and encouraged territorial control.'

No innocence, then, in these travellers' accounts but a great deal of variety, colour, surprise, excitement, even humour.

## 2

## *Exploring Holes and Corners: Emma Roberts*

At 10 a.m. on 1 September 1839 a plump, middle-aged woman embarked at Tower Stairs on the Thames on board the hundred-ton French steamship the *Phénix* for Le Havre. Her ultimate destination was Bombay.

'To the majority of readers, in these days of universal travelling,' Emma Roberts would write in her account of that journey, 'it will be superfluous to describe a steamboat.' It was, however, her first voyage on such a vessel after a lifetime of sailing packets, 'and though the tremulous motion and the stamping of the engine are anything but agreeable, I prefer it to the violent rolling and pitching of a sailing vessel.'

One of the more interesting and lively of the early nineteenth-century travellers in India, Roberts held the conviction that at this time India was insufficiently known and that it was her task to remedy that defect. In a short guide for the benefit of those thinking of following her example by heading East, *The East India Voyager or Ten Minutes Advice to the Outward Bound* (1839), Emma Roberts claimed that this 'large and most important territory belonging to Great Britain in the East is comparatively neglected'. Her notion was that enterprising women like herself should seize the opportunity to pursue 'a career of adventure in the Honourable Company's territories'. Dissatisfied with existing accounts and guides written by military men and servants of the Crown, she declared: 'The want of sympathy, but too frequently manifested by Europeans with the natives of India, in all cases when not proceeding from malevolence of disposition, arises from ignorance of their true character, and the claims they possess to a higher degree of consideration, and that such ignorance should exist at all is much to be lamented, especially when there are so many noble examples which shew that it must entirely originate in idleness or apathy.'

Roberts's writing is peppered with passages of this kind which rebuke the (generally male) Anglo-Indian settler for his ignorance of or hostility towards local culture. Her sharp tongue, however, did not prevent her from giving vent to occasional prejudices of her own.

It was natural that India, the jewel in the crown of the British Empire, should attract the interest of British travel writers and the public they catered for. Avoiding mostly the savage jungle encounters and heroic penetration into dark interiors that characterized the narratives of the African explorers, the Indian travellers tended to focus more on social mores, customs, scenery and landscape and, of course, colonial life. Many of the travellers were colonial administrators or officials or their spouses. They tended to pursue the familiar theme of knowledge as power, gathering facts and figures in order to be more efficient rulers and retainers of imperial sway. They reflected the changes in the British approach to India in the Victorian period, which tended to swing between the poles of anglicization and acknowledgement of degrees of native difference. The former is embodied in the notorious *Minute on Education* recorded by Lord Macaulay in 1835, mentioned below, in which he said that 'a single shelf of a good European library was worth the whole native literature of India and Arabia'. These attitudes were also shared by early missionaries who wanted to extirpate indigenous ways and replace them with Western Christianity. But after the trauma of the Indian Mutiny of 1857 the British came to believe that perhaps they needed to understand the native mind a little better. The travellers' accounts presented here, while at times displaying European prejudice, some decidedly so, nevertheless at their best amounted to an attempt to understand what lay around them.

Emma Roberts was born on 27 March 1791 in London but came

from what her first memoirist called 'a Welsh family of great respectability', her grandfather having been High Sheriff of Denbighshire. His three sons were all in the army, the eldest having in his time officiated as Gold Stick in Waiting to George the Third. Emma's father, William, the youngest son, died in service. After her father's death she lived with her widowed mother in Bath. Emma's first work, a history of the rival houses of York and Lancaster published in 1827, did not, as her anonymous memoirist puts it tactfully, 'take hold of public attention'. Soon after her mother's death she found herself sailing to India, in February 1828, on the *Sir David Scott* with her sister, who had just married Captain MacNaghten, who was bound for the Bengal Army. 'There cannot be a more wretched situation,' she later wrote, 'than that of a young woman in India who has been induced to follow the fortunes of her married sister under the delusive expectation that she will exchange the privations attached to limited means in England for the far-famed luxuries of the East.'

In fact Roberts turned this predicament into an opportunity to witness Anglo-Indian society at a certain angle. She would spend 1829 and 1830 in the Upper Provinces, at the military stations of Agra, Cawnpore and Etawah, but when she returned to Calcutta after her sister's death in October 1830 her literary career began in earnest. She was an industrious writer of poems, sketches, travelogues and essays and edited a newspaper in Calcutta called the *Oriental Observer* and later another, the *Bombay United Service Gazette*. Overwork finally persuaded her to return to London, where she wrote widely on history, biography, topography and cookery. She claimed that her volume of poems *Oriental Scenes* was the first book of poetry written by a British woman in India.

Roberts's first book about India, *Scenes and Characteristics of Hindostan*, appeared in 1835 and was a compilation of many sketches that had already appeared in periodical form at home and that had proved very popular. She described the life of Calcutta and its manners and customs with a keen eye for detail, her instinctive sympathy not preventing her from expressing criticisms of the social torpor and stifling conventions of Anglo-Indian life. A woman, she believed, 'must possess the courage of an Amazon to attempt any innovation upon ancient customs, amid such bigoted people as the Indians, Anglo and native'. Even the slowly circulating punkah, that iconic image of tropical languor, was not spared her trenchant assessment:

> The punkah also is very inimical to occupation; there is no possibility of enduring existence out of the reach of the influence of this enormous fan, and while it is waving to and fro, weights are requisite to secure every light article upon the table: should they be unadvisably removed, away flies the whole apparatus to different parts of the room, and the degree of irritability produced by trifling circumstances of this nature, superadded to the excessive heat and the perpetual buzzing and stinging of musquitoes, can scarcely be imagined by those who have never experienced the difficulty of pursuing any employment under the infliction of so many annoyances.

Roberts soon decided to quit this static society for a journey to a large outlying station where she intended to spend the rainy season. Victorian travellers had no conception of travelling light and twelve camels were required to transport Emma, her female travelling companion and her baggage: 'Our train consisted of a *khansamah* [head servant], who had the direction of the whole journey, three *khidmutghars* [attendants], a *sirdar-bearer* [valet], the tailor, the washerman, the water-carrier, the cook and *mussaulchees* [scullions], twelve bearers for each palanquin, and *claishees* [tent-pitchers], *banghie-bearers* [box bearers] and *coolies* almost innumerable.' She knew so little Hindi that she could not have very much conversation with her servants. Some of these would go on ahead with tents so that the rest of the party could lunch – sometimes quite luxuriously – at noon under canvas and move on to find, at the end of the day, tents pitched and waiting for them. Roberts gave due praise to the 'civilized' nature of this mode of travel. Most East India

Company employees rarely strayed from the presidency, or admin-
istrative area, where they were posted but state employees were
always on the move using the *dák* method of travelling, a form of
stage or post where one set of bearers replaced another along the
journey. Roberts, who, her memoirist explained, was handsome in
early life, though 'latterly her figure had attained some degree of ful-
ness', travelled in a palanquin carried by native bearers. With her
customary attention to detail, she describes this vehicle widely used
by the colonial travellers in India:

> An oblong chest will convey the truest idea which can be given of
> this conveyance; the walls are of double canvas, painted and
> varnished on the outside, and lined with chintz or silk; it is
> furnished on either side with sliding wooden doors, fitted into
> grooves, and when unclosed disappearing between the canvas
> walls; the roof projects about an inch all round, and is sometimes
> double, to keep off the heat of the sun. In front, there are two
> small windows, furnished with blinds, and beneath them run a
> shelf and a shallow drawer. The bottom is made of split cane
> interwoven like that of a chair, and having a mattrass, a bolster,
> and pillow covered either with leather or chintz: some are also
> supplied with a moveable support for the back, in case the
> traveller should prefer sitting upright to reclining at full length.
> The poles jet out at each end near the top; they are slightly
> curved, and each is long enough to rest upon the shoulders of
> two men, who stand one on each side, shifting their shoulders as
> they run along. Could the palanquin be constructed to swing
> upon springs, no conveyance would be more easy and agreeable;
> but mechanical art has made little progress in India; no method
> has yet been struck out to prevent the vehicle from jolting.

Eight men carried each palanquin, relieving each other by turns,
four on, four off. At night two *mussaulchees* joined the team as
torch-bearers. Progress was less than four miles an hour and bearers
were exchanged every ten to fourteen miles. Although this was an

expensive means of travel – a shilling a mile – the bearers remained very poor men. Travel rarely took place in the afternoon because of the heat and, comfortable as the palanquin might have been in comparison with other kinds of conveyance, the necessity to keep the doors partially closed to ward off the sun rather restricted what one saw: 'however the eye may still find amusement in contemplating the passing objects, and, particularly in Bengal, the gambols of monkeys crashing amid the boughs above, and the fireflies irradiating the leaves of whole groves, shooting in and out in coruscations of emerald light, afford gratification to those who are willing to be amused'.

The next phase of the journey, along the River Ganges, was by boat and from this vantage Roberts observed 'the splendour of the Anglo-Indian style of living'. The famous bungalow, however, was not to her taste. 'Out of the numberless bungalows which disfigure the face of British India, very few, and those only which are built partly of stone, and nearly hidden in embowering groves, are in the slightest degree picturesque.'

Generally Roberts counselled understanding of local customs – especially after hearing reports of an incident in which some 'raw young men' of the white tribe played some cruel tricks on their bearers only to find that the latter retaliated. That event made her conclude that 'policy as well as humanity should teach Europeans to treat the natives of India with kindness'. Yet she was not always ready to endorse indigenous customs such as suttee. Its official outlawing by the British government would, she hoped, 'pave the way to more enlightened notions on the subject of female privileges'.

As she travelled Roberts was puzzled at the lack of interest of so many Anglo-Indians in the beauty of the country. 'In this age of tourists,' she declared, 'it is rather extraordinary that the travelling mania should not extend to the possessions of the British Government in India; and that so few persons are induced to visit scenes and countries in the East, embellished with the most gorgeous productions of nature and art.' Agra, for example, seemed to her unrivalled – though her terms of praise were couched in the conventions of Orientalism: 'The reader of Eastern romance may here [at the Taj Mahal] realize his dream of fairy land, and contemplate those wondrous scenes so faithfully delineated in the brilliant pages of the *Arabian Nights*.' Anticipating the arrival of Thomas Cook, she speculated that improved transport infrastructure would mean that: 'Persons weary of Cheltenham, Baden, Spa, and other springs of fashionable resort, may take a trip to the Himalaya, and visit the Ganges by way of variety.'

Always as she travelled about India, Roberts was looking for the telling detail, the most important talent of the good travel writer, and her dissection of Anglo-Indian society was particularly acute. She noticed, for example, that this society was less obsessed by rank and its marks than would have been the case at home: 'It is sufficient that the party shall have the *entrée* of government-house, the grand test of gentility in India . . . no rank is recognized in India, excepting that which is held by the civil and military servants of the Company.' She urged the importance of sensitivity to local mores and predicted that British retention of India would depend upon 'the conciliation of a class of persons, whom it appears to have been hitherto the policy to depress and neglect, if not to insult'. She was critical of the reluctance of many of the colonial class to adapt to indigenous culture: 'An Englishman always finds it very difficult to accommodate himself to foreign usages and customs.' She was frustrated by the stiff protocols and lack of natural warmth in the Company men's comportment towards the local people: 'It is highly honourable to the British character that, in spite of its want of urbanity, and the little personal affection which it created, its uprightness and steadiness have secured the fidelity of immense multitudes bound to a foreign government by the equal distribution of justice and the security of property. It is unfortunate that we cannot unite the more endearing qualities with the moral excellencies for which we are distinguished.'

Yet she also noticed how quickly the process of absorption could proceed where it was allowed to, recording that in British India the children were 'seldom taught a word of English until they are five or six years old, and not always at that age. In numerous instances, they cannot make themselves intelligible to their parents, it being no uncommon case to find the latter almost totally ignorant of the native dialect, while their children cannot converse in any other.'

One of the more striking encounters on this trip was with an Englishman who had partly 'gone native', one of the famous 'white moghuls', Colonel Gardner. He had originally come out to India with the British Army but became one of those who 'follow the banners of native princes'. He had married 'a Mahommedan princess' and when Roberts meets him his 'tall, commanding figure, soldier-like countenance, and military air render his appearance very striking'. She was attracted to his 'romantic story', which was in such stark contrast with the stuffiness of the Anglo-Indian society she knew: 'So little of the spirit of adventure is now stirring in India, that the Misses Gardner, or the young Begums, or whatsoever appellation it may be most proper to designate them by, have not attracted the attention of the enterprising portion of the European community.' Gardner's lifestyle, which involved these daughters living in the zenana (the place where high-caste women in India lived secluded from the rest of the household), was, she decided, 'half Asiatic'. But he was drab compared with 'the Begum Sumroo' (Roberts gives her name as Zaib ul Nissa), who had married a German adventurer called Sumroo by the local people. He had deserted from the British Army and taken command of the force of the native ruler of Bengal, during which period he had massacred a number of English residents of Patna. Long widowed, the Begum presented a powerful image to Roberts: 'She is rather under the middle size, delicately formed, with fine-chiselled features, brilliant hazel eyes, a complexion very little darker than that of an Italian, and hands and arms, and feet which Zoffani, the painter, declared to be models of beauty. Of these, though now grown fat and wrinkled, she is justly proud.'

After the death of her German husband the Begum married a French adventurer called Monsieur L'Oiseaux, who wanted to drag her back to Europe. She pretended to go along with his plan but secretly arranged for her palanquin to be attacked by her soldier followers and it was given out that she had been killed. Monsieur L'Oiseaux shot himself in despair at the news. The Begum was then borne back to camp by her men 'with shouts and acclamations'. However much Roberts might have been attracted to these rather colourful characters, she conceded that the Begum was something of a monster and that 'respect for her talents is merged in abhorrence for her crimes'. The most grisly of these was when she became jealous of one of the females in her household. 'The unfortunate girl was buried alive under the floor of the apartment occupied by her mistress, who slept upon the spot in order to feast her ears with the dying groans of her victim, and to prevent the possibility of a rescue.'

After this Roberts's next destination, Delhi, was bound to be a let-down. Once again she was angered by the insensitive arrogance of the British: 'Native opinion is held in great scorn, and set at defiance by the European residents of India, who, with the solitary exception of a few, refusing to eat pork, out of deference to the prevailing prejudice, indulge themselves in the very thing that appears to be most hateful to the surrounding multitude.' Not that Roberts herself, as noted already, was an uncritical admirer of local customs, especially religious ones. She was revolted by the religious procession at Juggernaut, where pilgrims threw themselves under the 'monstrous vehicle' to be crushed to death: 'At Juggernaut there is nothing save unalloyed horror . . . a scene associated with all that is most fearful and disgusting in religious error.' She expressed the hope that 'a purer creed will be established upon the ruins of that monstrous fabric of superstition, which has so long tyrannized over the mental faculties of the Indian world'. Yet she concluded her first journey of exploration with regret at the aesthetic disparity between the imported manners of the British and those of the local population: 'The exceeding ugliness of the dress adopted by the most refined nations of Europe is in no place more apparent than in India, where it is contrasted with the flowing garments of the natives.'

Exhausted and ill from her literary labours, Roberts returned to England in 1832 and began to write about her experiences. But evidently she longed to return and was waiting for an opportunity to do so. In September 1839 she eventually made her decision to return to India. She resolved this time to make the journey in a completely different way, overland through France and Egypt, after taking the *Phénix* to Le Havre, recording the journey in *Notes of an Overland Journey through France and Egypt to Bombay* (1841).

Bad weather delayed her arrival at Le Havre, so she missed the steamer to Rouen, which compelled her and her companion (who is described merely as 'Miss E.') to perform the duties of a tourist – 'Like all English travellers, we walked about as much as we could, peeped into churches, made purchases of things we wanted and things we did not want, and got some of our gold converted into French money' – and to take tea. She caught the next available steamer to Rouen, where she changed to another, *L'Etoile*, which took her along the Seine towards Paris. At Meulan she transferred to rail for the last leg to the French capital. As usual she was precise about all the minor practicalities of travel and equipment:

I had reduced all my packages to four, namely, two portmanteaus, a bonnet-box, and a leather bag, which latter contained the medicine-chest, a kettle and lamp, lucifer-matches, &c.; my bonnet-box was divided into two compartments, one of which contained my writing-case and a looking-glass; for as I merely intended to travel through a portion of our British possessions in India, and to return after the October monsoon of 1840, I wished to carry every thing absolutely necessary for my comfort about with me.

Having noted Paris only for its 'bad smells', Roberts was off in a overnight diligence on 13 September, the heavy luggage having been dispatched to Marseilles by *messagerie*. After an unimpressive lunch at Auxerre ('A bad English dinner is a very bad thing, but a bad French one is infinitely worse') and a night in a gloomy provincial inn at Lyons, the next phase of the journey was the Rhône steamer to Marseilles. She noted the things tourists notice – at Avignon 'a half-finished bridge, apparently of ancient date, projects rudely into the middle of the stream' – and on finally reaching the Mediterranean was delighted at the contrast of the blue sea with the green Rhône water. She was less pleased by a German tourist who excitedly levelled his gun at a shoal of leaping fish which surrounded the boat, a 'wanton act of barbarity'.

Although Roberts was attracted to Marseilles as 'the handsomest and cleanest town we had yet seen in France' and in spite of having found a very comfortable lodging at the Hôtel des Ambassadeurs, the departure the next morning of a French boat, the *Megara*, to connect with the Bombay steamer at Suez left her with no option, given 'the ticklish state of affairs in Egypt', but to book two ladies' cabins for herself and Miss E. Mehmet Ali, the pasha of Egypt, she explained for her readers, was at this moment 'so obstinately determined to retain possession of the Turkish fleet, and the British Government so urgent with France to support the Porte against him'.

Glad to escape the vexatious demands of passport officials at Marseilles, Roberts sailed on 21 September for Malta, where she changed to another vessel, the *Volcano*, a government mail boat, for Alexandria. Roberts was long enough in Malta to perform her usual surgical anatomy of local society, its rankings and rivalries, and to visit the opera house and some churches where 'the mummeries of Roman Catholicism . . . afford amusement to the lovers of the grotesque'. Her most memorable encounter in Malta was with a young Egyptian, who, in spite of the condescension of the Maltese, who felt he had got above himself, impressed her as one of a new breed of Europeanized Egyptians encouraged by Mehmet Ali: 'Strongly attached to European customs, manners, and institutions, he will lose no opportunity of improving the condition of his countrymen, or of inducing them to discard those prejudices which retard the progress of civilisation.' This is a familiar note in Victorian travel writing, the frequently expressed wish that the indigenous populations would become so enamoured of the civilizing mission of the British imperialist as to slough off ancient superstitions, in order to enter the modern world (whose estimable values turned out to resemble more or less exactly those of the colonial power).

On arrival at Alexandria on 25 September, Roberts found the Turkish and Egyptian fleets were very much in evidence. Although Alexandria presented, from the sea, a very imposing appearance, the landing stage was 'a confused crowd of camels, donkeys, and their drivers, congregated amidst heaps of rubbish' but they got themselves through this 'rabble' to the civilized sanctuary of Rey's Hotel. 'In the day time,' she observed the following morning, 'the prevailing sound of Alexandria is the braying of donkeys, diversified by the grunts and moans of the almost equally numerous camels.' She found time to ride her first donkey, though she was slightly taken aback when a servant put his hand on her waist to steady her at certain rough points on the road. 'I could not help shrinking from such close contact with a class of persons not remarkable for cleanliness either of garment or skin.' The donkey ride was to deliver her to a filthy canal boat to Atfee (present-day Atfih) infested by cockroaches, rats and flies. Here she saw the Nile for the first time and was 'dreadfully disappointed' by the absence of the expected groves of rustling palm trees. Nevertheless she did her best. 'We looked eagerly out, pleased when we saw some illustration of old customs with which the Bible had made us acquainted.' Miss E. flattered herself that she caught sight of a crocodile but they decided in the end that it had been merely a water buffalo yawning.

The voyage had its *longueurs* and at times Roberts was reduced to dipping into her volume of Wordsworth in order to pass the time, but finally they glimpsed the pyramids. They did not disappoint. 'When informed that they were in view, my heart beat audibly as I threw open the cabin door, and beheld them gleaming in the sun, pure and bright as the silvery clouds above them . . . We were never tired of gazing upon these noble monuments of an age shrouded in impenetrable mystery.'

After three rough shipboard nights on the Nile they finally arrived at Boulak on 4 October. The gates of the city were closed because it was late in the evening but they eventually found an open gate and created quite a stir by their presence. Roberts was determined to explore the desert. Her imagination had been prepared for the desert encounter by childhood reading of *The Arabian Nights* and more recent reading of the latest translation of that work by the great Orientalist Edward William Lane. 'This study had given me a strong taste for every thing relating to the East, and Arabia especially. I trust that I am not less familiar with the writings of the Old and New Testament, and consequently it may easily be imagined that I should not find three days in the desert tedious, and that I felt anxious to enjoy to the uttermost the reveries which it could not fail to suggest.'

She set off on a conveyance known as a donkey-chair: 'Nothing could be more comfortable than these vehicles; a common arm-chair was fastened into a sort of wooden tray, which projected in front about a foot, thereby enabling the passenger to carry a small basket or other package; the chairs were then slung by the arms to long bamboos, one upon either side, and these, by means of ropes or straps placed across, were fastened upon the backs of donkeys, one in front, the other behind.' Passing an occasional party of 'fierce' Bedouin, she arrived at Suez on 9 October and was able to enjoy the comforts of Hill's Hotel, where she met a young Scotsman who was intending to 'make an attempt to explore the sources of the Nile' – that ruling preoccupation of so many Victorian travellers.

The steamer *Bérénice* next took her to Aden, where the whining British, who lamented the servant problem, got her down ('there is very little to interest European residents in this arid spot'). Roberts was always impatient with the bad behaviour of her compatriots towards local people and was outraged at their propensity to beat boat men and donkey men 'and others of the poorer class . . . No sooner have we been permitted to traverse a country in which formerly it was dangerous to appear openly as a Christian, than we abuse the privilege thus granted by outrages on its most peaceable inhabitants.' She believed that the British stewardship of Aden had not been a distinguished one and she was not particularly impressed by the attitudes of the expatriate population she had met on her journey across Egypt:

> A short residence in Cairo proves very captivating to many Englishmen; they like the independent sort of life which they lead; their perfect freedom from the thralls imposed by society at home, and, when tired of dreaming away existence after the indolent fashion of the East, plunge into the surrounding deserts, and enjoy all the excitement attendant upon danger. Numerous anecdotes were related to me of the hardships sustained by young English travellers, who, led by the spirit of adventure, had trusted themselves to the Bedouins, and, though escaping with life, had suffered very severely from hunger, thirst, and fatigue.

One of these 'enterprising tourists' even told her that he had anticipated the famous exploit of Sir Richard Burton by passing through Mecca in disguise.

From Aden, Roberts sailed to Makallah and then to Bombay, arriving on 29 October. Renewing her contact with India, she plunged into fresh descriptions of everyday life, showing she had lost none of her old attention to social nuance. She regretted the failure of curiosity among the British in this rising presidency. 'My predilection for exploring holes and corners of the native town is not shared by many of the Anglo-Indian residents of Bombay, who prefer driving to the Esplanade, to hear the band play, or to a place on the sea-shore called the Breach.' She was unimpressed by prolix government reports of inquiry into the state of affairs in India ('the foolscap is a weighty evil') and complained that 'the intellectual community of India' had failed to keep the British public informed in such a way that would 'lead those who are employed in legislating for our Eastern territories to inquire more deeply into those subjects which so materially affect its political, moral, and commercial prosperity'.

That public was soon to be deprived of any further attempts by Roberts herself to enlighten it. She planned to visit Gujarat and other places for a statistical work and had several schemes of social improvement for Indian women in mind, but on a visit to Colonel Ovans, the British Resident at Satara, in April 1840 she fell ill, probably once more from overwork and stress. She tried a change of air at Poona, where she stayed at the house of Colonel Campbell, but on 17 September, the day after her arrival, she died. Her last book was published posthumously. She was, according to contemporary obituary comments, much missed by Indians who appreciated her compassion and attempts at understanding.

A BENGALEE WOMAN

# 3

## *A Most Delightful Country: Fanny Parks*

'How I love this life in the wilderness! I shall never be content to vegetate in England in some quiet country place.'

Frances 'Fanny' Susanna Parks, another spirited woman traveller, was on the River Ganges in December 1844, drifting towards Allahabad in the company of her husband, Charles Crawford Parks (sometimes given as 'Parkes'), a civil servant in the customs department of the East India Company.

Everything that Fanny saw on this trip entranced her and fascinated her. 'Oh! the pleasure of vagabondizing over India,' she declared. Charles, taking advantage of one of the rare occasions when he was able to escape his desk in order to accompany her, found himself once again drawn along in her wake. 'My husband objects to accompanying me through the bazars, because such a crowd collect after me; – he goes along quietly, but with me it is different: – the moment I stop to sketch, a crowd collects, and the attendants are obliged to drive them off to enable me to see the object,' Fanny recorded in one of the entries in the copious diaries of her travels in India between 1822 and 1845. That this unusual woman should be noticed everywhere she went is not hard to understand. The title of her published account of these journeys, *Wanderings of a Pilgrim in Search of the Picturesque during Four-and-Twenty Years in the East; with Revelations of Life in the Zenana* (1850), hints at her sketching mania as well as the unique promise of her privileged accounts of the life of women in the zenana. The interest of the Victorian reading public was aroused by the prospect of what might be revealed.

Like Emma Roberts – coincidentally another Welsh traveller – Fanny Parks was passionately interested in everything around her, rejecting the incurious apartness that characterized many in Anglo-Indian circles. She had enormous reserves of energy and enthusiasm and a passion for travel and, like Roberts, she had powers of observation of a precision that is not always found in the published accounts of more celebrated travellers. She taught herself to be fluent in Hindustani and used the Persian script to sign her drawings and to display her name on the title page of her beautifully produced two-volume description of her wanderings. She even played the sitar. Her experience was mostly of the higher levels of society but her curiosity was wide-ranging. Sometimes her enthusiasm was considered indecorous by her fellow countrymen.

The Honourable Emily and the Honourable Frances Eden, both of whom published accounts of their own travels in India in the 1830s, were a little sniffy about Fanny's highly unsuitable and un-English lack of restraint: 'We are rather oppressed just now,' wrote Fanny Eden in her journal, 'by a lady, Mrs Parks, who insists on belonging to our camp . . . She has a husband who always goes mad in the cold season, so she says it is her duty to herself to leave him and travel about. She has been a beauty and has remains of it, and is abundantly fat and lively. At Benares, where we fell in with her, she informed us that she was an independent woman.' In that last observation to Fanny Eden, Fanny Parks spoke no less than the truth. In her own later account of this meeting, however, she was scrupulously polite about 'the Misses Eden'.

Frances Susanna Archer was born on 8 December 1794 at Conwy in north Wales. When, in 1834, she glimpsed the fort at the confluence of the Jumna and Chumbal rivers in India she would reach for Conwy Castle as a comparison. The landscape of north Wales stayed with her throughout her life. Returning for the first time in December 1839 she discovered:

> William Thomas, an old servant, who formerly lived with my grandmother; he keeps a small inn: the man was very glad to see one of the family, and he became my escort to the house in which I was born, which having been sold by my father, is now the property of the Castle Inn . . . in the room formerly my nursery were a couple of twins . . . I could not find a harper in Conway; it being the winter season . . . With great pleasure I revisited the old castle, admired the great hall, and the donjon keep; the pilgrim was not born in the latter, but in 'the flanking walls that round it sweep', that is, within the walls of Conway . . .

Her father, Captain William Archer, retired from the 16th Lancers, later moved the family to Lymington in Hampshire, where Fanny married Charles Crawford Parks, who was three years her junior. Within weeks the couple shipped to India. Charles already worked, in the jargon of the East India Company, as a 'Writer' and would spend his life in customs, first at Calcutta, then at Allahabad. While he was tied to his desk for twenty-two years, earning his pension, Fanny was off travelling, sketching and observing. 'For four and twenty years have I roamed the world,' she announced in the introduction to her book.

The couple left England on 19 June 1822 on the *Marchioness of Ely*, bound for Bengal. Fanny was 'happy with my lord and master', as she pliantly puts it, and when they eventually touched the Nicobar Islands she received her first exotic impressions – in the form of naked men ('like Adam when he tasted the forbidden fruit') surrounding the vessel. She dashed back to her cabin in shock but on later reflection decided that the natives were 'beautifully formed, reminding one of ancient statues'. She was mollified by their offer of fruit, which she paid for with brass rings cut from the curtains in the couple's cabin. Her curiosity mounted steadily until she went ashore longing 'to see the women, and know how they were treated' and by the time she sailed on she was 'completely island struck'.

The sea journey to India from England at this time took around five months and it was not until 13 November 1822 that they finally reached Calcutta and established themselves in a house in Park Street, Chowringhee, at 325 rupees a month. Using a metaphor highly appropriate for this vigorously determined woman, she declared: 'and thus opened our Indian campaign.'

The first month was fascinating for Fanny. 'I thought India a most delightful country.' The December climate was pleasant and there were horses to ride and balls to attend, including a magnificent farewell ball for the departing Governor-General, the Marquis of Hastings. Newcomers like Fanny were nicknamed 'griffins' for their first year by the old India hands but that was of no account to her: she was immediately off exploring and observing. 'I was much disgusted, but greatly interested,' she declared after witnessing a religious festival in honour of the goddess Kalee during which the devout pierced their tongues with skewers.

Fanny's first four years in India, however, were rather confined to Calcutta, which she describes in great detail, in a manner reminiscent of Emma Roberts. There was plenty for her to do managing a household with an enormous complement of servants, but by the spring of 1826 she had begun to get restless: 'The perusal of Lady Mary Wortley Montague's work has rendered me very anxious to visit a zenana, and to become acquainted with the ladies of the

East. I have now been nearly four years in India, and have never beheld any women but those in attendance as servants in European families, the low caste wives of petty shopkeepers, and *nach* women [professional dancers].' Curiosity vied with a residual sense of distance and enduring traces of Anglo-Indian snobbery when eventually her wish was granted:

I was invited to a *nach* at the house of an opulent Hindu in Calcutta, and was much amused with an excellent set of jugglers; their feats with swords were curious: at the conclusion, the baboo [gentleman] asked me if I should like to visit his wives and female relatives. He led me before a large curtain, which having passed I found myself in almost utter darkness: two females took hold of my hands and led me up a long flight of stairs to a well-lighted room, where I was received by the wives and relatives. Two of the ladies were pretty; on beholding their attire I was no longer surprised that no other men than their husbands were permitted to enter the zenana. The dress consisted of one long strip of Benares gauze of thin texture, with a gold border, passing twice round the limbs, with the end thrown over the shoulder. The dress was rather transparent, almost useless as a veil: their necks and arms were covered with jewels. The complexion of some of the ladies was of a pale mahogany, and some of the female attendants were of a dark colour, almost black. Passing from the lighted room, we entered a dark balcony, in front of which were fine bamboo screens, impervious to the eye from without, but from the interior we could look down upon the guests in the hall below, and distinguish perfectly all that passed. The ladies of the zenana appeared to know all the gentlemen by sight, and told me their names. They were very inquisitive; requested me to point out my husband, inquired how many children I had [Fanny never had children], and asked a thousand questions. I was glad to have seen a zenana, but much disappointed: the women were not ladylike; but, be it remembered, it was only at the house of a rich Calcutta native gentleman. I soon quitted the apartments and the *nach*.

By August 1822 Fanny was ready to set off on a proper journey, afforded by Charles's posting upcountry to Allahabad, of 800 miles by river and 500 miles by land. After selling their furniture and horses they set off on 22 November along the Grand Military Road. After a hundred miles both of them felt quite rejuvenated: 'The change of air and change of scene have wrought wonders in us both. My husband has never felt so well in health or so *désennuyé* since he left England. I am as strong as a Diana Vernon [a thoroughbred], and ride my eight or ten miles before breakfast without fatigue.' Fanny was not the first Victorian traveller to find that making a journey cured the many ills of a sedentary English middle-class life. Covering about fifteen miles a day, they reached Allahabad on 1 January 1827 and took possession of a new house 'very prettily situated on the banks for the Jumna, a little beyond the Fort'. On the trip they had crossed the Ganges at Benares, and this had given Fanny her first opportunity to witness forms of religious worship at length. She experienced a mixture of curiosity and prejudice: 'Long as I had lived in Calcutta, I had seen very little of native life or the forms of pooja [worship]. The most holy city of Benares is the high place of superstition. I went into a Hindoo temple in which pooja was being performed, and thought the organ of gullibility must be very strongly developed in the Hindoos.' She also noted the 'numerous uncouth idols in the temple'. Climbing the minarets to look down on Benares and the Ganges, she observed shrewdly: 'Young men prefer ascending them at early dawn, having then a chance of seeing the females of some zenana, who often sleep on the flat roof of a house, which is surrounded by a high wall.'

Life in Allahabad consisted of the usual colonial rituals of visiting and dining but the January climate suited Fanny, as she told her readers, 'we have, indeed the finest of climates of which you, living in your dusty, damp, dull fuliginous *England*, have no idea'. But by June the heat of Allahabad – known as 'the oven of India' – had become too much for her: 'A novel and a sofa is all one is equal to during such intense heat, which renders life scarcely endurable.' In the ensuing months she continued to record the scenes around her.

The controversial practice of suttee was much discussed at the time and she had the opportunity to witness such a ceremony near the gate of her grounds. The wife of a deceased corn chandler, in spite of the opposition of the local magistrate, insisted on committing herself to the flames in front of a crowd of five thousand which had gathered. 'After having bathed in the river, the widow lighted a brand, walked round the pile, set it on fire, and then mounted cheerfully.' But she did not see it through and escaped as the flames took hold. The magistrate, who with Charles had watched events, explained that now the widow would be branded an outcast and the Company would have to look after her. Not long after this Fanny was to welcome the abolition of the practice in 1830: 'Women in all countries are considered such dust in the balance, when their interests are pitted against those of the men, that I rejoice no more widows are to be grilled, to ensure the whole of the property passing to the sons of the deceased.'

In the early part of 1830 Charles was given an eight-month posting at Cawnpore, where they found another house, a bungalow on a platform of stone rising out of the Ganges, which at this point was about three miles wide. Fanny had her hands full running the new establishment: 'The rooms of our house are lofty and good; the dining-room forty feet by eighty feet, the swimming-bath thirty feet by twenty one, and all the other rooms on a suitable scale. There is a fine garden . . . In India the kitchen and all the servants' offices are detached from the dwelling on account of the heat . . . Our servants at present amount only to fifty-four, and I find it difficult enough to keep them in order; they quarrel amongst themselves, and when they become quite outrageous, they demand their discharge.' Watching the local boys swimming and sporting in the river in the evenings, she thought them 'much better off than the poor people in England'. She had some sympathy too for those less fortunate sections of Anglo-Indian society:

What can be more wretched than the life of a private soldier in the East? His profession employs but little of his time. During the heat of the day he is forced to remain within the intensely hot barrack-rooms; heat produces thirst, and idleness discontent. He drinks arrak [a cheap local liquor] like a fish, and soon finds life a burden, almost insupportable . . . The great source of all this misery is the cheapness of arrak mixed with datura [a narcotic plant], and the restlessness arising from the want of occupation; although a library is generally provided for the privates by the regiment.

Another problem was fever, which carried off many European soldiers at this time. The data on mortality of British soldiers and their families in nineteenth-century India are remarkably detailed and give a very clear idea of the kinds of diseases faced by Europeans. It is plain that travellers would have faced the same kinds of health threats as military personnel. The greatest single killer was malarial fever but yellow fever, cholera, typhoid and beriberi were also lethal. To take just one example: in 1889 Bengal's Sanitary Commissioner estimated that malarial fever was responsible for 75 per cent of all mortality in the province, or nearly one million deaths a year. Between 1817 and 1865 cholera caused fifteen million deaths in India and affected British military personnel particularly severely. Between 1818 and 1854 more than 8500 British troops died of the disease. The average annual mortality in European soldiers was 69 per 1000. In one severe epidemic in northern India in 1861 almost 2000 British soldiers and their families were affected and two-thirds of these died. Prodigious efforts were made to fight the disease, leading the Viceroy of India, Lord Curzon, to announce to a medical conference in 1899 that in the field of medicine alone justification for British rule could be found. It was, he declared, 'built on the bedrock of pure, irrefutable science . . . a boon . . . offered to all, rich and poor, Hindu and Mahommedan, woman and man'.

The facts seem to bear Curzon out. Death rates among British and Indian troops in India fell from 31.85 per 1000 in 1860 to 13.03 in 1900. In the wake of a Royal Commission set up in 1859 to inquire into the sanitary conditions of the army in India mortality rates began to fall. In the province of Madras, for example, deaths from malarial fever had already fallen by 60 per cent between the 1840s and the 1860s thanks to the growing use of quinine, which went into commercial production for the first time in the USA in 1823. From the 1870s onwards tropical medicine developed rapidly with the application of the germ theory of Pasteur, Koch and other microbiologists and the eventual foundation of new schools of tropical medicine in London and Liverpool.

At least Fanny's soldier casualties would have a conventional burial, unlike the poor corpse she witnessed from the bungalow at Cawnpore, floating down the Ganges: 'I have been more disgusted to-day than I can express: the cause is too truly Indian not to have a place in my journal . . . I beheld the most disgusting object imaginable.' A corpse of a poor man was floating down the river. He had been put on a funeral pyre covered with ghee (clarified butter) 'and fire enough had been allowed just to take off all the skin from the body and head, giving it a white appearance; any thing so ghastly and horrible as the limbs from the effect of the fire was never beheld, and it floated almost entirely out of the water, whilst the crows that were perched upon it tore the eyes out'.

Fanny continued to take every opportunity to travel, visiting Lucknow, where she rode out on an elephant in the evening to view the old part of the city. 'I like this . . . living *en prince*, in a climate so fine as this is at present [January 1831] it is delightful.' Back in Allahabad, where Charles at last had a permanent customs posting, she enjoyed the social life: 'Allahabad is now one of the gayest, and is, as it always has been, one of the prettiest stations in India. We have dinner-parties more than enough; balls occasionally; a book society; some five or six billiard-tables; a pack of dogs, some amongst them hounds, and (how could I have forgotten!) fourteen spinsters!' But the spinsters mocked her indefatigable travels and investigations into all aspects of Indian life: 'I study the customs and superstitions of the Hindoos so eagerly, that my friends laugh and say, "We expect some day to see you at pooja in the river!"'

At the end of 1834 Fanny purchased a small pinnace called the *Seagull.* On 9 December she set off along the River Jumna to Agra to see the Taj Mahal. The weather was cold by now and the boat was rocked by winds and drenched in thunderstorms but there were plenty of exciting things to see: 'Off Belaspoor, on one sand-bank, I saw ten crocodiles basking in the sun . . . on the river's edge were three enormous alligators, large savage monsters, lying with their enormous mouths wide open, eyeing the boats . . . I would willingly have taken the voyage for this one sight of alligators and crocodiles in their native wildernesses; the scene was so unusual, so wild, so savage.' The exoticism of the scene and the slightly risky nature of her position as a white woman without her consort no doubt intensified the pleasure for her (as it heightened her language) as she looked on her crew: 'just what in my youth I ever pictured cannibals must be: so wild and strange-looking, their long, black, shaggy hair matted over their heads, and hanging down to their shoulders; their bodies of dark brown, entirely naked, with the exception of a cloth around the waist, which passes between the limbs.'

When a titled visitor arrived from England just before the next stage of her voyage on the *Seagull,* Fanny waved away her guest's astonished reaction, explaining that on these extended solitary river voyages: 'I have books, and employments of various sorts, to beguile the loneliness; and the adventures I meet with, give variety and interest to the monotony of life on the river. Could I follow my inclinations, I would proceed to Delhi, thence to the Hills, and on to the source of the Jumna; this would really be a good undertaking.' She passed the time also by sketching and modelling little temples or ghats in soapstone and recording the dozens of varieties of birds as she drifted towards Agra. During her residence in India she collected many specimens which she preserved in arsenical soap.

She arrived at Agra after fifty-one days on the river, ill with exhaustion and suffering severe pains in her head. Finally confronted with the Taj Mahal, she was overawed by its magnificent proportions but appalled by the behaviour of the tourists: 'Can you imagine anything so detestable? European ladies and gentlemen have the band to play on the marble terrace, and dance quadrilles in front of the tomb!'

Indian tourism had begun to develop very slowly in the second half of the nineteenth century, the landmarks being Murray's *Hand-Book* to some of the regions of India in 1859 (a book which warned of all the dangers and disadvantages so that only the most venturesome would risk it) and the decision of Thomas Cook (whose activities are discussed in more detail in Chapter 8) to open a Bombay office in 1881. The first major railway line between Bombay and Calcutta opened in 1870 and some very luxurious hotels on the grand European model had opened at Calcutta and Bombay in 1860. India became part of Cook's round-the-world tour in 1872 but his business did not really take off until the 1880s, when he was still apologizing to customers for the standard of Indian hotels – outside the splendour of the Great Western and Great Eastern. The cost of a first-class ticket from London to Bombay via Brindisi with Cook was £74.

Soon after her visit to the Taj Mahal, Fanny was joined briefly by Charles and they went together to visit Colonel Gardner, mentioned in the previous chapter. Fanny remained behind, after Charles went back to Allahabad, in order to witness a wedding between the Colonel's granddaughter, Susan, and one of the princes of Delhi. There was clearly a great deal of mutual admiration between her and the Colonel, who died not long after this encounter. This was a unique opportunity for a European woman to be present at such a ceremony: 'I might have lived fifty years in India and never have seen a native wedding. It is hardly possible for a European lady to be present at one.' The 'native ladies' were shocked at Fanny's dining with men who were not her immediate relations and not covering her face. As for her independent journeys: 'A lady's going out on horseback is monstrous.'

Fanny remained enduringly fascinated with the zenana and the life of native women. She showed a marked sympathy for the sequestered occupants of these quarters. She learned that a man had murdered both his wives after finding a male in the zenana and was indignant: 'A man may have as many wives as he pleases, and mistresses without number; – it only adds to his dignity! If a woman take a lover, she is murdered, and cast like a dog into a ditch. It is the same all the world over; the women, being the weaker, are the playthings, the drudges, or the victims of the men; a woman is a slave from her birth; and the more I see of life, the more I pity the condition of the women.'

For all the interest of these passing scenes, Fanny was often frustrated by periods of inactivity and prone to occasional bouts of homesickness: 'How weary and heavy is life in India, when stationary! Travelling about the country is very amusing; but during the heat of the rains, shut up in the house, one's mind and body feel equally enervated. I long for a bracing sea breeze, and a healthy walk through the green lanes of England; the lovely wild flowers; – their beauty haunts me.'

In August a violent storm finally wrecked the *Seagull* (which was anyway being attacked by white ants) and that phase of travelling was over for Fanny: 'Alas! my beautiful Seagull; she has folded her wings for ever and has sunk to rest!' But within a few months a group of friends came to anchor their group of boats beneath her bungalow: 'the sight of their little fleet revived all my roaming propensities' and she was off once more in the direction of Calcutta. At one point on the river she thought she had seen one of the wonders of the East: a man walking on water. But the elephant on which he had been standing suddenly revealed its back above the water.

In December 1836 the little party of friends reached the Rajmahal Hills, where they left the boats to go shooting and Fanny had an adventure 'which, bringing for the second time in my life uncivilized beings before me, quite delighted me'. Since even the most sympathetic Victorian traveller routinely used terms such as 'savage' and 'uncivilized', Fanny's language would not have seemed at all inappropriate to her first readers. Descending a footpath from the interior of the hills there came 'a most delightful group, a family of savages, who attracted my attention by the singularity of their features, the smallness and activity of their bodies, their mode of gathering their hair in a knot on the top of their heads, and their wild-looking bows and arrows'. They had come to help with the rice harvest. Only five feet tall, they had 'the piercing and restless eye that is said to be peculiar to savages'. They showed Fanny how to fire an arrow from their bow after 'laughing excessively' at her method of firing, which was quite unlike that of these mountain people. Delighted with this little encounter Fanny presented the leading man with a pink silk handkerchief 'for his wife in the hills'. After this, arrival at Calcutta would simply usher in a predictable round of balls and race meetings and further encounters with society women such as the Misses Eden.

Back in Allahabad in the summer of 1837, Fanny was bored and ill, longing for the elixir of travel: 'Why should I keep a journal? There is nothing to relate in the monotony of an Indian life at home. The weary heavy day . . . nerves that are suffering from fifteen years' residence in India; – all this I feel most strongly, and must either return to England or go to the hills to recruit my weary frame.' She did not have to wait long before she was off again, visiting Delhi, where she met a princess, 'Hyat-ool-Nissa Begam', who had adopted James Gardner, son of the Colonel, whose grave she had recently visited.

She went next to the hills of Saharanpur, where she made the acquaintance of some more hill men who carried her on a kind of seat called a jampan: 'Eight of those funny little black Hill fellows were harnessed between the poles, after their fashion, and they carried me up the hill.' After a seven-mile ascent the delicious mountain air made her forget her recent fevers: 'I felt a buoyancy of spirit, like that enjoyed by a child.' She spent some time here in a bungalow recuperating and gazing on the peaks of the Himalaya. Here she learned of the death of her father; it was time to make a visit home to see her mother.

Fanny left India at the beginning of 1839 and her arrival at Plymouth on a wet, cold, gloomy day in May 'disgusted' her. Her mother found her anxious and careworn: 'No wonder, – for years and anxiety had done their work.' England did not impress Fanny. Even the appearance of people contrasted unfavourably with the grace and ease of Indian dress: 'What can be more ugly than the dress of the English?' she asked. But there was much to record after seventeen years' absence, including the inauguration of the railway age: 'Of all the novelties I have beheld since my return, the railroads are the most surprising, and have given me the best idea of the science of the present century. The rate at which a long, black, smoking train moves is wonderful; and the passing another train is absolutely startling.'

On returning to the beloved Conwy of her youth she enjoyed 'a leg of the most delicious Welsh mutton' and admired the landscape of north Wales. After a visit to Ireland she came back through Liverpool, where, on 10 January 1840, she was able to witness another milestone along the road of Victorian progress: 'Today the penny postage commenced: a great crowd collected at the post office, putting in letters, – which were in vast number, as people had refrained from writing, awaiting the opening of the penny post. The band was playing in front of the office.'

Back in Plymouth, Fanny went on board the *Wilberforce* steamer, named after the anti-slavery campaigner, whose pious memory she treated with a certain astringency: 'The crockery on board is shown to the lady visitors, who are expected to weep on beholding the appropriate design printed upon it: – a negro dancing with broken chains in his hands! It made me laugh, because there is much humbug in the whole affair – but it is the fashion.'

In spite of these wanderings around Britain and Europe (she visited France, Belgium and Germany) Fanny's interlude at home was not a happy one. She buried her mother in 1841 and fell seriously ill for three months: 'One by one all those I loved had sunk into the grave: mental suffering, united to anxiety and bodily exertion, brought on severe illness, and that buoyancy of spirit which had hitherto supported me was gone.' It was probably with some relief that Fanny finally sailed from Portsmouth on 8 February 1843 in the

*Carnatic*, bound for Cape Town. Charles, who was convalescing from a serious illness, would meet her there on 26 April. Fanny did not show towards the local people of the Cape the same sympathy she had evinced for the Indians: 'The Africanders are very dirty in their person, and they rub their bodies with a vile-smelling oil; the presence of a musk-rat is quite as agreeable as that of a Hottentot in a room.'

At the beginning of 1844 Fanny and Charles left Cape Town to return to Calcutta, where on 1 April they took a new house in Chowringhee. They stayed until October before starting the journey to Allahabad: 'It is delightful to be in the country once more.' Along the way they visited the sati tombs at Ghazipur, where Fanny reflected on the hard lot of women all over the world, her feelings no doubt intensified by the recent loss of her mother:

> It is very horrible to see how the weaker are imposed upon; and it is the same all over the world, civilized or uncivilized – perhaps some of these young married women, from eleven to twenty years of age, were burnt alive, in all the freshness of youth . . .
>
> The laws of England, relative to married women, and the state of slavery to which those laws degrade them, render the lives of some few in the higher, and of thousands in the lower ranks of life, one perpetual sati, or burning of the heart, from which they have no refuge but the grave, or the cap of liberty, – i.e. the widow's, and either is a sad consolation.

On 17 December they reached Allahabad: 'I shall be quite sorry to end my voyage, and feel the greatest reluctance to returning into society.' They were visited by all their old friends but by the end of January Fanny was bored and ill: 'This life is very monotonous, and the only variety I have is nervous fever now and then.' Soon Charles received permission for furlough and the arrangements to return to England were made. They left Calcutta on 19 August 1845 on board the *Essex*. It was a gloomy voyage – even the captain died and was buried at sea – and all sorts of premonitions came to her: 'I thought of the festering and air-poisoning churchyards of London, and felt, as far as I am concerned, how much I should prefer a sailor's grave.' They landed at Folkestone on 2 January 1846 'and took refuge at the Pavilion Hotel, where a good dinner and the luxuries of native oysters and fresh butter made us forget all the ills that flesh is heir to.'

When Fanny reached London she knew that her days as a traveller were over, 'her wanderings are ended – she has quitted the East, perhaps for ever: – surrounded in the quiet home of her native land by the curiosities, the monsters and the idols that accompanied her from India, she looks around and dreams of the days that are gone.'

Charles now had his pension and the couple retired to St Leonard's-on-Sea in Sussex, where Fanny prepared her journals for publication, a successful and lavish two volumes illustrated by her own sketches and coloured illustrations by herself and others. Charles died in London on 22 August 1854 of Bright's disease. Fanny survived him for more than twenty years, dying eventually of shingles on 21 December 1875 at her London home, 7 Cornwall Terrace, Regent's Park. She was buried with Charles in Kensal Green Cemetery on 28 December.

## 4

### *A Devilish Fascination: Richard Burton in Goa*

The story ends in a tangled, overgrown churchyard in Surrey. Amid the crooked and crumbling gravestones of St Mary Magdalen Catholic Church at Mortlake rears one of the more bizarre mausoleums of the nineteenth century, in the form of an Eastern traveller's desert tent, its Forest of Dean stone carved to imitate the folds of canvas. It is the tomb of Sir Richard Francis Burton: traveller, soldier, linguist, translator, swordsman, anthropologist, sexologist, poet and much else besides. At the rear of the tomb, between it and the cemetery wall, a ladder is placed which one can climb to peer through a small window into the tomb. Two coffins – containing the remains of Burton and his wife Isabel – are ranged side by side. A pious religious painting hangs on each of the two side walls, and a collection of what looks like North

African metalware (fetched perhaps from Burton's famous 'Moroccan Room' at Trieste, where the explorer ended his life as British Consul in 1890) is coated in thick dust. One descends the ladder, not quite sure what to make of what one has just witnessed. The choice of a Catholic burial was rather odd. It was the decision of Isabel, who was descended from a branch of the famous English Catholic family the Arundells, and it was controversial at the time, for Burton was considered by some of his contemporaries to have been so close in his attachment to Islam as to have secretly converted. The Dean of Westminster had already declined to have this mocking atheist buried alongside the pious David Livingstone in Westminster Abbey and most of Burton's friends stayed away from the ceremony at Mortlake. His close friend and drinking companion the poet Algernon Swinburne was furious with Isabel, whom he accused of having 'befouled Richard Burton's memory like a harpy' with her 'popish mendacities'. Undeterred, Isabel visited the tomb regularly and even held four seances there in the hope of contacting her husband on the other side of the grave.

Richard Burton was one of the most famous – certainly the most controversial and colourful – of the Victorian travellers and explorers. A bold and arresting figure, six feet tall with dark, glittering eyes, as captured in Sir Frederick Leighton's portrait in the National Portrait Gallery, and possessing, in Swinburne's words, the jaw of a devil and the brow of a god, Burton combined, with a very English dexterity, the roles of rebel and knight of the realm and spent a lifetime of wandering in search of experience and knowledge. As one of his biographers, Fawn Brodie, puts it: 'Burton's real passion was not for geographical discovery but for the hidden in man, for the unknowable, and inevitably the unthinkable.' There was about him something of the night, his contemporaries sometimes felt. The poet and critic Arthur Symons talked of 'a tremendous animalism, an air of repressed ferocity, a devilish fascination', though the scientist Francis Galton shrewdly noted that he had a habit of 'dressing himself, so to speak, in wolf's clothing, in order to give an idea that he was worse than he really was'. For all Burton's ardent exploration of Arabic literature, culture and religion, the writer Frank Harris claimed that 'deep down in him lay the despairing gloom of utter disbelief'. A Catholic grave in Surrey seems a queer resting place.

Unique as Richard Burton was, he was representative nonetheless of a certain kind of English traveller, and one by no means rare, who is both restlessly on the run from his own culture and expert at the construction of his own legend. 'England is the only country where I never feel at home,' he once said, and this could be the motto of a great many English travellers. In the late twentieth century Bruce Chatwin, another self-mythologizer, could be observed fitting himself into a very Burtonian template. Like so many travellers, Burton was largely the architect of his own mystique. In the British travel narrative the traveller is in charge, independent witnesses are few, the experience must be accepted at his or her own valuation without external corroboration. Writer and reader are locked into an exclusive contract which admits no other point of view. The temptations to dramatize, to rearrange the facts, to monopolize the interpretation, are irresistible. The phrase 'traveller's tale' is charged with an ambivalent connotation of exoticism and artful mendacity.

A case in point is Burton's legendary command of languages – he is said to have spoken twenty-nine plus associated dialects, bringing the total to forty. Undoubtedly he was a skilled linguist, passing competitive army translation tests and translating classics of Eastern literature, but in the end we have only Burton's word for this facility and countless other exploits of a convivial but secretive man who boasted that as a child he was 'a resolute and unblushing liar'. Burton was a very early example of the self-conscious traveller, mindful of his developing fame, attentive to the growth of the legend, of how he looked on stage. 'Please don't make me ugly, don't,' he pleaded to Leighton as he sat for his portrait.

Burton's style of writing was as idiosyncratic as the man.

Mannered, facetious in the fashion of mid-Victorian studied levity, studded with literary quotations in a variety of languages, sometimes desperately overworked, it can be exhausting. His books are often ill-constructed, piled high like some load-bearing camel, whose burden the reader watches, heart in mouth, fearing that one more package heaped on its back will send the whole lot crashing down. He was assiduous in amassing detail and anthropological, political and historical data – necessarily, as much of his travelling was done in the service of military intelligence and colonial administration – but often one misses the note of intimacy, the captured flavour of individual local people, the sense of character. The British traveller is frequently a lonely figure in the landscape. But, whatever his faults, Burton is impossible to ignore.

Born in Torquay on 19 March 1821 to Joseph Burton, a strict former soldier of partly Irish descent, and Martha Baker, whose indulgence of certain kinds of bad behaviour no doubt contributed to Richard's disorderly youth, in which fisticuffs and brawling played a prominent part, Burton was already on the move before he was one year old. The family moved to France and settled in Tours, where there was a substantial English colony, 'an oasis of Anglo-Saxondom in a desert of continentalism', as Burton later put it. It was a pleasant start for a child on the banks of the Loire at the small château of Beauséjour, where the children played and their father, kept by his wife's inheritance, hunted wild boar. But when Richard was nine the family suddenly uprooted and a life of gypsy-like wandering began – fourteen moves in ten years – and even Joseph Burton realized that he had to do something to provide his two boys with a stable education. This meant, in England, the horrors of a brutal preparatory school. Used to a certain kind of sensual freedom in France, the boys were dismayed to arrive back in England: 'Everything appeared so small, so prim, so mean, the little one-familied houses contrasting in such a melancholy way with the big buildings of Tours and Paris. We revolted against the coarse and half-cooked food, and, accustomed to the excellent Bordeaux of France, we found port, sherry, and beer like strong medicine; the bread, all crumb and crust, appeared to be half-baked, and milk meant chalk and water.'

Burton had arrived in what another compulsive expatriate, Lawrence Durrell, would later dub 'Pudding Island'. The love-hate relationship with England, the need constantly to escape it while always maintaining a distance from the country to which one has escaped, is a dominant theme in British travel writing. Lacking a clear sense of English identity as a result of his childhood wanderings, Burton called himself 'a waif, a stray . . . a blaze of light without a focus'.

His sister, Maria, he later wrote, described him at this time as 'a thin, dark little boy, with small features and large black eyes . . . extremely proud, sensitive, shy, nervous, and of a melancholy, affectionate disposition'. This nicely captures the paradox of Burton, the outward bluster and bellicosity concealing a sensitive and vulnerable interior life. The prep school in Richmond certainly brought out, in self-defence, the aggressive streak.

But Joseph Burton soon pined for his boar-hunting forests and the family returned to France – to the delight of the boys: 'We shrieked, we whooped, we danced for joy. We shook our fists at the white cliffs, and loudly hoped we should never see them again.' They arrived at Orléans, then moved on to Blois, and then suddenly – the legend was that Burton senior wished to be reunited with his Italian mistress – the family headed for Italy, where Richard's love of art was ignited at Perugia and Florence. He also learned to fence – a lifelong obsession – but another setback was waiting in the form of H. R. DuPré, an English tutor who was hired by Joseph Burton to take charge of the education of his ten-year-old son and his younger brother, Edward. DuPré was 'an awkward-looking John Bull article' whose chief teaching aid was a horsewhip which he used liberally until the boys were big enough to fight back. At the age of eighteen, Burton recalled: 'We had thoroughly mastered our tutor and threw our books out of the window if he attempted to give a lesson in Greek or Latin.' Although Burton's education was rather random and disrupted, his linguistic gifts were strong and well-developed. He is said to have acquired during his childhood wanderings in France and Italy a command of various dialects, which he claimed made him popular with the people he encountered: 'Nothing goes to the heart of a man so much as to speak to him in his own patois.' In an escapade in which he and Edward visited a Naples brothel there would be more opportunity to practise intimate dialogues even though 'a tremendous commotion' awaited them both at home afterwards when they were found out.

In 1840, when Burton was nineteen, his father sent him to Oxford with the idea that he would become a clergyman. It was another unwelcome renewal of acquaintance with 'mean' and 'ugly' England but, as a rather unorthodox undergraduate with some remarkable experiences behind him already, Burton found himself being invited out to dine frequently, meeting famous Oxford men such as Thomas Arnold, John Henry Newman and Benjamin Jowett. In a biographical sketch written in 1852, Burton described his career at Trinity College as 'highly unsatisfactory':

> I began a 'reading man', worked regularly twelve hours a day, failed in everything – chiefly, I flattered myself, because Latin hexameters and Greek iambics had not entered into my list of studies, – threw up the classics, and returned to old habits of fencing, boxing, and single-stick, handling the 'ribbons', squiring dames, and sketching facetiously, though not wisely, the reverend features and figures of certain half-reformed monks, calling themselves 'fellows'.

Burton claimed that the outbreak of the Afghan War in 1841 made him want to leave Oxford and join the army but he glosses over the real reason: he had been rejected for a Fellowship at Trinity (which his father was desperately keen for him to attain) after he insisted on reading his Greek not in the peculiar Oxford manner but using the pronunciation of the living Greeks he had met in Marseilles: 'The devil palpably entered into me,' he later admitted, 'and made me speak Greek Romaically by accent, and not by quantity, even as they did and still do at Athens.' In reaction, Burton resolved to leave Oxford without obtaining a degree and to start, under his own steam, the study of Arabic. He made sure that he got himself rusticated from the university, the clinching offence being to have attended with a group of undergraduates a race meeting in place of a lecture, which act meant that Burton – clearly identified as the ringleader – was expelled. That failure, however, rankled with him and drove him on to make his mark in other fields.

And so it was that, on 28 October 1842, Burton disembarked from the *John Knox* in Bombay harbour, eager for action but destined to discover almost immediately that the war was over and his hopes of distinguishing himself in battle were dashed. The urgency of the war, however, had been the factor that persuaded his father to withdraw his objections to an army career and stump up the £500 required to buy his son a commission in the Bombay Army. The latter was controlled by the East India Company and Ensign Burton was stationed with the 18th Bombay Native Infantry. This could have been a pleasant posting for an unambitious ensign: 'He has a horse or two, part of a house, a pleasant mess, plenty of pale ale, as much shooting as he can manage, and an occasional invitation to a dance, where there are thirty-two cavaliers to three dames, or to a dinner party when a chair unexpectedly falls vacant. But some are vain enough to want more, and of these fools was I.'

Burton worked out that there were two roads to preferment in India. 'The direct highway is "service"; getting a flesh wound, cutting down a brace of natives, and doing something eccentric, so that your name may creep into a despatch.' The other route was to study the local languages but this was 'a rugged and tortuous one'. It was the one that Burton chose. Already, on board the *John Knox*, he had studied Hindustani with Professor Duncan Forbes of King's College London so well that he was able to 'astonish the throng of palanquin bearers that jostled, pushed, and pulled me at the pier head, with the vivacity and nervousness of my phraseology'.

Once landed, Burton studied under a white-bearded Parsee called Dosabhai Sorabjee, who had taught generations of British Army personnel. 'I remained friends with the old man till the end of his days,' Burton later wrote. He was stationed at Baroda in Gujarat and at the end of six months, after what he claimed were twelve hours a day of study, he had qualified as an interpreter in Hindustani, coming top in an examination sat by twelve candidates. Next he studied Gujarati and some Sanskrit and in due course many other languages and dialects. Anything was better than the Anglo-Indian society – bands, billiards and picnics – which he loathed, but he seems to have had, like many of the British military men, a native mistress in Baroda.

In October 1844 Burton's regiment was sent to the more northerly province of Sind, where he found himself under Sir Charles Napier, who, learning of his linguistic accomplishments, began to employ him in intelligence work. Burton had sailed to Karachi ('the town is a mass of low mud hovels') on a government steamer, the *Semiramis*, and had met on the voyage another figure who was to be influential in his life, Lieutenant-Colonel Walter Scott (nephew of the novelist) of the Bombay Engineers. After nine months of interpreting at courts martial, Burton was transferred to Scott's staff, to work on a survey aimed at rebuilding the Indus irrigation system: 'My new duties compelled me to spend the cold season in wandering over the districts, levelling the beds of canals, and making preparatory sketches for a grand survey.'

By the end of his first year he had 'Persian at my finger's ends', sufficient Arabic to read, write and converse fluently 'and a superficial knowledge of that dialect of Punjaubee which is spoken in the wilder parts of the province'. He next dedicated himself to the systematic study of the Sindian people, their language and customs, but he felt that the only way to do this properly was to 'pass for an Oriental', his first adult flirtation with the idea of disguise. This was necessary, he argued, to counteract the negative image of the British colonial official in the region:

> The European official in India seldom, if ever, sees anything in its real light, so dense is the veil which the fearfulness, the duplicity, the prejudice and the superstitions of the natives hang before his eyes. And the white man lives a life so distinct from the black, that hundreds of the former serve through what they call their 'term of exile', without once being present at a circumcision feast, a wedding, or a funeral. More especially the present generation, whom the habit and the means of taking furloughs, the increased facility for enjoying ladies' society, and, if truth be spoken, a greater regard for appearances if not a stricter code of morality, estrange from their dusky fellow subjects every day and day [*sic*] the more.

Burton was representing himself as someone who was more in touch with the local population on the strength of his ability to talk to them but his reason for wanting to penetrate deeper into the culture of Sind was to acquire the knowledge that would make British rule more effective and absolute. After trying various disguises he settled on a half-Arab, half-Iranian character, knowing that the Sindians would quickly realize from his accent that he was not one of them but would expect someone from the Gulf to speak like a foreigner. For a self-dramatizing character like Burton the whole enterprise was perfectly fashioned. He called himself Mirza Abdullah, a wandering salesman of fine linen, calicoes and muslins, and his trade won him an entrée to many private houses and, he claimed, won him many hearts in the process. He grew his hair long, had a long beard and his face and hands, arms and feet were stained with henna. During the day he was probably taken for 'a kind of Frank in a sort of Oriental dress' but in the evening, as he explored the encampments and settlements, he pretended, as a means of strengthening his act, to be serving a foreign master. This unorthodox intelligence-gathering technique – normally British

officers relied on native agents – led Burton into places where few
if any had previously ventured:

> Sometimes the Mirza passed the evening in a mosque listening to
> the ragged students who, stretched at full length with their
> stomachs on the dusty floor, and their arms supporting their
> heads, mumbled out Arabic from the thumbed, soiled, and
> tattered pages of theology upon which a dim oil light shed its
> scanty ray, or he sat debating the niceties of faith with the long-
> bearded, shaven-pated, blear-eyed and stolid-faced *genius loci*,
> the Mullah.

He played chess or rubbed up against 'hemp-drinkers and
opium-eaters' in wayside inns and gained a great deal of knowledge
from one particular old woman near Hyderabad, Khanum Jan, a
matchmaker, and her husband. 'Thus it was,' claimed Burton, 'I
formed my estimate of the native character.' He was confident that
it could be summed up by saying that 'the Eastern mind . . . is
always in extremes; that it ignores what is meant by "golden mean",
and that it delights to range in flights limited only by the *ne plus
ultra* of Nature herself'. The cost of acquiring this knowledge after
four months' wandering in disguise was, he estimated, six shillings
in various disbursements.

In his account of his sojourn in Sind, *Scinde; or The Unhappy
Valley* (1851), Burton put on display his boisterous and colourful
prejudices about everything he saw, much of it addressed in jocular
and rather creaking fashion to a representative John Bull at home.
There were five thousand British and native soldiers in Karachi
when he arrived and the Sepoy or native soldier regiments struck
him as 'grotesque' because, as he saw it (overlooking his own ventures into disguise) there was 'a total want of "fitness of things" in an
Ultra-European dress, upon an Ultra-Asiatic person'. But he conceded that these men were very important to his British readers:
'they have fought for your cotton and pepper many a year, and you
may still rely upon their faith and loyalty'. Although the 'society of

ladies' in official contexts was not something Burton sought out, individual amours seem to have been very much in his line and, outside Karachi, he came across the encampment of some Persians 'escorting one of the prettiest girls ever seen to her father's house'. The enraptured Burton immediately dashed off a billet-doux in flowery, romantic prose 'upon a sheet of bright yellow notepaper' which he sealed with wax of the same colour and sent by a slave boy. The girl had 'features carved in marble like a Greek's, the noble, thoughtful Italian brow, eyes deep and lustrous as an Andalusian's, and the airy, graceful kind of figure with which Mohammed, according to our poets, peopled his man's paradise'.

Lovestruck, Burton waited for his reply but he was destined only to see her emerge in her burka and wait as her dromedary knelt to pick her up. As she mounted, he watched her 'turning her latticed face towards us' and with 'a tiny giggle' she departed. This may have influenced Burton's later judgement on the burka and on female adornment in general: 'Uncivilised and semi-barbarous people can never rest content with the handywork of nature: they must gild refined gold, tattoo or tan, paint or patch a beautiful skin, dye or chip pearly teeth, and frizzle or powder "hyacinthine locks"'.

The readiness with which Victorian travellers threw out words such as 'barbarian' and 'savage' has been noted, but sometimes there was wistful envy of the qualities of the people thus apparently dismissed. 'One of the first things the Eastern traveller remarks,' Burton recorded, 'is how palpably inferior we are, and we ever have been, with all our boasted science and knowledge, in general astuteness, private intrigue, and public diplomacy, to the semi-barbarous people with whom we have to deal.' Occasionally he and his travelling companions adopted native dress for comfort rather than to deceive and John Bull is treated to an account of how to tie a turban and spurn the English collar: 'Remember, Sir, we are not in a civilised land.'

Burton's rather rambling narrative of his journey through Sind, interspersed with long passages of history and ethnography, is rarely revealing of the man. One exception is a passage on the love of

Sindian women for their children, which he calls 'the great female virtue in the East, [it] is an all-absorbing passion, beautiful, despite of its excess . . . in this point at least civilisation gains nothing by contrast with barbarism. The parents are engrossed by other cares – the search for riches, or the pursuit of pleasure – during the infancy of their offspring.' The allusion is to the habits of the English in general and the absence in his own life of affection from his mother. He also reveals his drug-taking experiments: 'I have often taken the drug [hashish] rather for curiosity to discover what its attractions might be, than for aught of pleasurable I ever experienced . . . I recollect on one occasion being persuaded that my leg was revolving upon its knee as an axis, and could distinctly feel as well as hear it strike against and pass through the shoulder during each revolution.'

A picture begins to emerge of a man with strong opinions, expressed in a cavalier fashion, though he claimed that he had no interest in politics, 'detesting nothing more than political discussion'. He was a believer in the strong hand when dealing with native insurgency: 'The natives of Central Asia are to be controlled only by strange and terrible punishments,' which John Bull's liberal friends would no doubt have deprecated: 'Some claptrapping journalist never fails to catch and dress up for your taste some tale about the horrors of the last siege, or the few acts of violence which soldiers will commit after the excitement of a battlefield.'

Burton eventually left Sind in May 1849 on the *Eliza*, a return of the imperial traveller which he renders at the end of his book in the jocose terms of his extended dialogue with the long-suffering listener, John Bull:

Two days down the Indus – three more to Bombay; thence the last Indian voyage to the coal-hole of the East, and the Anglo-European baby-depot. Next the short discomforts of the desert and old Egypt, so delightful to the same homeward-bound. Then the P&O's noble steamer. And lastly, to conclude the panorama passing rapidly before my spiritual eye, the joyful jump on English soil – the rail-carriage, second class – the cab – the knock at the door – the tumbling up stairs, reckless of box or fare – the falling into Mrs Bull's extended arms – the proud look at Billy, who has grown prodigiously these last nine months – the huggings of all the dear little creatures that dance on your toes ecstatically – the first glass of London stout!

In reality Burton was extremely ill in the summer of 1849, so much so that he thought his days were numbered as he began his return journey. It was not his first brush with serious illness, for in February 1847 he had been granted two years' sick leave after a bout of cholera during the 1846 epidemic in Sind. This period resulted in another book published in 1851, the same year as his Sind travels, *Goa and the Blue Mountains; or Six Months of Sick Leave.* Dedicated to his cousin Elizabeth Stisted, whom he was courting at the time of writing, the book describes a pleasant interlude of six months (he never took the full two years granted to him) travelling south from Bombay. Burton set off on the *Durrya Prashad* (Joy of the Ocean) after satisfying the Medical Board – 'a committee of ancient gentlemen who never will think you sufficiently near death to meet your wishes' – of his entitlement to sick leave.

The style of his account is light and facetious, Burton at his most determinedly jaunty. The reader is introduced to the boat and its captain, who is constantly watched by a 'grim-looking bushy-bearded Moslem, who spends half his days in praying for the extermination of the infidel, and never retires to rest without groaning over the degeneracy of the times, and sighing for the good old days of Islam, when the Faithful had nothing to do but to attack, thrash, rob, and murder, the Unfaithful'. The first stage of the journey, south along the 'pirate coast', was uneventful and Burton feared that he was going to be bored but on arrival at New Goa after three days' sailing the scene comes alive.

After landing and finding a guide called John Thomas who promised that he would 'show de Goa to de Bombay gentlemens', one of Burton's first excursions was to the barracks where Phonde Sawunt, who had raised a revolt against the Indian government, was imprisoned, surrounded by 'about a dozen stalwart sons'. Burton decided they were 'negro Robin Hoods and Dick Turpins', folk heroes who rejected the rule of the British imperialist. He often threw out comments which suggested that, in spite of his habitually racist language, he was not a dyed-in-the-wool version of the latter. He was an admirer of Sir Charles Napier, who, in spite of his military ruthlessness, tried to introduce progressive reforms and in a private diary confessed his misgivings about the colonial mission: 'The whole system of Indian government is constructed for robbery and spoliation, not for conquest, not for good to the multitude, not for justice!' Burton had witnessed at first hand the hostility of the ordinary people of Sind towards the colonial power and wrote: 'Everyone knows that if the people of India could be unanimous for a day they might sweep us from their country as dust before a whirlwind.' Looking on this group of men in the Goa barracks he reflected that they had 'a well-defined idea of what patriotism means, and can groan under the real or fancied wrongs of the "stranger" or the "Sassenach's" dominion as loudly and lustily as any Hibernian or Gael in the land'.

Old Goa, Burton felt, was 'a city of the dead', the old Portuguese buildings full of a melancholy feeling of departed grandeur. Burton hated the Catholic religious art in the cathedral frescoes, where 'Boiled, roasted, grilled and hashed missionaries, looking more like seals than men, gaze upon you with an eternal smile.' The nunnery of Santa Monaca, however, was the site of one of Burton's most romantic escapades. As the prioress was showing him around his eye fell on 'a very pretty white girl' who was a Latin teacher to the nuns. Burton then relates a tale alleged to be about someone else but in fact, as was confirmed later by other sources, it is autobiographical. Having established the girl's willingness to be abducted, he came back to the nunnery at night, with 'an Afghan scoundrel' called Khudadad as his accomplice, and disguised in native dress. Burton's local interpreter, Salvador, confessed when he saw the pair of them: 'I never saw an English gentleman look more like a Mussulman thief.'

Armed with knives, the pair arrived just after midnight, with a boat ready and waiting, and positioned themselves outside the little door leading to the back garden of the nunnery. Opening the door with a false key, they entered the building, the girl having drugged the guards' tobacco with a little datura earlier, and entered the room where she was sleeping. They bore her off in triumph. They threw away the key and ran towards the arranged meeting place only to find that they had made a horrible mistake. The body in their hands was not that of the young girl but the sub-prioress: 'Instead of the expected large black eyes and the pretty little rose-bud of a mouth, a pair of rolling yellow balls glared fearfully in his face, and two big black lips, at first shut with terror, began to shout and scream and abuse him with all their might.' Gagged and bound, the sub-prioress was abandoned where she lay and the two men fled.

While in Sind Burton had already proved himself an accomplished practical joker and this exploit had all his favourite ingredients of play-acting, disguise and romantic assignation. Returning to more sober pursuits, he explored the local society, which he considered to be ruined by the Portuguese policy of allowing intermarriage, 'a most delusive and treacherous political day dream. It has lost the Portuguese almost everything in Africa as well as Asia.' He believed that the products of these mixed-race marriages were 'in plain English, mongrels' and he spilled a great deal of ink fulminating against this 'ugly' and 'degraded' race who, in his colourful diatribes, were alleged to exhibit 'a mixture of sensuality and cunning about the region of the mouth'. Burton seems to have been particularly exercised by the equality of manners of the 'Black Christians', who shocked his sense of decorum by indulging 'in a favourite independence of manner utterly at variance with our Anglo-Indian notions concerning the proper demeanour of a native towards a European'.

Burton rowed the fifteen miles from Old Goa to Seroda, where more than twenty establishments with dancing girls were to be found. He visited there the grave of a retired British major who had resigned his commission in a native regiment when the nautch girl he wanted to marry said that she would not marry an infidel until he resigned from the army. This 'Major G' had become a Hindu and an expert in esoteric lore and the sight of his grave stirred emotion in Burton: 'It is always a melancholy spectacle, the last resting-place of a fellow-countryman in some remote nook of a foreign land . . . The wanderer's heart yearns at the sight. How soon may not such fate be his own?'

Burton would later become involved, through membership of the Anthropological Society, in the fashionable contemporary delusion of so-called 'scientific racism'. Given his passion for racial stereotyping it was inevitable that he would be drawn into this field and in Goa he had plenty of opportunity to hold forth on his pet topic. He believed that Europeans were bound to 'degenerate' in the tropics after a time and that intermarriage with local people would prove fatal. 'Neither British nor Portuguese India,' he asserted, 'ever produced a half-caste at all deserving of being ranked in the typical order of man.' Burton believed that imperial rule depended on a fragile basis of mutual awe or respect, on maintained distance between the races: 'Our Empire in the East has justly been described as one of opinion, that is to say, it is founded upon the good opinion entertained of us by the natives, and their bad opinion of themselves.'

He was sceptical of the missionary endeavour, so ardently pursued by the Portuguese: 'some years spent in Western India have convinced us that the results hitherto obtained are utterly disproportionate to the means employed for converting the people'. This opinion he delivered in the full knowledge that his candour 'may not be appreciated' by the earnest mid-Victorian reading public. Burton rode his hobby-horse hard into some strange thickets. He believed that the missionaries had failed to appreciate that in the East the Christian was actually inferior in 'strength, courage and principle' to the native tribes and that this 'deficiency of personal vigour' was all down to 'the use of impure meats, and the spirituous liquors in which he indulges'. Goa, Burton judged, was a lesson to the British imperialist. 'She compelled or induced good Hindoos and Moslems to become bad Christians. The consequence has been the utter degeneracy of the breed.'

Burton sailed on to Calicut, leaving Goa at night under a silvery moon aboard the *San Ignacio*, reflecting as the old city was left behind that 'they are epochs in the traveller's life, these farewells to places or faces we admire'. He saw the Blue Mountains, the Neilgherry Hills, from the sea, and went to Malabar, where he covered pages with detailed anthropological descriptions of the Hindu population. He continued by land south along the seashore, preferring the horse to either the palanquin or the mancheel (which consisted 'merely of a pole, canvas sheet hung like a hammock beneath it, and above it a square, moveable curtain, which you may draw on the sunny or windy side'): 'In the core of the nineteenth century you may think this style of locomotion resembles a trifle too closely that of the ninth, but trust to our experience, you have no better.' He stayed in travellers' bungalows even though they were 'dirty ill-built ruinous roadside erections, tenanted by wasps and hornets, with broken seats, tottering tables, and populous bed-steads for the use of which, moreover, you were mulcted at the rate of a rupee a day'. Eventually he hired some bullocks and 'a score of naked savages' to carry the baggage: 'What a scene of human and bestial viciousness, of plunging and bellowing, of goading of sides, punching of stomachs, and twisting of tails!'

The scenery improved greatly after he reached the foot of the Neilgherries, looking back down at the plain four thousand feet below and away to the blue mist covering the distant hills of Malabar. His final destination was Ootacamund, or 'Ooty' as the British called it, with its lake that reminded him of Windermere and the military sanatorium he had come for. Ootacamund was a growing European settlement where the invalids were carried about by native bearers – 'eating the air' in the local idiom. In addition to the palanquin there was a new form of conveyance, the tonjon. This was 'a light conveyance, open and airy, exactly resembling the seat of a Bath chair, spitted upon a long pole, which rests upon the shoulders of four hammals or porters'.

Most of the residents were people from the Madras presidency on leave or from Bombay on sick leave, added to a few retired coffee planters. Military uniforms, except at balls, were banished, which came as a refreshing change for Burton, who was weary of army life. There was a Masonic lodge, a Protestant church, a library and other facilities for the European. 'You dress like an Englishman, and lead a quiet gentlemanly life – doing nothing . . . You sit up half the night [because no early parades were required] . . . At the same time your monthly bills for pale ale and hot curries, heavy tiffins, and numerous cheroots, tell you, as plainly as such mute inanimate things can, that you have not quite cast the slough of Anglo-Indian life.'

Burton enjoyed dissecting this little world which was divided into two types: those from the Madras presidency and those from the Bombay presidency. The Madrassees – known as 'Mulls' from their fondness for mulligatawny soup, the Bombay people being of course 'Ducks' – were again split into three divisions: '1, the very serious; 2, the *petit-sérieux*; and 3, the unsanctified'. There was a British club with newspapers and periodicals, billiard tables, tiffin, cigars and glasses of pale ale. When life in the settlement became too boring there was the diversion of hunting wild hog, bison, woodcock, leopard, ibex, elephants, wolves, bears or ant-eaters or 'excursionizing'. The government paid £7 for every elephant slaughtered and ivory found a ready sale.

At the same time Burton explored and anatomized the indigenous people of the surrounding hills but once again he saw the negative consequences of contact with the European when 'savage felicity' was dissolved by the touch of 'semi-civilized or civilized life'. The races of the Blue Mountains had been, Burton believed, 'morally ruined by collision with Europeans and their dissolute attendants. They have lost their honesty: truth is become almost unknown to them; chastity, sobriety and temperance, fell flat before the strong temptations of rupees, foreign luxuries, and ardent spirits. Covetousness is now the mountaineer's ruling passion.'

And so, cutting short his stay, Burton moved on, though he was entitled to a longer period of leave: 'But is not man born with a love of change – an Englishman to be discontented – an Anglo-Indian to grumble?' As he boarded the *Eliza* not long after his return to Bombay he would reflect that his Indian period was over. No doubt he was pleased to move on to other plans and other travels, but one incident would continue to haunt him, leaving an ambivalent odour adhering to his Indian career.

In 1845 Napier had asked Burton, as the only officer who was fluent in Sindi, to investigate a scandal which horrified the upright soldier, the continued existence of male brothels in Karachi. Burton threw himself into the task with his usual thoroughness and vigour, disguising himself once again, and sparing no detail in his report, sexual matters always being a special field of interest to him. The detail in this report allowed a construction to be put on it that Burton had experienced as well as observed the services of male prostitutes. The report was filed away but was leaked two years later in 1848 by some in the military who had succeeded Napier and, for obscure reasons, possibly anger at having been mocked or insulted by the outspoken captain, wanted to thwart Burton's career. They forwarded the report to Bombay, where it resulted in an attempt to get him cashiered. That failed but his reputation was damaged and the whiff of scandal would follow him for the rest of his career.

Burton arrived in London in the summer of 1849 and soon joined his family at Pisa, then followed them shortly after to Boulogne, where he spent the next four years writing furiously and seeking (and finding) a wife. After this his travels would resume. Apart from the two books on Sind and Goa he produced in this French period of recuperation another, drier but formidably detailed and researched, tome on Sind and a short book called *Falconry in the Valley of the Indus* (1851) which is of interest now mostly for its autobiographical appendix. Burton enjoyed the pleasures of falconry in Sind, in the full knowledge that it was considered deeply unfashionable, and that he would be pronounced a medieval relic in pursuing it in the middle of the nineteenth century in an age of steamships and railways: 'The Knight no longer rides out with his hawk on fist, and falconers, and cages, and greyhounds behind, to chase the swift curlew, or to strike down the soaring heron. In these piping days of peace and civilisation ... the Knight's lady thinks a drive round Hyde Park, or a canter down Rotten Row, quite sufficient exercise in these times for her highly nervous and thoroughly civilized constitution.'

## 5

## The Tables Turned: William Sleeman in Oudh

British travellers in India in the nineteenth century could hardly have imagined themselves to be unconnected with the imperial project. Richard Burton, who was a soldier in the Bombay Army and an official military surveyor in Sind, was never in doubt that his researches would bear fruit in knowledge useful for the colonial administration. He believed that one could not govern a population without devoting oneself to understanding it. His genuinely scholarly passion for the languages and the culture of India was always applied to the discharge of his role as an employee of the East India Company. His ambivalence about British imperialism, however, has been observed, and he was not alone in having periodic misgivings about the future of the British presence in India and about the right way to administer it in the present.

Sir William Henry Sleeman, born in Cornwall in 1788, entered the Company's Bengal Army in 1809 and took part in the Anglo-Nepal war of 1814–16 but subsequently held a variety of civil and political appointments. In 1828, as an administrator in the Central Provinces, he tried to abolish the practice of suttee but he is best known for his successful attempts to eradicate the phenomenon of thuggee. This practice had caught the imagination of the Victorian reading public who enjoyed Meadows Taylor's 1839 best-seller *Confessions of a Thug*. Travellers often gratified this taste with lurid tales of the actions of the thugs, professional murderers who worshipped the goddess Kali and attacked travellers, strangling them with a cord of twisted silk and hastily burying them. When Lord

Bentinck became Governor-General of India in 1835 he appointed Sleeman as head of a Commission for the Suppression of Thuggee and Dacoity. Sleeman investigated thuggee thoroughly (publishing a book on it in 1836) and between 1826 and 1840 more than fourteen thousand thugs were hanged, transported or imprisoned.

By 1848 the practice had more or less ended and in this year Sleeman was appointed British Resident at Lucknow, where in 1849–50 he made a *Journey through the Kingdom of Oude* (1858), the findings of which persuaded his superior Lord Dalhousie, Governor-General, to annex the kingdom. This was in contradiction to Sleeman's belief that native rule, suitably reformed, was the best course. Forcible annexation, he argued, would lead to a mutiny of the sepoys, or native soldiers. In an angry letter published posthumously in *The Times* in November 1857 (it appears to have been written three years earlier) Sleeman argued that annexation of the Kingdom of Oudh (he spelled it 'Oude') by the British would simply crush 'all the higher and middle classes connected with the land. These classes it should be our object to create and foster, that we might in the end inspire them with a feeling of interest in the stability of our rule.'

Sleeman warned that Dalhousie's illegitimate attempt at military annexation, his 'aggressive and absorbing policy, which has done so much mischief of late in India', would result in popular resentment leading to terrorist attacks: 'when the popular mind becomes agitated by such alarms . . . fanatics will always be found ready to step into Paradise over the bodies of the most prominent of those from whom injury is apprehended'. He threatened to resign if any unprincipled course was taken: 'To confiscate would be dishonest and dishonourable.' He made the stark prophecy, emphasizing its import with italics, '*We shall find a few years hence the tables turned against us.*' Sleeman was clearly a man who believed that imperial rule could continue only if it maintained moral legitimacy.

Sleeman's journey through Oudh was the result of a commission from Dalhousie on 16 September 1848 and he undertook it at the end of 1849 and the early part of 1850. The book was written in 1851 but not published until 1858, two years after Sleeman's death. His commitment was to the rule of law. 'We have no right to annex or confiscate Oude,' he wrote, 'but we have a right, under the treaty of 1837, to take the management of it, but not to appropriate its revenues to ourselves.' He was under no illusions about the 'prevailing anarchy and lawlessness' of Oudh and the incompetence or worse of its rulers. The King, in particular, who 'gave himself up to the effeminate indulgence of his harem and the society of eunuchs and fiddlers', was responsible for 'atrocious cruelties and oppression'.

Sleeman left Lucknow on 1 December 1849 mounted on an elephant 'the better to see the country' and soon he was finding confirmation of the moral chaos of the kingdom. Pausing on the road to hear the tale of woe of a poor Brahmin seeking redress for some wrong, he concluded: 'No Government in India is now more weak for purposes of good than that of Oude.' Poverty and fear were everywhere in evidence, and the people were miserable and suffering from diseases such as goitre caused by polluted water. The King's officers such as Rajah Sing and his agents were considered by everyone Sleeman saw 'more as terrible demons who delighted in blood and murder than as men endowed with any feelings of sympathy for their fellow-creatures; and the government, which employed such men in the management of districts with uncontrolled power, seemed to be utterly detested and abhorred'. For this reason, Sleeman became convinced, the people saw the British as being on their side, and everywhere he went he was besieged by petitioners seeking redress for their grievances, the King having no interest in public affairs but only 'the pursuit of his personal gratifications': 'He sometimes admits a few poets or poetasters to hear and praise his verses, and commands the unwilling attendance of some of his relations, to witness and applaud the acting of some of his own silly comedies, on the penalty of forfeiting their stipends; but any one who presumes to approach him, even in his rides or drives, with a petition for justice, is instantly clapped into prison, or otherwise severely punished.'

Towards the end of December 1849, in the neighbourhoou Sultanpoor, where wolves were a constant menace to the local population, especially children, Sleeman learned the story of a boy who had been found, a couple of years earlier, living in a wolf's den near Chandour, about ten miles from Sultanpoor. A soldier had noticed a female wolf leaving her den on the banks of the river: 'The boy went on all fours and seemed to be on the best possible terms with the old dam and the three whelps, and the mother seemed to guard all four with equal care.' After a determined chase the family retreated to their den, where they were dug out by the trooper and some local people. The boy was rescued but had to be tied up, 'for he was very restive, and struggled hard to rush into every hole or den they came near'. They tried to make him speak 'but could get nothing from him but an angry growl or snarl'. He rejected any cooked meat put before him with disgust 'but when any raw meat was offered, he seized it with avidity, put it on the ground under his paws, like a dog, and ate it with evident pleasure'.

Shortly afterwards the boy was sent to the European officer at Sultanpoor, Captain Nicholetts, who continued to try to tame him: 'A quilt stuffed with cotton was given to him when it became very cold this season, but he tore it to pieces, and ate a portion of it, cotton and all, with his bread every day.' The boy would not go near other children, preferring the company of animals, and eventually grew quieter, needing no restraint. In August 1850, having grown thin and ill, he put his hands to his head and spoke the first words anyone had ever heard him utter: 'It aches.' He then asked for water, drank it and died.

In January Sleeman was back in Lucknow, an 'overgrown city' in which there was 'a perpetual turmoil of processions, illuminations, and festivities'. He identified this as a key problem in the maladministration of the country, the King being indifferent to the feelings and opinions of the landed aristocracy and country people with whom he and his court had no sympathy. Instead he spent all that he could spare for the public 'in gratifying the vitiated tastes of the overgrown metropolis'. Sleeman concluded that the more

...w Muslims disliked these excessive proces-
...ons which seemed designed to divert the idle
...n rather than serve the needs of true piety. 'It is,
...prehensible departure from the spirit of their creed,
...the simple tastes of the early Mahommedans, who laid
...ir superfluities in the construction of great and durable
...s of ornament and utility.'

Sleeman's journey – included here because officials and invest-
igators were also an important category of travellers – ended on 28
February 1850 at Chinahut, where it had begun. 'I can safely say,' he
wrote, 'that I have learnt more of the state of the country, and the
condition and requirements of the people, than I could possibly
have learnt in a long life passed exclusively at the capital of
Lucknow.' The final picture is of a man of probity taking the trouble to understand the country through which he passed, surveying
it from on high on the back of an elephant but attentive to what
local people said to him, comprehending, patient and unhurried.
'The pace of a good elephant is about that of a good walker, and I
had generally some of the landholders and cultivators riding or
walking by my side to talk with.'

## 6

## *Scenes of Horror: Ruth Coopland and the Indian Mutiny*

In the accounts of many of the prominent Victorian travellers (but always incidentally, obliquely, mere footnotes to the grand imperial narrative) apprehensions and doubts about the British presence in their colonial territories sporadically occur. Not every British traveller was a diehard imperialist. But one event in India raised the stakes in a dramatic way and shook the entire basis of the British presence: the Mutiny of March 1857. A direct challenge to British authority, it was successfully put down but it marked a turning point. The next year the lands of the East India Company were annexed to the Crown and a Secretary of State was made responsible for Indian affairs. British India continued its forward march and nearly twenty years later Queen Victoria was proclaimed Empress of India, but the memory of the uprising lingered.

There was as yet no significant 'anti-imperialist' movement but, as stories leaked out about the brutal suppression of the revolt, many felt unease. There were public debates about the need to rule Indians in a more ethnically sensitive fashion, to move away from the spirit of Lord Macaulay's *Minute on Education*, in which, as noted above, he proclaimed that 'a single shelf of a good European library was worth the whole native literature of India and Arabia' and outlined an education policy whose aim was to create not a free and autonomous intelligentsia but 'a class who may be interpreters between us and the millions whom we govern – a class of persons Indian in blood and colour, but English in tastes, in opinions, in morals and in intellect'. The Victorian preoccupation with difference, with the idea that the peoples of the British dominions were not like us, that they were another breed or essence, lay behind such assumptions.

One of the most dramatic accounts of the Mutiny from the British perspective was Ruth Coopland's *A Lady's Escape from Gwalior and Life in the Fort of Agra during the Mutinies of 1857* (1859). This tale of a plucky individual woman's courageous escape from the hands of the dastardly mutineers was a great success. It was her only book and virtually nothing is known about her apart from the fact that she was the wife of the Reverend George William Coopland, who was a Fellow of St Catherine's College, Cambridge, and Chaplain to the East India Company. George was posted to Gwalior, a hundred miles south of Agra, shortly after his marriage to Ruth, but within weeks they were drawn into the violence.

The newly married couple reached Calcutta on the afternoon of 17 November 1856 and joined the expectant crowd on the deck of the ship. 'Some, who were returning to homes and relations, welcomed this country of their adoption as an old friend. Others, like myself, examined with a critical eye the new and strange land which they believed would be their home for many years,' wrote Ruth. The British public was very familiar with Calcutta, a city, she believed, better known to it than Paris or Rome as a result of the copious published descriptions of life there: 'There is scarcely a family in the three kingdoms that has not sent home an account of Calcutta, its splendid mansions, its balls, races, and the luxurious life of its inhabitants.' She was very favourably impressed: 'The carriages and horses were equal to those seen daily in Hyde-park, and the ladies were most exquisitely dressed. Dresses from Paris arrive every fortnight, and the climate only requires a very airy style.'

A month later, however, on 21 December 1856, she was off on the 121-mile train journey to Raneegunge, where the line stopped and she transferred to a *dák* gharry ('it is something like a small caravan on four wheels, and is drawn by one horse') to Benares, which she reached on 26 December. Three days later she left for Agra, via

Allahabad and Cawnpore, arriving on 3 January 1857. She left her ritual tribute of praise at the foot of the Taj Mahal ('one could scarcely fancy it built by mortal hands') but was soon off again for the final leg of the journey to Gwalior, travelling in a 'dhoolie', or litter:

> We left for Gwalior on the 7th of January, and though I was wrapped in a cloth jacket and plaid, I was glad of a warm Siberian rug, the weather was so cold . . . We were accompanied by a tribe of thirty natives; banghy wallahs [luggage porters], to carry our boxes, two torch-bearers, and additional ones for the dhoolies; they were headed by our kitmutghar [butler] in a warm lebada [quilted cloak], or tight kind of cassock, brilliant green turned up with red, and a shawl turban of red lui [blanket], or native blanket; he rode a queer little pony, which looked as though it had not a leg to stand upon, and was attended by a village boy, screaming and yelling, and ummercifully thumping the poor animal with a thick stick, the boy shivering with cold, and complaining it made his pêté [stomach] ache.

Much as Ruth enjoyed the sights and sounds and sensations of the new country, she was happy to take solace during the journey from two very English books: the latest volume of Macaulay's *History of England* and Charles Kingsley's recent novel *Westward Ho!* 'I felt grateful to the famous authors of these books for giving us so much interest and amusement when away from civilised life.' In contrast with earlier women travellers in India who showed degrees of understanding of Indian culture and religion, Ruth Coopland invariably expressed only irritation, although her experiences at this historical moment would certainly have hardened her later attitudes. At Dholpore she was struck by the appearance of the local men, whose warlike and bold aspect made her think of 'the absurd notions many people at home have of the natives of Hindoostan; they think India is solely peopled with "mild Hindoos", dressed in white garments, gliding about with graceful movements, and cringingly submissive: I only found them obsequious when they wanted anything from me.' The unpleasantness of the phrase 'cringingly submissive' was the prelude to an attack on those people whom she characterized as 'the Mahrattas, Bheels, and Pindarees', calling them 'a strong, savage, martial race' who differed from the Hindus of Benares and Calcutta:

> They are not bad-looking, with their black hair and moustaches, and rather harshly-marked features; but at heart most of them are cruel and bloodthirsty, and are only kept by our superior power from burning alive, swinging on hooks, crushing under the car of Juggernaut, and otherwise sacrificing victims to their vile religion: were it not for this, they would again return to Thuggism, Sutteeism, and burying alive. I think we have had sufficient proof of their treachery; yet actually, since my return home, people have asked me if I did not think the 'poor Hindoos much maligned and harshly treated'.

This interest in the nuances of racial stereotyping also extended to her own people. Arriving finally at Gwalior ('the Gibraltar of India') on 8 January 1857, to a gratifyingly full church, she and George went out to a military dinner where, she observed, 'everyone nearly in India is Scotch or Irish . . . I do think there were only half a dozen *genuine* English in the room, including my husband.' After six weeks the couple eventually got a house of their own and Ruth 'gradually became initiated into the minutiae of life at a small station'. This involved joining a book group which made available issues of *Blackwood's* and *Frazer's* magazines, the Indian papers and the *Delhi Punch*, which sadly turned out to be 'a bad imitation of its witty namesake in England'.

Some early disturbances reported from Dumdum and Barrackpore were premonitions of what was to come and then, in March, the Mutiny broke out. Ruth quoted two of her husband's letters home which show him to have been made of the same stuff: 'This is God's punishment upon all the weak tampering with idolatry and flattering vile superstitions. The sepoys have been allowed to have their own way as to this and that thing which they pretended was part of their religion, and so have been spoiled and allowed to see that we were frightened of them.' In a second letter he reported: 'The insubordination in our own servants is most remarkable. They look as if they would like to cut our own throats . . . Here we are in the midst of a lot of savages (for most of them are nothing better) seventy miles from any European regiment, and the insurgents are not far from us.' After a massacre of Europeans at Meerut Ruth noticed how 'the people eye us, when we drive out, in the most sinister and malicious way'. After another massacre at Delhi the servants became bolder and more insubordinate.

The Cooplands felt trapped and as if they were waiting for death. Eventually, after a warning from their ayah that the sepoys planned to kill them, they fled in the night. George was killed but Ruth and the women escaped and fled to the Rajah for protection, helped by a faithful servant, Muza. They were then enabled to reach Agra, where they arrived on 19 June and were lodged in the fort and Ruth gave birth. 'Life was a blank to me for many days,' she wrote of her arrival at the fort.

She stayed in Agra for the whole of that summer and autumn, eventually leaving on 12 December for Delhi, which she christened the 'City of Horrors' because of what had happened there. She was enraged by the local people and the 'impudent, self-satisfied expression on their faces' but also able to note the returning signs of normality: 'European ladies riding on immense elephants, and gentlemen on camels, horses and ponies.' Back in control, the British were punishing the offenders. On 23 December, up to 500 people having been hanged since the siege of Delhi, the Nawab of Jhujjhur was also hanged pre-emptively, 'to show our contempt for the natives' who had threatened an uprising on Christmas Day. Ruth was glad to leave the city: 'I could not but think it was a disgrace to England that this city, instead of being rased to the ground, should be allowed to stand, with its blood-stained walls and streets, – an everlasting memorial of the galling insult offered to England's honour.' She wanted to see Delhi annihilated and on the ruins a church or monument built inscribed with a list of all the victims of the massacres and paid for by a tax on every native implicated in 'the mutinies'.

At the end of December 1858 Ruth Coopland began her journey home, via Umballah and Simla. In spite of her indignation she was alive to the beauty of the landscape on the journey to Simla: 'It is utterly vain for me to attempt to give the most faint idea of the surpassing beauty of this mountain scenery. It would require the pencil of a Turner, and the pen of a Scott, to convey any idea of it.' She went next to Lahore, the only white person in the party with her baby. 'At times I met officers going down the country; but ladies and etiquette are too closely allied to allow of my speaking to them: between gentlemen there is a kind of freemasonry, which is very pleasant, and indeed needful in a wild country with no Europeans near you.'

From Lahore she travelled to Karachi and then Bombay, where she shipped on the Peninsular and Oriental Company steamer *Oriental,* the passage paid for by the Relief Fund. 'I had soon taken my last look of India, and its myriads of people, – most of whom are black at heart, – its burning sun, and all the scenes of horror I had witnessed.' She stopped for a week in Egypt and then arrived at Southampton on the *Ripon* on 26 April 1858, to be met at the quay by her father and to find herself back in 'dear old England', a place where 'Christianity is universal, and which is ruled by a sovereign, who sets to all her subjects a good and noble example'.

## 7

## *An Alien Caste: Wilfrid Scawen Blunt and Indian Freedom*

Wilfrid Scawen Blunt was that rare thing, a political traveller. His journey through India in the autumn of 1883 – a time he categorized as 'the awakening hour of the new movement towards liberty in India, the dawn of that day of unrest which is the necessary prelude to full self-assertion in a very subject land' – was that of someone who called himself unambiguously 'a Home Ruler in the East'.

Blunt was born in 1840 at Petworth House in Sussex to a family of landowners of long lineage. From his prep-school days he placed himself, he claimed, on the side of the underdog and became a very English Tory radical. After entering the diplomatic service at the age of eighteen he served for more than a decade in Europe and South America. Always prone to showing off, he galloped about Athens in the late 1850s on a white horse in imitation of the swagger of Byron and had many passionate affairs throughout his diplomatic period, later writing in one of his poems: 'Pleasure is duty, duty pleasure/In equal measure.' By 1869 he had settled down a little and married Byron's granddaughter, Lady Annabella Noel King. Inherited wealth allowed him to abandon the diplomatic service (and by now his cradle Catholicism) and the couple embarked on travels on horseback through Turkey, Algeria, Egypt, Palestine, Syria and Arabia. In 1878 they started to breed Arab horses and Blunt's collection of poetry *Proteus and Amadeus* appeared.

Blunt next moved into active politics and, through his establishment contacts, particularly a friendship with Gladstone's private secretary, E. W. Hamilton, he began to advance the cause of Islam. He was living in Cairo in September 1881 when the nationalist uprising of Arabi Pasha against the Ottoman Turks took place and he immediately returned to London to put Arabi Pasha's case. After some initial success in persuading Gladstone, to whom he gained direct access, in the policy of 'Egypt for the Egyptians', Blunt's line fell increasingly out of favour and in May 1882 Alexandria was bombarded and Egypt occupied by the British. Arabi Pasha was forced into exile. Blunt, who described the British invasion and occupation as 'an act of brutal and stupid aggression, a war and an intrigue, undertaken in the interests of cosmopolitan finance and in defiance of both law and principle', was also banished from Egypt.

Accordingly, in September 1883 Blunt set off for India. He claimed that the current viceroy, Lord Ripon, had originally been sent to India in 1880 at the behest of Queen Victoria rather than Gladstone, whom Blunt accused of pursuing a policy of 'aggressive imperialism in the East'. He added that 'the dissatisfaction of her Indian subjects distressed her, and hardly less the arrogance with which they were treated by their fellow subjects of British origin'. Ripon soon enraged the conservative forces in Britain, including *The Times*, when in 1883 he backed the Ibert Bill, which for the first time gave jurisdiction over Englishmen in criminal cases to native judges, a measure aimed at removing the impunity with which English members of what Blunt called 'the planter class' could maltreat their native servants. Anglo-Indian officials were said to have encouraged press attacks on their Viceroy. Always an anti-imperialist, Blunt had found his views sharpened by his experience of Egypt, where he had witnessed 'European intrigue' at close quarters in 'a struggle where I knew the right to be with the native reformers, the wrong with our obstinate officials'.

Blunt arrived in India cordially hated by the British imperial class but with the sympathy of the Panislamic movement in Egypt behind him, which he believed gave him 'my passports to the confidence of their Indian co-religionists'. The press campaign against Blunt stirred up by British Egyptian officials who tried to get Ripon to ban this political agitator from India 'insured me a welcome with the Hindus . . . wherever I went I was an object of pleased curiosity with the disaffected'.

On 13 September 1883 Blunt left London for Paris to meet some exiled Egyptian nationalists who said that Indian nationalists were discouraged by the British Government spies everywhere and by a belief that there was no sympathy for them among the English, whose officials, in the words of Sheykh Jemal-ed-Din Afghani, 'never smiled when they spoke to them'. Blunt took a train the next day to Marseilles, where he caught a steamer of the Messageries Maritimes line to Egypt for a futile fortnight's lobbying of the British official, Sir Evelyn Baring, before embarking at Suez on a British ship, the *Ghoorkha*, bound for Colombo.

As well as developing a malarial fever on board (in the absence of a sick bay he was stretched out on a table in the saloon of the verminous vessel) Blunt found himself despised by the 'rough set of Colonial English and planters from India, Assam and Burmah', who hated what he stood for and the Ibert Bill in particular. Blunt read the Qur'an on board and felt: 'There are moments when I could arise and proclaim a *jehad* on board.' One of the men, an indigo planter, advised Blunt that if the Bill were passed all the planters would leave India and added that 'the niggers were all rogues from the first to the last'. He advised severe punishment of them with the proviso that it was not overdone, for 'they are capable without any exaggeration of dying to spite you'. Blunt couldn't get off the ship quickly enough at Colombo.

Blunt spent three delicious weeks of recuperation in a beautiful country house, watching the fishing boats from its verandah, where he had a view of a banana grove full of leaping squirrels 'looking into the bunches to see if there are any ripe enough to eat' and copious exotic birds, flowers, butterflies and lizards. When he felt better he attended a dinner with the Governor of Ceylon, Sir Arthur Gordon, who was 'a very excellent man, who was on the best of terms with the various native communities' as a result of the island's being a Crown colony with greater equality between local people and Europeans. 'There is none of that extreme and open arrogance we find in Northern India.'

On 11 November Blunt left behind these three weeks, 'the happiest of my life', and sailed on a steamer for Tuticorin, the southernmost point of the Indian peninsula. On arrival he transferred to a train which puffed through attractive countryside, made lush green by the rains, as far as Madura ('the most interesting Hindu city in India'), where the Muslim community came to greet him and set out their grievances. The same night he went on by train to Trichinopoly.

He was woken the next morning by the sound of an old English general barking out orders in a hoarse voice to two thousand massed Madras Infantry. These sounds 'were like the breaking of a spell' because until this point he had seen no signs of the British presence. He reflected: 'It is hateful to be here as members of the alien ruling caste, reverenced and feared, and secretly detested.' Yet his views of the local people were not necessarily couched in sensitive terms: 'The common peasants here have all the appearances of savages, so much so that one expects to see bows and arrows in their hands.' Blunt had more sympathy for the dispossessed descendants of the former native rulers of Madras: 'The dispossessed Princes of India always reminded me of captive wild beasts shut up in their cages, lame and diseased, and dying of their lack of moral exercise.'

In Madras, where Blunt stayed for a week at Lippert's Hotel facing the sea, he canvassed more local opinion and made some very shrewd observations about the Anglo-Indian officials, whose behaviour he contrasted with the 'old-fashioned personal rule of the Indian princes, with whom there was always the possibility of a personal appeal to the head of the State'. This was in sharp opposition to the 'blank seclusion of the English rulers, who were walled off from all knowledge of what was going on by their ignorance of native life and their complete severance from native society'. He claimed that in the days of the East India Company, when communication with England was rare and difficult, the English officials and even the Governors and Governors-General were thrown to a large extent for their society on the Indians of rank and position, whose language they had been obliged to learn and with whom they lived on a footing of something like equality. Now they lived wholly among themselves and were almost without intercourse with natives of any class, except perhaps the lowest, whom they treated at best with good-humoured contempt. Thus they heard nothing and cared nothing for the feelings and opinions of the people, and the abyss between the rulers and the ruled was every year increasing.

Blunt painted a rather disobliging picture of the Governor of Madras, Grant Duff, as a 'thin, sickly, querulous man . . . out of temper with everything around him, yet paid ten thousand a year by the Madras Indians for ruling them'. The feeling was mutual, and Grant Duff, aware of Blunt's reputation, was perhaps understandably 'reserved and suspicious'.

On 27 November Blunt took the overnight train to Hyderabad, where he was invited, in spite of his reputation (the local newspapers were now following his progress), to stay in a wing of the Palladian British Residency. The Resident, Mr Cordery, was pleasant enough but Blunt assumed he was under surveillance 'and I suspect our entertainment at the Residency is designed to keep us out of mischief'. Taken out the next day to view the town from the back of an elephant, Blunt was favourably impressed: 'The town is most interesting, being after Cairo the most gay and busy in the Mohammedan East . . . like a great flowerbed, crowded with men and women in bright dresses and with a fine and cheerful air of independence, more Arab than Indian.'

But Cordery soon became alarmed at Blunt's independent excursions around the city. In the course of one of these Blunt was asked by a native schoolmaster to explain 'the tyranny of the English officials and their brutal manners'. How was it, the man asked, that Blunt was different from the others, that he made him sit down on the same sofa with him, that he addressed him politely and did not treat him as a slave? Blunt replied that 'there were degrees of good breeding among us' and that the men who came out to India as government servants 'were, many of them, taken from a comparatively low rank in life, and that, being unused to refined society, or to being treated with much consideration at home, they lost their heads when they found themselves in India in a position of power'. Why did Blunt want to help them? 'I explained that in youth I had led a life of folly, and that I wished to do some good before I died, and that I had received much kindness from the Moslems, and learned from them to believe in God, and so I spent a portion of every year among them.'

On 10 December, to the relief of the Resident, Blunt left Hyderabad by the early train and the next day arrived at Poona ('an uninteresting place, without a vestige of Eastern colour'), moving on immediately to Bombay (about which he had little to say, having spent all his time looking for Arab horses to buy) and then to Calcutta, arriving on 17 December. As soon as he could he visited Lord Ripon for a meeting that he had anticipated nervously but which in the event went well and lasted an hour: 'Since my famous interview with Gladstone in March, 1822, I have not been so favourably impressed by any statesman that I have conversed with.' Blunt did the rounds of all the people who mattered in Calcutta, including newspaper editors such as Kristo Das Pal of the *Hindu Patriot* and a member of the Legislative Council who claimed that the British 'had no sympathy with India or its people. They came and went like birds of passage.' Blunt did admit to being impressed by the Bishop of Calcutta, Dr Johnstone, 'a good specimen of his class, with more liberal views than nearly any Englishman I have talked to in India. He does not want to convert anybody or Anglicize them.'

Blunt paid two visits to the National Conference, the only European present at this national parliament in embryo, and on his second visit on 29 December he addressed the delegates, saying that he believed that all nations were fit for self-government and few more so than India. He invited them to consider the case of Greece, which, before it won its independence, was 'a conglomeration of robber chieftains, piratical seafarers and an absolutely uneducated peasant population' – and look at it now. 'This produced much cheering.'

But Blunt did not merely go about listening to what he wanted to hear. He met the pro-British Siva Prasad (burnt in effigy by Hindus in his native town), who believed 'that India was worse off in the matter of peace and order before [the British] came'. He also listened to a debate at Government House on the Ibert Bill before leaving on 6 January 1884. 'On the whole I leave Calcutta much satisfied with all I have done, heard, and seen, though not sorry to be once more on the move.'

The following day he arrived in Patna, a Muslim stronghold, and, after a day of meetings with prominent Muslims, he left on 8 January on the morning train. At the station an incident occurred which symbolized for Blunt everything that was wrong with the British demeanour and presence in India. He was being seen off by his Muslim friends, including Vilayet Ali Khan, the chief nobleman of Patna, when a Scottish doctor, who later turned out to be the Chief Medical Officer of the Punjab, Brigadier-Surgeon B. C. Kerr, though Blunt does not name him in the book, thrust his head out of a carriage window and, 'with an insolent air of authority', violently threatened the party with his stick if they did not remove themselves from the vicinity of his window. Blunt was outraged, calling the doctor a blackguard and giving him in charge at the next station, Dinapore. The train had already started to move off, so it was not until it stopped again at the second of Patna's stations that Blunt could summon the railway authorities, who initially tried to defend the doctor. Blunt demanded the doctor's card, which was from the Army and Navy Club in Sealkote, and threatened to report the stationmaster to Lord Ripon if he did not intervene. Blunt would write a stiff letter the next morning to Ripon 'warning him of the state of things, and of the bitterness of native feeling in consequence of their habitual ill treatment by the English' but for now he forced the man to identify himself, helped by several of his

Patna friends who had by this time boarded the train and come to his aid. 'The matter being treated in this way made a prodigious sensation, as it was the first time an Englishman had openly taken part with the natives against his fellow countrymen.'

Blunt arrived at Benares and the following day visited 'the last representative of the Moguls' in India, Bahadur Shah Zafar, who lived rather mournfully on a pension provided by the British 'in lieu of his Indian Empire'. Blunt was moved by this

> Sad old relic perched in a half ruinous house, like a sick eagle, looking down on the river and the crescent-shaped city, with his little group of tattered servants. We were pitying him from our hearts, melted at his pedigree, when he suddenly changed his tragic tone, and asked whether we would like to see a cock fight, and, when we assented, jumped briskly on his legs and led the way to the palace yard, where cocks had already been brought in crowing.

The fight, however, was rather listless and short. 'I would not have missed this visit to the last of the Moguls for millions.'

The next afternoon Blunt went to Allahabad to stay with Sir Alfred Lyall at Government House, where he was treated to a tedious official dinner. 'How dull Anglo-Indian society is!' he complained, adding that his visible presence among the government officials put a distance between him and the Muslims with whom he would normally have entered into dialogue: 'I feel suddenly shut out from all light, as when one goes through a tunnel on a railway journey.' Nevertheless, Blunt insisted that his conversations with Lyall made quite clear that 'my ideas do not really run counter to any liberal interpretation of the continuance of British rule in India'. In Calcutta he had actually advocated a system of administration in which each Indian province had its English government, but proposed that the whole civil administration, legislation and finance should be devolved to local control. The anti-imperialist and self-professed 'Home Ruler' seemed to draw back from total

British withdrawal and the local newspaper, *The Pioneer*, even printed 'a vicious little paragraph', which it was later persuaded by Blunt to correct, claiming that he was a paid spy of the British Government. When he moved on next to Lucknow, however, *The Pioneer* returned to the attack by accusing him of stirring up sedition in Patna and other Muslim centres. 'Good hearty abuse as a revolutionist,' Blunt observed, 'can do me nothing but good.'

From Lucknow, Blunt travelled to Delhi, where he witnessed the key sites of the Mutiny, drawing a very different moral from Ruth Coopland when he saw the place where 'the English soldiers slew and destroyed some thousands of innocent men in revenge for the death of about one hundred'. A local chief claimed that twenty-six thousand people were killed by the British following its capture from the rebels, and that whole quarters and suburbs were rased to the ground: 'Such are the resources of civilization . . . I suppose no Englishman will ever dare write the real history of that year.' Blunt believed that if there were a second mutiny everyone would join it and he had long conversations with a prominent member of the military, Colonel Moore, who evinced real understanding of the local people: 'We talked over the whole situation in India, and agreed that it was impossible so absolutely unsympathetic a Government should not come into collision, some day, with the people. The Indians were the gentlest people in the world, and the easiest to govern, or we could not maintain our rule for an hour. As it was, they had only to combine against us passively to make the whole machine stop working.'

Blunt went on to Bombay and Hyderabad, where, as usual, he was wined and dined, in spite of his views, by the Residency. He continued to discuss 'the Patna affair' – Ripon earlier having asked him to tone down his letter of complaint in order to make life a little easier for him in making representations about the incident – and, at dinner with the Viceroy, a man called Lambert who was head of the secret police claimed to be surprised that such an incident should have happened.

Back in Bombay in the middle of February, Blunt took up with his other passion, Arab stallions, and, after visiting various stables and dealers, arranged for some horses to be shipped back to England, where he intended to race them at Newmarket. The dining continued ('It is astonishing the amount of liquor consumed here in India') with the local Governor, Sir James Fergusson: 'He is a good fellow of the old Tory type, believing that all is for the best in the best of all possible worlds, and firmly convinced that the Anglo-Indian administration is worked perfectly by high-minded and disinterested men, having the welfare of the natives at heart.' At the same dinner he met a woman who 'complained of the shabby way the Anglo-Indian officials were treated by Government, and thought it hard India should not be governed entirely for their benefit. They all hated India so much that they ought to be handsomely treated for being obliged to live there. What would India do without them, and what would England do without India?' Blunt added sniffily. 'She had been four months in India, and has not yet gone beyond Bombay.'

Meanwhile the decent Tory Fergusson warned Blunt not to go around stirring people up and 'exciting the native mind' by appearing to sympathize with local grievances: 'He could not understand how, as an Englishman, I could reconcile it with my conscience to do this. The Government of India was a despotism of a paternal and beneficent character, which was day and night working for the people's good, and any agitation would only impede its efforts . . . I had not the heart to say how precisely his good faith proved all the native argument.'

Blunt's last evening in India was on 29 February 1884. 'There was a beautiful sight in the heavens to-night, the crescent moon with the evening star exactly over it and quite close, like the Mohammedan device. This should mean a victory for the Mahdi either at Suakin, where they talk of an imminent battle, or perhaps the fall of Khartoum. I never saw a moon and star like this before.' He sailed on 1 March and would never return. He later regretted this 'failure' to pursue what he had started: 'I might have brought about great permanent good for the people whose interests I had espoused, and perhaps with the Mohammedans encouraged them to a real reformation, social and intellectual, if not political.' But the personal sacrifice would have had to have been total and Blunt seems to have held back in some way. 'It would have required something more than sympathy to bring me to the point; and I suppose my mind lacked the impetus of a full faith, without which complete devotion to a cause more than half religious could not be.'

Blunt continued to fight for Home Rule for Ireland, standing without success for Parliament in that cause and being imprisoned for his opposition to the Balfour Bill, which was designed to crush the Home Rule movement. Always controversial in his private life (a diary in the Fitzwilliam Museum, Cambridge, opened for the first time in 1972, catalogues his sexual exploits), Blunt numbered Wilde and other leading poets among his acquaintance. He died in 1922 and was buried in his own Sussex woods. E. M. Forster called him 'an English gentleman of genius'.

## 8

## *A Digression on Tourists*

One of the many themes introduced permanently into the tradition of English travel writing by the Victorian period was the conflict – in which one could march beneath only one campaign banner or the other – between the Traveller and the Tourist.

Representative of the dismay caused by the new phenomenon of mass tourism is the predicament of Isabella Bird, one of the most lively and observant of the great Victorian travellers, who found herself at the Niagara Falls in 1854. Already rather put out by the burgeoning industrial landscape of paper mills on the way to the Falls, on arrival she encountered with distaste 'a great fungus growth of museums, curiosity-shops, taverns, and pagodas with shining tin cupolas' and complained that, instead of being allowed to 'sit quietly on Table Rock, gazing upon the cataract', the tourist was dragged into a routine called 'doing Niagara'. She was handed oil-skins 'in order to "do" Niagara in the "regulation manner"'. After completing this duty she purchased a few items at a native American Indian curiosity shop for which she paid, in her estimation, six times their real value and then at last managed to find a vantage point for quiet contemplation of the Falls: 'I was not distracted by parasitic guides or sandwich-eating visitors; the vile museums, pagodas, and tea-gardens were out of sight: the sublimity of the Falls far exceeded my expectations, and I appreciated them the more perhaps from having been disappointed with the first view.'

Here the denunciation by traveller of tourist – the former is what we wish to be, the latter is what we profess to loathe – is already well established in its classic form in this passage with its attendant themes: the awareness of the gap between standardized image and reality, the pressure of other people at tourist bottlenecks, the ugliness of modern tourist facilities, the sense that one is being herded about or infantilized by the bossy tourist entrepreneurs, the impression that, as a tourist, one must do what one is told and not fail to complete the task obediently in the stipulated manner.

Quite early in the Victorian period the word 'tourist', which had been used neutrally enough in the late eighteenth century, began to acquire its present-day, rather sniffy, overtones and many other modern responses to travel and tourism had their origin in the century of Thomas Cook. One of these was the feeling of regret at the damage likely to be done by the growth of travel itself. In *Twenty Five Years in British Guiana* (1898) Henry Kirke, who had spent the last quarter of the nineteenth century in that corner of South America, wrote, in a passage commenting on the changes he had witnessed:

> . . . railways and steam vessels are now hurrying through vast territories only known twenty years ago to the fierce Carib or placid Arawak; gold diggers and diamond searchers are swarming up every great river and gloomy creek, and the whole face of the country is being rapidly changed . . .
>
> And with this change of circumstances the people have changed. Their old quaint manners and habits have disappeared; the old legends are vanishing; the people dress and talk as others; the electric light illuminates their houses; the tramcar patrols their streets; the silk chimney-pot of civilization is constantly in evidence; and they are as other men. The world is gradually acquiring a painful similarity; in a few hundred years every one will dress alike and speak the same language, and the human race will be reduced to one dull commonplace level of uniformity.

Mrs Archibald Little, travelling in China in the 1890s, although she noted the advantages of the new steamers on the River Yangtze, nevertheless expressed a characteristic lament: 'Yet it will be sad if steamers introduce an unappreciative crowd to the grand solitudes of the ravines and precipices, the rocks and rapids of the Yangtse.'

The distinction between 'tourist' and 'traveller' intensified during the great surge of British travelling after 1815, facilitated by trains and steamships and ever speedier forms of transport, and guided by the handbooks of Baedeker and Murray and the entrepreneurship of Thomas Cook. The word 'tourist' increasingly took on a pejorative tone. Surveying the crowd in the great dining room of the Shepheard Hotel in Cairo at the start of the 1873 Egyptian season, the writer Amelia Edwards claimed that, in less than two days, the traveller 'knows everybody's name and everybody's business; distinguishes at first sight between a Cook's tourist and an independent traveller'. In the pecking order of travel, the independent traveller is the true aristocrat, the shepherded tourist a mere peasant.

In his *Diary* the Reverend Francis Kilvert angrily observed, after encountering some tourists, one of them 'discoursing learnedly to his gaping companion and pointing out objects with his stick', at Llanthony Abbey in Wales in April 1870: 'If there is one thing more hateful than another, it is being told what to admire and having objects pointed out to one with a stick. Of all noxious animals too the most noxious is a tourist. And of all tourists the most vulgar, ill-bred, offensive and loathsome is the British tourist.' Three months later in Cornwall he bumped into another 'noisy rabble of tourists, males and females, rushing down the rocks towards Land's End as if they meant to break their necks, and no great loss either'.

Wordsworth famously protested in 1844, in letters to the *Morning Post* about the threat, so perceived, of the extension of the railway to his beloved Lakes. In the sonnet *On the Projected Kendal and Windermere Railway* he asked: 'Is then no nook of English ground secure | From rash assault?' and referred disparagingly to 'the pausing traveller's rapturous glance'. The railway, symbol of nineteenth-century progress, was a wreaker of destruction on rural beauty and tranquillity. In addition the railway-borne tourist was indicted for preferring speed to contemplation, his or her attention span fatally shortened by the new technology. The *noxiousness* of tourism was being established as a dominant theme in English travel writing. In the summer of 1848 *Blackwood's Magazine* declared: 'The merits of the railroad and steamboat have been prodigiously vaunted and we have no desire to deprecate the advantages of either . . . But they have afflicted our generation with one desperate evil; they have covered Europe with Tourists.'

Thirty years after Wordsworth, Ruskin was fulminating at the 'stupid herds of modern tourists' dumped on the shores of Windermere 'like coals from a sack'. The theme would prove constant throughout the twentieth century also. Evelyn Waugh in his travel book *Labels* (1930) observed that 'every Englishman abroad, until it is proved to the contrary, likes to consider himself a traveller and not a tourist'. And D. H. Lawrence in the 1920s observed: 'When a few German bombs fell upon Rheims Cathedral up went a howl of execration. But there are more ways than one of vandalism. I should think the American of five-minutes tourists has done more to kill the sacredness of old European beauty and aspiration than multitudes of bombs would have done.'

Travellers are never objective. They carry baggage. They represent what they see in particular ways, seeing countries and peoples through the prism of their time. In the eighteenth century travellers went in search of the picturesque. They would climb mountains in search of views using the famous 'Claude glass', a tinted convex mirror held up to the scene on which one had turned one's back in order to view it as if it were a moody and tenebrous landscape painting. Today we hold up our digital cameras in much the same way. Representations are just that, versions of reality, partial accounts, the 'sight' – that key term in the lexicon of the tourist industry – dependent on the nature of the seer, on the assumptions governing what he or she judges to be worthy of notice.

Just occasionally, however, some Victorian travellers would have flashes of self-knowledge. 'In Africa we always appear to consider the country ours and the natives the intruders,' wrote Helen Caddick in *A White Woman in Central Africa* (1900). David Livingstone, also in Africa, noted: 'There must be something in the appearance of white men, frightfully repulsive to the unsophisticated natives of Africa; for, on entering villages previously unvisited by Europeans, if we met a child coming quietly and unsuspectingly towards us, the moment he raised his eyes, and saw the men in "bags", he would take to his heels in an agony of terror, such as we might feel if we met a live Egyptian mummy at the door of the British Museum.'

Perhaps the most frank of the self-reflective Victorian travellers in this respect was Mansfield Parkyns, whose *Life in Abyssinia* (1853) contains many observations on the anomalous role of the white man in Africa. He observes, for example:

> It is a difficult task for any man to form a just opinion of the character of a nation through whose country he may have passed, or among whom he may have sojourned only for a short space of time. Travellers are far too apt to attribute to an entire population traits which they may have observed in the townspeople, or even in their immediate followers. Such an estimate is evidently unfair: the servants usually chosen by foreigners, in all parts of the world, are of a stamp peculiar to themselves, and often but poor samples even of the class to which they nominally belong . . .

and:

> Wherever travellers, no matter of what nation they be, are in the habit of passing, they spoil the people with whom they come into contact; or rather perhaps it is, that the people who volunteer their services to them are usually of not a very high grade. The newly-arrived tourist, from ignorance of the language, localities, and prices of the country, naturally applies to his interpreter to ascertain where he may best purchase anything that he may need; the servant as naturally directs him to the

shops of those tradesmen from whom he anticipates the highest percentage – thus our friend gets among a bad set of tradesmen. And so on . . .

We are too apt also to compare the manners of other nations with our own, and to judge of the people accordingly . . . I don't believe that there exists a nation, however high in the scale of civilization, that can pick a hole in the character of the lowest, without being in danger of finding one nearly, if not quite, as big in its own.

If the travellers encountered in the present book, toiling through the more remote or difficult parts of the unmapped globe, could see themselves as lonely explorers, shining the lamp of civilization into the darkness of tropical forests, there were others, far more numerous, who travelled in a different way, with the inevitable pains of the journey having been reduced or removed altogether by a new breed of entrepreneur. The tourist industry was in the ascendant, and one name stands out above all others: Thomas Cook.

Thomas Cook was born in 1808 in Melbourne, Derbyshire, to a poor but pious Baptist rural family. Leaving school at ten to work as a gardener's boy on the local estate, he soon became a Sunday school teacher and, by the age of twenty, a wandering village missionary, preaching, handing out tracts and establishing Sunday schools across the Midlands. Soon he became an active temperance campaigner and started to organize alcohol-free picnics and on 5 July 1841 he led an excursion on the Midland Counties Railway from Leicester to Loughborough consisting of 570 temperance supporters all of whom had paid a shilling each. It was a unique combination of entrepreneurial flair and evangelical zeal which Cook described fifteen years later as 'the starting point of a career of labour and pleasure which has expanded into a mission of goodwill and benevolence on a grand scale'. The Loughborough trip was quickly followed by other railway excursions and Cook declared characteristically: 'We must have RAILWAYS FOR THE MILLIONS.'

The Victorian age of steam had barely begun when Cook seized his opportunity. Although often opposed by the local landowners (the reason why so many rural stations today are positioned so far from the villages they serve), the railways surged forward in the 1830s. One of the earliest railway companies, the Liverpool and Manchester Railway, carried 445,000 passengers in 1830, the first year of its operation. By 1841 mail coaches had more or less ceased and the mail was carried by railways and by 1842 most stagecoaches had been withdrawn. The early train services were slow – in 1838 passengers travelling between London and Birmingham had to break the journey at one point to take a linking coach – and it was not until 1873 that dining and sleeping cars were introduced. Similar development of the railways was taking place across Europe and steam was simultaneously revolutionizing sea travel. By 1821 a regular ferry service was operating between Dover and Calais and ocean vessels steadily increased in size and speed throughout the nineteenth century.

Thomas Cook was always at the cutting edge of new travel opportunities. In 1845 he organized a trip from Liverpool to Caernarfon in north Wales, including the ascent of Snowdon, which was such a success it had to be repeated. This was a milestone in modern mass tourism, with Cook making a preliminary survey of accommodation and facilities and issuing a *Handbook of the Trip to Liverpool* (1845). This included all sorts of useful information such as tables of distance and eagerly reported that the announcement of this trip 'has excited an interest in these parts which has scarcely a parallel in the annals of Special Pleasure Trains'. Revealing of how Cook was here writing the first draft of tourism's future script, he added that the guide was published 'with the view of assisting the tourists in the most economical disposal of their time'.

The need for tourists to see as much as possible in the shortest possible time, preferably as a result of being told what to see and what not to see and the order in which to see it, was firmly established as a priority of modern mass tourism, though the *Handbook* was wistful about this urgent necessity: 'A great disadvantage connected with Railway travelling is the impossibility of minutely inspecting the interesting scenes which nature presents or art exhibits: a rapid glance is all that can be obtained of places and objects on which the antiquary, the philosopher, the naturalist, and scientific might luxuriate for hours or days. For this there is no remedy . . . the prevailing desire of excursionists is to reach the terminus as soon as possible . . .'

Cook went on to offer railway excursions to Scotland, the Lake District, the Isle of Man and Ireland and in 1848 inaugurated the first trip to a 'stately home', Belvoir Castle, whose doors were thrown open to the excursionists by the Duke of Rutland. But Cook's ambitions were not confined to Britain: 'I had become so thoroughly imbued with the Tourist spirit that I began to contemplate Foreign Trips, including the Continent of Europe, the United States and the Eastern Lands of the Bible.' His beginnings as a missionary were never obscured and this was linked to a fundamental egalitarianism and a belief that mass travel was an instrument of democratization. Accordingly he organized in 1861 a special excursion to Paris of 1600 people to attend a workers' demonstration. He described his loss of £120 on this venture as a 'labour of love minus profit' and in the later *Letter to the American Press* (1866) he claimed that he saw his work as a travel agent as 'appertaining to the great class of agencies for the advancement of Human Progress'.

But it was not all plain sailing. The cross-Channel ferry companies blocked Cook's plans for an all-in tour to the 1855 Paris Exhibition but by 1862 he was running what can properly be seen as the first 'package tours' with all transport and accommodation taken care of and the travellers being of modest means. Throughout the 1860s he conquered Europe, declaring in 1864, in an idiom straight from the missionary's soapbox lexicon: 'France and Switzerland now present to me new and almost unlimited fields of tourist labour.' In 1866 he made his first tour to America, a year after he opened his first London office, at 98 Fleet Street, and by the end of that decade he was offering tours at the luxury end of the market, to Palestine and Egypt. He was also broadening his influence. In

1870 his son, John Mason Cook, was officially appointed by the Egyptian government to act as its agent for passenger traffic on the Nile and in 1880 the Cooks were given exclusive control of all passenger steamers. The democratic populist was increasingly involved in both luxury tourism and the activities of British imperialism in Egypt, transporting soldiers, for example, during the revolt of Arabi Pasha. This tendency was cemented in the 1880s when Thomas Cook & Son set up in India to organize trips for wealthy Indians to see (and it was hoped approve) the metropolitan heart of Empire, an initiative that had the personal backing of Gladstone.

In contrast with its democratic beginnings, the empire of Thomas Cook had become associated in the colonies with a superior tourism of palatial hotels which had a part to play in the segregation and hierarchical ordering of those societies. Yet Cook always retained the belief with which he had started: that travel was a healer of global divisions. After his first round-the-world tour in 1873 he said he hoped to 'pioneer the way for the golden age when nations shall learn to war no more'.

In 1873 Cook published a collection of peripatetic letters to *The Times*, written on his own travels to research new tours. The English Baptist was not taken, on his journey to India, with the religious practices of the local people. Guided by 'Mr Etherington of the Baptist Mission', he was shown round the holy city of Benares, passing 'through centres of idolatrous filth and obscenity, combining bull, peacock, monkey, and other nameless objects of worship', and saw, from the deck of a boat on the Ganges, people washing corpses for burning. 'The whole of these heathen scenes were revolting in the extreme, and we turned with pleasure to see the contrast of 200 or 300 intelligent youths being educated in Queen's College, in the library of which I was pleased to see a file of *The Mail*, the offspring of *The Times*, and the *Illustrated London News*.'

Equally disappointing was Constantinople with its wretched hotels, while China remained 'the most impregnable of all Eastern nations. They are opposed to railways and telegraphs.' But for the most part Cook was anxious on these tours to smooth the way for organized travel, by putting pressure on local facilitators and squeezing their margins in the same way as tour operators do today: 'We wish to rub off a few ugly angles from the fares, and to make the figures popular, on the principle of all our tourist arrangements.'

In the end Thomas Cook saw his work as a travel agent in much the same terms as the colonialists saw their work of empire-building, and those terms were lofty:

I have learnt the way to circumnavigate the globe; have seen what may be done and what should be avoided; what time is required and the best season for making the tour; what detours may be made to the best advantage; what are the respective denominations and the proportionate values of moneys of all the states and countries visited. In a word, I think I comprehend the whole of this 'business of pleasure' around the world, and it now remains to be seen how far the various transit companies will respond to my views and proposals, with a view to popularising tours to and through America, on one side; India on the other, and round the world. I have collected facts of routes, countries, and people, that will serve for thought and guidance to the end of my days . . . Transition is written on every land . . . Japan is rising from seclusion and semi-barbarism to light and civilization. China must open her doors to the march of events and the progress of liberty, commerce, and religion and India, freed from the shackles of caste and superstition, will, ere long, embrace that truth to which England owes her greatness.

PART TWO

# THE EAST

TOWER OF GALATA.

# 9

### *Queenly Stamboul: Julia Pardoe in Constantinople*

When Alexander Kinglake published in 1844 his book on his travels through parts of the Ottoman Empire and what is now termed the Middle East (a twentieth-century coinage) he called it *Eothen* or 'from the East'. The Ottoman Empire long ago vanished. Another term popular with travellers in this region, 'the Levant', is equally outmoded. The political geography of the region through which the next group of travellers wandered (and, being travellers, they have a habit, in crossing borders indiscriminately, of inconveniently straying out of the neat boxes within which an author seeks to confine them) has changed so much that, as a general label, the term 'East' seems as serviceable as any.

The lands of what was largely the declining Ottoman Empire were first described as the Middle East in 1902 by the US naval historian Alfred Thayer Mahan. As early as 1838 an Anglo-Turkish Convention had started the process of opening up free trade and removing protectionist barriers. Although transport improvements such as railways were slower here to make an impact, and the camel retained its pre-eminence, travellers increasingly ventured into the Near and Middle East, lured in many cases by Orientalist dreams. The usual mix of motives drew the travellers on: trade, archaeology, espionage, diplomacy, missionary activity, science, botany, ornithology and sheer taste for adventure symbolized by Richard Burton's famous exploit of penetrating the holy city of Mecca in disguise.

Burton was also a scholar and a linguist and observed in his preface to his translation of *The Arabian Nights* that 'England has forgotten, apparently, that she is at present the greatest Mohammedan empire in the world, and in her Civil Service examinations she insists on a smattering of Greek and Latin, rather than a knowledge of Arabic'. One of the milestones in modern Middle Eastern studies is Edward William Lane's *Manners and Customs of the Modern Egyptians* (1836), which proved very popular and encouraged Burton to go on to translate *The Thousand and One Nights* between 1838 and 1841 and to compile an *Arabic-English Lexicon* (which was never completed). The Victorian taste for the Middle East, attested to by so many writers of the period, was now being catered for. The discovery of Egypt as a tourist destination and a place of ancient remains, together with the attraction of the Bible lands to devout evangelical Christians, ensured that the region would see more and more travellers. As well as the travellers encountered below, Thomas Cook was playing his part in ensuring an increase in numbers of British tourists.

It was in the spirit of blowing away some of the perfumed mists of Orientalism in order to reveal the actuality beneath that Julia

Pardoe resolved to write her account of her long stay in the mid-1830s in the Ottoman capital, then called Constantinople. *The City of the Sultan; and Domestic Manners of the Turks* appeared in 1837 and in it Pardoe was determined to try to describe accurately a city and a culture that she felt had been misunderstood by European travellers. Pardoe's first raptures, however, as she anchored in the Golden Horn on 30 December 1835 were entirely conventional: 'my long-indulged hopes were at length realized, and the Queen of Cities was before me, throned on her peopled hills, with the silver Bosphorus, garlanded with palaces, flowing at her feet.' No matter that snow had fallen on the city, she was seized with 'unalloyed delight. How could it be otherwise? I seemed to look on fairyland – to behold the embodiment of my wildest visions – to be the denizen of a new world.'

Born in Beverley, Yorkshire, in 1804, the younger daughter of Thomas Pardoe, an army officer (who was with his daughter on her Istanbul trip), and his wife Elizabeth, Julia Pardoe had a track record of literary romanticism, having published in her teens *The Nun: A Poetical Romance* and then an anonymous novel entitled *Lord Morcar of Hereward* (1829). Travelling for her health because of fear of consumption, she had already completed a travel book on Portugal in 1833 before she arrived in the Bosphorus. Her declared aim was to cut through the obstacles of language and culture to present a true picture of life in the Ottoman capital. She recognized that prejudice operated in both directions: from the 'Frank', as Europeans were called, and from the Turks themselves, 'particularly the Turkish females', though she understood why the latter would be unwilling to make the effort to overcome their anti-European prejudices 'when they remember how absurdly and even cruelly they have been misrepresented by many a passing traveller, possessed neither of the time nor the opportunity to form a more efficient judgement'. Pardoe resolved to give herself both those things and to counter the effects of being trapped in a narrow social élite in the fashionable district of Pera, which 'always reminded me of an ant-hill; with its jostling, bustling, and racing for straws and trifles; and its ceaseless, restless struggling and striving to secure most inconsequent results'.

Julia Pardoe had originally left England with her father intending to visit Turkey, Greece and Egypt but after three months in Constantinople she decided to stay on in order to write a book that would offer readers 'a more just and complete insight into Turkish domestic life, than they have hitherto been enabled to obtain'. Her first impressions of 'Queenly Stamboul' were those of a conventional traveller. She was struck by the way the houses were so close to the sea that 'they positively overhang' and she noted how, in the harbour, 'the languages of many lands came on the winds'. As they waited to disembark, caiques would pass the ship 'now freighted with a bearded and turbaned Turk, squatted upon his carpet at the bottom of the boat, pipe in hand, and muffled closely in his furred pelisse, the very personification of luxurious idleness; and attended by his red-capped and blue-coated domestic, who was sometimes a thick-lipped negro'. The veiled women had 'the appearance of an animated corpse'.

None of these observations seemed to bode well for a self-professed dispassionate researcher but Pardoe was a romantic, captivated by the glittering scene and the night-time mosques illuminated for Ramadan, and impatient, 'in these days of utilitarianism', with prosaic accounts of the marvels she saw: 'I detest the spirit which reduces everything to plain reason, and pleases itself by tracing effects to causes, where the only result of research must be the utter annihilation of all romance and the extinction of all wonder.'

From the moment Pardoe landed at the Custom House stairs at Galata on New Year's Day, 1836, 'amid a perfect storm of snow and wind', she applied herself to the task. Her first ambition was to get inside a Turkish family – 'this difficult, and in most cases impossible achievement for a European' – and very quickly a respectable Turkish merchant allowed her into his house, where she was able to visit his harem with a female Greek interpreter and observe the beauty of the daughter, 'whose deep blue eyes, and hair of golden brown, were totally different from what I had expected to find in a Turkish harem'.

Soon it was night and time for the breaking of the Ramadan fast with a sumptuous meal: 'Nineteen dishes, of fish, flesh, fowl, pastry, and creams, succeeding each other in the most heterogeneous manner – the salt following the sweet, and the stew preceding the custard – were terminated by a pyramid of pillauf.' In spite of this abundance Pardoe decided that 'gastronomy is no science in the East' and that 'the Osmanlis only eat to live, they do not live to eat' but she paid tribute to the 'simple and beautiful hospitality of the Turks, who welcome to their board, be he rich or poor, every countryman who thinks it proper to take a seat at it'. She retired with 'the ladies' to the harem, where a storyteller entertained them and the eldest woman present lit her pipe, which caused Pardoe a violent fit of coughing. She was impressed by the seeming tolerance of Ottoman religion: 'The Turks are extremely tolerant with regard to religious opinions; their creed being split into as many sects as that of the Church of England; and each individual being left equally free to follow, as he sees fit, the dictates of his own conscience.'

Lodged, however, in the fashionable European quarter of Pera ('the St James's of the capital'), Pardoe found time for *soirées dansantes* at the Russian palace, masked balls and other entertainments, but also for excursions around the city, to the Greek quarter at Fanar, for example, where the Greek Carnival was in full swing 'under one of those bright suns which make the Bosphorus glitter like a plate of polished steel'. The warmth of her reception touched her: 'Nowhere do you feel yourself more thoroughly at home at once than among the inhabitants of the East; they *may* be what we are accustomed to call them – semi-barbarians – but, if such be the case, never was the aphorism of a celebrated female writer more thoroughly exemplified that "extreme politeness comes next to extreme simplicity of manners".'

One Greek in particular, Nicholas Aristarchi, whom she terms 'Great Logotheti [Head of the Clergy] and Chargé d'Affaires for Wallachia', 'was to me an object of surpassing interest . . . his bright and restless eyes appear almost to flash fire during his moments of excitement'. The feeling was mutual and Aristarchi was clearly dazzled by the lively thirty-one-year-old and insisted on dancing with her nearly the whole evening and talking to her for the remainder. She in turn was fascinated by his talk 'and it was with sincere pleasure that I heard him promise that he would get up an extempore ball for us the following night'. In the end she spent 'three days of unalloyed gratification' with the Great Logotheti and his circle.

Returning to her self-imposed task of illuminating the domestic manners of the modern Turks, Pardoe faced frankly the difficulties impeding an insight into Turkish character, chief of which was language. But she was aware, too, of the problems of representation, the distorting lens of Orientalism and the exotic veils thrown over this part of the world by European writers and travellers:

> The traveller hazards undigested and erroneous judgements on the most important facts – traces effects to wrong causes – and deciding by personal feeling, condemns much that, did he perfectly and thoroughly comprehend its nature and tendency, he would probably applaud. Hence arise most of those errors relative to the feelings and affairs of the East, that have so misled the public mind of Europe; and, woman as I am, I cannot but deplore a fact which I may be deficient in the power to remedy. The repercussion of public opinion must be wrought by a skilful and a powerful hand. They are no lady-fingers which can grasp a pen potent enough to overthrow the impressions and prejudices that have covered reams of paper, and spread scores of misconceptions.

This strikes a relatively new note among the travellers' narratives explored so far. Pardoe showed herself aware of the great gap that existed between the outside visitor and the local culture, and she saw it as her mission to try to close it. She noted scathingly that there were people who had lived for fifteen years in Constantinople yet were as ignorant of it 'as though they had never left their own

country' and even in the high diplomatic circles to which she had
entrée 'the great question of Oriental policy is never discussed'.
Anticipating by nearly 150 years Edward Said's influential critique of
Western attitudes, *Orientalism* (1978), which will be discussed later,
she went on:

> It is also a well-attested fact that the entrée of native houses, and
> intimacy with native families, are not only extremely difficult,
> but in most cases impossible to Europeans; and hence the cause
> of the tissues of fables which, like those of Scheherazade, have
> created genii and enchanters *ab ovo usque ad mala*, in every
> account of the East. The European mind has become so imbued
> with ideas of Oriental mysteriousness, mysticism, and
> magnificence, and it has been so long accustomed to pillow its
> faith on the marvels and metaphors of tourists, that it is to be
> doubted whether it will willingly cast off its old associations,
> and suffer itself to be undeceived.

She noted how easy it was to condemn easily identifiable flaws
such as the ubiquity of bribes but it was 'the reverse of the picture
that has been so frequently overlooked and neglected', prejudiced
eyes neglecting to look at 'the moral state of Turkey' in which capital crime, she claimed, was absent and social cohesion remarkable.
One could note 'the contented and even proud feelings of the lower
ranks, and the absence of all assumption and haughtiness among
the higher'. There were no riots or murders or gambling houses, the
streets were quiet and a mere 150 police covered a population of
600,000. This greater equality in social relations, she believed,
derived from the fact that throughout the Ottoman Empire 'nearly
every man is the owner of a plot of land, and is enabled to trim his
own vine, and to sit under the shadow of his own fig-tree – he has
an interest in the soil – and thus, although popular commotions are
of frequent occurrence, they merely agitate, without exasperating
the feelings of the people'. The Turks, in her view, were kinder to
animals than the English (who seemed to want to shoot everything

that moved) and there was deep parental affection and maternal respect: 'These are strong traits, beautiful developments, of human nature; and, if such be indeed the social attributes of "barbarism", then may civilized Europe, amid her pride of science and her superiority of knowledge, confess that herein at least she is mated by the less highly-gifted Musselmauns.'

Pardoe also detected a more positive attitude to death and stronger religious feelings and challenged directly the assumption that Muslim women were kept down, arguing that they were 'the freest individuals in the Empire . . . It is the fashion in Europe to pity the women of the East; but it is ignorance of their real position alone which can engender so misplaced an exhibition of sentiment.' This positive assessment was somewhat vitiated by her view that the source of the contentment of Turkish women was their almost total absence of education: 'They have no factitious wants, growing out of excessive mental refinement; and they do not, therefore, torment themselves with the myriad anxieties, and doubts, and chimeras, which would darken and depress the spirit of more highly-gifted females . . . a woman in person, but a child at heart . . . Were I a man, and condemned to an existence of servitude, I would unhesitatingly chuse that of slavery in a Turkish family.'

In spite of her repeated claims to be divesting herself of Orientalist prejudice in the interests of preferring 'the veracious to the entertaining', Pardoe knew that her readers wanted to hear about harems and Turkish baths. Her description of the latter is particularly vivid:

> For the first few moments I was bewildered; the heavy, dense, sulphureous vapour that filled the place, and almost suffocated me – the wild, shrill cries of the slaves pealing through the reverberating domes of the bathing-halls, enough to waken the very marble with which they were lined – the subdued laughter, and whispered conversation of their mistresses murmuring along in an under-current of sound – the sight of nearly three hundred

women only partially dressed, and that in fine linen so perfectly saturated with vapour, that it revealed the whole line of the figure – the busy slaves, passing and repassing, naked from the waist upwards, and with their arms folded upon their bosoms, balancing on their heads piles of fringed and embroidered napkins – groups of lovely girls, laughing, chatting, and refreshing themselves with sweetmeats, sherbet, and lemonade – parties of playful children, apparently quite indifferent to the dense atmosphere which made me struggle for breath – and to crown all, the sudden bursting forth of a chorus of voices into one of the wildest and shrillest of Turkish melodies, that was caught up and flung back by the echoes of the vast hall, making a din worthy of a saturnalia of demons – all combined to form a picture, like the illusory semblance of a phantasmagoria, almost leaving me in doubt whether that on which I looked were indeed reality, or the mere creation of a distempered brain.

Her connections, her boldness and animation, and the simple fact that she was a young European woman with a lively interest in what she saw around her caused many doors to be thrown open to Julia Pardoe and enabled her to see most of the people who mattered in Constantinople in the 1830s. At the Kourban-Bairam festival of sacrifice on 28 March 1836, the Sultan Mahmoud stopped in his progress to ask who she was and she also visited Mustapha Pasha, who asked her searching questions about the Thames Tunnel and the operation of fire insurance companies. She sailed out into the Sea of Marmara, where 'Europe was beside and behind us – Europe, with its palaces, its politics, and its power – and the shadowy shore of Asia, with its cypress-crowned heights, and its dusky mountains, seemed to woo our approach'.

Pardoe also took the risk of visiting St Sophia, at the time out of bounds to the infidel. Demonstrating that it was not only male adventurers like Richard Burton who could play at disguise, she transformed herself in order to stand under the great dome: 'I stained my eyebrows with some of the dye common in the harem;

concealed my female attire beneath a magnificent pelisse, lined with sables, which fastened from my chin to my feet; pulled a *féz* low upon my brow; and, preceded by a servant with a lantern, attended by the Bey, and followed by the Kiara [house-steward] and a pipe-bearer, at half past ten o'clock I sallied forth upon my adventurous errand.' The Kiara warned her that if discovered she would be torn to pieces. 'This assertion somewhat staggered me, and for an instant my woman-spirit quailed.' But St Sophia was worth it:

> To me it seemed like a creation of enchantment – the light – the ringing voices – the mysterious extent, which baffled the earnestness of my gaze – the ten thousand turbanned Moslems, all kneeling with their faces turned towards Mecca, and at intervals laying their foreheads to the earth – the bright and various colours of the dresses – and the rich and glowing tints of the carpets that veiled the marble floor – all conspired to form a scene of such unearthly magnificence, that I felt as though there could be no reality in what I looked on, but that, at some sudden signal, the towering columns would fail to support the vault of light above them, and all would become void.

She had looked on all this 'at a moment when no Christian eye had ever heretofore looked on it; and when detection would have involved instant destruction'.

In the summer there were new excursions, to the old Ottoman capital, Broussa, at the end of May and in June to Mount Olympus, to lunatic asylums, fez factories, cemeteries, until, as autumn approached, it was time to leave, in tears, on the steamer *Ferdinando Primo*, which took Pardoe and her father (and a Prussian baron, a German noble, a colonel of the Coldstream Guards, a Hungarian cavalier and a Russian-Greek artist, not to mention a deck crowded with 'Turks, Greeks, and Jews') to the mouth of the Danube and through Bulgaria and Hungary, where she brings her narrative to a halt at Budapest. She travelled back to London via Vienna.

Pardoe's account of her travels was published in 1837 and was immediately popular, running to three editions. She produced a further volume on *The Beauties of the Bosphorus* (1838) and later travel books on France and Hungary, the latter greatly admired for its 'word-painting' by Elizabeth Barrett Browning. In 1842 ill-health persuaded her to leave London and live in Kent with her parents – she never married – where she wrote more indifferent novels, articles for *Frazer's* and other magazines and works of French history. This prolific literary toil earned her a civil list pension in 1860 and she died on 26 November 1862 at 24 Upper Montagu Street in London after a chronic illness of the liver.

'I cannot part from the reader who has lingered with me in strange lands,' she wrote at the conclusion of *The City of the Sultans*, 'without a feeling of regret; and as I look back upon the pages that I have written, and the scenes that I have sketched, a heaviness of heart comes over me, as though I were looking upon the face of a dead friend.'

## A Longing for the East: Alexander Kinglake in Smyrna

A certain facetious, self-deprecating tone has always been found in English travel writing but nowhere more notably in the Victorian period than in the work of Alexander Kinglake, whose *Eothen* (1844) has rarely been out of print and who himself conceded that his book was written in an 'almost boisterous tone'. He took great pleasure in announcing at the outset his commitment to frivolity: 'It is right to forewarn people (and I have tried to do this as well as I can, by my studiously unpromising title-page\*) that the book is quite superficial in character. I have endeavoured to discard from it all valuable matter derived from the works of others, and it appears to me that my efforts in this direction have been attended with great success; I believe I may truly acknowledge, that from all details of geographical discovery, or antiquarian research . . . the volume is thoroughly free.' (\* 'Eothen,' notes Kinglake, is 'almost the only hard word to be found in the book'.)

In fact Kinglake had some interesting things to say about the nature of travel writing and the 'jarring discord between the associations properly belonging to interesting sites, and the tone in which I speak of them'. He argued that 'my notion of dwelling precisely upon those matters which happened to interest me. and upon none other, would of course be intolerable in a regular book of travels . . . Now a traveller is a creature not always looking at sights . . . he will sing a sadly long strain about Self; he will talk for whole pages together about his bivouac fire, and ruin the ruins of Baalbec with eight or ten cold lines.' He stressed the 'egotism' of the traveller and 'his habit of referring the whole external world to his own sensations'. Yet even in the 'regular book of travels' the relationship between the travelling eye and the thing seen, the way in which the meaning of what is seen is constructed according to certain assumptions brought by the traveller, the value-laden 'discourses' he or she might have chosen, the whole manner in which countries are represented, are matters the thoughtful reader will always want to confront. It is no surprise that in recent decades the study of travel writing and the making of theories around it has become a rapidly expanding area of academic criticism. Yet, paradoxically, many readers feel that as a genre it has rather lost its way.

Kinglake in truth was rather more serious than he claimed to be and he did say that he was not 'flying from his country because of ennui' but 'strengthening his will, and tempering the metal of his nature for that life of toil and conflict in which he is now engaged'. That life began in 1809 at Taunton in Somerset, where as a young boy he was introduced to Homer by his mother. He was educated at Eton and Trinity College, Cambridge, where he was up at the same time as Tennyson and Thackeray. He studied law at Lincoln's Inn and was called to the Bar in 1837 but did not have a particularly distinguished legal career. Although active in sports and horsemanship as a student, he was too short-sighted for military service, and, after his law studies were complete, he set off on an eighteen-month trip through Europe and the Ottoman Empire which resulted in one of the most famous Victorian travel books, its style often said to echo Lawrence Sterne's eighteenth-century account of *A Sentimental Journey through France and Italy* (1768).

*Eothen* opens at Semlin, on the border of the Austro-Hungarian and Ottoman empires, with Kinglake contemplating 'the Splendour and Havoc of the East' symbolized by the sight of the Ottoman fortress of Belgrade. From here he travelled a hundred miles across the 'great Servian forest', jogging along at five miles per hour on horseback, delighted to have turned his back on 'the stale civilization of Europe' and mocking the 'state of utter respectability' of those he has left behind. The first stopping point of Kinglake and his companion, 'Methley' (actually Lord Pollington, an old Eton friend), was Adrianopolis, where Methley became ill and both were thoroughly soaked, their carpet bags seeming 'to contain nothing but mere solutions of coats and boots, escaping drop by drop'.

They crossed the Golden Horn and arrived in Constantinople fifteen days after setting out, struck like so many travellers to Istanbul up to the present day by the fact that 'nowhere does the sea come so home to a city'. The plague was raging in Constantinople and this, Kinglake believed, 'lent a mysterious and exciting, though not very pleasant interest to my first knowledge of a great Oriental city; it gave tone and colour to all I saw, and all I felt'. With Methley on his sickbed, Kinglake passed his time wandering around Constantinople, occasionally bumping into 'one of those coffin-shaped bundles of white linen which implies an Ottoman lady' and learning Turkish well enough to appreciate the eloquence and rhetoric of the market traders.

Shortly after Kinglake glimpsed Mount Olympus in the distance, Methley suddenly recovered and the two, both well-equipped classical scholars, set off for the Troad, the land of Troy, all too aware of the inevitable disappointments in store when, for example, the River Scamander of poetic imagination would be seen in reality (it had changed its course in the intervening centuries). Taught by his mother to read Homer in a spontaneous and 'rapturous' way rather than with the tools of the dry pedant, Kinglake was an imaginative classicist all too aware that: 'One's mind regains in absence that dominion over earthly things which has been shaken by their rude contact.' On the other hand, when he looked on the Aegean and the position of, for example, the island of Samothrace, he was convinced that Homer had stood where he was standing.

When Methley reached Smyrna it was time for him to return home, so he left Kinglake to reflect on his own on the nature of the Greeks in that relatively newly independent kingdom. Although he enjoyed the cosmopolitan flavour of Smyrna and its role as the main point of commercial contact between Europe and Asia, Kinglake felt that 'there was more heartiness, and strength in the

Greeks of the Ottoman Empire than in those of the new kingdom – the truth is, that there is a greater field for commercial
enterprise, and even for Greek ambitions under the Ottoman scep-
tre, than is found in the dominions of Otho.' But he did not despise
the Greeks, in spite of having reservations about their business
ethics: 'For myself, I love the race; in spite of all their vices, and even
in spite of all their meannesses, I remember the blood that is in
them, and still love the Greeks.' He praised in particular the beauty
of the women.

From Smyrna, Kinglake set sail in a Greek brigantine, the
*Amphitrite*, towards the coast of Syria with a new attendant,
Mysseri. He believed that sailors were the true Greeks 'because their
pursuits, and their social condition are so nearly the same as those
of their glorious ancestors', though he couldn't help noticing how
Greek sailors had a tendency to hug the coast: 'Indeed they have a
most unsailor-like love for the land.' His experience of Greek navigation (the voyage to Cyprus took forty days) taught him how
wrong he was to express surprise at the time taken by Ulysses to
reach Ithaca.

Kinglake left the ship at Limassol in a violent storm and became
the guest of the Greek who was British Vice-Consul there, regret-
ting that in spite of 'stately receptions' and generous hospitality,
only rarely 'does one gain an opportunity of seeing the familiar, and
indoor life of the people'. He visited the temple of Paphos but he
was not by temperament a ruin-bibber: 'I take no antiquarian interest in ruins, and care little about them, unless they are either
striking in themselves, or else serve to mark some spot on which my
fancy loves to dwell.' He was more interested in the beauty of Greek
women and soon sailed off again to Beirut.

One of Kinglake's first tasks was to pay a visit to a remarkable
English eccentric, Lady Hester Stanhope, who lived in 'an old con-
vent on the Lebanon range' about a day's journey from Beirut.
Niece of the Prime Minister William Pitt and, in Kinglake's phrase,
'Chatham's fiery grand-daughter', the imperious Lady Hester had
travelled widely in the Middle East in a style of epic grandeur,

arriving in the ancient city of Palmyra, for example, at the head of a troupe of hired Bedouin, to be greeted by the inhabitants in such a manner that she believed that they were crowning her 'Queen of the Desert'. By the time Kinglake found her in 1834 she was grounded at Dar Jun, where she lived in the semi-restored convent with around thirty servants and slaves. It was where she would die five years later, in her early sixties. Her glory days were over and she lived as a virtual recluse, nursing her grievances and elaborating her alternative philosophies. 'I can hardly tell why it should be,' Kinglake reflected, 'but there is a longing for the East, very commonly felt by proud-hearted people, when goaded by sorrow.'

Although he believed Lady Hester exercised 'something like sovereignty' over the wandering tribes around her, her loss of personal power and influence, which had once been significant in the region, had made her compensate with the search for spiritual power. The unlucky visitor was doomed to listen for hours 'to this wondrous white woman babbling about the occult'. She did her best to try to impress upon the witty scepticism of Kinglake 'the vanity and falseness of all European creeds' but he was unmoved by the putative magic of the East.

Kinglake travelled on to Galilee and to Nazareth, where he confessed to being deeply moved by the early-Christian shrine and met some monks who gratifyingly served up wine 'in the very midst of water-drinking infidels'. He visited the Sea of Galilee and bathed in the Dead Sea and, finally, encountered in the desert a true Arab encampment: 'The low, black tents which I had so long lusted to see were right before me, and they were all teeming with live Arabs – men, women, and children.' Unfortunately these poor Bedouin turned out to be 'awfully ugly'. In spite of his 'entire ignorance of the Arabic', Kinglake negotiated with some local Arabs to cross the Jordan on a kind of raft of inflated animal skins. His enthusiasm for Nazareth was not rekindled at Jerusalem and the 'Babel of worshippers' at the Church of the Holy Sepulchre did not attract him. In fact he gave full vent to his prejudices: 'I could not help looking upon the Jews of Jerusalem, as being in some sort the representatives, if not the actual descendants of the rascals who crucified our Saviour.'

Nor did the Muslims escape his criticism. He disliked the 'sad and sombre decorum' that ruled throughout the world of Islam: 'The Mahometans make beauty their prisoner.' Fortunately, in Kinglake's eyes, Bethlehem, after an insurrection against Mehmet Ali which left it a wholly Christian settlement, had been freed from 'the hateful laws of Asiatic decorum' and he was able to delight in 'the voice of free, innocent girls' and drink at 'this gushing spring of fresh, and joyous girlhood'.

Kinglake next set out on a nine-day journey across the desert to Cairo on a camel. On hiring these beasts, he reflected: 'You will find, I think, that one of the greatest drawbacks to the pleasure of travelling in Asia, is the being obliged more, or less, to make your own way by bullying.' He managed to secure four camels, one for himself, one for each servant and one for his baggage, and set off, soon to discover that the desert is not such a solitary place: 'If you adopt the Arab life for the sake of seclusion, you will be horridly disappointed, for you will find yourself in perpetual contact with a mass of hot fellow-creatures.' One night, looking out at the desert around the encampment, he enjoyed a moment of self-sufficiency before recalling that 'wherever man wanders, he still remains tethered by the chain that links him to his kind'. In fact the simple nomadic life contained much in a small space, for 'within my tent, there were heaps of luxuries, – dining rooms, dressing-rooms, – libraries, bed rooms, drawing rooms, oratories, all crowded into the space of a hearthrug'.

On reaching Cairo after this desert journey Kinglake found himself the only European traveller in the city because the plague was raging. By the time he left, nineteen days later, people would be dying at the rate of twelve hundred a day. He welcomed the chance to speak to people after his journey, though 'I felt a sort of consciousness that I had a little of the wild beast about me.' In fact most of the people he got to know died of the plague and everywhere were taking place funerals attended by professional mourners.

One of his new friends, Osman Effendi, showed him his harem: 'The rooms of the hareem reminded me of an English nursery, rather than of a Mahometan paradise.' When he eventually left the city he suddenly realized 'how much alarm and anxiety I had really been suffering'.

His next stop was the Pyramids, whose awesome size reignited his childhood fears of 'immensity', yet he found himself resistant to the notion that they belonged to some other realm, not human, 'the sheer giant-work of some old dismal age weighing down this younger planet':

> Fine sayings! but the truth seems to be, after all, that the Pyramids are quite of this world; that they were piled up into the air for the realization of some kingly crotchets about immortality, – some priestly longing for burial fees; and that as for the building – they were built like coral rocks by swarms of insects, – by swarms of poor Egyptians, who were not only the abject tools and slaves of power, but who also ate onions for the reward of their immortal labours! The Pyramids are quite of this world.

The great Sphinx, however, did chasten Kinglake. He found it 'more wondrous, and more awful than all else in the land of Egypt . . . You dare not mock the Sphynx.'

The next stage on his journey was Suez and from thence to Gaza and Nablus, a beautiful town, Kinglake felt, but 'the very furnace of Mahometan bigotry'. As ever, he searched for the signs of female beauty and found them but alas: 'It was always, however, with a sort of Zoological expression of countenance that they looked on the horrible monster from Europe.' One exception was Mariam, a beautiful sixteen-year-old loved by a sheikh who wanted her to convert to Islam in order to marry him, the act of conversion automatically annulling her existing marriage to a Christian. Kinglake's help was sought by the family of the girl, who was presently imprisoned in a mosque until her conversion could be accredited.

Kinglake realized that he had better keep out of this, although his dislike for the Christian family made him wish Mariam would be successful in marrying her sheikh.

At Damascus Kinglake was pleased to find that a city formerly very dangerous for Europeans had now been rendered 'safer than Oxford' thanks to the efforts of the new Consul General and he was delighted by this 'city of hidden palaces, of copses, and gardens, and fountains, and bubbling streams'. He enjoyed the baths and the great café and the gardens and 'rushing waters', which enacted an 'idea of bliss'. He finally ended his journey by crossing 'the Pass of the Lebanon' and, at the summit, catching sight of the distant sea. Kinglake had become used to what he called 'the people and the scenes of forlorn Asia – well used to tombs and ruins, to silent cities and deserted plains, to tranquil men, and women sadly veiled' and he now looked forward to his journey home to the West. He felt himself at a crossroads 'between the birthless Past, and the Future that has no end' and set out an Orientalist contrast between the slumbering, benighted East and the progressive dynamism of the European nineteenth century:

> Behind me I left an old and decrepit World – Religions dead and dying – calm tyrannies expiring in silence – women hushed, and swathed, and turned into waxen dolls – Love flown, and in its stead mere Royal and 'Paradise' pleasures. – Before me there waited glad bustle and strife – Love itself, an emulous game – Religion a Cause and a Controversy, well smitten and well defended – men governed by reasons and suasion and speech – wheels going – steam buzzing – a mortal race, and a slashing pace, and the Devil taking the hindmost – taking *me*, by Jove (for that was my inner care), if I lingered too long, upon the difficult Pass that leads from Thought to Action.
>
> I descended, and went towards the West.

Kinglake's travels were not over. He later visited Algeria, and in 1854 he went to witness at first hand the invasion fleet on the

Crimean coast and recorded the battle of the Alma in sketches. In 1857 he became the Liberal MP for Bridgwater until he was unseated in 1869 as a result of a case of bribery involving his election agent. He concentrated on a massive eight-volume history of the Crimean War. An active social life – for a rather shy and weak-voiced man who did not shine in his Commons speeches – included membership of the Travellers' Club and the Athenaeum but eventually ill-health ended his days as a clubman and he died aged eighty-two of gout and throat cancer at his home in Bayswater Terrace, London.

II

*Hairy Saints: Robert Curzon in Search of Icons*

It is hard not to warm to a writer who opens his book with the words: 'In presenting to the public another book of travels in the East, when it is already overwhelmed with little volumes about palm-trees and camels, and reflections on the Pyramids, I am aware that I am committing an act which requires some better excuse for so unwarrantable an intrusion on the patience of the reader than any that I am able to offer.' The note of patrician languor came easily to Robert Curzon, fourteenth Baron Zouche of Harringworth and the first Viscount Curzon. His best-selling *Visits to Monasteries in the Levant* (1849) describes his travels in the 1830s through Egypt, the Holy Land and Greece in search, controversially by present-day ethical standards, of rare manuscripts which he acquired from various Orthodox monasteries. He exemplifies a certain type of English traveller – relaxed, witty, well-informed, ready to be amused and, without being self-important, never quite letting go of his sense of himself as a discreetly superior Englishman at large in strange countries. He had none of that single-minded, sometimes self-righteous, earnestness which characterizes the scientific explorer and he had a talent for vivid re-enactment of scenes which, as has been suggested above, is rarer than one might think among the Victorian composers of travel narratives.

Robert Curzon was born in 1810 and educated at Charterhouse and Christ Church, Oxford. Leaving without troubling to take a degree, he entered Parliament as the Member for the rotten borough of Clitheroe in 1831, only for the borough to be disenfranchised a year later by the great parliamentary reforms of 1832, following which he set off on his travels with his close companion Walter Sneyd.

The idea for his book came to Curzon while he was staying 'in a country house belonging to my family' and leafing idly through various ancient manuscripts, most of which had been collected by himself (and are now in the British Museum). It occurred to him that he should 'write down some account of the most curious of these manuscripts, and the places in which they were found, as well as some of the adventures which I encountered in the pursuit of my venerable game'. He had what every travel writer needs, a pretext on which to hang his random adventures. Curzon believed that the monasteries of 'the East' were especially interesting because 'they are the most ancient specimens extant of domestic architecture' after the remains of Pompeii. 'The refectories, kitchens, and the cells of the monks exceed in point of antiquity anything of the kind in Europe.' The actual church architecture of these monasteries, by contrast, Curzon felt, was seldom distinguished, though their well-fortified nature was striking: 'I have been quietly dining in a monastery, when shouts have been heard, and shots have been fired against the stout bulwarks of the outer walls, which, thanks to their protection, had but little effect in delaying the transit of the morsel between my fingers into the ready gulf provided by nature for its reception.'

Curzon may have been criticized for stripping Orthodox monasteries of their heritage but the manuscripts he acquired were often very poorly cared for and some might not have survived without his intervention. Monks sometimes used old illuminated volumes to stand on to keep their feet warm and he was unimpressed by the 'ignorance and superstition' of many of them.

At the end of July 1833, on the cusp of the new era of accelerated travel, Curzon took a passage from Malta to Alexandria in a merchant sailing vessel, the *Fortuna*, 'for in those days there were no steam-packets traversing every sea, with almost the same rapidity and accuracy as railway carriages on shore'. Writing in 1865 in a preface to one of the many reprints of his book, Curzon delivered a representative lament that would echo across the nineteenth century, a keening for the lost Arcadia of true travel before everything was made accessible and uniform by mass tourism:

> Those countries were, however, much better worth seeing at that time than they are now; they were in their original state, each nation retained its own particular character, unadulterated by the levelling intercourse with Europeans, which always, and in a very short time, exerts so strong an influence that picturesque dresses and romantic adventures disappear, while practical utility and a commonplace appearance are so generally disseminated, that in a few years more every country will be alike, and travellers will discover that there is nothing to be found in the way of manners and customs that they may not see with greater ease in their own houses in London.

However, when Curzon reached Alexandria and saw his first Arab sailor, he made the conventional observation: 'He was just the sort of man that I imagine Sindbad the Sailor must have been.' He put up at what he believed was the only hotel in Africa, the Tre

Anchore, and soon was inspecting various 'savage-looking Bedouins', marvelling that 'anything so like a wild beast could exist in human form'. He was well aware of the contrast between a formally attired early-Victorian English aristocrat and the freedom of manners and unconventionality of the Bedouin: 'An English gentleman in a round hat and a tight neck-handkerchief and boots, with white gloves and a little cane in his hand, was a style of man so utterly and entirely unlike a Bedouin Arab that I could hardly conceive the possibility of their being only different species of the same animal.'

The next day the gentleman removed his hat in the presence of Boghos Bey, the Armenian Prime Minister of the Egyptian ruler, Ali Pasha, the first of Curzon's many encounters on his trip with people who mattered. He also discovered that stock character of nineteenth-century Eastern travel, the dragoman – guide, interpreter and much else besides: 'The newly-arrived European eats and drinks whatever his dragoman chooses to give him; sees through his dragoman's eyes; hears through his ears; and, although he thinks himself master, is, in fact, only a part of the property of this Eastern servant, to be used by him as he thinks fit, and turned to the best account like any other real or personal estate.'

On first seeing the Nile, Curzon knelt down and drank its 'muddy taste' and at Cairo he stayed, naturally, at 'the hospitable mansion of the Consul-General' and paid a visit with him to Ali Pasha, who, with his 'quick sharp eye', looked like 'an old grey lion'. Curzon delighted in the sights of Cairo: 'Nothing can be conceived more striking than a great assemblage of people in the East: the various colours of the dresses and the number of the white turbans give it a totally different appearance from that of a black and dingy European crowd; and it has been well compared by their poets to a garden of tulips.' But he noted how rapidly the presence of Europeans had generated all sorts of cheating and touting by the locals in contrast with 'the unsophisticated times, before steamers came to Alexandria, and what is called the overland journey to India was established'. Curzon preferred a more leisurely pace of travel and was delighted when the Minister of Finance lent him a magnificent *dahabieh*, a large sailing boat, on which to glide along the Nile: 'I like to take my time and look about me, and sit under a tree on a carpet when I get to an agreeable place, and I am in no hurry to leave it; so the heavy quality of the vessel suited me exactly – we did nothing but stop everywhere.'

Curzon returned to England after this short trip but soon came back to visit the Coptic monasteries of Egypt in earnest. At the monastery of Baramous the monks gave him a 'half-ruined cell' in which to sleep on a carpet where he was attacked by 'a multitude of ravenous fleas'. He went on to another monastery, Souriani, on the Natron lakes (in present-day northern Tanzania), where he was horrified to see some Coptic vellum manuscripts being used as coverings for jars of preserves and which he judged to be 'among the oldest manuscripts in existence'. Curzon started to ply the abbot with rosaglio, or rosé wine, in order to break down his resistance. The abbot insisted that there was no truth in the rumour that there was a cellar with a secret store of books but Curzon managed to persuade the monk to let him enter an oil store full of empty jars: 'taking the candle from the hands of one of the brethren (for they had all wandered in after us, having nothing else to do) I discovered a narrow low door, and, pushing it open, entered into a small closet vaulted with stone which was filled to the depth of two feet or more with the loose leaves of the Syriac manuscripts which now form one of the chief treasures of the British Museum'.

As he pursued his tour of the monasteries Curzon abandoned his necktie and cane for 'the long robes of a merchant of the East' but was under no illusion that this disguise would provide invisibility: 'there were my servants armed to the teeth and laden with old books; and one and all we were so covered with dirt and wax from top to toe, that we looked more as if we had been up the chimney than like quiet people engaged in literary researches'. At an Abyssinian monastery he entered the library: 'The strange costumes and wild appearance of these black monks, and the curious arrangement of their library, the uncouth sounds of their singing and howling, and the clash of their cymbals in the ancient convent of the Natron lakes, formed a scene such as I believe few Europeans have witnessed.'

After this tour of acquisition Curzon pressed on by horse to Jerusalem, arriving from the direction of Gaza: 'It is not easy to describe the sensations which fill the breast of a Christian when, after a long and toilsome journey, he first beholds this, the most interesting and venerated spot upon the whole surface of the globe . . . I do not think that anything we saw afterwards during our stay in Jerusalem made a more profound impression on our minds than this first distant view.' Outwardly, however, Curzon maintained his composure in contrast with the raptures all around him: 'we, who consider ourselves civilized and superior beings, repressed our emotions; we were above showing that we participated in the feelings of our barbarous companions'. He was in fact sceptical about the claims of the tourist industry that had grown up around the holy places:

> Whether all the hallowed spots within these walls really are the places which the guardians of the church declare them to be, or whether they have been fixed on at random, and consecrated to serve the views of a crafty priesthood, is a fact I shall leave others to determine . . . The main error on the part of the priests of modern times at Jerusalem arises from an anxiety to prove the actual existence of everything to which allusion is made by the evangelical historians, not remembering that the lapse of ages and the devastation of successive wars must have destroyed much, and disguised more, which the early disciples could most readily have identified.

Curzon spent several weeks at Jerusalem, partly because he wanted to stay on to witness the Greek Easter ceremonies, and he made many excursions, reflecting on the quality of the travel guides available to him:

In addition to the Bible, which almost sufficed us for a guide-book in these sacred regions, we had several books of travels with us, and I was struck with the superiority of old Maundrell's narrative over all the others, for he tells us plainly what he saw, whilst other travellers so encumber their narratives with opinions and disquisitions, that, instead of describing the country, they describe only what they think about it; and thus little real information as to what there was to be seen or done could be gleaned from these works, eloquent and well written as many of them are; and we continually returned to Maundrell's homely pages for a good plain account of what we wished to know.

Curzon left Jerusalem on 6 May 1834 but not before witnessing a horrifying event at the Church of the Holy Sepulchre, where a large crowd was trampled in a panic: 'I saw full four hundred wretched people, dead and living, heaped promiscuously one upon another, in some places above five feet high . . . When the bodies were removed many were discovered standing upright, quite dead.' The deaths affected Curzon deeply. In the middle of the night he looked out at the court where the corpses were laid out: 'In the morning I had walked with them, living men, such as I was myself, and now how changed they were! . . . What little difference there is in appearance between the same men asleep and dead!'

On Friday 31 October 1834 Curzon arrived at Corfu, where he was rowed across to the Greek mainland at Igoumenitsa, heavily guarded by Albanians ('great dandies about their arms') to protect him from pirates. On arrival he hired packhorses and guides and set off for the rock-perched monasteries of the Meteora. However, at a pass through the Pindhos mountains at Métsovo the party was seized by robbers, who ended up offering their services as guides, which, in the circumstances, were politely accepted. When he finally reached the Meteora Curzon was overwhelmed: 'nothing can be more strange and wonderful than this romantic region, which is unlike anything I have ever seen either before or since'. But he was not so impressed by the various religious hermits living in caves and holes all about them: 'It is difficult to understand by what process of reasoning they could have persuaded themselves that, by living in this useless, inactive way, they were leading holy lives . . . they did nothing whatever to benefit their kind.'

Curzon's robber-guides woke up the monks at the first monastery, of Barlaam, by firing off their guns. This produced, one hundred feet up, 'the face and grey beard of an old monk' who demanded to know the identity of this wild party. A thin cord was let down, to which Curzon attached his letter of introduction, and then 'a much larger rope was seen descending with a hook at the end to which a strong net was attached'. Two servants were put into this net, 'twisting round and round like a leg of mutton hanging to a bottle-jack', which rather put Curzon off and he resolved instead to climb up a series of ladders which were suspended by large wooden pegs on the face of the precipice. After 'hanging in the air like a fly on a wall' and suffering a fit of dizziness he clambered through a small iron door and was soon quaffing rosaglio with the abbot.

Later they let Curzon down on a winch and he sent his things on to the Megálou Meteórou, the Great Monastery, where he was later bundled into a net and 'slowly drawn up into the monastery, where I was lugged in at the window by two of the strongest of the brethren, and after having been dragged along the floor and unpacked, I was presented to the admiring gaze of the whole reverend community, who were assembled around the capstan'. He soon began his inspection of the monastery and its frescoes, but was unimpressed by the depictions of 'little ugly saints, very hairy and very holy . . . These Greek monks have a singular love for the devil and everything horrible and hideous. I never saw a well-looking Greek saint anywhere.'

After dining with the monks – seated on the floor and using his hands – Curzon began his negotiations. He paid gold for two rare Byzantine gospel manuscripts: 'Such books as these would be treasures in the finest national collection in Europe.' All seemed to be proceeding smoothly until a row broke out between the *agoumenos*,

or abbot, and the librarian about the division of the spoils of this
sale. Soon all the other monks were drawn into the rumpus 'and
everyone began to quarrel with his neighbour, the entire community
being split into various little angry groups, chattering, gesticulating,
and wagging their long beards'. Asserting his authority, the abbot
announced that the sale must be cancelled. This was not the
announcement they had been hoping for: 'the monks all looked
sadly downcast at this unexpected termination of their noble
defence of their principles'.

When Curzon rejoined his robbers they enthusiastically offered
to sort out the problem by dashing off to steal back the books but
he restrained them. On the way back he left them at Métsovo,
though they wanted him to continue to employ them, and he
returned to the Corfu ferry at the end of 'the most dangerous and
rapid expedition that it ever was my fortune to take'.

Three years later Curzon, in the spring of 1837, was back. He presented himself in the lobby of the Palace of the Patriarch of
Constantinople clutching a personal letter from the Archbishop
of Canterbury which recommended him as suitable person
to view the libraries of the monasteries of Mount Athos. 'Who
is the Archbishop of Canterbury?' the Patriarch demanded. After
various coffee ceremonies, however, he was mollified and furnished
Curzon with a *firman*, an official letter which was to prove very
useful throughout this trip since it announced him grandly as 'the
Honourable Robert Curzon, of a noble English family' and opened
many doors.

Next Curzon hired a Greek factotum and interpreter ('an ugly,
thin little fellow'), whose right eye 'had a curious obliquity of vision,
which was not particularly calculated to inspire confidence'. Curzon
had himself a leather belt made containing a number of sections in
which pieces of gold could be concealed without announcing themselves by their jingling and then was ready to leave his hosts, Lord
and Lady Ponsonby at the British Embassy at Therapia, to board a
steamer which passed down the Dardanelles. He then switched to a
sailing vessel to travel through the Aegean islands en route to

Lemnos: 'I thought how little changed things were in these latitudes since the brave Captain Jason passed this way in the good ship Argo.'

After a brief but distasteful experience of the flea-ridden beds of Lemnos, Curzon arrived by sea below the great monastery of St Laura at Athos to begin his manuscript hunt. While his man went off to find mules for 'the celebrated Milordos Inglesis, the friend of the Universal Patriarch', Curzon went to inspect a venerable hermit who was living in a Byzantine tower nearby and who made him feel that he had stepped back briefly into the twelfth century. The monks of St Laura, most of whom had never seen a stranger before, settled him in and allowed him to inspect the frescoes, which were of yet more hairy saints: 'these are all old men with beards . . . These personages are severe and grim of countenance, and look by no means comfortable or at home; they each hold a large book, and give you the idea that except for the honour of the thing they would be much happier in company with the wicked little sinners and merry imps in the crimson lake below.' Curzon enjoyed the company of the monks, who, though they renounced meat, tippled 'famously'. Although Athos was famous for its exclusion of the female, even down to the female domestic animal, Curzon, as he tried to sleep, discovered that this rigid law was 'infringed by certain small and active creatures who have the audacity to bring their wives and large families within the very precincts of the monastery'.

After breakfast of a sort of white paste composed of cloves of garlic crushed with sugar and mixed with oil, shreds of cheese 'and sundry other nice little condiments', Curzon set off to explore the five thousand volumes of the library of St Laura and its nine thousand manuscripts. To his eye, however, there was nothing really valuable and he resolved to press on to the Monastery of Karakálou, where, spotting a loose leaf of a Gospel of St Matthew, he asked the *agoumenos* if he might buy some more manuscripts. The abbot wanted to know what on earth he wanted such a thing for and Curzon's man chipped in with the suggestion that they would be useful for covering jam pots or vases of preserves. '"Oh!" said the *agoumenos*, "take some more" and, without more ado, he seized upon an unfortunate thick quarto manuscript of the Acts and Epistles, and drawing out a knife cut out an inch thickness of leaves at the end before I could stop him. It proved to be the Apocalypse, which concluded the volume, but which is rarely found in early Greek manuscripts of the Acts: it was of the eleventh century.'

Promising to be back to purchase more of these items, Curzon continued his circuit of the monasteries, occasionally encountering resistance, and occasionally horrified by the neglect of precious material. At the monastery of Xenophou he found 'an immense quarto Evangelistarium sixteen inches square, bound in faded green or blue velvet, and said to be in the autograph of the Emperor Alexius Comnenus . . . it was amongst the finest Greek MSS that I had ever seen'. For five hours he haggled over this item with the monks, 'but in the end I got the great book of Alexius Comnenus for the value of twenty-two pounds . . . bearing with perfect resignation the smiles and scoffs of the three brethren, who could scarcely contain their laughter at the way they had done the silly traveller'. At the monastery of St Paul he discovered an illuminated Bulgarian manuscript: 'I had seen no book like it anywhere in the Levant. I almost tumbled off the steps on which I was perched on the discovery of so extraordinary a volume.' The monks told him that they had no use for old books and asked if there was anything he wanted, so he coyly asked for the Bulgarian MSS: 'Perhaps the greatest piece of impertinence of which I was ever guilty . . . I felt almost ashamed . . . to salve my conscience I gave some money to the church.'

Curzon then returned to the Karakálou monastery, where he purchased 'a curiously carved cross set in silver . . . It is one of the most ancient as well as one of the finest relics of its kind now existing in England.' Smelling the English lord's gold, the *agoumenos* led him to a vast store of hazel nuts and tried to interest him in purchasing them for export but Curzon's appetite for trading was done.

The next day he shipped out his treasures and caught a Smyrna boat, the *Stamboul,* back to Constantinople.

Subsequently Curzon was appointed attaché at the Embassy in Constantinople, where he combined the role of Private Secretary to Sir Stratford Canning with further manuscript explorations and acquisitions. After subsequent diplomatic missions, which resulted in a book on Armenia, he returned to England and eventually married at the age of forty. His study of manuscripts continued and he became an expert on handwriting. After succeeding to the barony in 1870 he concerned himself with the family estates in Sussex and Staffordshire until his death in August 1873.

## 12

## *Laughing Heartily: Esmé Scott-Stevenson in Asia Minor*

Little is known of the author of *Our Ride through Asia Minor* (1881) but the lively and trenchant style of Esmé Scott-Stevenson's account makes it a refreshing addition to the corpus of Eastern travels. Although she travelled with her husband, Captain Andrew Scott-Stevenson of the 42nd Royal Highlanders ('Black Watch'), she boasted that it had been written in 'a natural womanly way' and that she had sent off the manuscript without showing it to him for fear that he would tone down her more outspoken comments. 'I have no literary pretensions whatever,' she announced. 'The attempt to describe things just as I found them is, therefore, responsible for the unvarnished opinions of places and people which I have recorded.'

In fact this trope of plain observation plainly recorded was not uncommon among Victorian travellers and rather obscures the vigorous prejudices and partialities that generally attended such accounts. Esmé Scott-Stevenson claimed that the country through which she and her husband journeyed had been 'almost unexplored' and she saw it as her mission to encourage travel in that region: 'I earnestly hope that, not only strong energetic men, but also clever and cultivated ladies, may be tempted to share the pleasure I have enjoyed; and instead of going to India, America, or Africa for new sensations and enchanting scenery, come out to Karamania.'

Scott-Stevenson had written an earlier account of *Our Home in Cyprus* (1879), where her husband was British Commissioner at Kyrenia. She had been in the habit of going down to the beach to

admire 'the picturesque-looking Turk with his long beard, his knot-
ted staff and flowing robes, vividly calling to mind the pictures of
the patriarchs' and watching the caiques unloading their exotic
cargoes. The sailors had gratified her taste for 'improbable tales' of
the Orient, the result of which was to 'fire me with an uncontrol-
lable wish to see for myself the wonders hidden by the distant
hills'. And so, on 2 April 1880, the couple set off from Cyprus
bearing a *firman* obtained from the Porte by Sir Robert Biddulph,
Governor of Cyprus, with their friend Dr Johnstone, a civil surgeon living in Kyrenia. Captain Scott-Stevenson supplemented his
wife's motives with an intention to gauge Asia Minor's potential as
rich country for exploitation and as a future recruiting ground for
England against her dastardly Russian foe. They both expected to
confront 'that incarnation of organised hypocrisy and injustice, of
brute force and cruelty – the Russian Government and the Russian
people'.

Ignoring all warnings of the dangers they faced, which included
the 'fanatical and barbarous' people and the fact that 'a lady had
never been seen in these countries' and would undoubtedly meet
with various sorts of 'unpleasantness', the Scott-Stevensons acquired
a tent and laid in supplies of 'preserved provisions and wine', waterproof clothing, saddles and bridles, and sent to England for a copy
of Kiepert's map of *Klein-Asien* – reputed to be the best there was
but destined to prove 'little better than a delusion and a snare'.
Letters of credit from the Ottoman Bank were also obtained, as well
as a map very useful for propaganda purposes which showed how
the English at the Treaty of Berlin had stopped the Russians from
depriving the Turks of a large amount of territory.

The couple's first stop was Nicosia, and then Larnaca, where the
weekly steamer of Bell's Asia Minor Line left for the Syrian coast.
Scott-Stevenson was keen to be away from the stultifying male society of Larnaca: 'I cannot divine how civilised people exist in
Larnaca . . . Gentlemen possibly can manage; for they can smoke
and read the papers comfortably enough in the club, which is good.
But for ladies – diversion is simply conspicuous by its absence.' So,

on 4 April 1880, they set sail and twelve hours later, at 7 a.m., Scott-Stevenson came out on deck to look on the beauty of Beirut. Soon she was being handed down the ship's side 'and passed on from one brawny arm to another' to face her first encounter with corrupt Turkish officialdom, which demanded bribes to avoid their bags being searched. The couple were soon mollified, however, by Bassoul's Hotel, where two hundred guests, mostly Americans, sat down to dinner and where the floors were of cool marble, the host's civility was beyond reproach and the fresh butter and cream unstinting.

For the next four days Scott-Stevenson toured the bazaars of Beirut, scandalized at their filth and their prices: 'Alas! these Eastern cities – veritable whited sepulchres, fair to the eye yet foul within! . . . The town is shockingly dirty and about as odiferous as Valetta.' Luxury was soon put behind them as they boarded another Bell steamer, the *Clutha*, for Tripoli, making the acquaintance on the boat of a Mr Bertram, a gentleman who had wintered on the Nile 'and wished if possible to go home through Anatolia' and who now joined the party (which also included a Greek interpreter brought from Cyprus, Theodore Vassilio). They seem to have enjoyed quarrelling with café owners over their prices and criticizing their breakfasts ('all we could get was some coffee, boiled with grounds in Turkish fashion') until they began to appreciate the Arab bread and 'delicious fresh butter', which, they conceded, 'effaced all recollection of the tinned meats which had been so carefully stowed away amongst the other treasures in our saddle-bags'. Mr Bertram offered the opinion that the food constituted 'very good tackle'. There were a great many outbursts of hearty laughter, especially when Scott-Stevenson fell off her horse into a stream. When they saw the rotten mule that had been assigned to Dr Johnstone it was promptly christened 'Dr Johnstone's Ruins'.

At Aleppo they made the acquaintance of a Mr Boscawen from the British Museum, who was busy shipping out antiquities, and the English consul, Mr Henderson, who boasted of having killed thirty-six foxes in the past year. With his collection of fine Arab horses and greyhounds for coursing the hunting was good, especially gazelle. His courtyard was stacked with antiquities he had 'dug out of the ruins' of the old Hittite capital, Yerabblus.

They also visited prominent Turkish officials, who seemed strongly Anglophile, including the regional military commander, Djemel Pasha, who laid out English afternoon tea with 'bread-and-butter cut in the orthodox fashion and Minton's ware'. After a visit to the barracks, Scott-Stevenson pronounced her verdict on the Ottoman Turks. 'Yet much as I like the Turk, it is impossible to be blind to the fact that he is not born to govern.' Corruption, intrigue and general inefficiency meant that their Empire was doomed to collapse 'unless we step in and force upon it the reforms which are so sadly needed'.

As they penetrated farther into Armenia, laughing heartily at their various mishaps, Scott-Stevenson decided that she did not like the Christian villages and was 'disgusted' by the Christian missionaries and their tales of alleged persecution by the Turks. 'It is perhaps not a lady's part to raise an argument,' she declared, before doing so in splendidly vituperative fashion on the subject of missionaries:

But how do they go about? and what do they do? Why, in frockcoats and chimneypot hats, preaching, nay forcing upon the people – in their own land remember – dogmas and customs which from their childhood they have been taught to regard as simply abominable. Is this not enough to arouse, now and then, the indignation of an ignorant peasantry! What would the rector of an English village do, if a Turk with his fez and baggy trousers were to come and sit cross-legged with his Koran, and tell them that they would go to a place unmentionable unless they believed his dogmas? If he were not stoned, he would at least be chucked into the nearest horsepond, and the magistrates would order him on for creating a disturbance . . . I hate the injustice of it all. We, in England, are apt to forget that there are two sides to the question.

On the road to Adana some Circassians were injudicious enough to get in her way: 'I cried out in Turkish: "Circassian savages, when the English come you will all be sent back to your own country in chains."' Here too the two jocular Englishmen decided they had had enough: 'Mr Bertram declared he could no longer stand the fatigue of such travelling as we had undergone, without the aid of bottled beer and champagne.' Dr Johnstone was worried about overstaying his leave. And to cap it all Theodore had proved 'perfectly incapable' as an interpreter: 'When at a loss for a word he used to excuse himself by saying I had ordered him to leave his dictionaries behind – two huge volumes that would have required a special donkey for their porterage.' A new translator, Nahli Sabbagh, was hired to replace him and the party, including Scott-Stevenson's fifteen-stone, largely silent, husband, Andrew, set off for Kaisariyeh, with her throwing out vigorous anathema against various objects such as modern killims ('very ugly') and the Turks in general. ('Oh these poor Turks! how ignorant they are. I am truly sorry for them.') Along the way they encountered some robbers who reminded her of her faithful promise to Andrew that in such an emergency she would defer to him and let him take charge – which he did, frightening them with a discharged rifle: 'Oh! how I longed to be a man to join in the chase.' The new interpreter was in awe of this marvel of Anglo-Saxon late-Victorian womanhood, who recorded:

> I am so dreadfully strong-minded and determined and so insistent on getting what I want from the khanjis and villagers. I can ride such long distances, too, and give him such terrible lectures about being brave and courageous. At the same time, I am not very imposing to look at, and do so thoroughly enjoy all that is beautiful and interesting in our journey and laugh 'like a schoolgirl' as my husband says, when anything comical happens, that Nahli is fairly puzzled. He has only known one English lady before; and she dressed in trousers like her husband, and was as good a shot as he was, and did not care in

the least about her personal appearance. So a mixture of temerity and ladyhood, which I suppose I represent, is quite incomprehensible to Nahli.

Scott-Stevenson expressed satisfaction at the increasingly tough going as they penetrated deeper north: 'I began to feel that, *at last,* we were leading the life of roughing and adventure I had often longed to experience.'

The Scott-Stevensons took violently against Kayseri, an important Turkish town on the caravan route and the first base of the missionaries, finding it filthy, and its inhabitants greedy and exploitative. They visited the local Pasha ('We always made it a rule to call on the chief authorities') but he was 'very fat with dull eyes' and did nothing to lessen their conviction that: 'The Armenians may be an industrious thriving people, but God forbid we should have anything to do with them. If we do, they will be an everlasting thorn in our side.' By contrast, they render the Turks, whose faults have been exaggerated by 'bigoted and narrow-minded' missionaries, all the more sympathetic. Scott-Stevenson preferred 'the poor downtrodden Turk' to the 'grasping Armenian and the wily Greek' but was most contemptuous of the missionaries, the results of whose money and labours over forty years were 'very small'.

The couple pushed on to Nevsehir, where they tried to buy some overpriced candlesticks from a trader but 'unfortunately for his chance of sale I noticed his nose, and there was no mistaking the sign of the Armenian, so we left the shop without purchasing anything'. Two 'unctuous and oily hypocrites' converted by missionaries stepped forward looking for baksheesh but 'with such specimens as these I have not the slightest sympathy'. It was not until an encounter with some Turcomans that Scott-Stevenson appeared to have met her match: 'The Turcoman women seem a fine sturdy race, large boned and huge limbed, very industrious and clean, but quite uncivilised. They looked on me with utter contempt; and could not contain their astonishment at seeing the men of our party waiting assiduously on me, instead of me on them . . . I suspect I would have had rather a rough time of it, if I had been left alone with these ladies.'

At Eregli they found the town more or less under siege from a band of Circassians who were terrorizing the inhabitants and plundering the shops. Andrew got into 'a towering rage' at this and made it known in the market-place that he would shoot the first Circassian who even looked at him: 'We had thrown discretion to the winds; and if these people gave us the slightest cause, my husband was determined to show them that they could not, at any rate, insult or bully an Englishman with impunity. These people are cowards at heart . . . they used to slink away when they saw us.' Nonetheless they were very relieved to move on to Konya, where they saw a fine show of the celebrated whirling dervishes ('the dresses of the dancers floated round them like an extinguisher') and where, in spite of the fact that it was 'in the very heart of Asia Minor, in a town that is filled with the most bigoted of Moslems', the people were much less irksome than those of Kayseri, where Esmé had sometimes been forced to 'open my umbrella in their faces and stand under its shelter with my back towards them'.

Despite these shows of violent prejudice, she insisted that she was becoming more in touch with the people, and she offered a useful 'hint to the traveller'. This was not to arrive at a place bawling 'I want this' or 'I want that' but to wait and see what the local people were eating and then 'they bring you always the best they have. We discovered many little things like that by experience, and found that every day of our progress we were getting on better with the people.'

Towards the end of their trip the Scott-Stevensons arrived at Zena in the Taurus mountains, where they had a letter of introduction to the Hadji Ibrahim Aga, who was at his summer camp there, and for the first time the couple slept out in the open air, leading Esmé to declare: 'How much of our lives we waste by living within the four walls during the grandest time of the twenty-four hours!' They were enchanted with the beautiful scenery in 'one of the fairest spots in the created world'. After this they sailed from Killindryeh on 19 May for Cyprus but not before Scott-Stevenson had pronounced her verdict on their travels:

> I went to sleep that night very happy. I felt that I had accomplished a feat that few ladies would undertake; that I had travelled through a country that was almost unknown, and gone through trials and dangers that required great tact and endurance to overcome them. I hope people won't laugh when I say that I felt, for once in my life, that I had done something really of use to my fellow creatures; and that if I should succeed in writing a readable account of our travels, I might be the means of attracting attention to an almost unknown land, where health is to be found by those who seek it, grand sport by the hunter, and unexplored treasures by the traveller, the botanist, the geologist, and the antiquary.

Back in Cyprus, Scott-Stevenson considered that, notwithstanding the shortcomings of the Osmanli government, her sympathies were with its long-suffering people, and she was full of 'deep commiseration for the unfortunate Mussulman'.

# 13

## *A Digression on Guidebooks*

The modern British guidebook was born in 1836. A clear and uncluttered line of descent runs from John Murray's pioneering *A Hand-Book for Travellers on the Continent* (1836) to the Rough Guides and Lonely Planet Guides of today. The combination of authoritative bossiness (what to see and what not to see, what to do and what not to do) and eagerness to please the traveller has remained largely unchanged. The word 'Murray' became synonymous as the nineteenth century progressed with reliability and accuracy. It also came to symbolize a certain kind of travel, characterized by the earnest desire to see the sights, and to do what every other traveller had done, a disposition to rubberneck rather than to hack one's way through virgin forest or untrodden plain.

The Preface to the first Murray (covering Europe north of the Alps) lays down the template of the travel guide. Just as the two modern guides mentioned above boast of their origins in spontaneous student travel by their founders, so the anonymous *Hand-Book* writer claims to have written his guide 'partly for his own amusement, partly to assist his friends going abroad' and to that end made 'copious notes of all that he thought worth observation, and of the best modes of travelling and seeing things to advantage'. There was the tantalizing suggestion that some fresh doors would be opened (he had 'visited many spots to which his countrymen rarely penetrate') but the book's solidity rested on its guidance along 'beaten routes'.

The writer of the first Murray dismissed the existing guidebooks as either inaccurate general accounts often written by people who had not actually visited the places they wrote about or local histories written by those who knew all too much and simply piled on the detail without discrimination, leaving the user in the dark about 'what are the curiosities of the place'. The unique selling point of Murray, by contrast, was the notion of discrimination, of sifting the needful from the otiose in the traveller's itinerary, of discriminating between 'what is peculiar to the place, and what is not worth seeing, or may be seen equally well or to greater advantage somewhere else'. Murray promised faithfully to confine itself to 'matter-of-fact descriptions of what *ought to be seen* at each place . . . calculated to interest an intelligent traveller, without bewildering his readers with an account of all that *may* be seen'. Today's harried tourist, anxiously visiting, and photographing every 'sight', fearful to have missed some obligatory stopping point, with little time for serendipity, has been trained and disciplined by Murray's descendants in the art of logging what 'ought to be seen'.

Descriptions by 'authors of celebrity' such as Byron, Scott, Southey and Bulwer (conveniently on Murray's publishing list) were appended but the guidebook writer himself adopted the brisk, no-nonsense style in vogue today: 'as simple and condensed a style as possible, avoiding stilted descriptions and exaggerated superlatives'. This anti-style was enhanced by that other key feature of the modern guidebook: savvy. Murray was the product of 'the writer's personal inquiries' and great pains had been taken 'to acquire the most recent information from the best authorities, and to bring it down to the present time'. Like readers of today's cool, in-the-know travel guides, Murray's first customers were being offered the latest low-down on each location.

The guide promised another feature: utter self-sufficiency in its prescriptions. There was simply no need of any other vade-mecum: 'This volume is complete in itself as far as it goes, and is intended to preclude the necessity of resorting to any other Guide Book in the countries which it describes.' Like today's Rough Guides, it boasted its superiority to its predecessors 'because it is based on personal knowledge of the countries described . . . many of the descriptions have already served to guide travellers abroad, and have thus been verified on the spot'. And like that series of modern guides which requests users to email their suggestions and improvements, the first Murray '*most particularly requests all who make use of it* to favour him, by transmitting, through his publisher, *a notice of any mistakes or omissions which they may discover* [original italics]'. The author was well aware that books for the armchair traveller were one thing 'but a book of this kind, every word of which is weighed and verified on the spot, is subjected to a much more severe test and criticism'.

Murray's *Hand-Book* began with a series of maxims about travel from writers such as Francis Bacon, Samuel Rogers and Lawrence Sterne, then quickly got down to brass tacks. In advice that would these days be toned down for an English guidebook, where the consumer is not expected to make any exertion of this kind, it said firmly: 'No one should think of travelling before he has made some acquaintance with the language of the country he is about to visit. This should be the first, as it is the best, preparation for a journey.' It suggested that the user should 'lay in a stock of good temper and patience as is not likely soon to be exhausted, whatever mishaps may befall him; and that he should divest himself, as soon as possible, of his prejudices, and especially of the idea of the amazing superiority of England, above all other countries, in all respects'. There was practical advice on money, recommending, in preference to letters of credit, 'circular notes' that could be cashed through a network of two hundred agents and correspondents in Europe, and advice about keeping one's cool at passport checks: 'Of all the penalties, at the expense of which the pleasure of travelling abroad is purchased, the most disagreeable and most repugnant to English feelings is that of submitting to the strict regulations of the continental police, and especially to the annoyance of bearing a passport.'

Murray warned that English servants taken abroad were 'worse than useless' because they could not speak a word of any language other than English, so couriers, admittedly 'an expensive luxury', were strongly recommended and an address was given of an agency at 7 Old Compton Street, Soho, where they could be hired for £8–10 a month. Advice was given on carriages and on dress: '*shoes ought to be double-soled, provided with iron heels and hobnails, such as are worn shooting in England*'. In general: 'A frock-coat is better than a shooting-jacket, which though well enough in remote places, is strange, and will attract notice in the streets of a foreign town.' A flask and a telescope (from Carey the optician at 181 The Strand) were essentials and 'Berry's patent inkstands and fire-boxes are much to be recommended for their portability'.

The book included lists of steamboat sailings, on which information was obtainable from the General Steam Navigation Company at 69 Lombard Street or 37 Regent Circus, Piccadilly. By 1836 an all-inclusive service from London to Calais was running three times a week with first-class cabins available for a pound. Daily ferries between Dover and Calais started at ten shillings. The special guide-book tone of insider knowingness about the peculiarities of the foreigner is captured in a section on 'Landing on the Continent' which is reminiscent of passages in the *Rough Guide to Greece* warning backpackers what to expect on arrival at a Greek island ferry port:

> When the steam-boat reaches its destined port, the shore is usually beset by a crowd of clamorous agents from the different hotels, each vociferating the name and praises of that for which he is employed, stunning the distracted stranger with their cries, and nearly scratching his face with their proffered cards. The only mode of rescuing himself from these tormentors, who often beset him a dozen at a time, is to make up his mind *beforehand* to what hotel he will go, and to name it at once. The Agent or Commissionaire of the house then steps forward and the rest fall back while he takes the new arrival under his protection, extricates him from the throng, and conducts him to his quarters.

This advice would work today.

As one turns the pages of Murray at random, the eye might fall on an entry on Bruges which, in its up-to-the-minute pen portrait, briskly judgemental tone and shrewd assessment of how much time is worth devoting to the place, would not be out of place in a modern guide: 'This city, the Liverpool of the middle ages . . . is now reduced to 43,000 inhabitants, of whom 15,000 are paupers . . . At present it wears on the whole an air of desolation . . . Its appearance is the more mournful from its great extent, and the size and unaltered splendour of many of the public buildings and private houses, which are so many vestiges of its former wealth and prosperity.' After a brief quote from Southey the *Hand-Book* concedes: 'It has still many objects of interest, which deserve at least a day to be devoted to them.' After enumerating these – the Grande Place, Hôtel de Ville, the Academy of painting and so on – information about means of forward travel is given, including diligences to Ostend and Ghent and canal boats.

For the earnest Victorian traveller Murray could be supplemented by several more exacting tomes such as Colonel Julian Jackson's *What to Observe; or the Traveller's Remembrancer* (1841): 'The object of the present work is simply, as its title indicates, to point out to the uninitiated traveller what he should observe, and to remind the one who is well informed, of many objects which, but for a remembrancer, might escape him.' This awesome volume – six hundred pages of close-packed print – was aimed at generating that very characteristic early-Victorian phenomenon 'useful knowledge' by giving advice about what to look for and what to record when travelling. Mere dilettante travellers were letting the side down by failing to make the most of their travels and the *Remembrancer* aimed to teach its readers 'what an immense field of physical and moral research lies open to his investigation . . . when we consider the total absence of anything like solid information given to us by the legion of those who quit their native country to roam for a while over the various parts of the globe, we cannot but think that some good must result from pointing out how their peregrinations may be turned to better account than they have hitherto been.' It went on: 'Our book is intended for general use, and we therefore hope it will prove acceptable alike to those who travel luxuriously over civilized Europe, and to those adventurous and ardent spirits who wander undaunted among hostile tribes, braving every obstacle and enduring every hardship in search of knowledge.'

This formidably organized work breaks down by category the potential knowledge that could be gleaned by a serious-minded traveller. The chapter on 'Morals and Manners' observes: 'Among savages the manners and moral habits are simple, and their origin easily discovered; while in civilized countries they are of a complex character, often difficult to understand, frequently contradictory, and their origin obscure'. This assertion is developed by arguing that: 'The great facility afforded in the present day for rapid communication between the several parts of the same country, and between one country and another, has so blended the manners of the whole population, so amalgamated foreign with domestic usages, that all the civilized parts of the world present a family likeness, in which the peculiarities of each are only to be discerned by the closest inspection.' To help the earnest seeker after useful knowledge to be an effective anthropologist a series of questions is proposed:

> Are the inhabitants generally an imaginative or a reflecting people? Are they lively or phlegmatic? Are they distinguished by any particular virtues or vices, and what are these? Are they brave or cowardly; proud or modest; hospitable or inimical to strangers; cruel or humane; confiding or distrustful; witty or obtuse? Are they peaceable or warlike; patriotic or cosmopolite; industrious or idle; sober or debauched; frank or deceitful; religious or profane; liberal or parsimonious; honest or thievish?

The guide had more down-to-earth pieces of advice for the traveller, such as how to walk in a straight line: 'It may appear to many, that any one who is sober can walk in a straight line, and that directions for such a simple operation are altogether superfluous; but this is by no means the case.' There is equally fascinating advice about how to climb trees. Nor were politics shied away from. When it came to the colonies, the necessary questions to be put were as follows: 'What benefits have accrued from the colony to the country which sent it, to the country which received it, and to the colonists themselves; has it been favourable, or is it likely to be favourable to the purposes of civilization, by spreading throughout a barbarous country, the arts, the sciences, the industry of Europe, and the Christian religion?' The terms of the question here rather determine the likely answer.

This genre of expert guidance on what to look for became popular and the Royal Geographical Society (RGS) established a committee to prepare a publication called *Hints to Travellers*, which was first published in 1830 as a tiny guide costing two shillings and sixpence and bearing the gilt crest of the Society but which grew and grew in subsequent editions throughout the century and into the following one, reaching 921 pages by 1938. The Preface to the third, 1871, edition explained that: 'Applications are frequently made by travellers to the Royal Geographical Society, for instructions by which they may make their labours useful to Geography.' The Council of the RGS promised that it would always answer such applications 'when they proceed from persons who are zealously engaged in preparing themselves for arduous enterprises'. This does not quite sound like the readership of Murray. The *Hints* are very technical and the advice is clearly to those whose aims are primarily scientific. A section of Examination of Instruments urges: 'Let every Instrument be tested and its errors determined and tabulated at the Kew Observatory. This is done for a trifling fee.' There is good advice on how to pack instruments: 'The corners of all instrument cases should be brass-bound; the fittings should be screwed, and not glued . . . Thermometers travel best when slipped into india-rubber tubes . . . Instruments travel excellently when packed in *loose, tumbled* cloths.'

The *Hints* were the product of experience and some of the

famous explorers of the day reported back on their procedures and their equipment. One of these was Livingstone's companion John Kirk, who wrote in the fourth edition:

> When Dr Livingstone and I crossed the mountains and reached Lake Shirwa, our outfit was as follows: one six-inch sextant, one mercurial horizon, one pocket chronometer, two prismatic compasses, one pocket compass, one field-glass, one aneroid barometer, two common thermometers, two boiling-point thermometers (the brass apparatus commonly supplied is quite superfluous), botanical paper, arsenical soap, one wide-mouthed bottle containing spirits of wine, pocket-lens, knives, note-books, water-colours, mathematical tables, nautical almanac, and wax candles.

In 1849 there appeared another publication, *A Manual of Scientific Inquiry* (sometimes known as 'The Admiralty Manual'), written by some of the leading scientists of the day, including Herschel on meteorology, Hooker, director of the Royal Botanic Gardens at Kew, on botany and Darwin on geology. Its aims were similar to those of *Hints to Travellers*. Writing ten years before *The Origin of Species* made him famous, Darwin paints an attractively simple portrait of the geologist and his tools: 'The geologist fortunately requires but little apparatus; a heavy hammer, with its two ends wedge-formed and truncated; a light hammer for trimming specimens; some chisels and a pickaxe for fossils; a pocket-lens with three glasses (to be incessantly used); a compass and a clinometer, compose his essential tools.' The chapter on ethnology by J. C. Prichard stresses the vital importance of this science: 'On almost every topic now enumerated our acquaintance with remote nations is at present much more extensive than it was a quarter of a century ago; but on all it is still very defective.' Prichard noted: 'The rudest or most simple stage of human society is not without its appropriate arts. Some of these indicate as much enterprise and ingenuity, and as great activity of the intellectual faculties, as the practices of more civilized men . . . In every nation, however, barbarous, it is probable that some sort of morality exists in the sentiments of men.'

In 1855 Francis Galton, later more renowned for his forays into the tricky field of eugenics, published *The Art of Travel*, a highly successful blend of the scientific manual and the guide for, if not readers of Murray, then at least the sort of adventurous traveller who may not necessarily have been a scientist. Born in 1822 in Birmingham, and a grandson of two of the founding members of the Birmingham Lunar Society, Galton was reputed to have been a child prodigy who was reading at the age of two and a half and discussing Homer's *Iliad* at six. He read mathematics at Trinity College, Cambridge, but failed to achieve success and, after leaving with a pass degree, pursued the study of medicine in a desultory fashion until in 1844 his father died and left him a very large inheritance.

Galton's travels began in the Middle East, where he learned Arabic, and in 1850 a visit to south-west Africa led to a book *Tropical South Africa* (1852) and the Royal Geographical Society's Founder's Medal for 1854. He next decided to write *The Art of Travel*, prompted, he said, by the fact that he had found it impossible to learn even the rudiments of survey and mapping techniques in England. The guide grew steadily as each edition appeared and was enriched by new knowledge of the African interior brought back by mid-century explorers such as Baker, Burton, Speke and Grant, and the beginnings of Arctic travel. The lack of knowledge of camp-craft during the Crimean War led Galton to lecture troops at Aldershot in 1856 on the 'arts of travelling and camping'. He had a taste for gadgetry and was one of the pioneers of fingerprinting.

Galton always insisted that 'the traveller must enjoy his journey rather than strive anxiously for a goal; travel is an experience rather than a quest' and in his Preface he stated his ambition to 'do welcome service to all who have to rough it, – whether explorers, emigrants, missionaries or soldiers'. The scientist in him, however, wanted to organize rationally the fruits of his contributors' travels, 'collecting the scattered experiences of many such persons in various circumstances, collating them, examining into their principles, and deducing from them what might fairly be called an "Art of Travel" . . . I made a point of re-testing, in every needful case, what I had read or learned by hearsay.' And like, the other guide writers, he wanted to hear from his readers who were encouraged to write in to his publisher: 'Mr. Murray, 50, Albemarle Street, London.'

The book begins with an injunction to 'those who meditate travel':

> *Qualifications for a Traveller.* – If you have health, a great craving for adventure, at least a moderate fortune, and can set your heart on a definite object, which old travellers do not think impracticable, then – travel by all means. If, in addition to these qualifications, you have scientific taste and knowledge, I believe that no career, in time of peace, can offer to you more advantages than that of a traveller. If you have not independent means, you may still turn travelling to excellent account; for experience shows it often leads to promotion, nay, some men support themselves by travel. They explore pasture land in Australia, they hunt for ivory in Africa, they collect specimens of natural history for sale, or they wander as artists.

Galton went on to cover all the things that such a traveller would need to know, with an emphasis on practical knowledge and skills. He dismissed the commonly supposed dangers of travel, including the threat from 'savages', who were said to 'rarely murder new-comers; they fear their guns, and have a superstitious awe of the white man's power'. Galton's shrewdly opportunist side came through occasionally in the text, as when he underlined the advantages of travel: 'It is no slight advantage to a young man, to have the opportunity for distinction which travel affords. If he plans his journey among scenes and places likely to interest the stay-at-home public, he will probably achieve a reputation that might well be envied by wiser men who have not had his opportunities.' He also dismissed the idea that women did not make good travellers:

> I believe there are few greater popular errors than the idea we have mainly derived from chivalrous times, that woman is a weakly creature . . . It always seems to me that a hard-worked woman is better and happier for her work. It is in the nature of women to be fond of carrying weights; you may see them in omnibuses and carriages, always preferring to hold their baskets or their babies on their knees, to setting them down on the seats by their sides.

One has the sense that personal experience lay behind many of the practical tips, such as those for dealing with wasp and scorpion stings: 'The oil scraped out of a tobacco-pipe is a good application.' The experiences of famous travellers were also drawn on: 'Captain Burton wrote very much in the dark, when lying awake at night; he used a board with prominent lines of wood, such as is adopted by the blind.' We know that Burton was a reader of Galton because his annotated personal copy of *The Art of Travel* survives in the Huntington Library in California. Against a passage concerned with how to hang clothes from a smooth tent pole, Burton has scribbled 'always have hooks'.

The overall tone of the guide – brisk and down to earth – can be seen in some remarks on 'the management of savages' where it is advised that: 'A frank, joking, but determined manner, joined with an air of showing more confidence in the good faith of the natives than you really feel, is the best . . . If a savage does mischief, look on him as you would on a kicking mule, or a wild animal, whose nature is to be unruly and vicious, and keep your temper quite unruffled.'

Galton's English traveller, as he flipped to the index entry on 'natives' to find the rubric 'see Savages', was innocent of any idea that the indigenous peoples might actually be fellow humans.

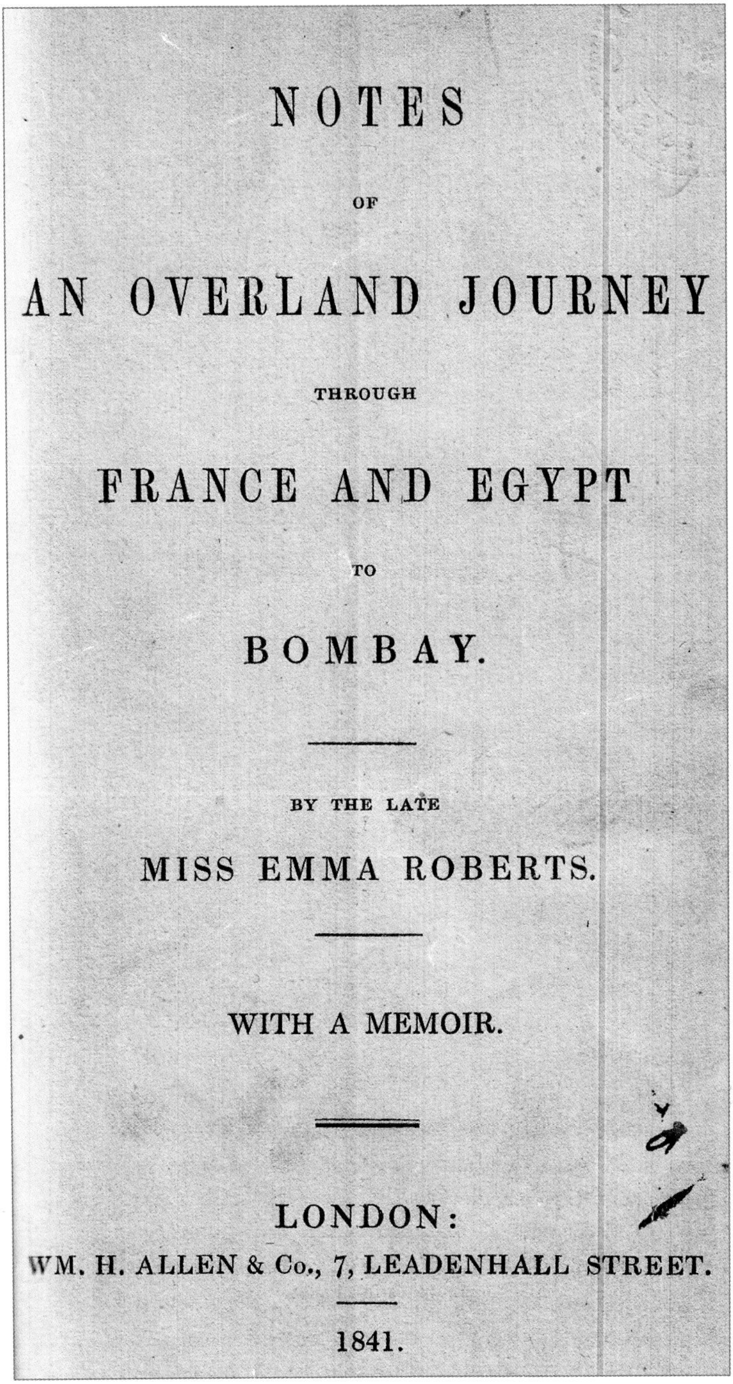

# NOTES

OF

# AN OVERLAND JOURNEY

THROUGH

# FRANCE AND EGYPT

TO

# BOMBAY.

---

BY THE LATE

## MISS EMMA ROBERTS.

---

**WITH A MEMOIR.**

---

## LONDON:

WM. H. ALLEN & Co., 7, LEADENHALL STREET.

1841.

The frontispiece of Emma Roberts's India memoir.

The grass cutter and gram grinder – sketch from Fanny Parks's *Wanderings of a Pilgrim in Search of the Picturesque during Four-and-Twenty Years in the East*, 1850.

David Hogarth and natives in the Taurus mountains, Turkey.

Robert Curzon, surrounded by locals at Souriani Monastery on the Natron lakes (in present-day northern Tanzania).

'The Queen of cities was before me': Julia Pardoe on arriving in 1835 in the Ottoman capital, then called Constantinople.
(National Portrait Gallery)

A studio portrait of
Richard Burton.

Burton in disguise
as a Mecca pilgrim.

'I have followed my husband everywhere, gleaning only woman's lore': Isabel Burton.

The great self-conscious stylist among nineteenth-century travel writers: Charles Doughty, in Arab dress.

'A very solid and substantial little person': Isabella Bird.
(Topfoto)

Bird's drawing of one of the Aino at Noboribetsu on the Japanese island of Hokkaido.

'Possessing hair which is not black adds immensely to the interest of inspecting foreigners': Constance Gordon-Cumming, Beijing, June 1879.

The original caption read: 'Dinner party in the garden of a member of the Hanlin College, – white cloth spread in complement to Europeans. By Mrs Archibald Little'.

A sketch by Richard Burton of British travellers in East Africa.

Annie Hore, the author of
*To Lake Tanganyika in a Bath Chair* (1886).

# PART THREE

# THE MIDDLE EAST

## 14

*Orientalizing: Richard Burton on the Road to Mecca*

Richard Burton's visit in 1853 to the holy places of Islam at Mecca and Medina, disguised as a pilgrim, was his most famous exploit, giving full rein to his love of disguise and self-invention. He was not the first English traveller to attempt this journey to the 'mysterious *penetralia* of Mahommedan superstition'. William Pitts of Exeter in the late seventeenth century had preceded him, and the Swiss traveller Burckhardt had performed the same feat in 1811.

Central to the glamour of Burton's expedition was the idea of danger overcome through the triumph of disguise, but we have only his word for it that the deception was a success. It was certainly necessary to adopt the disguise because an infidel discovered in the holy city might well have been killed, but Oriental mystery cuts both ways, and it is possible that his survival may have been assured by the courteous discretion of his Arab hosts who did not wish to reveal that they had seen through his imposture. In later editions of his *Personal Narrative of a Pilgrimage to Al-Madinah and Meccah* (1855) Burton was obliged to defend himself against attacks on his motives for carrying out this journey – from fellow Christians rather than outraged Muslims – who saw it as a kind of blasphemy.

It is unlikely that any twenty-first-century traveller, for many reasons, would think of repeating such an adventure. The truth will never be known with certainty and we have little choice but to put ourselves in the hands of Burton himself, who controls the narrative.

Introducing a posthumous reprint of the book, his widow Isabel stressed the dedication of Burton to his task of creating a new persona:

My husband had lived as a Dervish in Sind [see Chapter 4], which greatly helped him; and he studied every separate thing until he was master of it, even apprenticing himself to a blacksmith to learn how to make horse-shoes and to shoe his own horses. It meant living with his life in his hand, amongst the strangest and wildest companions, adopting their unfamiliar manners, living for nine months in the hottest and most unhealthy climate upon repulsive food; it meant complete and absolute isolation from everything that makes life tolerable, from all civilisation, from all his natural habits; the brain at high tension, but the mind never wavering from the *rôle* he had adopted; but he liked it, he was happy in it, he felt at home in it, and in this Book he tells you how he did it, and what he saw.

Isabel Burton's description provides an answer to the question: why did he then do it? He did it because 'he was happy in it, he felt at home in it'. Burton was not the first and would not be the last English traveller to find deep satisfaction in reinventing himself in a strange country.

Burton's plans for the trip began in the autumn of 1852 when he offered his services to the Royal Geographical Society, now entering its third decade of existence and consolidating its role as the orchestrator of the great Victorian expeditions. With a characteristic verbal flourish he described his goal as 'removing that opprobrium to modern adventure, the huge white blot which in our maps still notes the Eastern and the Central regions of Arabia'. His current employers, the Honourable East India Company, would not grant him furlough of three years to perform what they considered too risky an enterprise but he was allowed a year off to pursue his Arabic studies in the region, and with the RGS's backing he used it also to make his pilgrimage to Mecca. His own description of his motives reveals their complexity:

> Being liberally supplied with the means of travel by the Royal Geographical Society; thoroughly tired of 'progress' and of 'civilisation'; curious to see with my eyes what others are content to 'hear with ears', namely, the Moslem's inner life in a really Mohammedan country; and longing, if truth be told, to set foot on that mysterious spot which no tourist had yet described, measured, sketched and daguerrotyped, I resolved to resume my old character of a Persian wanderer, and to make the attempt.

In strictly geographical terms he defined his object as being: 'To cross the unknown Arabian Peninsula, in a direct line from either El Medinah to Muscat, or diagonally from Meccah to Makallah on the Indian Ocean.' There were also secondary objectives, including opening up trade in horses between central Arabia and India, and eliciting information about the famous Empty Quarter, 'the vast expanse marked Ruba el Khali (the empty abode) in our maps'. He also wanted to pursue some ethnological speculations about the racial origins of the Arab peoples. But in spite of the support of the RGS and these official purposes, Burton deliberately labelled his book a *Personal Narrative* because 'it is the personal that interests mankind' and people would be curious to see 'what measures I adopted, in order to appear suddenly as an Eastern upon the stage of Oriental life'. He made no attempt to disguise the theatrical aspect of the whole show, ending by saying: 'I make no apology for the egotistical semblance of the narrative.' He was convinced that the Victorian reading public would want to take its seat in the stalls for the performance.

And so, on 3 April 1853, Richard Burton, described on his title page as 'Lieutenant Bombay Army', left London for Southampton. The next day he embarked on the 'magnificent screw steamer' (he had already forgotten his tirade against progress) of the Peninsular and Oriental Company, the *Bengal* already reborn as a 'Persian Prince', the first of the disguises he tried on before starting on his pilgrimage. After thirteen days of practice it was the Persian Prince who arrived at Alexandria, where he immediately perceived that the disguise was working, proof being the fact that he was not pursued by tourist touts: 'the infant population spared me the compliments usually addressed to hatted heads'.

Burton went straight away to the home of his friend John Larking, where, stretched out on a midnight divan, he savoured for the first time the exotic languor of this new world, trying to define its special quality, which he believed inhered in the word *Kaif* or *khif*. His definition is important because it shows how Burton arrived in the Arab world with a pre-existing template or set of antitheses which would shape his narrative and constitute its under-lying framework of assumptions. He set out his stall as a European half in love with an ideal that was at the opposite pole from mid-Victorian earnest purposefulness:

And this is the Arab's *Kaif.* The savouring of animal existence; the passive enjoyment of mere sense; the pleasant languor, the dreamy tranquillity, the airy castle-building, which in Asia stand in lieu of the vigorous, intensive, passionate life of Europe. It is the result of a lively, impressible, excitable nature, and exquisite sensibility of nerve – a facility for voluptuousness unknown to northern regions; where happiness is placed in the exertion of mental and physical powers . . . No wonder that *Kaif* is a word untranslatable in our mother-tongue!

Burton's interest in the 'facility for voluptuousness' would eventually lead to his studies and translations of Arab erotic classics.

During a month spent in Alexandria he visited baths and coffee houses, bazaars and mosques, honing his disguise as a (very successful, for he had always been a dabbler in medicine) Indian doctor. At the end of this period he decided finally to adopt the persona of a wandering Dervish called Shaykh Abdullah: 'No character in the Moslem world is so proper for disguise as that of the Dervish . . . no one asks him – the chartered vagabond – Why he comes here? or Wherefore he goes there? . . .' He paid a dollar to the British Consulate for a passport defining him as 'an Indo-British subject named Abdullah, by profession a doctor aged thirty, and not distinguished – at least so the frequent blanks seemed to denote – by any remarkable conformation of eyes, nose, or cheek'. This was endorsed by the Egyptian authorities. Dr Abdullah was born.

Burton/Abdullah took great pleasure in describing the costume and properties in which he stepped out on to the stage for the opening scene:

The silver-mounted dressing-case is here supplied by a rag containing a miswak [a stick of soft wood chewed at one end used as a brush], a bit of soap and a comb (wooden), for bone and tortoiseshell are not, religiously speaking, correct. Equally simple was my wardrobe; a change or two of clothing. The only article of canteen description was a zemzemiyah, a goat-skin water-bag, which communicates to its contents, especially when new, a ferruginous aspect and a wholesome, though hardly an attractive flavour of tann-gelatine . . . For bedding and furniture

I had a coarse Persian rug – which, besides being couch, acts as chair, table, and oratory – a cotton-stuffed chintz-covered pillow, a blanket in case of cold, and a sheet, which does duty for tent and mosquito curtains in nights of heat . . . a huge cotton umbrella of Eastern make, brightly yellow, suggesting the idea of an overgrown marigold . . . a substantial housewife . . . it was a roll of canvas, carefully soiled, and garnished with needles and thread, cobblers'-wax, buttons, and other such articles . . . A dagger, a brass inkstand and pen-holder stuck in the belt, and a mighty rosary, which on occasion might have been converted into a weapon of offence, completed my equipment.

A cotton purse in a breast pocket contained silver pieces and small change (the latter vital to avoid drawing attention to one's wealth). 'My gold, of which I carried twenty-five sovereigns, and papers, were committed to a substantial leathern belt of Maghrabi manufacture, made to be strapped round the waist under the dress . . . A pair of common native khurjin or saddle-bags contained my wardrobe, the "bed", readily rolled up into a bundle, and for a medical chest I bought a pea-green box with red and yellow flowers, capable of standing falls from a camel twice a day.'

At the end of May the well-equipped Dr Abdullah stepped on to a Nile steamer for Cairo. He was travelling deck class and, as a Muslim, was unable to eat the relatively decent food of the infidels: 'So the Dervish squatted apart, smoking perpetually . . . he drank the muddy water of the canal out of a leathern bucket, and he munched his bread and garlic with a desperate sanctimoniousness.' Burton was bored by the Egyptian scenery, which reminded him of Sind and which, as a result of copious past travellers' accounts that rendered 'all things perfectly familiar to us', made it impossible to see things with any freshness. Even the pyramids 'only suggest the remark that they have been remarkably well-sketched'.

On the boat Burton met an Indian, Miyan Khudabakhsh, who invited him to stay with him on arrival, after three days, at Cairo.

Burton revealed much about himself in describing this encounter. 'My host,' he reported, 'had become a civilised man, who sat on chairs, ate with a fork, talked European politics, and had learned to admire, if not to understand liberty – liberal ideas! and was I not flying from such things?' He declared that 'of all orientals, the most antipathetical companion to an Englishman is, I believe, an Indian. Like the fox in the fable, fulsomely flattering at first, he gradually becomes easily friendly, disagreeably familiar, offensively rude, which ends by rousing the "spirit of the British lion".'

These observations led Burton to reflect on British imperial power in India. He judged that British rule was popular in the three presidencies but elsewhere the people would welcome change 'and how can we hope it to be otherwise, – we, a nation of strangers, aliens to the country's customs and creed, who, even while resident in India, act the part which absentees do in other lands? Where, in the history of the world, do we read that such foreign dominion ever made itself popular?' Such comments show the deep ambivalences in Burton's sensibility, his peculiar mix of the progressive and the retrogressive, the empathetic and the obtuse, the way in which he partly opened himself to what he saw and partly remained imprisoned in his most long-running role, that of a British Victorian imperialist, knowing where he stood in relation to the other inhabitants of the globe, but conscious of the permanent feeling of distance and difference: 'I am convinced that the natives of India cannot respect a European who mixes with them familiarly, or especially who imitates their customs, manners and dress.'

Burton moved next to a *wakalah*, or caravanserai, in the Greek quarter of Cairo, where he met another friend from the Nile boat, an Alexandrian merchant called Haji Wali, with whom he smoked hashish and from whom he received some valuable advice about tweaking his disguise. Out went the large blue pantaloons and the short shirt and the gown which marked him out as a Persian and in came the dress of an Afghan or Pathan. The new story was that he was born in India of Afghan parents who had settled in the country, had been educated in Rangoon and had been sent out to wander. 'To support the character requires a knowledge of Persian, Hindostani and Arabic, all of which I knew sufficiently well to pass muster; any trifling inaccuracy was charged upon my long residence at Rangoon . . . I assumed the pliant manners of an Indian physician, and the dress of a small Effendi, still, however, representing myself to be a Dervish, and frequenting the places where Dervishes congregate.'

After beginning to practise his medical profession in and around the caravanserai, Burton found himself an Arabic teacher under the pretence that as an Indian doctor he needed to be able to read Arab medical texts. Once Ramadan was over at the end of June he bought himself a pilgrim's garb, furnished himself with supplies and travel documents and, after a drunken brawl with an Albanian captain at the caravanserai who tried to snatch his pistol, set off with his servant on two hired dromedaries for Suez. After the pullulating life of Cairo the desert was austere and serene and the 'fantastic desolation of the place' wonderfully restorative:

> The wildness and sublimity of the scenes around you stir up all the energies of your soul . . . Your *morale* improves: you become frank and cordial, hospitable, and single-minded: the hypocritical politeness and the slavery of civilisation are left behind you in the city. Your senses are quickened . . . There is a keen enjoyment in a mere animal existence . . . And believe me, gentle reader, that when once your tastes have conformed to the tranquillity of such travel, you will suffer real pain in returning to the turmoil of civilisation . . . The air of cities will suffocate you, and the care-worn and cadaverous countenances of citizens will haunt you like a vision of judgement.

On arrival at Suez the next evening, his bones aching from the eighty-four-mile camel ride, Burton was 'lamenting my degeneracy and the ill effects of four years' domicile in Europe', further evidence that this pilgrimage was in large measure about searching for

an antidote to the ills of modern civilization. After protracted negotiations at Suez in the course of which Abdullah the Dervish nearly
gave the game away by letting his companions catch sight of his
Western sextant, and where a British sub-vice consul, George West,
saw through Burton's disguise and discreetly sorted out his papers,
his party took passage, on 6 July 1853, on the *Golden Thread*, packed
with north African pilgrims who poured over the side of the ship
'like ants into the Indian sugar-basin' and proceeded to fight one
another for space. Burton paid a sailor to be allowed to use a bed
frame slung to the ship's side and thus avoid the hell-hole of the
cabin.

As the ship sailed out he reflected wistfully on the British flag
over the Consulate:

> But the momentary regret was stifled by the heart-bounding
> which prospects of an adventure excite, and by the real pleasure
> of leaving Egypt. I had lived there a stranger in the land, and a
> hapless life it had been: in the streets every man's face was the
> face of a foe as he looked upon the Persian. Whenever I came in
> contact with the native officials, insolence marked the event;
> and the circumstance of living within hail of my fellow
> countrymen, and yet in an impossibility of enjoying their
> society, still throws a gloom over the memory of my first sojourn
> in Egypt.

After twelve days at sea Burton reached Yanbu al-Bahr, the port
for El Medinah, and began to treat for some camels. Pilgrims always
wore a pocket Qur'an, or 'Hamail', slung by red cords over the left
shoulder, so Burton craftily displayed a lookalike which comprised
three compartments, one for his watch and compass, the second for
ready money and the third contained penknife, pencils, and slips of
paper which he could conceal in the palm of his hand. It was inad-
visable to be seen sketching, particularly in the presence of Bedouin,
who would suspect the sketcher of being 'a spy or sorcerer'. In
Cairo Burton had got himself made up a diary-book, a long, thin

volume that he could hide in his breast pocket and take notes in, at first in Arabic and later, when such a precaution appeared unnecessary, in English. He carried an Egyptian brass ink-stand and English ink as being more resistant to water. 'For prudence sake, when my sketches were made, I cut up the paper into square pieces, numbered them for future reference, and hid them in the tin canisters that contained my medicines.'

Armed, and nervous of attack, Burton's party set off at dusk on twelve camels that made about two miles progress an hour. The first phase of their journey eastwards, via Bir Abbas, which included being attacked by armed Bedouin and experiencing intense heat, ended on 25 July at El Medinah, where they relished the gardens and orchards about the town after the pitiless desert landscape. Burton stayed at the house of Sheykh Hamid, one of the party from Suez, and carefully began his religious observances. Earlier Burton had injured his foot and it was giving him a great deal of pain. He made his visit to the Prophet's tomb on a donkey – 'raw-backed, lame of one leg, and wanting an ear' – although he was not impressed by the actual mosque, the second of the three most venerable Islamic holy places, finding it 'mean and tawdry'. Nor could he gain admittance to the actual tomb. 'It is not, like the Meccan mosque, grand and simple – the expression of a single sublime idea: the longer I looked at it, the more it suggested the resemblance of a museum of second-rate art, a curiosity-shop, full of ornaments that are not accessories, and decorated with pauper splendour.' He continued to explore all the neighbouring sites, which drained his purse to such an extent that when he eventually reached Mecca he had to forgo some of the holy places because he could not afford the price of admission.

On Sunday 28 August the great caravan from Damascus arrived and Burton was captivated by 'the vivacity, the variety, and the intense picturesqueness of the scene' in this town of tents which immediately sprang up: 'fine old Arab Shaykhs of the Hamidah clan . . . performing the Arzah or war dance . . . firing their duck guns upwards, or blowing the powder into the calves of those before them, brandishing their swords, leaping frantically the while, with their bright-coloured rags floating in the wind, tossing their long spears tufted with ostrich feathers high in the air, reckless where they fall'. Burton was impressed with the religious devotions of the pilgrims and after visiting the nearby battlefield of Uhud, where the custodian shook his bunch of keys violently 'to warn the souls of the martyrs having "spiritual converse" that profane eyes are approaching', he declared admiringly: 'What grand pictures these imaginative Arabs see!' He contrasted this with European superstition and 'such puerilities as clairvoyance and table-turning'.

Burton originally hoped to press on to Muscat but he was running out of furlough and the Bombay Army wanted him back before the end of March 1854, so he set off for Mecca with the Damascus caravan on 28 August: 'I had reason to congratulate myself upon having passed through the first danger. Meccah is so near the coast, that, in case of detection, the traveller might escape in a few hours to Jeddah, where he would find an English vice-consul, protection from the Turkish authorities, and possibly a British cruiser in the harbour. But at El Medinah discovery would entail more serious consequences. The next risk to be run was the journey between the two cities, on which it would be easy for the local officials quietly to dispose of a suspected person by giving a dollar to a Bedouin.'

Burton travelled by the 'eastern road', the Darb El Sharki, a route which he believed had never been taken by a European: 'The appearance of the caravan was most striking, as it threaded its slow way over the smooth surface of the Khabt [low plain]. To judge by the eye there were at least 7,000 souls, on foot, on horseback, in litters, or bestriding the splendid camels of Syria.' There were eight gradations of pilgrim: 'The lowest hobbled with heavy staves . . . only the wealthy and the noble rode in Takhtrawan (litters), carried by camels or mules . . . The morning beams fell brightly . . . upon the scarlet and gilt litters of the grandees. Not the least beauty of the spectacle was its wondrous variety of detail: no man was dressed like his neighbour, no camel was caparisoned nor horse clothed in uniform, as it were.'

His chief disappointment was that the necessity of travelling in the cool of the night prevented him from seeing very much. Although he found the Bedouin women unattractive, he admired, in the usual fashion of English desert explorers, the noble simplicity of the people, contrasted, in the familiar trope, with the ills of the decadent West:

> The manners of the Bedouins are free and simple: 'vulgarity' and affectation, awkwardness and embarrassment, are weeds of civilised growth, unknown to the people of the desert . . . The true Bedouin is an abstemious man, capable of living for six months on ten ounces of food per diem; the milk of a single camel, and a handful of dates dry, or fried in clarified butter, suffice for his wants. He despises the obese and all who require regular and plentiful meals, sleeps on a mat, and knows neither luxury nor comfort, freezing during one quarter and frying three quarters of the year.

Moreover, the experience of desert life was necessary to understand the nature of Arab art and culture: 'I cannot well explain the effect of Arab poetry to one who has not visited the Desert. Apart from the pomp of words, and the music of the sound, there is a dreaminess of idea and a haze thrown over the object, infinitely attractive, but indescribable.' But the desert was a place 'peopled only with echoes, – a place of death for what little there is to die in it, – a wilderness, where, to use my companion's phrase. there is nothing but He [Allah]. Nature, scalped, flayed, discovered her anatomy to the gazer's eye.'

Burton was now approaching his final destination, El Zaribah, where:

> Having pitched the tent and eaten and slept, we prepared to perform the ceremony of El Ihram (assuming the pilgrim-garb),

as El Zaribah is the mikat, or the appointed place. Between the noonday and the afternoon prayers a barber attended to shave our heads, cut our nails, and trim our mustachios. Then, having bathed and perfumed ourselves – the latter is a questionable point, – we donned the attire, which is nothing but two new cotton cloths, each six feet long by three-and-a-half broad, white, with narrow red stripes and fringes . . . we were placed with our faces in the direction of Meccah and ordered to say aloud, 'I vow this ihram of hajj (the pilgrimage) and the umrah (the little pilgrimage) to Allah Almighty!'

The pilgrims were then informed: 'We must so reverence life that we should avoid killing game, causing an animal to fly, and even pointing it out for destruction; nor should we scratch ourselves, save with the open palm, lest vermin be destroyed, or a hair uprooted by the nail. We were to respect the sanctuary by sparing the trees, and not to pluck a single blade of grass . . . For each infraction of these ordinances we must sacrifice a sheep.'

Shortly afterwards, at one in the morning, Burton was woken by cries of 'Meccah! Meccah!' and he entered the city on the morning of Sunday 11 September 1853, one day before the official beginning of the pilgrimage. 'The House of Allah has been so fully described by my predecessors,' he rather disarmingly told his readers, 'that there is little inducement to attempt a new portrait.' In fact he describes dressing himself at dawn the next day in his pilgrim garb and entering the sanctuary by the principal northern door to contemplate the final object of his quest:

There at last it lay, the bourn of my long and weary pilgrimage, realising the plans and hopes of many and many a year. The mirage medium of Fancy invested the huge catafalque and its gloomy pall with peculiar charms. There were no giant fragments of hoar antiquity as in Egypt, no remains of graceful and harmonious beauty as in Greece and Italy, no barbaric gorgeousness as in the buildings of India; yet the view was strange, unique, and how few have looked upon the celebrated shrine! I may truly say that, of all the worshippers who clung weeping to the curtain, or who pressed their beating hearts to the stone, none felt for the moment a deeper emotion than did the Haji from the far north. It was as if the poetical legends of the Arab spoke truth, and that the waving wings of angels, not the sweet breeze of morning, were agitating and swelling the black covering of the shrine. But, to confess the humbling truth, theirs was the high feeling of religious enthusiasm, mine was the ecstasy of gratified pride.

Burton admits here that his motives differed from those of the true pilgrims and in saying that this crowded, populous shrine is one 'few have looked upon' he unwittingly underlines his Eurocentric vision: until a thing is looked on ('discovered') by a British traveller it cannot be said properly to exist.

Dutifully Burton performed his pilgrim's rituals such as the perambulation, though the press of people around the black stone meant that he could not at first manage to touch it until his boy beat a way through for him. By the end of the session Burton confessed to being 'thoroughly worn out with scorched feet and a burning head' when he finally left the mosque. Returning later in moonlight to the 'Navel of the World' its solemnity impressed him: 'One object, unique in appearance, stood in view – the temple of the one Allah, the God of Abraham, of Ishmael, and of his posterity. Sublime it was, and expressing by all the eloquence of fancy the grandeur of the One Idea which vitalised El Islam, and the sternness and steadfastness of its votaries.'

Burton continued to visit the various shrines and to perform the required rituals such as throwing stones at the devil at Mount Arafat (where he was distracted by a beautiful eighteen-year-old pilgrim he nicknamed 'Flirtilla') but he had performed his feat and it was time to return to India (though his real wish would have been to travel farther in the region). He travelled forty-six miles in one eleven-hour night donkey ride from Mecca to Jeddah, issuing into the plain like 'a captive delivered from his dungeon'. On arrival at Jeddah he felt at home, for 'the British flag was a restorative and the sight of the sea acted as a tonic' and so 'my peregrinations ended'. Worn out, he embarked on the *Dwarka* for Suez.

However, Burton, had not finished with disguise and a new idea of penetrating another forbidden city was forming in his mind.

# 15

## *Bible Truths: Josias Porter and Henry Tristram in the Holy Land*

Aware of the flood of what Robert Curzon called 'little volumes about palm-trees and camels', many Victorian travellers were keen to point out that their accounts were based on more substantial and enduring engagement with the countries they had visited. The Irish missionary the Reverend Josias Leslie Porter claimed that his *Five Years in Damascus* (1855) was emphatically 'not a book of travels, penned during a "summer's ramble" or a "winter's residence". It is the result of researches extending over a period of more than five years.' He added sternly that it was his object 'not so much to amuse as to instruct'. In addition, by choosing the area around Damascus in Syria, which had been a city since the time of the prophet Abraham, Porter was trying to connect with the patriarchal age. 'Lebanon and Hermon will not cease to be remembered with liveliest feelings so long as the Word of God continues to bless the world.'

Such narratives which sought to make connections between past and present in the Holy Land were not rare in the Victorian period. William Hepworth Dixon's *The Holy Land* (1865) and David Urquhart's *The Lebanon* (1860) were two notable examples, the former written with an occasionally cloying piety ('It is the Holy Land on which we gaze: – the country of Jacob and David, of Rachel and Ruth; the scene of our sweetest fancies, of our childhood prayers, and of our household psalms. Among yon hills the prophets of Israel taught and the Saviour of all men lived and died . . .').

Porter, never guilty of false modesty, was convinced that he had outdone previous travellers in Syria by the 'minuteness' of his attention to detail and his overarching ambition was to demonstrate the veracity of the Bible:

> While wandering through Bible lands my chief object has been to illustrate Bible truths; and the result of extensive travel, and no little research, has been to impress upon my mind the fact that the more we extend our labours in Palestine, whether as antiquarians, geographers, or politicians, the more strongly are we convinced of the literal fulfilment of prophecy, and of the minute accuracy of the topographical and statistical sketches contained in the Word of God.

Born in Carrowan, County Donegal, in 1823, to a farming family, Porter was trained for a ministry in the Irish Presbyterian Church, whose board of missions sent him in December 1849 to Damascus, where he remained for ten years, travelling extensively in Syria and Palestine. As well as his account of the Damascus years he wrote the

Murray *Hand-Book for Travellers* for Syria and Palestine in 1858. On his return from the Middle East he became Professor of Biblical Criticism in the Presbyterian College in Belfast and devoted the rest of his life to education. He died in 1899.

When Porter arrived in Beirut by steamer on the morning of 12 December 1849 he applied with success the advice of Murray noted above:

> Numbers of little boats, with fantastically dressed occupants, already danced upon the swelling waves round our vessel; and scores of eager porters shouted their deep gutturals in the ears of impatient travellers, as if an excess of sound would render their unknown tongue intelligible. Hotel proprietors and servants, in bad French and worse English, set forth the superiority of their respective establishments. Experience had taught me how to get rid of the annoyance of a multitude, by committing myself into the custody of one. I therefore expressed my determination to take up my abode at the 'Hotel de Belle Vue' of Antonio Tremetsi.

As early as 1849 the sense that the new age of mass travel was dawning, and with it the flight of exoticism, had taken hold of travellers like Porter: 'In this age of locomotion the romance of travel is gone, and a Library of Researches, Narratives, and Memorials makes the wanderer familiar with every object of interest, and with all its associations, classic or sacred, ere his eye rests upon it. Still the first sight of the Syrian shores, and of the mountains of Israel, is not soon forgotten. There is a magic power in the living reality which neither poet's pen nor painter's pencil can ever appropriate.' Porter relished the magnificent scenery of Lebanon in these first weeks at the Belle Vue, during which time he made many local excursions and hired a dragoman who would start to teach him Arabic. When another missionary, Dr Paulding of the Damascus Mission, turned up, Porter and his wife resolved to join him on his return journey to Damascus.

They set off at noon on Thursday 3 January 1850: 'It was a new an interesting sight to us to observe our little caravan winding through the narrow cactus-lined lanes, and then emerging into the broad sand avenues of the pine-forest. The strange garb of our native attendants and muleteers, the gay trappings of our baggage animals, adorned with innumerable little shells and bits of red, white, and green cloth, and the odd-looking tasseled bridles of our own steeds, formed a fantastic picture.' Guided by his 'careful and wiry Arab', Porter began the ascent into the mountains 'along paths where an English foxhunter would deem it madness to risk his neck', noting with satisfaction the adherence of many villagers to the Protestant Church that had been formed by the American Board of Commissioners for Foreign Missions.

At one of these villages, however, there was a shock to Porter's sense of propriety when they discovered that they were expected to sleep in the same room as an entire family: 'And feelings of indignation began to arise when our servants and muleteers wrapped themselves in their *capotes*, and one after another dropped asleep at our side . . . For a lady, it must be confessed, this was rather a rough introduction to Syrian life; we said nothing, however, and, only pushing our travelling beds as far as possible out of reach of strange feet, composed ourselves to rest.'

Porter's travelogue was interspersed with detailed summaries of his researches which, he promised, would avoid the errors of those previous travellers whose descriptions 'have been the creations of poetic imaginations' and who in consequence offered him 'but little assistance'. Damascus, he argued, was the most securely identified of the Scripture sites and was one of the oldest cities in the world and 'a connecting link between the most remote antiquity and modern times'. Yet in spite of his determination to avoid the snares of the poetic, Porter was clearly moved by what he saw in the 'gay bazaars' and the street life. He was delighted by the interior of a fine house built by Ibrahim Pasha's Secretary to the Treasury, Ali Aga, with its beautiful *harim*: 'It resembles, in fact, some scene in fairyland; and one feels, on beholding it, that the glowing descriptions in the

"Arabian Nights" were not mere pictures of the fancy.' He was clearly impressed by 'the splendour of oriental life'.

Porter made many journeys and excursions from his Damascus base and one of these was to Palmyra. On 1 April 1851 he set off with the Reverend Smylie Robinson, another missionary, both of them seated on dromedaries. Descriptions of mounting a camel or an elephant were one of the stock motifs of Victorian travel writing (see Chapter 41) and Porter's is a fine example of the genre:

> I had often heard that the first mounting of a dromedary formed a kind of era in a man's life, and I confess that, when I saw mine with open mouth, growling savagely, and struggling to free itself from the grasp of the driver, I felt a little trepidation. No sooner had I leaped into the saddle than the brute, giving a sharp lurch backwards, and a heavy one forward, and then another backwards, gained its feet and ran a few yards at a smart trot; it then wheeled about, and suddenly, by a similar but reversed series of lurches, was again upon the ground. A second time it went through this pantomime, and was preparing for a third, when its driver seized and pinioned it by placing his foot upon its knee . . . it was with no little anxiety I looked forward to a ride of nearly two hundred miles on such an animal. The pace was dreadful when it trotted; and then the sittings-down and risings-up and sudden jerks had almost dislocated my spine. In walking, however, when I became a little accustomed to the rocking motion, I found the pace easy, and even pleasant.

The camel continued to misbehave and when the missionary dismounted at one small village 'the small dimensions of my nether garments became visible' and 'laughter broke forth' among the local boys, causing Porter to reflect 'whether, had I appeared in like costume in any of the villages of old England, a similar reception would have awaited me'. He had many conversations with local people and one night, around the fire, he was having a classic traveller's conversation about the differences to be observed between

Syria and his home country. One man claimed that the English could travel anywhere they liked because they had an instrument that showed them the way by day and by night. Realizing that they referred to a compass, Porter produced his pocket compass, pointing out how the direction of Mecca was always shown, but then he took a metal object and drew away the magnetic needle. His host shouted in astonishment: 'There is no God but God!' and an old man by his side marvelled: 'The Franks have the power of *Janns!*'

The next day Porter observed a young boy placing his hands on his father's neck and kissing each cheek: 'Precisely similar was the scene at the meeting of Jacob and Esau nearly four thousand years ago: "And Esau ran to meet him, and embraced him, *and fell on his neck*, and kissed him."' Constantly Porter was reminded of the Biblical parallels and echoes in everything that he saw:

> The whole scene and circumstances were to us intensely interesting. The numerous tents grouped together on the parched desert soil, the wide-spreading flocks and herds browsing peacefully on every side, and the picturesque and primitive costumes of those who tended or wandered forth among them, pictured vividly before our minds the days when Abraham dwelt in tents, and when Jacob led his family and flocks across this same desert to the land of promise.

Equally, when a lamb was slaughtered for them at a desert encampment: 'It seemed as if we had been carried back more than three thousand years in the world's history, and by some mysterious providence permitted to mingle with the people of patriarchal times.' There were dangers, however, in such travel and later Porter was captured by armed robbers who demanded money to escort him out of their territory until he pointed out that if anything happened to him his captors' future income from conducting English travellers would be in jeopardy.

Another excursion in August 1852 was to the Valley and Fountain of the Barada – ancient Abana – this time in the company of the

Reverend Mr Frazier and a Mr Peck, 'an American traveller, whose lively sketches of the East have appeared in the columns of the "New York Observer"'. But what most interested Porter was the ancient provinces of Batanoea, Auronitis and Trachonitis, a region then occupied by a mixed population of Christians, Druze and Muslims. He wanted to see if missionary schools could be established in their villages and whether he could sell Christian literature to them in order to 'open up the way to more important labours'.

On another trip in January 1853 Porter joined a caravan to the Hauran region: 'A single change of clothes, a substantial *lehâf* to serve as bed and coverlet, a pocket sextant, a large and small compass, with my note and sketch books, formed my whole luggage.' He had plenty of time to reflect on the clash of civilizations: 'Civilisation and education have not given to the poor Arab that suavity of manner and that courtesy to which we are accustomed in the West. Lying and deceit are here universal, and therefore every man distrusts his fellow; and it requires vociferation and oaths innumerable to convince him that he is in earnest. It speaks well for the English character, that, wherever Englishmen have dealings, this stage-play is almost wholly dispensed with.'

However, Porter was not always so lucky. At Kunawat one night he was surrounded by a party of mountain Arabs who seemed determined to rob him, notwithstanding his English *sang froid* (he seems regularly to have forgotten that he was Irish). He reported a conversation conducted 'with the greatest composure' as follows:

'But why would you plunder us? We are strangers, and not your enemies.'

'It is our custom.'

'And do you strip all strangers?'

'Yes, all we can get hold of.'

'And if they resist, or are too strong for you?'

'In the former case we shoot them from behind trees; and in the latter we run.'

'How do the people of your tribe live? Do they sow or feed flocks?'

'We are not *fellahin*. We keep goats and sheep, hunt partridges and gazelles, and steal!'

'Are you all thieves?'

'Yes, all!'

But in spite of these risky encounters Porter kept coming back to his sense of the unbroken line of communication from the Biblical past to the lived present and its daily tasks and habits and manners: 'Could stronger evidence be given of the truth and faithfulness of a narrative some three thousand years old, than the witnessing of every little circumstance attending it realized in the ordinary customs of the people now residing on the spot where it was first enacted? Bible story assumes a living character when studied in this land.'

Many other Victorian travellers in the Holy Land shared Porter's belief in the value of matching the topography to the Bible story. Henry Baker Tristram, a geologist and naturalist before he became Anglican Bishop of Jerusalem, managed in his *The Land of Israel* (1865) to moralize the landscape, seeing in its natural history the actual sources of the peculiar strength of the parables and scriptural narratives: 'Though Palestine boasts in its productions neither the tropical splendour of India, nor the gorgeous luxuriance of Southern America, yet from *its* fowls of the air are drawn for us our lessons of faith and trust, from the flowers of *its* fields our lessons of humility.' Two things struck Tristram particularly about the Holy Land: 'the absence in its scenery of the *romantic* – of all that could bewilder the imagination or foster a localized superstition' and: 'the marvellous variety of its climate, scenery, and productions . . . No land could have been found more capable of providing illustrations for a book which was to be read and understood by the men of North and South alike – which was to teach the lessons of truth equally to the dweller in the tropics and under the pole – than this, in which the palm, the vine, and the oak flourish almost side by side.'

Tristram sailed with companions on an overnight boat from Cyprus to Beirut for a determined exploration of the geology. A typical example of his approach was the discovery that the destruction of Sodom in the Bible by fire and brimstone was not the result of a volcanic eruption. After examining evidence of sulphur and bitumen by the Dead Sea, he took the view that:

> The kindling of such a mass of combustible material, either by lightning from heaven, or by other electrical agency, combined with an earthquake ejecting the bitumen or sulphur from the lake, would soon spread devastation over the plain, so that the smoke of the country would go up as the smoke of a furnace . . . The simple and natural explanation seems . . . to be this: that during some earthquake, or without its direct agency, showers of sulphur, and probably bitumen, ejected from the lake, or thrown up from its shores, and ignited perhaps by the lightning which would accompany such phenomena, fell upon the cities and destroyed them. The history of the catastrophe has not only remained in the inspired record, but is inscribed in the memory of the surrounding tribes by many a local tradition and significant name.

He concluded his book with the words:

> We passed through the land with our Bibles in our hands, – with, I trust, an unbiassed determination to investigate *facts*, and their independent bearing on sacred history . . . I can bear testimony to the minute truth of innumerable incidental allusions in Holy Writ to the facts of nature, of climate, of geographical position . . . that prove the writers to have lived when and where they are asserted to have lived . . . I can find no standpoint here for the keenest advocate against the full inspiration of the scriptural record. The Holy Land not only elucidates but bears witness to the truth of the HOLY BOOK.

## 16

### *Romancing Narratives: William Palgrave in Arabia*

The assumption of many local people around the globe that
the British Victorian traveller was a spy was not, on the face
of it, unreasonable. Travellers such as Richard Burton were quite
frank about the military usefulness of their travels and knowledge
gained by many a traveller in remote and politically turbulent
parts of the world was fed back helpfully into the imperial
machine. Without this underlying pattern of expectation of
intrigue in foreign places much of the charm of Kipling's *Kim*, for
example, would be lost and everyone loves the idea of a spy in the
hot desert sand. Not all travellers, however, were spies and a man

or woman with a notebook may well have been doing nothing more than sketching an Assyrian ruin or a group of peasants at a well.

One traveller who was an agent (originally of the French) in Egypt and later an official British diplomat was William Gifford Palgrave – brother of the compiler of the most famous of English verse anthologies, *The Golden Treasury of Songs and Lyrics* (1861). Palgrave, in disguise, made a dangerous and pioneering journey across the Arabian desert in the early 1860s and recorded his trip in 1865 in his *Narrative of a Year's Journey through Central and Eastern Arabia*. Some have questioned the veracity of this work but it remains one of the first major pieces of nineteenth-century British travel writing about that region.

Palgrave was born in London in 1826 and educated at Charterhouse and Trinity College, Oxford. After graduation in 1846 he went out to India and was commissioned lieutenant in the 8th Bombay Native Infantry regiment in 1847. Two years later he converted to Catholicism (his ancestry was Jewish) and entered the Jesuit College in Madras, working as a Jesuit missionary until 1853, when he went to study in Rome. Two years later he transferred to Syria and was active there as a missionary, reportedly making many converts, an outcome not always guaranteed by Victorian missionaries. Based in the town of Zahlah, he nearly lost his life in the 1860–1 Druze massacres of Christians, about which his first book was written in 1861. Next he became a French agent trying to facilitate a French invasion of Syria from Egypt and then, in 1862, he made his journey into Arabia. Palgrave's long residence in the region as much as his adoption of disguise contributed to the success of this risky expedition.

In his preface to the *Narrative* Palgrave claimed that his journey had been undertaken 'with the purpose of observing rather than publishing' – tardy publication, it is perhaps worth pointing out, has matured some of the greatest English travel books. He admitted that the adoption of 'native disguise' had its disadvantages in preventing him from carrying out proper scientific inquiry because it was not possible to be seen with instruments of scientific measurement. Worse than this: 'I was at times unable to take down a single note, much less could I display a sketching book or photographic apparatus, however fair the landscape and tempting the sun'. His literary resources thus became his principal ones:

> On the other hand long years, the best part of my life indeed, passed in the East, familiarity with the Arabic language till it became to me almost a mother tongue, and experience in the ways and manners of 'Semitic' nations, to give them their general or symbolic name, supplied me with advantages counterbalancing in some degree the drawbacks enumerated above. Besides, the men of the land rather than the land of the men, were my main object of research and principal study. My attention was directed to the moral, intellectual, and political conditions of living Arabia, rather than to the physical phenomena of the country, – of great indeed, but to me, of inferior interest.

Palgrave was a thoughtful analyst. His own complex identity (he marked his conversion to Catholicism by retrieving the family name of Cohen) helped him to negotiate the intricacies of the region, which he felt previous writers had failed to understand at all adequately, not least because they had succumbed to the romantic distortions of Orientalism. He had a very ambitious aim in his exploration of Arabia:

> The hope of doing something towards the permanent social good of those wide regions; the desire of bringing the stagnant waters of Eastern life into contact with the quickening stream of European progress; perhaps a natural curiosity to know the yet unknown, and the restlessness of enterprise not rare in Englishmen; these were the principal motives. The author may add that at the time of the undertaking he was in connection with the Order of the Jesuits, an Order well known in the annals

of philanthropic daring; he has also gratefully to acknowledge that the necessary funds were furnished by the liberality of the present Emperor of the French . . . It is a matter of real importance to form a correct idea of nations with whom events tend to bring us ever more and more into contact, and of whose future destinies we seem likely to be in no small measure, under Providence, the arbitrators. Ideas which, I regret to say, appear to me often distorted and exaggerated, prevail in the West regarding our Eastern fellow-men; ideas due in part to the defective observation, perhaps the prejudices, of travellers, too preoccupied by their own thoughts and fancies to appreciate or even understand the phases of mind and manners among nations other than their own; while at times an enthusiastic imagination has thrown a prismatic colouring over the faded East. My principal object and endeavour in this work has been, accordingly, to give a tolerably correct notion of the Arab race, – of their condition, intellectual and political, social and religious; such at least as it appeared to me; and should it be my good fortune to have effected this, I ask no more.

At the eastern gate of the city of Ma'an, now in Jordan, on the evening of 16 June 1862, Palgrave and his 'hardy, young, and enter-prising', but unidentified, companion, on their long-necked 'meagre' camels, set their faces to the east, saying to themselves: 'It is time to fill up this blank in the map of Asia, and this, at whatever risks, we will now endeavour; either the land before us shall be our tomb, or we will traverse it in its fullest breadth, and know what it contains from shore to shore.' In front of them stretched a wide and level plain 'blackened over with countless pebbles of basalt and flint, except where the moonbeams gleamed white on little inter-vening patches of clear sand'. Their first destination was Djowf (Al Jawf in modern Saudi Arabia), two hundred miles away, and the journey was perilous because of robbers and the difficulty of finding water. The leader of their Bedouin companions, Salim-el-'Atneh, was little better than an outlaw: 'Lean in make and swarthy of features, his thin compressed lips implied settled resolution and daring purpose, while the calmness of his grey eye showed a cool and thoughtful disposition, not without some possible intimation of treachery.' This is the sort of deft, economic character portrait that so often eluded a writer like Burton, with his wordy bombast. Palgrave wrote a leaner, sharper prose, without mannered flourishes, and right at the outset challenged the sentimental Orientalist view of the Bedouin: 'On the contrary, deeds of the most cold-blooded perfidy are by no means uncommon among these nomades . . . To lead travellers astray in the wilderness till they fall exhausted by thirst and weariness, and then to plunder and leave them to die, is no infrequent Bedouin procedure.'

Salim's companions, Alee and Djordee, were likewise 'utter barbarians in appearance no less than character', scruffy and heavily armed. Palgrave and his companion were dressed like 'ordinary middle class travellers of inner Syria' and had been so since leaving Gaza: 'Our dress then consisted partly of a long stout blouse of Egyptian hemp, and under it, unlike our Bedouin fellow-travellers, we indulged in the luxury of the loose cotton drawers common in the East, while our coloured head-kerchiefs, though simple enough, were girt by akkals or head-bands of some pretension to elegance; the loose red leather boots of the country completed our toilet.' Neatly concealed in the camels' travelling sacks were 'suits of a more elegant appearance, carefully concealed from Bedouin gaze, but destined for appearance when we should reach better inhabited and more civilised districts'. Like Burton, Palgrave pretended to be a travelling doctor and defensively maintained that disguise was necessary so that the reader would have 'the satisfaction, whatever that may be, of making their journey across the great Peninsula book in hand and by their snug fireside, with somewhat less risk than the travellers themselves had in their time to undergo'.

Palgrave and his party marched for fifteen to sixteen hours a day under a 'well-nigh vertical sun' with only two- or three-hour breaks for sleep and he soon succumbed to tertian fever which made him delirious. A typical day would start long before dawn and then halfway through the morning they would breakfast on a sort of flour cake cooked over an open fire 'till at last half-kneaded, half-raw, half-roasted, and more than half-burnt, it was taken out to be broken up between the hungry band, and eaten scalding hot, before it should cool into an indescribable leathery substance, capable of defying the keenest appetite'. Then they would set off again and march until an hour before sunset when the same meal was taken again, with the addition of dried dates (while they lasted). At midnight they lay down 'for just enough sleep to tantalise, not refresh', then were off again.

On 23 June they encountered the seimoom, the 'deadly wind of the desert', but were, fortunately, in the vicinity of some black nomad tents into one of which they all piled, provoking screams when its sole female occupant was discovered. Soon Palgrave reached the Wadi Sirhan, a district of very poor Arabs. Although he received hospitality from them, he was not impressed: 'Here you may see human nature at its lowest stage, or very nearly.' Nevertheless, he found the Arab to be at least capable of improvement, glimpsing 'the groundwork of a manly and generous character, such as Persian or a Turk seldom, if ever, offers' under the surface of 'fickleness proper to men accustomed to no moral or physical restraint'. Thus launched on a characteristically Victorian wave of race speculation, Palgrave surfed on: 'I only wish that those who indulge their imagination in ideal portraits of desert life, and conceive the Bedouins and their condition to be worthy of admiration or of envy, would pass but three days in a Sherarat encampment, and see, not through the medium of romancing narratives written *a priori* as they say, for ready currency, but with their own eyes, to what a depth of degradation one of the noblest races earth affords can descend under the secular influence of nomade life.'

He insisted that the true Arab, rather than this 'degenerate' specimen of nomad, was of a noble race: 'Indeed, after having travelled much, and made pretty intimate acquaintance with many races, African, Asiatic, and European, I should hardly be inclined to give the preference to any over the genuine unmixed clans of central and

Eastern Arabia.' They are the same blood and tongue as the Bedouin: 'Yet how immeasurably superior! The difference between a barbarous Highlander and an English gentleman . . . is hardly less striking.' Once again, extensive knowledge of Arab language and culture could not save the traveller from this obsessive preoccupation with racial (and class) stereotyping and ranking.

Palgrave moved on from the desert to Djowf – 'our first transition from desert to inhabited Arabia' – which was a sort of oasis lying between the northern desert and the southern sandy waste. Once again the local people did not quite measure up: 'In manners, as in locality, the worthies of Djowf occupy a sort of half-way position between Bedouins and the inhabitants of the cultivated districts. Thus they partake in the nomade's aversion to mechanical occupations, in his indifference to literary acquirements, in his aimless fickleness too, and even in his treacherous ways.' Palgrave, however, conceded their liberality and pronounced the Arabs in general to be, at their best, 'the English of the Oriental world' in their love of liberty, aptitude for commerce and hatred of petty rules and regulations. On the other hand, he could dimly perceive the trouble that might be in store given the persistent failure of the West to understand this region: 'So little is the East and its inhabitants understood by the West . . . that I do not see much probability of serious moral or religious change being brought about in Arabia or in any Asiatic elsewhere by European agency, unless indeed for the worse.'

After three weeks at Djowf, Palgrave moved on again, not before issuing a brief apology: 'My readers may have already observed that my narrative resembles somewhat the journey it describes, full of divergences and circuitous passages.' In fact such randomness is intrinsic to the genre. It was the wrong time of the year – 20 July – when Palgrave entered into the desert region of the Nefood, a burning expanse of sand, and even the Bedouin lost their customary 'boisterous gaiety' as they plunged more deeply into a terrain and an experience that would become well known in the English tradition of desert writing through Doughty and Thesiger:

We were now traversing an immense ocean of loose reddish sand, unlimited to the eye, and heaped up in enormous ridges running parallel to each other from north to south, undulation after undulation, each swell two or three hundred feet in average height, with slant sides and rounded crests furrowed in every direction by the capricious gales of the desert. In the depths between the traveller finds himself as it were imprisoned in a suffocating sand-pit, hemmed in by burning walls on every side; while at other times, while labouring up the slope, he overlooks what seems a vast sea of fire, swelling under a heavy monsoon wind, and ruffled by a cross-blast into little red-hot waves. Neither shelter nor rest for eye or limb amid torrents of light and heat poured from above on an answering glare reflected below . . . Add to this the weariness of long summer days of toiling – I might better say wading – through the loose and scorching soil, on drooping, half-stupefied beasts, with few and interrupted hours of sleep at night, and no rest by day because no shelter, little to eat and less to drink, while the tepid and discoloured water in the skins rapidly diminishes even more by evaporation than by use, and a vertical sun, such a sun, strikes down till clothes, baggage, and housings all take the smell of burning and scarce permit the touch.

Only later did Palgrave discover that some of his Bedouin guides had been plotting to rob the travellers and leave them to die in the desert sand.

Eventually Palgrave reached the mountains of Djebel Shomer and, on arrival at Ha'yel (Ha'il), the party created something of a stir and was greeted by the court chamberlain of the monarch, Telal. The danger now was that the disguise of Damascan doctors adopted by Palgrave and his companion, without which 'all intimate access and sincerity of intercourse with the people of the land would have been irretrievably lost, and our onward progress to Nejed rendered totally impossible', would be compromised. To his horror, Palgrave was spotted by a Damascus merchant who knew him and who hailed him, and then by two more people, who threatened to expose his true identity. Fortunately the court chamberlain decided that these witnesses were each as unreliable as the other and Palgrave was taken to an audience with the monarch, a shrewd and bright-eyed ruler whose courtiers surrounded him:

'How many of those I know would give half their having to be present at such a scene and in such a locality,' thought I, while almost wondering at our own quiet and secure position amid the multitude; for, to say truth, how little of Arab rule or life has yet been witnessed by Europeans, how little faithfully described? Half-romantic and always over-coloured scenes of wild Bedouins, painted up into a sort of chivalresque knight-errants and representatives of unthralled freedom; or, perhaps, the heavy and hollow formalities of some coast or frontier courtlet, more than half Ottomanized: apocryphal legends, like those of Lamartine, and the sentimental superficialities of his school, – such is almost all that we possess on these subjects, and from which we are invited to form our criterion and appreciation of Arabia and its people.

Palgrave thus persisted in seeing himself as the truly objective observer freed from the distortions of romantic Orientalist fantasy. He was impressed by Telal and his rule: 'After all, nationality is a good thing, and foreign rule but a poor compensation for it. Here was an Arab governing Arabs after their own native Arab fashion.' Palgrave felt the same principle of self-rule applied to Asia, where: 'I would unhesitatingly say that its specific remedy . . . is to be found first and foremost in the reintegration of its nationality.'

In order to rehabilitate his disguise Palgrave began the next day to practise as a doctor, though conscious that it was 'a horrid, a most scandalous imposture, an unpardonable cheat . . . I sat in cross-legged state, with a pair of scales before me, a brass mortar, a glass ditto, and fifty or sixty boxes of drugs, with a small flanking line of bottles.' One thing that was never disguised was the vigour of

Palgrave's prejudices and, like several other distinguished Arabian travellers, he was far from enchanted with the indigenous culture. At the root of the region's difficulties, he declared without hesitation, was Islam: 'When the Coran and Mecca shall have disappeared from Arabia, then, and then only, can we seriously expect to see the Arab assume that place in the ranks of civilization from which Mahomet and his book have, more than any other individual cause, long held him back.'

The Turks were hardly any better and 'have hardly ever appeared on the world's scene except to destroy, rarely to construct; neither literature nor arts owing aught to the Turk but progressive debasement and decay'. And the Persians are 'in their national character, essentially and irretrieveably rotten', their influence 'productive of extravagance in speculation, bad taste in literature, and perversity in art'. While Palgrave practised as a doctor throughout the summer, Telal continued to probe his guests about their true intent and eventually they opened up to him, especially as they would be dependent on him for a passport to enable them to complete the next stage of their journey. 'Were what passes between us to be known at large,' Telal wisely observed, 'it might be as much as your lives are worth, and perhaps mine also.'

Finally, on 8 September 1862, Palgrave, or, as he was described in the new passport, Seleem-el'Eys-Abour-Mahmood, together with his associate Barakat, 'physicians seeking their livelihood by doctoring', moved off across the elevated table land of central Arabia in the direction of Riyadh, the capital of the Wahhabis, of whom Telal warned them to be careful. This stage of the journey approached the route of the Medina pilgrims, which meant that robbers flourished. Joined at one point by some dervishes from Kabul, Palgrave reflected on those Westerners who had adopted disguise in order to visit the holy places. Without mentioning Richard Burton by name, he observed: 'Passing oneself off for a wandering Darweesh, as some European explorers have attempted to do in the East, is for more reasons than one a very bad plan . . . To feign a religion . . . seems hardly compatible with the character of a European gentleman, let alone that of a Christian.' Palgrave believed that it would be very difficult, given the theological niceties involved, for a European to pass himself off as a dervish and he questioned the motives of those who tried, regarding their real aim as merely 'to boast of the impunity with which they have made a jest of Oriental religion'. He also insisted – and the charge is very important in assessing the truthfulness of Burton's claims – that local people had told him that the various 'alleged Darweesh-personifiers' had actually been rumbled though they remained blissfully unaware of the fact.

At the beginning of October Palgrave finally reached Riyadh, 'the main object of our long journey, the capital of Nejed and half Arabia, its very heart of hearts'. He spent fifty days in the city, where he and his companion were given quarters near the palace of King Feysul and where they set up as doctors once more, their first patient the King's treasurer, a splendidly dressed Negro girt with a gold-hilted sword. The court was deeply suspicious of the two doctors, convinced that they were spies sent by the Egyptian government, and when they eventually tried to leave they discovered it was almost as hard to quit Riyadh as to enter it. They were in the end directly accused by Feysul's son, Abd-Allah, of being spies and threatened with execution. Palgrave argued that this would be to violate his father's hospitality, and after much discussion and the offering of other such arguments, the threat receded: 'What amused me not a little was that the Wahhabee prince had after all very nearly hit the right nail on the head, and that I was snubbing him only for having guessed too well.'

Shortly before he left, Palgrave witnessed a remarkable and rare public audience of King Feysul: 'It was a scene for a painter. There sat the blind old tyrant, corpulent, decrepit, yet imposing, with his large broad forehead, white beard, and thoughtful air, clad in all the simplicity of a Wahhabee; the gold-hafted sword at his side his only ornament of distinction.' Palgrave left secretly during evening prayers with a band of travellers whose camels had been discreetly loaded during the afternoon. Passing through the unattended gate, he and his companion breathed sighs of relief 'like men just let out of a dungeon' but the city cast its awful shadow after them:

> I slept little that night . . . looking back to that huge dark outline of wall and tower amid the shades of the valley; we remembered those whom it encircled, we thought of what influence it had already exercised and might yet exercise over the entire Peninsula; how stern yet how childish a tyranny; how fatal a kindling of burnt-out fanaticism; a new well-head to the bitter waters of Islam; how much misdirected zeal; what concentrated though ill-applied courage and perseverance; and what might be in the end!

Fearful that their role as spies – which in effect is what they were – would be discovered, they pressed on across the red desert towards the Persian Gulf at Hofhoof (Al Hufuf), where the coastal people impressed Palgrave with their greater openness resulting from regular contact with strangers: 'Free intercourse with other races has indeed in all lands . . . this excellent effect, that, while it nowise lessens, nay even strengthens, national and patriotic feelings, it encourages at the same time a kindlier and a more generous way of thought and action towards other branches of the great human family, and renders men more social to all, without disuniting them among themselves.'

Palgrave enjoyed his stay, the good food and the women, who were especially beautiful in his judgement. His personal 'beauty-scale' began at zero with the Bedouin women, increasing to five or six here at the coast, 'and lastly, by a sudden rise of ten degrees at least, the seventeenth or eighteenth would denote the beauties of Oman.' On 19 December he moved on to Kateef (Al Qatif) to find a boat to Bahrain but was unimpressed by 'the dead shallow flats of the bay . . . How different from the bright waters of the Mediterranean, all glitter and life, where we had bidden them farewell eight months before at Gaza!'

They sailed on 23 December, arriving on Boxing Day at Bahrain, where Palgrave waited for quite a time for his servant, Aboo-'Eysa, to rejoin him. The new party then set off, Palgrave disguised once again 'under the scientific character of a deep-read physician, on the look-out for I know not what herbs or drugs, which I was to suppose discoverable in the south-eastern regions'. He spent the early months of 1863 exploring the coast of Oman, which he found 'pre-eminently a land of amusement, of diversion, of dance and song, of show and good-living'. Slavery, it is true, was part of the picture but he considered that, as practised by the Arabs, it 'had little in common with the system hell-branded by those atrocities of the Western hemisphere, the end of which, under God's blessing, appears now imminent'. Palgrave's argument was a variant on the traditional imperialist thesis that civilization was being brought in the nick of time to the barbarian and that black people should be grateful to be 'taken from an existence befitting only the boars and tigers of a jungle, to lead henceforth a life somewhat more resembling that of reasonable bipeds'. But it was not an argument he wished to prolong since 'the strong sensual passions of the African race' were for him 'a disagreeable subject'.

In the first week of March Palgrave was caught in a violent storm on the way to Masqat, in the course of which the boat sprang a leak and he was forced to dive overboard and swim towards the lifeboat, which he saw 'dancing like an empty nutshell on the ocean'. In desperate straits, and with his fellow passengers reciting the Qur'an constantly, he steered on until the storm returned and he felt there was no choice but to jump overboard into the 'white yeast of raging waters' and allow himself to be washed ashore. He survived, without his notes of the year so far and with no money or gifts, but local hospitality was offered that allowed him to take a boat to Masqat, where 'an old acquaintance from Bombay' gave him further financial assistance. However, his health was not good and soon, on a boat to Aboo-Shar, he came down with typhoid fever. His travels were now necessarily at an end. On 10 April he boarded an Indian steamer to Basra which took a seven-day voyage up the Tigris to Baghdad and from there he returned via Aleppo to Syria.

Palgrave returned to England to write his *Personal Narrative*, then – in spite of a spirit not entirely suited to taking orders – he joined the British foreign service, which took him to Abyssinia and Asia Minor. He was subsequently British Consul at St Thomas in the West Indies and at Manila and then Consul General in Bulgaria. Sent next to Bangkok, he developed an interest in Eastern religions, having by now abandoned Catholicism. In 1884 he was appointed Resident Minister in Uruguay, where he died of bronchitis at Montevideo on 30 September 1888, once again reconciled to Catholicism.

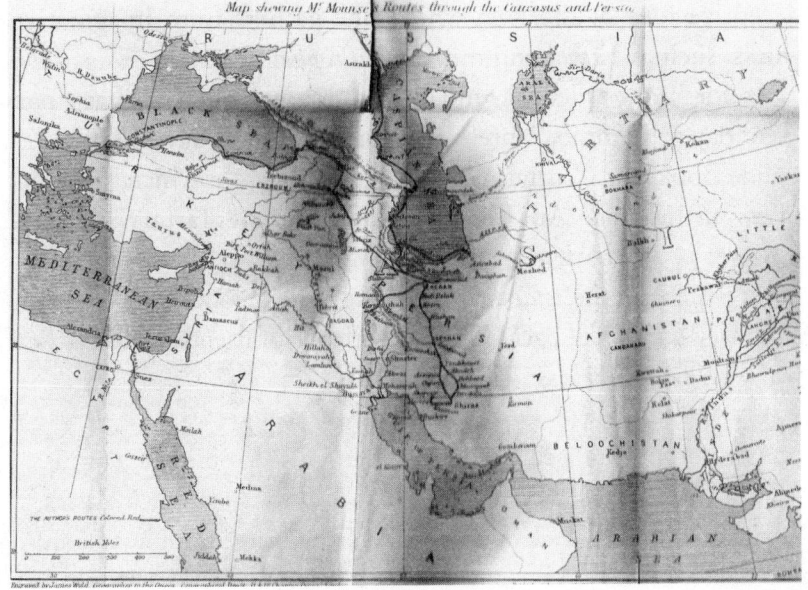

17

*Feringhistan: Augustus Mounsey in Persia*

When the British diplomat Augustus Henry Mounsey set off on a journey to Persia in November 1865 he cast himself in the role of a thoroughly representative British Victorian traveller. His knowledge of the country, he frankly admitted, was 'of the most meagre description', and even that little was derived almost wholly from romantic literary sources. Managing at least to avoid the ritual genuflection before *The Arabian Nights*, Mounsey cited two non-fiction works, James Morier's popular 1828 translation *The Adventures of Hajji Baba of Ispahan* and a book which he calls *A Diplomate's Residence in Persia* (actually *Journal of a Diplomate's Three Years' Residence in Persia* by Edward Backhouse Eastwick). For the rest he had 'merely that hazily golden, but, alas!

deceptive idea of the East which one gathers from imaginative works, such as *Vathek* and the *Veiled Prophet*.

As for more practical guidance, there was none at that time: 'The day will come, I presume, when we shall have "Murray's" Guide Books for Central Asia and the vast regions which the compilers of English Atlases term Independent Tartary. As yet, however . . . we have none in the style of those well-known red volumes which are the *vade-mecum* of the British continental tourist.' Mounsey had to fall back on the experience of friends whose advice was worse than useless:

> As to outfit, one gentleman who had passed some years of his youth in Iran, recommended me to take a supply of watch-glasses and crystal wine-coolers; another, lately returned from it, said an English saddle and a portable bed were all the kit I should require; and a third, who had sojourned in the land for four or five years, hesitated at counselling me to provide myself with a supply of brandy and sherry, and pronounced a fur coat for the journey to be completely superfluous.

By the time he came to record the narrative of his experiences, Mounsey was able to produce his own definitive list, based on hard experience, of what should be brought along:

> Fowling-piece, revolver and ammunition; light bedstead (the lightest I know are made in Russia, and occupy little more space than an ordinary gun-case); sheets, blankets, &c., and waterproof covering; portable India-rubber bath, japanned iron washhand-basin, plates and cups; knives (a large one for the pocket, with corkscrew, is most useful), forks and spoons; English saddle, fitted with holsters and saddle-bags, and bridle; portable medicine-chest; a small supply of brandy; preserved meats and soups. The traveller should be prepared for the extremes of heat and cold, and accordingly provide himself with a pith helmet, strong riding-boots, and breeches; veils and spectacles for

protection of the eyes; several linen suits for summer; fur coat, felt boots (reaching to the knee), and a plentiful outfit of woollen and flannel clothing for winter.

Mounsey, who an otherwise sturdy biographical source such as Frederic Boase's *Modern English Biography* has to concede was 'a somewhat obscure figure', began his diplomatic career at the Lisbon embassy in 1857, progressing through Hanover in 1861 and Vienna in 1862. He held several central European appointments and was acting Consul General in Budapest in 1873 and in Paris in 1875. He was later Secretary of the British Legation in Tokyo and Athens and Resident Minister and Consul General in Bogotá, where he died on 10 April 1882. He belongs to that attractive strain of Victorian travel writing, the agreeably relaxed and amused, and he was an early example of a traveller returning with a message to his fellow countrymen that Something Should Be Done in the form of overseas aid. Dry winters in 1870 and 1871 had caused an eighteen-month famine in Persia at the time of publication in 1862 of his *A Journey through the Caucasus and the Interior of Persia* and he hoped that the fund-raising efforts of the Persian Relief Fund, a struggling 'committee of gentlemen' in London, would be boosted by the book. Mounsey wrote his narrative with a slight fear that he had been a little too negative about the 'moral obliquity' of the Persian character, which he said was 'formed, to a very great extent, by the system of government under which he has so long lived' whereas in truth the Persian's natural disposition was to be 'amiable, intelligent, imaginative, and docile'.

And so: 'On a cold drizzling November morning in 1865, I left the great metropolis shrouded in congenial fog, and rolled down with the mail to Dover.' From Calais he took the train to Cologne and Passau, deprecating on the way the 'democratic universal-suffrage idiosyncrasy' of the French and Belgian railway personnel in contrast with the formal manners of the Germans and Austrians. From Vienna he travelled by train to Trieste, then by a steamer of the Austrian Lloyd line to Istanbul, casting anchor in the Golden

Horn on 7 December and taking 'an excellent dinner at the ambassadorial table'. On 17 December he steamed up the Bosporus and out across 'the dreaded Black Sea' towards an increasingly 'stern and inhospitable'-seeming Asiatic coast. The weather deteriorated and the Dalmatian captain took refuge from the storms and blizzards in Sinop, which allowed Mounsey the chance of a little grebe shooting.

A little farther along the Black Sea coast at Samsun he left the ship intending to take a poorly maintained post road to Mosul and Baghdad ('let Macadam be forgotten, and the results of the labours of parish overseers and district boards be consigned to oblivion'). In fact the weather improved and he rejoined the ship for Trabzon (Trebizond), where on arrival another 'capital déjeuner' was had at the house of the Russian Consul General, for Mounsey's companion since Vienna had been 'Count L', principal aide-de-camp of the Grand Duke Michael. The following morning, after a night voyage, Mounsey arrived at the Bay of Batoum (Batumi in modern Georgia) and soon afterwards caught his first glimpse of 'the great Caucasian Alps, and their tall snow-covered peaks sharply defined against the clear blue sky'.

On 23 December Mounsey cast anchor at the mouth of the River Rioni and took a barge from the boat upstream to the town of Poti, where he checked in to the Hôtel Colchide. The next day he paid 400 francs to hire a steamer upriver but left it halfway to transfer to some grand carriages arranged by the Count, each drawn by six horses, that took them to Kutaisi, the chief town of Colchis, where Jason was said to have found the Golden Fleece. It was hard work, Mounsey complained, travelling in a 'half-civilized country' like Russia, especially in the comfortless *telega*, or post vehicle: 'In the Caucasus it may be described as an oblong wooden box of the roughest sort, placed, without springs, upon four wheels, and capable of holding one traveller and his traps most uncomfortably.'

The next stage of the journey was over the mountains of the Suram chain to Tbilisi, the capital of Georgia, 'a stranger mixture of Asiatic and European architecture, and yet hardly European'. The companionship of Count L delivered plenty of elevated social life and more of those splendid dinners because the Count's boss, the Grand Duke Michael, brother of the reigning Emperor of Russia, had his residence in the city. Mounsey dined well and thoroughly enjoyed himself in spite of 'my complete ignorance of the Russian and Georgian languages' and a growing conviction that the Georgians were 'lazy, indolent, apathetic, and ignorant, without ambition to rise in the world, and content to live on in their own sluggish way'. He celebrated the Russian New Year on 12 January 1866 by skating on the frozen River Kura, 'to the great stupor of the inhabitants, who have never seen skates in their lives'.

On 15 January Mounsey left Tbilisi for the final leg of the journey into Persia, a distance of four hundred *versts* (265 miles). This time he travelled in a carriage with springs and took care to invest in 'huge felt boots and a portable bed weighing some ten pounds'. The carriage was also stuffed with 'tongues, chickens, preserved meats, bread, butter, wine, brandy, tea, and sugar'. He passed through Armenia, 'one of the oldest nations in the world', and visited the Church of St Gregory at Ejmiadzin, a tour which terminated in the great refectory, where two hundred monks and priests and seminarists were hard at work 'making a hearty midday meal off boiled beef and a pilau of grits. I did not find either of these dishes very good, but cannot speak too highly of the convent wine, very much resembling Sauterne, which stood in great abundance on the long tables, and seemed to be as much relished by my hosts as by myself.'

The next day, after glimpsing Mount Ararat, he pressed on to cross 'the swift-flowing yellow Araxes' on a 'species of rudely-constructed raft' into Persia. The local food, especially the kebabs, appealed greatly to Mounsey, who pronounced that 'all European cooks ought to be sent to the East in order to learn how to boil rice'. But he had his reservations about the much-mentioned largesse of Eastern hosts:

One hears a great deal about Oriental hospitality. Anything very profuse or splendid in this line in Europe is sure to be termed Oriental, and one might almost imagine that Easterns pass their lives in giving magnificent *fêtes* to the strangers who visit them. As far as Persians are concerned, this idea is certainly erroneous . . . on being asked to dine in a Persian house, I have often found I was only doing the proper thing in taking half the dinner with me, and have not infrequently received hints through the servants of my host, a few hours previous to the meal, that a supply of wines or spirits would be most welcome.

On Mounsey's arrival at Tabriz the authorities impounded all his luggage on the pretext that he was smuggling gold lace and it was only when he called on the British Consul General's help that he was able to retrieve it. He stayed with the Consul General and rode out with him the next day into the bazaar, where he heard shouts from the crowd of 'Feringhee, Feringhee' (foreigner). For the mass of people in the East, Mounsey concluded, 'there is in Europe, or rather westwards of Constantinople, but one land, "Feringhistan" and one race, that of the "Feringhee"'.

On 28 January Mounsey embarked on a 370-mile journey to Tehran but on reaching his goal he was a little disappointed: 'Arrived within sight of Teheran, I could perceive but a long low line of brown mud wall capped here and there by the brown domes, very like ant-hills, of some insignificant mosques, rising above the snow-covered plain and backed by huge snow-covered mountains.' Inside the city much was ruinous, whereas 'I had dreamt of tall minarets, gilded domes, and lofty bazaars.' After the usual good dinner with the English envoy Mounsey went out the next day to explore the capital and decided: 'Teheran, which can hardly be said to contain any architectural building at all, is simply insignificant.'

Mounsey faced the imminent prospect of being bored in the Persian capital. He went on several hunting excursions, had a short and inconsequential audience with the Shah and searched for amusement. 'There was a billiard-table at the English Mission, but one can't always play at billiards.' Since there was only one 'European lady' in the entire city he was driven to take solace in cards. An excursion by mule caravan to Ispahan which consisted of 'twenty-nine quadrupeds and thirteen bipeds' was a welcome diversion and taste of splendour, as were the other ruins such as Persepolis. 'The Nomad instinct,' Mounsey reflected, 'which is said to be innate in us all, but is repressed in Europe by education and civilization, develops itself rapidly in a country like Persia, where there is no obstacle to its indulgence: impelled by it, and weary of the monotony of a residence in town . . . I determined to pass the interval of five or six days . . . on the plain of Merdasht, in preference to further inactivity at Shiraz.' But this expedition resulted in an encounter with some hostile nomads who had to be persuaded to deliver hospitality to the Feringhee. Annoyed by this, Mounsey addressed a high imperialist oration to his readers:

> Previous and subsequent experience has brought me to the conclusion that Persians, whether nomads or the contrary, must be treated with a high hand. The European traveller owes his safety to the fear which he inspires, and to nothing else: if he be not really able to enforce obedience, he must act as if he were. His prestige is luckily still so great that a display of firmness generally obviates the necessity of a recourse to extreme measures; but he must always be prepared for them, and show that he is so. Then he will, as a rule, find little difficulty in procuring all that a traveller can justly demand, and have no reason to complain of his reception amongst them; for, except when roused by religious fanaticism, they are naturally amiable, docile, and serviceable.

A couple of days later further refusal by a postmaster at a caravanserai to supply foreigners with fresh horses led Mounsey's party to ram the stable door with a telegraph pole to release a horse, and to flourish revolvers to force the angry local people to put away their brandished knives. Mounsey's narrative was drawing to an end not a moment too soon as he seemed to be losing interest ('little else of interest occurred during the summer and autumn of 1866,' he observed wearily). Fishing and snipe shooting and, by the winter, some skating, amused him but by the early summer of 1867 he was ready to leave on a steamer from Rasht to Baku and on northwards across the Caspian Sea to the mouth of the River Volga, where another steamboat took him west: 'Of the broad swift-flowing Volga I have little to say: its banks are flat and its scenery is monotonous.' He stopped at Sarepta, Saritzin, Samara 'and at many other places which are all duly described in the pages of Murray' but he was longing for home and the grouse moors. After steaming seven days and nights he arrived at Nizhni Novgorod on 1 August 1867, then took a train across Europe to Calais, then took 'the Dover express which was to carry me into Charing Cross on the 8th of August, and more important than all, the limited mail which was to land me amongst heather and grouse on the 12th'.

## 18

*Avoiding Politics: Isabel Burton and*
*Laurence Oliphant in Palestine*

The life – or more properly the legend – of Richard Burton was carefully stage-managed by his wife Isabel, who posthumously edited (where she did not feed to the fire) his writings, wrote his life and massaged his image. Recent biography has tried to rehabilitate her image but the literary evidence still points to her subservient role in the legend and the preface to her book *The Inner Life of Syria, Palestine, and the Holy Land from My Private Journal* (1875) is not calculated to dispel one's reservations. Unlike the majority of distinguished Victorian women travellers, who were simply

resourceful, able and experienced (a perception not helped sometimes by what one might call the Plucky Gel mode of literary
criticism) and who produced narratives that are in no need of being
patronized, Isabel went out of her way to disparage herself. 'I have
followed my husband everywhere, gleaning only woman's lore,' she
announced, adding that: 'This book contains little History,
Geography, or Politics; no Science, Ethnography, Botany, Geology,
Zoology, Mineralogy, or Antiquities . . . Exploration and the harder
travels, such as . . . the . . . wilder parts of Syria, have been described
by Captain Burton and myself in "Unexplored Syria"; but for all
that, this book contains things women will like to know.' What
women liked to know, apparently, was the life of the harem but,
alas, this 'would not be suitable for English girls, and I wish to
write a book which may be read by everybody'.

Isabel Burton's book, though very long, is a disappointment. It
has her husband's prolixity without its redeeming qualities.
Burton was British Consul at Damascus during their residence in
Syria and she claimed that, as the wife of a consular official, 'I
avoid politics', but male writers in military or government service
seem not to have imposed such a constraint on themselves. What
she did seem prepared to do was to indulge some Orientalist
imaginings and produce some pastiche of her husband's effusive
style. In the opening chapter she declares that there are times
when 'a horror of the common groove, of the cab-shafts of civilization, of the contamination of cities, of the vulgarities of life,
takes its hold of me, and I yearn for the desert to recover the
purity of my mind and the dignity of human nature – to be
regenerated amongst the Arabs.' This could be achieved by com-
muning with 'the solemn, silent mystery, the romantic halo, of
pure Oriental life'.

Writing five years after Isabel Burton, Laurence Oliphant, in
*The Land of Gilead* (1880), had an avowed political purpose in his
travels in this region and went 'in pursuance of an idea': to establish
a Jewish colony in Palestine. In the wake of the Treaty of Berlin he
believed that the Sultan of Turkey would have to initiate reform in

order to prevent international intervention across Asia Minor. Oliphant had travelled widely in Turkey and believed that as well as reform at the centre what was needed was a series of experiments in decentralized government. His 'experiment on a small scale' would, he thought, appeal to the Turkish ruler. A Colonization Company would be set up to channel overseas capital into the project and the Jews were selected for the experiment because they were 'rich enough, proven loyal subjects to the Ottomans, and historically associated with "the province of Asiatic Turkey"'.

Oliphant selected the provinces east of the Jordan for his site because: 'Situated between the Holy Places at Jerusalem and the Asiatic frontier of Russia, between the Mediterranean and the Red Sea, between Syria and Egypt, their strategic value and political importance must be apparent at a glance.' He explicitly disavowed the 'theological chimera' of the restoration of the Jewish homeland in Palestine and was simply interested in establishing a successful colony which might serve as 'a model for the rest of Syria and Asia Minor' and both the Prime Minister, Disraeli, and the Foreign Secretary, Lord Salisbury, smiled on his project.

Laurence Oliphant had plenty of experience to offer. The son of the later chief justice of Ceylon, he was born in Cape Town in 1829 and after practising at the colonial Bar he travelled in Nepal, Russia and North America and became secretary to Lord Elgin during his negotiations in Canada. Subsequently in the Crimea and elsewhere he involved himself in diplomatic and intelligence work and was an early visitor to the newly opened territory of Japan. He made many unofficial missions after officially retiring from the diplomatic service in the early 1860s and was briefly a Liberal MP. Resigning his seat in 1867, Oliphant, who had always had an interest in mysticism, took up with the American religious 'prophet' Thomas Harris, who ran a community in America called the Brotherhood of the New Life at Brocton in New York State. Oliphant made over his money to Harris and became a subservient disciple. Although he resumed his journalistic activities, serving as correspondent for *The Times* in the Franco-Prussian War, he eventually broke with Harris.

Early in 1879 he set off on the journey recorded in *The Land of Gilead.*

In the middle of February Oliphant left England and based himself initially at Beirut to begin the search for 'the tract of waste land' he needed. To avoid any harassment he travelled in the most unostentatious manner possible with a companion, Captain Owen Phibbs, and the latter's servant instead of a dragoman, carrying, on one mule guided by a muleteer, very little money and no tents, just bedding, cooking utensils and food essentials. 'These consisted of a few tins of preserved meat, some Liebig's Extract, tea, coffee, sugar, a ham, some cheese, cakes of chocolate, a bottle of olives, dates &c. We also took a bottle of spirits of wine and a spirit-lamp, which we found to be the greatest possible comfort: a cup of hot tea, coming at the right moment, saves many a headache, if one is at all susceptible to the sun.'

Oliphant travelled south to Sidon, noting as he went the suitability of the country for railway building, and soon felt that he was travelling along 'the beaten track of the tourist and traveller from Jerusalem to Damascus'. He met his first Arabs, who seemed to him 'perfectly good natured and peaceable, though they bear a somewhat doubtful reputation' and experienced the hospitality of a Sheikh Ismail, who put them up at his home in what turned out to be a room shared with everyone else: 'As for sleep, it proved out of the question: each one of the five either snored, or moaned, or puffed, or talked in his sleep; and these noises, diversified with the incessant barking of dogs and a slight sprinkling of fleas, kept me awake, and indeed to some extent occupied, until the first streak of dawn warranted me in waking my companion and rousing the household generally.'

Like his predecessors in this region, Oliphant was alert to the Biblical significance of every scrap of land: 'It was impossible to pass the night upon a mound which popular tradition identifies with the dunghill upon which Job scraped himself with potsherds, without feeling a strong desire to trace its origin, and raise, however slightly, the veil which shrouds the mystery of his place of abode.' In spite of claiming that it was not his main purpose, his book is bulked out, like so many portly Victorian travel narratives, with much historical and antiquarian digression.

When Oliphant finally reached the region he called 'the land of Gilead, a hard, rocky region', he felt that he had put the beaten track behind him, and by travelling simply with two Kurdish guides he felt that he was closer to the people: 'We had, moreover, far better opportunities of seeing the inhabitants and judging of the actual condition of the country by living amongst them as we did, than if we had followed the ordinary custom of travellers, and isolated ourselves in our tents, limiting our contact with them to intercourse through a dragoman.' But the reality of life in the deserted region was a little harsher. At the village of Kefr Assad he put up in a circular hut of mud and stone where the bedroom was 'a small apartment, about ten feet square, partly excavated and partly built of stone, plastered with mud and cow-dung. The entrance was a hole three feet high, destitute of a door, through which came the entire supply of light and air, as there were neither windows nor chimney.' After a good meal from his own cook, who had a genius for rustling something up whatever the circumstances, Oliphant turned in, anticipating a good night's rest after the day's travelling:

A delusion which, unhappily, was soon dispelled; for no sooner had the sounds of the day died away, and the family and our servants gone to roost, than a pack of jackals set up that plaintive and mournful wail by which they seem to announce to the world that they are in a starving condition. They came so close to the village that all the dogs in it set up a furious chorus of defiant barking. This woke the baby, of whose vocal powers we had been till then unaware. Fleas and mosquitoes innumerable seemed to take advantage of the disturbed state of things generally to make a combined onslaught. Vainly did I thrust my hands into my socks, tie handkerchiefs round my face and neck, and so arrange the rest of my night attire as to leave no opening by which they could crawl in. Our necks and wrists especially seemed circled with rings of fire . . . So we groaned and tossed without closing an eye, eagerly watching for morning, and an hour before daylight roused the establishment.

The next day, after coffee and Arab bread, Oliphant renewed his quest, looking at the countryside around him with expectation that the day was not far distant when 'the vast tracts of rich land, now lying waste upon its slopes, may be cultivated by an emigrant population, who will develop their resources, and find in these beautiful and secluded vales a refuge from that persecution to which they are exposed in Christian countries'. At the ruins of Jerash an old rogue emerged to demand money on top of what the travellers had already paid. He brandished a testimonial in their faces which he assumed would provide a ringing endorsement but which, to the literate, revealed that he was an 'extortionate old thief'. He insisted that they read the document carefully, then he stowed it away complacently for future use. Oliphant looked beyond him to the hills, which in his judgement were eminently suitable for settlement: 'Except by a few wandering Arabs they are uninhabited, and consequently totally uncultivated, waiting, let us hope, to be reoccupied by the descendants of the same race which once pastured their flocks in their luxuriant valleys, and upon the rolling prairie-land which stretched beneath us.' Oliphant's confident projections of his colony east of the Jordan seem today, with the knowledge of the years of conflict and disastrous interventions to follow, not a little naive, as well as ominously dismissive of the Arab population:

The fact that this rich and luxuriant country should be only sparsely inhabited by a wandering population, possessing no legal title whatever to the soil, specially adapts it to settlement by a fixed and permanent population who could be established here without injury to the Arabs; for regulations might easily be devised under which the interests of both could be safeguarded and secured. In point of fact, however, the Arabs have very little claim to our sympathy. They have laid waste this country, ruined its villages, and plundered its inhabitants, until it has been reduced to its present condition; and if they were driven back to the Arabian deserts from which they came, there is abundant pasture in its oases for their camels and goats.

As he looked on approvingly, dreamed his dreams of railways (even producing a map of the network), Oliphant felt he was gazing on a new 'Land of Promise'. The actual land, however, was not without its disappointments. He made a visit to Jerusalem in Holy Week and for the Jewish Passover and decided that the Jews there were not likely to furnish the right kind of raw material as colonists: 'The Ashkenazim established there are a useless mendicant class, who are now a burden upon their co-religionists, and who would be equally so upon an enterprise, where not merely industry, but a small amount of capital would be essential.'

One of the last sights of Oliphant's trip was an evening among the dervishes and wonder-workers of Damascus, where he had gone to seek, successfully, the support of the Governor-General of Syria for the colonization of Gilead. He and his party watched skewers being put through the cheeks of young men without drawing blood or causing pain. Scorpions were devoured. Then the dervishes began to eat live snakes. A brazier was brought in and live coals became the next course: 'the smell of burning flesh becoming powerful and sickening as they crunched the glowing morsels'. But it was when Sheikh Ruslan Aboutou, the evening's master of ceremonies and spiritual leader of the order of Bedawi, proposed to put a curved knife about eight inches long and two inches broad through a man's stomach, that 'the repugnance of our party could not be overcome' and they left abruptly with 'a cry of horror from the ladies'.

After returning to Beirut Oliphant took a steamer to Constantinople at the end of May 1879. He was full of optimism that his scheme would be favourably received, that it would be to the advantage of the Ottoman Empire and that it was also a special responsibility of England: 'The population of Palestine in particular, of which 25,000 belong to the Hebrew race, is looking to England for protection and the redress of grievances.' In fact the subsequent approach to the Turkish Government failed and the scheme foundered in political complexities.

Oliphant continued to travel in Egypt and America, where the breach with Harris was finally achieved. He continued to push the Palestine plan and in 1882 he moved with his wife to Haifa, where he built a house and began to develop his odd mystical notions, later expounded in a book called *Sympneumata, or Evolutionary Forces Now Active in Man* and written with his wife. It was a scheme for the elect – in possession of the superhuman transcendental gift of insight, the sympneumata – to regenerate their fortunate fellow members of the human race.

After his wife's death in 1886 of a fever, Oliphant, who had dabbled in spiritualism, believed he was receiving messages from her. He went on to develop the concept, expounded in his *Scientific Religion, or The Higher Possibilities of Life*, of a new religion based on the power of sexual love. He married again in 1888 but died shortly afterwards from lung cancer at Surbiton on 23 December 1888.

## 19

### *The Travellers' School: Charles Doughty in Arabia Deserta*

Victorian travellers commonly prefaced their published narratives with self-deprecating disclaimers insisting that their
accounts possessed no literary merit. Charles Montagu Doughty, by
contrast, is the great self-conscious stylist among the nineteenth-
century travel writers and the language of his massive *Travels in
Arabia Deserta* (1888) is a remarkable mixture of Chaucerian and
Elizabethan English, infused with Arabic linguistic and speech patterns to create, as those with a knowledge of Arabic have attested, a
sense, particularly in the dialogues, of how the original Arabic

encounters would have sounded. The book's enormous length – over 600,000 words – was initially an obstacle to its publication and many publishers refused it. It was not until an abridgement by Edward Garnett appeared, with Doughty's sanction, in 1908 under the title *Wanderings in Arabia* that Doughty began to discover a significant readership. But even Garnett admitted that this first abridgement 'naturally both affrights and triumphs over the endurance of the ordinary man' and his second attempt, *Passages from Arabia Deserta* (1931), appeared at a quarter of the length of the original. But the style remained intact.

Doughty had originally set off on his travels as a philologist with the ambition to write a patriotic epic on, as he put it: 'The Nation's beginnings, to continue the older tradition of Chaucer and Spenser, resisting to my power the decadence of the English language.' It is not so much the quaintness of diction, which renders a camel as 'a great shuffle-footed beast', as the archaic syntax with its inversions and formal rhythms that forms the basis of this highly idiosyncratic prose. Early in the book he is hailed by an old friend 'in that long street of Damascus which is called Straight' and the friend takes him by the hand to say, in words that would not be heard in Albemarle Street in 1888: 'Tell me (said he), since thou art here again in the peace and assurance of Ullah, and whilst we walk, as in the former years, toward the new blossoming orchards, full of the sweet spring as the garden of God, what moved thee, or how couldst thou take such journeys into the fanatic Arabia?'

What moved Doughty to embark on his twenty-month trip through north-west Arabia in November 1876 was the wish to examine the ancient inscriptions at Medain Salih and to make impressions of them. He failed to persuade either the British Association or the Royal Geographical Society to fund his trip, which followed a year learning Arabic, but he set off regardless. Doughty was born in 1843 in Leiston, Suffolk, where his father was a clergyman and landowner. His parents both dying in his early childhood, he was cared for by relatives and educated privately, and planned a career in the Royal Navy until he was rejected because of a slight speech impediment.

Doughty's growing interest in geology and archaeology continued at Cambridge, where he graduated in natural sciences in 1865. His self-appointed mission to revive the decadent English of his fellow Victorians now took over and, in spite of his lack of funds, he travelled as a poor philological scholar in Holland, then went on to explore Provence and Italy (witnessing an eruption of Mount Vesuvius), North Africa, Spain, Greece and then the Holy Land. He went next to Egypt and undertook a three-month camel journey across the Sinai Peninsula. Moving on to Jordan, he planned the trip to record the Medain Salih inscriptions that forms the immediate pretext of the travels in Arabia.

At Damascus in November 1876 Doughty had sought permission from the Governor of Syria to join the Haj caravan of pilgrims to Medain Salih but the Waly referred the traveller to the British Consul, who would not hear of it. Doughty believed that the Consul's refusal of papers was 'the source to me of nearly all the mischief of these travels in Arabia'. He was determined not to leave Damascus, which was busy with preparations for the Haj: 'There is every year a new stirring of this goodly Oriental city in the days before the Haj; so many strangers are passing in the bazaars, of outlandish speech and clothing from the far provinces.' Eventually Doughty found a Persian camel driver, Mohammed Aga, who was prepared to take him. Accordingly, he became the latest Victorian Englishman in disguise in a strange country, calling himself Khalil: 'I was presently clothed as a Syrian of simple fortune, and ready with store of camel biscuit to ride along with him; mingled with the Persians in the Haj journey I should be the less noted whether by Persians or Arabs.' He was not trying to deceive in the Burtonian manner, merely to blend into the scene without drawing attention to himself, the wish, invariably frustrated, of every serious traveller.

Doughty moved off with his small party to a camp outside the city where pilgrims mustered for the journey proper. In spite of the antique and decorous prose, he was quite precise about such mundane matters as dates or the number of days a journey took. At ten o'clock in the morning of 13 November 1876 a cannon was fired and the pilgrimage officially started. It took twenty minutes for the long caravan to pass before Doughty and his party could join the rear of the procession. The six thousand pilgrims, leading ten thousand cattle, camels and mules and guarded by armed troops against the marauding Bedouin, set off across 'an empty waste, a plain of gravel, where nothing appeared and never a road before us'.

Although a frail child and reportedly a shy man, Doughty had a stubbornly individualist streak which led him into some undiplomatic wrangles with his Arab hosts during his wanderings. Not long after leaving Damascus he protested when an Arab caravan servant was beaten to force him to confess to stealing his Persian master's purse. Doughty's intervention was ignored but he was subsequently warned that this could have drawn attention to him and resulted in his being sent back. Like Palgrave before him, he had little love for the dominant religion of the region. As the caravan passed out of Syria into Arabia proper on 24 November he reflected on the many deaths that occurred along the pilgrims' way: 'How great is that yearly suffering and sacrifice of human flesh, and all lost labour, for a vain opinion, a little salt of science would dissolve all their religion!' He believed that the chief perils of Arabia were 'famine and the dreadful-faced harpy of their religion, a third is the rash weapon of every Ishmaelite robber'. For all his learning and scholarly interest in archaeology, there were limits to Doughty's traveller's empathy. He withheld respect for Islamic 'fanaticism', boasting that 'the sun made me an Arab, but never warped me to Orientalism'.

On arrival at Medain Salih, Doughty parted company with the pilgrims and settled in the garrison town for some time, seeing further evidence of the power of Islam: 'Are not Mohammed's saws to-day the mother of belief of a tenth part of mankind? . . . Islam and the commonwealth of Jews are as great secret conspiracies, friends only of themselves and to all without of crude iniquitous heart, unfaithful, implacable.' Nevertheless, Doughty exhibited much more interest than a traveller like Burton ever did in the character and personality of individual people he met along the way. His host and protector at Medain Salih, Mohammed Aly, who bargained with him to be his guide to the local monuments, is described vividly, with human insight, and in Doughty's inimitable idiom:

> A diseased senile body he was, full of ulcers, and past the middle age, so that he looked not to live long, his visage much like a fiend, dim with the leprosy of the soul and half fond; he shouted when he spoke with a startling voice, as it might have been of the ghrôl: of his dark heart ruled by so weak a head, we had hourly alarms in the lonely kella. Well could he speak (with a certain erudite utterance) to his purpose, in many or in few words. These Orientals study little else, as they sit all day idle at the coffee in their male societies: they learn in this school of infinite human observation to speak to the heart of one another. His tales seasoned with saws, which are the wisdom of the unlearned, we heard for more than two months, they were never ending. He told them so lively to the eye that they could not be bettered, and part were of his own motley experience.

Aly warned Doughty, as a Nasrâny or foreign Christian, to be careful in visiting those monuments judged to be holy places. Spotting some rusted ancient coins on the ground, Doughty reflected: 'Arabia of our days has the aspect of a decayed country . . . she is forsaken and desolate.'

When the Haj returned, he decided to 'go forth to wander with the Arab in the immense wilderness' and persuaded the local Pasha to guarantee his safe conduct by speaking to his Bedouin guides. The Russo-Turkish war at this time exacerbated the potential tensions between a Christian and his Muslim hosts – quite apart from Doughty's lack of documents and his outspokenness – so this was a dangerous journey. Out in the desert to the east he encountered a group of desert nomads with whom he stayed for several months, observing their daily life and patterns of behaviour in great detail. He noted in particular the 'weary servitude' of women and was called in on one occasion ('the guest's honourable office') to persuade a woman called Hirfa to return to her husband, Zeyd, after she had run away because he could not give her children.

This slow growth of acquaintance with the people of the desert gave Doughty deep satisfaction: 'Pleasant is the sojourn in the wandering village, in this purest earth and air, with the human fellowship, which is all day met at leisure about the cheerful coffee fire, and amidst a thousand new prospects . . . A pleasure it is to listen to the cheerful musing Beduin talk, a lesson in the travellers' school of mere humanity, – and there is no land so perilous which by humanity he may not pass, for man is of one mind everywhere . . .'

Doughty explored the surrounding landscape, visiting the volcanic hill of Anâz and the lava fields of the Harra and its 'iron desolation', where the barren extremity made him conscious of the littleness of man in such a terrain: 'What lonely life would not feel constraint of heart to trespass here! the barren heaven, the nightmare soil! where should he look for comfort? – There is a startled conscience within a man of his *mesquîn* [paltry] being, and profane, in presence of the divine stature of the elemental world! – this lionlike sleep of cosmogonic forces, in which is swallowed up the gnat of the soul within him, – that short motion and parasitical usurpation which is the weak accident of life in matter.'

After this time at Teyma, Doughty travelled east towards the Irnan mountain region with the Bishr tribe of the Western Nejd desert. He encountered a woman at one camp who came asking for gifts of needle and thread: 'I saw, with an aversion (of race), that all these Bishr housewives wore the *berkoa* or heathenish face-clout, above which only the two hollow ill-affected eyes appeared. This desolation of the woman's face was a sign to me that I journeyed now in another country.' Later he met a schoolmaster who asked him for a book. So pleased was he with Doughty's gift of a geography book written in Arabic by an American missionary in Beirut that 'he laid it on his head in token of how highly he esteemed it, – an Oriental gesture which I have not seen again in Arabia, where is so little (or nothing) of "*Orientalism*"'.

He was constantly aware of danger on this trip, being warned not to be seen writing in his notebook and finding himself accused of being a spy but he seems not to have made any concessions to the culture of his hosts, spotting another veiled woman whose 'feminine face was blotted out by the sordid veil-clout; in our eyes, an hea-thenish Asiatic villainy! and the gentle-blooded Arabian race, in the matter of the hareem, are become churls.'

On arrival at Hâyil (modern Ha'il in Saudi Arabia) Doughty's guide feared for his reception as a foreigner and made himself scarce. Fortunately an old friend, Abd-el-Azîz, spoke to the Emir on his behalf while Doughty paced up and down outside. Eventually he was called in, given coffee, then summoned to the Emir's pres-ence. The ruler was lying on his elbow on cushions and Doughty saluted him with a *Salaam*. The 'bird-like' Emir ordered Doughty to be seated on the stranger's seat to be interrogated about his jour-ney and where he had come from and what hospitality he had received from the desert tribes. Doughty said he was a doctor and the Emir asked what medicines he had to sell but most of all he wanted to know why he was travelling. Doughty replied that it was 'the liberal sciences' that provided the spur for his journey. 'And it is for this thou art come hither!' exclaimed the Emir. 'It was difficult to show him what I intended by the sciences, for they have no experience of ways so sequestered from the common mouth-labours of mankind.' Doughty was next asked to read from an Arabic text, which impressed the Emir, who promised to give him safe conduct to Baghdad.

The following day people came to be healed by the *hakim* (doctor) but their 'long hours bibble-babbling' left him no repose and he eventually closed the door on them. That evening he was disappointed by the meagreness of the food: 'The devil is not in their dish; all the riot and wantonness of their human nature lies in the Mohammedan luxury of hareem.' The next night he was summoned again to the Emir, who was interested to hear about Western exploration and discovery but: 'He listened coldly to my tale of finding the New Land over the great seas, and enquired, "Were no people dwelling in the country when it was discovered?"'

At Doughty's third meeting with the Emir his answers had been rather too candid and, although people mobbed him out of curiosity in the streets so that he 'passed like a cuckoo with his cloud of wondering small birds', he began to sense a cooling of his welcome. Even the coffee server tried to attack him with a camel stick.

Doughty had now been in Arabia for a year and his health was not good, he was 'worn and broken in this long year of famine and fatigues' and was 'fallen in a great languor'. He therefore set out for the oasis of Khaybar, which was 'as it were an African village in the Hejâz' and where he received a very hostile reception during which his possessions were examined and his books and papers went to the Pasha, who would pass judgement on him. 'If the Pasha's word be to cut his head off, we will chop off thy head, Nasrâny,' his hosts informed him. The dubious local Turkish ruler, Abdullah, kept Doughty imprisoned in 'black captivity' for two months until finally there came back from the Pasha a letter dated 11 January 1878 saying that he was satisfied with the aims of Doughty's journey. When the latter complained that not all his possessions had been returned to him, Abdullah struck him in the face.

When Doughty got away he journeyed across the Harra in very poor health, afflicted with weariness, nosebleeds and eyesight dimmed by ophthalmia. He felt rather desperate and unsure where next to head for safety and, after hearing one evening his companions planning to disappear during the night with his camels (a plot he foiled), he felt some relief at the approach of Buraydah, 'among the greater dunes of the Neféd', which loomed ahead, a 'dream-like spectacle'. Once again he was advised by the guides to disguise his foreign provenance and accentuate his role as *hakim*. He took lodging at the Emir's hostel and then waited for an audience with him. The great Arabist, after being sorely tried by the spectacle of the veil and the burka, was now afflicted by the sound of the evening call to prayer: 'Whilst I sat upon a clay bench, in the little moonlight, I was startled from my weariness by the abhorred voice of their barbaric religion! the muéthin crying from the minaret to the latter prayer.'

Six men then arrived and took him in to the Emir, in the process trying to rob him of his aneroid barometer, thinking it was an expensive watch. Luckily for Doughty the Emir's man arrived and chastised them, forcing the return of his money and valuables. His reception by the Emir – 'a sordid fellow' – was deferred to the next day and after it he returned to his lodgings, where shortly afterwards a 'sluttish young woman' knocked on his door and demanded of Doughty in Arabic: 'Suffer me to sleep in thy bosom.' He asked himself despairingly: 'Who could have sent this lurid quean?' He sent the 'baggage' packing and reflected that 'only for the name of a Religion, (O Chimaera of human self-love, malice and fear!) I was fallen daily into such mischiefs, in Arabia'.

Outside, whether prompted by the lurid quean or not, an angry crowd gathered baying for the Nasrâny's blood, since no Christian, they maintained, had ever entered the town before. The harem of the house took up his defence with their tongues and though the Emir's office, Jeyber, managed to disperse them, the prospects were not good and he offered to allow Doughty to escape to Unayzah. After threatening the Emir with the retribution of the Sultan, whose protection he claimed to be under, Doughty defeated the inconstant officials ('all their life is passed in fraud and deceit') and managed to leave with the Emir's grudging protection.

But his troubles were not over, for a camel driver charged with accompanying him abandoned him at a wady in the middle of nowhere. 'This was the cruellest fortune which had befallen me in Arabia!' Doughty wailed. Fearful that he would be taken for a spy, he tore his map into small pieces and threw himself on the mercy of a Negro man who helped him to make the journey to Unayzah, where he met a merchant called Abdullah-el-Kenneyny, who asked him why he was so foolish as to admit to being English 'in this wild, fanatical country'.

The combination of ill-health and hostility from the people began to tell on Doughty and his narrative becomes increasingly gloomy as it moves towards its conclusion. After weeks languishing in the vicinity of Unayzah, Doughty was offered the chance to join a caravan heading for Mecca. He summed up his state:

> I had passed many days of those few years whose sum is our human life, in Arabia; and was now at the midst of the Peninsula. A month! – and I might come again to European shipping. From hence to the coast may be counted 450 desert miles, a voyage of at least twenty great marches in the uneasy camel-saddle, in the midsummer flame of the sun; which is a suffering even to the homeborn Arabs. Also, my bodily languor was such now, that I might not long sit upright; besides I foresaw a final danger, since I must needs leave the Mecca kâfily [caravan] at a last station before the (forbidden) city.

In addition, a year previously in Wady Thirba, Doughty had been bitten in the knee by a greyhound and the wound had now developed an ulcer which seemed to be spawning further ulcers across his body: 'Ah! what horror, to die like a rabid hound in a hostile land,' he lamented. He got himself painfully on to a camel at the assembly place of the Mecca pilgrimage and travelled, in pain and with little water, for seventeen days before the Christian had to be put off and redirected to Jiddah on the Red Sea. The sea was only 'thirty leagues' away but he had no food and water 'and there was no strength left in me'. The climate was increasingly hostile to the Nasrâny and, just before setting off for Jiddah, Doughty was threatened by a knife-wielding fanatic who wished to kill the infidel and who was joined by 'a throng of loitering Mecca cameleers' who had come to witness the scene: 'Those Mecca faces were black as the hues of the damned, in the day of doom: the men stood silent, and holding their swarthy hands to their weapons.' After much threatening language and gesture the man was persuaded not to kill Doughty, though he was robbed of some of his saddlebags and clothing, and he was allowed to proceed to Taif.

This new stage of the journey, however, found Doughty once again among thieving cameleers – 'the most dangerous Arabs that I have met with' – and he was forced to draw a pistol on their leader, Sâlem. In another tense stand-off he had to decide whether to fire against these men armed with knives or to conciliate. Sâlem's confederate Fheyd went for Doughty, who stood up to him: 'There was not time to shake out the shot, the pistol was yet suspended from my neck, by a strong lace: I offered the butt to his hands. – Fheyd seized the weapon! they were now in assurance of their lives and the booty: he snatched the cord and burst it.' Then they robbed him and divided the spoils between them. Doughty considered that these men were so dangerous because 'the natural humanity of the Arabians was corrupted in them by the strong contagion of the government towns'. The verdict of the camel men was: 'Thou wast safe in thine own country, thou mightest have continued there; but since thou art come into the land of the Moslemîn, God has delivered thee into our hands to die.' Doughty was taken by them to Taif, where they assumed he would face the justice of the Sherîf. He was grateful to reach the town, which, 'after nigh two years' wandering in the deserts, was a wonderful vision'. He was met by a Turkish colonel and officer of the Sherîf who lodged him, and it was immediately clear that he would receive proper hospitality: his dangers were over. In this civilized environment Doughty could for the first time examine his state:

> The tunic was rent on my back, my mantle was old and torn; the hair was grown down under my kerchief to the shoulders, and the beard fallen and unkempt; I had bloodshot eyes, half-blinded, and the scorched skin was cracked to the quick upon my face. A barber was sent for, and the bath made ready: and after a cup of tea, it cost the good colonel some pains to reduce me to the likeness of the civil multitude . . . After this he clad me, my weariness and faintness being such, like a block, in white cotton military attire; and set on my head a fez cap.

In the evening Doughty was led to the Sherîf, who received him with 'gracious gravity' and told him that his danger was over. He then dealt with Sâlem and ordered him to restore the stolen goods.

From Taif Doughty travelled with an escort to Jiddah, where his wanderings finally came to an end on the shores of the Red Sea on 2 August 1878. From Jiddah he sailed to India, where he received medical treatment. Although he delivered an interim paper to the Royal Asiatic Society while in Bombay it was 1883 before he addressed the Royal Geographical Society and published his paper (not without a battle over its prose style) in the RGS's *Proceedings*. The full account of his travels would eventually be published ten years after he left Arabia. Later scholars would pay tribute to the accuracy of Doughty's portrayal of nineteenth-century Arabian society.

In the years following his great work Doughty married and wrote poetry, including the long-cherished, thirty-thousand-line epic *The Dawn of Britain*, which remains unread, and a drama, *Adam Cast Forth*, based on an Islamic Adam and Eve legend. He also wrote some science-fiction works and *Mansoul*, a medieval dream vision. He was honoured at the end of his life with the gold medal of the RGS and various honorary degrees and was greatly admired by T. E. Lawrence, who described *Arabia Deserta* as 'a bible of its kind'. He died at Sissinghurst in Kent on 20 January 1926.

## 20

## A Digression on Geography

Joseph Conrad's powerful novella *Heart of Darkness* (1902), one of the most memorable modern European fictional texts about Africa, ends with the following words about the great River Congo: 'The offing was barred by a black bank of clouds, and the tranquil waterway leading to the uttermost ends of the earth flowed sombre under an overcast sky – seemed to lead into the heart of an immense darkness.'

For the nineteenth-century European the continent of Africa was a largely unknown and unexplored space, a darkness that scientific explorations and missionary advances aspired to fill with light, the lamp of 'civilization' dispersing the shadows of 'barbarism'. Momentary reflection, however, on just one part of that continent, the Belgian Congo, is sufficient to dispel that simplistic idea and to compel the question: who were the barbarians and who were the civilized? Much of the 'darkness' of the Dark Continent was imported. Small wonder that the great Nigerian novelist Chinua Achebe, in his famous attack on *Heart of Darkness*, should write with exasperation: 'Can nobody see the preposterous and perverse arrogance in thus reducing Africa to the role of props for the break-up of one petty European mind?'

The famous 'blank spaces on the map' were the goal of nineteenth-century explorers. The nine-year-old Joseph Conrad in 1868 put his finger on one such blank space on a map of Africa, 'then representing the unsolved mystery of that continent', and determined to go there when he grew up. The incident is reworked in

*Heart of Darkness* when Marlow confesses: 'Now when I was a little chap I had a passion for maps. I would look for hours at South America, or Africa, or Australia, and lose myself in all the glories of exploration. At that time there were many blank spaces on the earth, and when I saw one that looked particularly inviting on a map (but they all look like that) I would put my finger on it and say, When I grow up I will go there.'

When the adult Conrad finally got to the region of which he had dreamed as a child it was on a 'wretched little stern-wheel steam-boat' on the Congo and in the wake of the enormities committed in the 'scramble for Africa' which left him with 'the distasteful knowledge of the vilest scramble for loot that ever disfigured the history of human conscience and geographical exploration'.

In another essay, 'Geography and Some Explorers', published in his posthumous *Last Essays* (1926), Conrad distinguished three phases of travel. The first of these was Geography Fabulous, the picture of the world we find in the early travel narratives where exotic scenes, bizarre marvels, supernatural events, are jumbled up with authentic reports. These were followed by more serious works, such as Marco Polo's records of travel, Sir John Mandeville's *Travels* (1357) and Richard Hakluyt's *The Principal Navigations, Voyages, Traffiques and Discoveries of the English Nation* (1589), which nonetheless retained many features of the old fabulating tendency. Hakluyt especially (a work more honoured in the shelving than the perusal, though abridged versions are readily available) suggests a connection between the Elizabethan and Victorian imperial imperatives in travel. In a Preface to the second edition of 1598 Hakluyt boasted that the colonization of Virginia for the Queen will 'increase her dominions, enrich her coffers, and reduce many pagans to the faith of Christ', a fair summary of the ambition of Victorian imperial explorers. The imaginary kingdoms, spouting dragons drawn in the corner of maps, fantastically implausible (but enormously entertaining) accounts of strange humans and animals – what Conrad called 'the mediaeval mind playing in its ponderous childish way with the problems of our earth's shape, its size, its character, its products, its inhabitants' – gradually ceded to the next phase, Geography Militant.

By this Conrad meant the period after the 'discovery' of the New World by Columbus when the great explorers started to chart the world as it actually was (and to stake their claims to it). 'The voyages of the early explorers,' he wrote, 'were prompted by an acquisitive spirit, the idea of lucre in some form, the desire of trade or the desire of loot, disguised in more or less fine words.' Africa, he believed, had been cleared by these scientific geographers of 'the dull imaginary wonders of the dark ages' and been replaced with 'exciting spaces of white paper' – not this time the whiteness of civilizing light blinding Africa's awesome and savage darkness but the blank canvas on which imperial cartography could do its work. Much of the white would be filled in with red. And after the great age of modern discovery the age of Geography Triumphant would be ushered in, with the world safely mapped and ordered.

One powerful Victorian institution which pre-eminently contributed to that process of cartographical conquest was the Royal Geographical Society, described by one modern critic, Felix Driver, in his *Geography Militant* (2001), as 'part social club, part learned society, part imperial information exchange and part platform for the promotion of sensational feats of exploration'. The RGS became, through its sponsorship of expeditions, its key role in disseminating the results of expeditions and in directing, validating and specifying the very detail of what travellers were engaged in doing, the virtual control centre of Victorian travel and exploration. To appear in a boiled shirt before the gentlemen (it was not until 1892 that the first lady, the redoubtable Isabella Bird, was permitted to address the Society) of the RGS to report one's discoveries when back from the field was the final consummation of a Victorian travel adventure.

Founded on 24 May 1830 – in that pivotal decade which also saw the first guidebook, the first package tour, the first steam train service, the first cross-Channel ferry and so many other key developments in modern travel – the RGS had been preceded by organizations such as the Royal Society, the African Association and the Raleigh Travellers' Club. The last of these, a dining club of forty members whose fortnightly dinners featured dishes from whichever part of the globe the evening's host had travelled in, approved a resolution on 24 May 'that a Society is needed whose sole object shall be the promotion of that most important and entertaining branch of knowledge – geography: and that a useful Society might therefore be formed under the name of the Geographical Society of London'.

The new Society's objectives were to remain in place throughout the century and beyond. They included collecting and disseminating information, accumulating a library of 'the best books on geography, and a complete collection of maps and charts from the earlier period to the present time', preparing 'instructions' for potential travellers about what to take and what to look for and corresponding with similar societies abroad – as well as other societies with an interest in geography. It also hoped to be able to fund expeditions, which it did indeed succeed in doing. The RGS founding committee of six was chaired by Sir John Barrow, Permanent Secretary to the Admiralty, and the youngest member, at thirty-eight, was the geologist Sir Roderick Murchison, who later played a dominant role in the Society. The close connection with the Admiralty was important and gradually the RGS took over the role of supporting voyages of discovery from the Royal Navy.

Debates at the RGS were lively and often provided a theatre for famous explorers to exhibit themselves in ways that did not always please all members. Like many British cultural institutions of the present day, the RGS could sometimes lurch from an austere sense of its mission in the direction of an opportunistic populism. In 1864 it all became too much for the scientist Joseph Hooker, director of the Royal Botanic Gardens at Kew, who declared exasperatedly: 'I hate the claptrap and flattery and flummery of the Royal Geographical, with its utter want of Science and craving for popularity and excitement, and making London Lions of the season of bold Elephant hunters and Lion slayers, whilst the steady, slow and scientific surveyors and travellers have no honour at all.' Hooker perhaps had in mind the phenomenon of the 'African nights' when the explorers strutted their stuff and showed off their trophies.

But there can be little argument that the RGS played a central role in Victorian travel and in such characteristic explorations as the search for a North-West Passage, hunting the source of the Nile, crossing the Australian deserts or exploring the north and south Poles.

# PART FOUR

# CHINA AND JAPAN

A KURUMA.

## 21

### *Curious Inventions: Isabella Bird in Japan*

Travelling for the good of one's health was a very common incentive for Victorian women travellers. Whether or not there was something peculiarly stultifying about the domestic lives of nineteenth-century British middle-class women, travel seems to have been a remarkably effective tonic for many of them. Isabella Lucy Bird, who suffered from childhood with a spinal complaint, nervous headaches and insomnia, was one of those whom healthy outdoor pursuits, particularly horse-riding, restored to vigorous health.

Born in 1831 in Yorkshire to an evangelical clergyman, the Reverend Edward Bird, and his wife Dora, Isabella Bird travelled on horseback through the United States (see Chapter 43) and Canada, New Zealand, Australia and what were then called the Sandwich Islands (Hawaii). In her *A Lady's Life in the Rocky Mountains* (1879) she describes a month on horseback in the snow-covered Rockies among cowboys who judged her 'a good cattle man' and where she developed a close friendship with a grizzly bear-scarred trapper and hunter, Jim Nugent, who later died in a gunfight. A contemporary described her as 'a very solid and substantial little person, short but broad, very decided and measured in her way of speaking'.

In 1876 Bird married an Edinburgh doctor, John Bishop, who was ten years younger than her – he later described her as having the appetite of a tiger and the digestion of an ostrich – but two years later, in April 1878, she was advised to travel again and so set off for Japan 'in order to recruit my health'. At the start of the Victorian period China and Japan had still not yet emerged from a long period of isolation from the West when neither country had been open to European travellers. Foreign contacts were not unknown – Jesuit missionaries, for example, had been in China in the sixteenth century – but both countries were determined to do what they could to exclude the foreigner in general until treaties were forced upon them in the middle decades of the nineteenth century. Before this the Chinese had themselves traded with the outside world through the port of Guangzhou (Canton) and the Japanese had used Deshima island near Nagasaki, which was a Dutch trading station. Japan proved more eager, when the time came, to embrace Western influence.

The key date in China was the Treaty of Nanjing in 1842 but even after this foreigners were hemmed into a narrow strip of land along the Pearl River outside the city boundary. Women were not allowed on Chinese soil and the wives of some traders were forced to live in Macao. After 1842 the new colony of Hong Kong was established and five ports were opened up between Guangzhou and Shanghai but few risked travelling to the prohibited areas. After the Opium Wars of 1839–42 and 1856–60, however, the treaties of 1858–60 finally opened up all of China to the foreigner and the era

of Far Eastern travel had begun. In 1872 Cook's Round the World
Tour included both Shanghai and Hong Kong as stopping-off
points and accounts from traders, government officials, missionaries and those who were now termed 'globetrotters' began to roll off
the presses. By the 1890s there were fortnightly steamers from
London to China, shortening the journey from three months to
two weeks, and trips onward to Japan were arranged from there. In
China there was still bitterness over the Opium Wars and travellers' accounts are punctuated by incidents of hostility from local
people.

In Japan the isolation was ended for Britain in 1858 when Lord
Elgin arrived to sign a treaty, five years after the dramatic arrival of
the American, Commodore Perry, in Tokyo Bay in July 1853, ending
250 years of isolation. The Japanese were quick to exploit the opportunities of trade and modernization and in the 1870s and 1880s
large numbers of *yatoi*, or foreign experts, arrived to help speed the
transition. It is noticeable in travellers' accounts that Japan had by
this time become more fashionable than China, which had a reputation for being less clean and less well ordered. The earlier fashion
for *chinoiserie* yielded to *japonaiserie*, symbolized by the performance of the opera *The Mikado* in London in 1885. Up-to-date
accounts of China and Japan therefore attracted a lively interest.

Bird was very precise about what kind of traveller she was and
took care to distinguish herself always from the common herd of
tourists (see Chapter 8). The title of her book *Unbeaten Tracks in
Japan* (1880) announces her approach. In her Preface she sets out her
manifesto:

> This is not a 'Book on Japan', but a narrative of travels in Japan,
> and an attempt to contribute something to the sum of knowledge
> of the present condition of the country, and it was not till I had
> travelled for some months in the interior of the main island and
> in Yezo, that I decided that my materials were novel enough to
> render the contribution worth making. From Nikkō northwards
> my route was altogether off the beaten track, and had never been

traversed in its entirety by any European. I lived among the Japanese, and saw their mode of living, in regions unaffected by European contact. As a lady travelling alone, and the first European lady who had been seen in several routes through which my route lay, my experiences differed more or less widely from those of preceding travellers . . . It was with some reluctance that I decided that they should consist mainly of letters written on the spot for my sister and a circle of personal friends; for this form of publication involves the sacrifice of artistic arrangement and literary treatment, and necessitates a certain amount of egotism; but on the other hand, it places the reader in the position of the traveller, and makes him share the vicissitudes of travel, discomfort, difficulty, and tedium, as well as novelty and enjoyment. The 'beaten tracks' . . . have been dismissed in a few sentences.

As well as indicating her method and recording her dismissal of the conventional travellers' itineraries, Bird made much of her concern with 'truth' and 'accuracy' even if the results were controversial: 'Some of the Letters give a less pleasing picture of the condition of the peasantry than the one popularly presented, and it is possible that some readers may wish that it had been less realistically painted; but as the scenes are strictly representative, and I neither made them nor went in search of them, I offer them in the interests of truth.'

In her opening chapter Bird returned to the fray, determined to scotch 'the curious inventions of some early voyagers', by which she meant such colourful stage properties of the Victorian imagination as hara-kiri, mikados and shoguns. In particular she rebuked the errors of senior politicians and civil servants who, she believed, had created a false picture of Japan since its relatively recent opening up to the West: 'So true is it that, unless we are going to travel in a country, to fight it, or to colonise it, our information is seldom either abundant or accurate, and highly imaginative accounts by early travellers, the long period of mysterious seclusion, and the changes which have succeeded each other with breathless rapidity during the last eleven years, create a special confusion in our ideas of Japan.'

Bird pointed out that Japan was only forty-two days by sea from England and that the process of modernization, now launched, would not be turned back. Although she believed that the Japanese of the treaty ports had been 'contaminated and vulgarised by intercourse with foreigners' she felt that those of the interior, far from being 'savages', were 'kindly, gentle, and courteous, so much so that a lady with no other attendant than a native servant can travel, as I have done, for 1200 miles through little-visited regions, and not meet with a single instance of incivility or extortion'. Finally, she was keen to emphasize that her Japan was the modern country not the ancient stereotype: 'Politically, Old Japan is no more. The grandeur of its rulers, its antique chivalry, its stately etiquette, its ceremonial costume, its punctilious suicides, and its codes of honour, only exist on the stage.'

Bird's first 'Letter' was written from the Oriental Hotel at Yokohama on 21 May 1878. Her first view of the coast of Japan, she admitted, offered 'no startling surprises either of colour or form' but it was nonetheless beautiful: 'Broken wooded ridges, deeply cleft, rise from the water's edge, grey, deep-roofed villages cluster about the mouths of the ravines, and terraces of rice cultivation, bright with the greenness of English lawns, run up to a great height among dark masses of upland forest.' And there was the 'wonderful vision' of Mount Fuji. Otherwise Yokohama did not impress her with its 'dead-alive look' and she couldn't wait to get away into 'real Japan'.

That utopian goal of all serious travellers, discovery of the 'real' country, lay before her but she was very nearly overwhelmed by this strange country and suffered from 'complete mental confusion, owing to the rapidity with which new sights and ideas are crowding upon me . . . the country presents itself to me as a complete blur, or a page covered with hieroglyphs to which I have no key. Well, I have months to spend here, and I must begin at the alphabet, see everything, hear everything, read everything, and delay forming opinions as long as possible'. This open mind, a spontaneous feeling of the way, contrasts sharply with the sometimes aggressive prejudice and peremptory judgement of so many Victorian travellers, including many eminent names.

Bird travelled by rail the eighteen miles from Yokohama to Tokyo. The line was built by British engineers, opened only in 1872 and followed closely the British model, the railway staff being 'Japanese in European dress'. She was met by an orderly from the British Legation with a brougham rather than one of the mass of *kurumas*, the term she preferred to 'the Chinese jin-ri-ki-sha' or rickshaw. Expatriate life did not excite her approval. She disliked the 'aggressions made here [in the Foreign Concession] by Western architectural ideas' and concluded that the social life of foreigners in Tokyo 'is much like life at home, except that it has fewer objects and less variety, and . . . talk runs in somewhat narrower grooves'. Nevertheless: 'As no English lady has yet travelled alone through the interior, my project excites a very friendly interest among my friends, and I receive much warning and dissuasion, and a little encouragement.'

Bird hired an eighteen-year-old youth called Ito as servant and, not being keen on 'the fishy and vegetable abominations known as "Japanese food"', she packed her own supplies, though: 'After several months of travelling in some of the roughest parts of the interior, I should advise a person in average health – and none other should travel in Japan – not to encumber himself with tinned meats, soups, claret, or any eatables or drinkables except Liebig's extract of meat.' The ambassador's wife, Lady Parkes, added to her supplies 'two light baskets with covers of oiled paper, a travelling bed or stretcher, a folding chair, and an india-rubber bath' and she was ready to go.

On 10 June 1878 Bird finally set off on her journey into the interior. Her luggage weighed 110 pounds and Ito's ninety. It is always fascinating to learn what people carry with them on their travels and fortunately Bird gave a very full description of the contents of the painted wicker boxes suspended on either side of the packhorse:

I have a folding chair – for in a Japanese house there is nothing but the floor to sit upon, and not even a solid wall to lean against – an air-pillow for *kuruma* travelling, an indiarubber bath, sheets, a blanket, and last, and more important than all else, a canvas stretcher on light poles, which can be put together in two minutes; and being 2½ feet high is supposed to be secure from fleas. The 'Food Question' has been solved by a modified rejection of all advice! I have only brought a small supply of Liebig's extract of meat, 4lbs of raisins, some chocolate, both for eating and drinking, and some brandy in case of need. I have my own Mexican saddle and bridle, a reasonable quantity of clothes, including a loose wrapper for wearing in the evening, some candles, Mr Brunton's large map of Japan, volumes of the Transactions of the English Asiatic Society, and Mr Satow's Anglo-Japanese Dictionary. My travelling dress is a short costume of dust-coloured striped tweed, with strong laced boots of unblacked leather, and a Japanese hat, shaped like a large inverted bowl, of light bamboo plait, with a white cotton cover, and a very light frame inside, which fits round the brow and leaves a space of 1½ inch between the hat and the head for the free circulation of air . . . infinitely to be preferred to a heavy pith helmet . . . My money is in bundles of 50 *yen* . . . I have a bag for my passport, which hangs to my waist. All my luggage, with the exception of my saddle, which I use for a footstool, goes into one *kuruma*.

Thus equipped, Bird set forth with a special passport giving her permission to travel through all of Japan north of Tokyo and virtually anywhere in Hokkaido without having to specify a route to the authorities. The first ninety miles were covered in three days by *kuruma* runners through rice fields and past wayside tea-houses. In the first night's lodging she was prevented from writing her journal because of the attentions of fleas and mosquitoes and the bed, a piece of canvas nailed to two wooden bars, collapsed in the night. The next night, at Tochigi, she stayed in another *yadoya*, or lodging house, where the room was enclosed by screens which were full of holes 'and often at each hole I saw a human eye'. She became such an object of attention that Ito, fearing the press of so many curious people at the screens, offered to take care of her money in case she was robbed.

The compensation the next day was the 'snow-slashed' Nantaizan mountains and arrival at Nikkō, where, after the night-long racket of the *yadoya*, she stayed at a pavilion owned by the chief man in the village with a garden and the mountain rising behind. She spent nine days at this spot, admiring its 'solemn grandeur, its profound melancholy, its slow and sure decay and the historical and religious atmosphere from which one can never alto-gether escape'. She then went to a village she called Irimchi, where she made close observations of the village customs and complained of the dampness of the climate: 'I don't wonder that the Japanese rise early, for their evenings are cheerless, owing to the dismal illumination.'

It was time to move on again and she decided that: 'My journey will now be entirely over "unbeaten tracks" and will lead through what may be called "Old Japan" . . . Comfort was left behind at Nikkō!' Saddled on two 'depressed-looking mares', she and Ito wound among ravines 'whose steep sides are clothed with maple, oak, magnolia, elm, pine and cryptomeria, linked together by fes-toons of the redundant *Wistaria chinensis*, and brightened by azalea and syringa clusters. Every vista was blocked by some grand moun-tain, waterfalls thundered, bright streams glanced through the trees, and in the glorious sunshine of June the country looked most beau-tiful.' But soon she began to notice the squalor of the people in the country areas, making no apology for referring to it ('I write the truth as I see it') even if her perception differed from that of the 'tourists'. She wanted to tell things as they were: 'But truly this is a new Japan to me, of which no books have given me any idea, and it is not fairyland.'

As Bird continued her journey northwards the kaleidoscope of images spun around her: 'Mountains and passes, valleys and rice swamps; poverty, industry, dirt, ruinous temples, prostrate Buddhas, strings of straw-shod pack-horses; long, grey, featureless streets, and quiet, staring crowds, are all jumbled up fantastically in my memory.' And although she continued to be preoccupied with the dirt and squalor for which she had been unprepared but which she felt a duty to record 'as a contribution to the general sum of knowledge of the country', she tried to balance the picture: 'In many European countries, and certainly in some parts of our own, a solitary lady-traveller in a foreign dress would be exposed to rudeness, insult, and extortion, if not to actual danger; but I have not met with a single instance of incivility or real overcharge, and there is no rudeness even about the crowding.' This last remark was elicited after a crowd of two thousand people milled around her at a place she called Bangé.

This abundant curiosity followed Bird as she moved northwards through Japan, recording details of the daily life of the people, revelling in the mountain scenery and the natural beauty. At Yusawa in the Yamagata region the combination of poor food and importunate gazing of the locals nearly proved too much for her:

> Yusowa is a specially objectionable-looking place. I took my lunch, a wretched meal of a tasteless white curd made from beans, with some condensed milk added to it, in a yard, and the people crowded in hundreds to the gate, and those behind being unable to see me, got ladders and climbed on the adjacent roofs, where they remained till one of the roofs gave way with a loud crash, and precipitated about fifty men, women and children into the room below, which fortunately was vacant.

A policemen soon arrived and demanded to see her passport and to know why she was travelling. Bird's reply was terse and to the point: 'To learn about the country.' The policeman demanded to know if she was making a map. It was partly the lack of laughter in these intent gazes that she found irksome: 'The great melancholy stare is depressing.' And so she pressed on, increasingly troubled by her spinal problem, which slowed her progress, and by the universal damp: 'I have lived in soaked clothes, in spite of my rain-cloak, and have slept on a soaked stretcher in spite of all waterproof wrappings for several days, and still the weather shows no signs of improvement, and the rivers are so high on the northern road, that I am storm bound as well as pain bound here [at Odaté].'

Eventually the sodden traveller reached Aomori Bay, where a steamer was waiting to take her to Hokkaido, reachable by a small paddle-boat in which she was buffeted all night by gales. Arriving at Hakodate harbour on 13 August 1878, she went straight to the Church Mission House in spite of considering herself, soaked and muddy, 'unfit to enter a civilised dwelling'. She relished a good bed, a door that locked and twenty-three letters from home to read. In addition: 'I felt a somewhat legitimate triumph at having conquered all obstacles, and having accomplished more than I intended to accomplish when I left Yedo.'

After the main island of Japan, Bird felt happier with the 'breeziness and freedom' of Hokkaido and spent longer at Hakodate than she had intended. She visited the local missionaries and judged their task 'very uphill' with only the medical missionaries getting anywhere, but her plans were now for another long expedition away from the beaten track. Armed with a *shomon*, or special letter, from the British consul, which ensured help from officials along the way, she set off on 'the first foray made by a lady into the country of the aborigines'.

Taking a steamer across Volcano Bay to Noboribetsu in which once again she became an object of attention, stowed in a cabin in the bows 'full of coils of rope, shut in, and left to solitude and dignity, and the stare of eight eyes, which perseveringly glowered through the windows', she arrived to see her first member of the 'aboriginal' race, the Aino. 'I think I never saw a face more completely beautiful in features and expression, with a lofty, sad, far-off, gentle, intellectual look, rather that of Sir Noel Paton's "Christ" than of a savage.' As she penetrated more deeply into the Aino country, she was fascinated: 'I am in the lonely Aino land, and I think that the most interesting of my travelling experiences has been the living for three days and two nights in an Aino hut, and seeing and sharing the daily life of complete savages, who go on with their ordinary occupations just as if I were not among them.' Her curiosity was eager and open, and she was able to question the people through an interpreter, but their 'savagery' (the word was repeated almost obsessively in these passages) troubled her. One night in the hut:

I never saw such a strangely picturesque sight as that group of magnificent savages with the fitful forelight on their faces, and for adjuncts the flare of the torch, the strong lights, the blackness of the recesses of the room and of the roof, at one end of which the stars looked in, and the row of savage women in the background – eastern savagery and western civilisation met in this hut, savagery giving and civilisation receiving, the yellow-skinnned Ito the connecting-link between the two, and the representative of a civilisation to which our own is but an 'infant of days'.

Bird was growing tired from her demanding travels – she reckoned she had crossed a hundred rivers and streams – 'yet I felt an intuitive perception of the passion and fascination of exploring, and understood how people could give up their lives to it'. She pressed on to Lebungé ('a most fascinating place in its awful isolation') through difficult mountainous terrain to reach the sea again at Oshamambe, where at night: 'My room was only enclosed by *shōji*, and there were scarcely five minutes of the day in which eyes were not applied to the finger-holes with which they were liberally riddled; and during the night one of them fell down, revealing six Japanese sleeping in a row, each head on a wooden pillow.' When she eventually arrived back at Hakodate she tried, unsuccessfully, to avoid the Consul because: 'I had the general look of a person "fresh from the wilds".'

In spite of her preoccupation with the clash of 'civilisation' and 'savagery', wholly characteristic of her time, Bird did make genuine efforts to reach out to the Japanese people. She defended their attempts to democratize and modernize, attacking the Western 'carping and sneering with which every fresh Japanese movement is received' as 'unbecoming, and very lacerating to the feelings of a people unduly sensitive to foreign criticism'.

Leaving Hokkaido and the faithful Ito, who had been such a solid source of information, she sailed to Yokohama, then Tokyo and Kobé, where she took a train to Osaka, deliberately choosing to travel third class 'as I was most anxious to see how the "common people" behaved . . . It is quite a mistake always to travel first class, for then one only hears the talk of foreigners, which is apt to be vapid and stale.'

After a stay at Miss Starkwether's American Mission School for Girls at Kyoto at the start of November, Bird made a few more excursions, then returned the following month to the British Legation in Tokyo. Just before Christmas 1878 she finally left Japan on the SS *Volga*: 'The snowy dome of Fujisan reddening in the sunrise rose above the violet woodlands of Mississippi Bay as we steamed out of Yokohama Harbour on the 19th, and three days later I saw the last of Japan – a rugged coast, lashed by a wintry sea.'

Bird then sailed to Hong Kong and Guangzhou and on to Saigon and Singapore, from where her letters to her sister Henrietta formed another book, *The Golden Chersonese* (1883). After the death of Henrietta in 1880, she married John Bishop and, after his death in 1886, she resumed her travels as a medical missionary, having studied at St Mary's Hospital in London. She visited medical missions in India and travelled in Tibet, Turkey, Persia and Kurdistan. In 1891 she became the first woman to address the Royal Geographical Society, having refused a previous offer to do so because 'it seems scarcely consistent in a society which does not recognise the work of women to ask women to read a paper'. Three years later she travelled in Korea and China and was planning a further Chinese trip when she fell ill and died at her Edinburgh home on 7 October 1904.

Isabella Bird remains one of the most vigorous and enterprising of the Victorian women travellers. She relished the freedom that travel gave her, once remarking that 'travellers are privileged to do the most improper things'.

## 22

### *Very Odd People: Constance Gordon-Cumming in China*

O n Christmas Eve 1878, while Isabella Bird was writing up her last Japan journal on board the SS *Volga* from Yokohama, another Far Eastern traveller, Constance Fredereka ('Eka') Gordon-Cumming, was at her writing desk on board the *Pei-Ho*, a steamer of the Messageries Maritimes line, approaching the harbour of Hong Kong. She too had just come from Japan, where she had spent four months 'nearly frozen, living in paper houses, without fires' and had 'fled southward with the swallows, and sailed from Nagasaki, intending to spend Christmas at Shanghai'.

However, Shanghai turned out to be a disappointment with its 'horrid river of yellow mud and the hideousness of the flat country round', not to mention the 'great dull hotel, where there was not a creature to be seen except Chinese servants, [which] depressed me to such a pitch, that I resolved to risk spending Christmas-Day at sea rather than remain there'. Not even Giles Gilbert Scott's Anglican Cathedral at Shanghai, with its ladies of the congregation decorating the church with imported real holly and moss, could detain her. She was happy to swap the city for her 'dreary ship' huddled around 'two wretched stoves in the large, dark uncomfortable cabin'. The problem with Shanghai was olfactory:

Never could I have conceived the possibility of such varied combinations of bad smells! and even the eye remains unsatisfied, for the streets are all narrow and crowded; and though the multitude of quaint figures, open shops, strange sign-boards, and occasional curly roofs cannot but be somewhat picturesque, the marvel is that they produce so little effect. Even the temples are mean and disgusting – a marvellous contrast to those of clean, delightful Japan . . . Much as I generally delight in Oriental cities, I felt it a relief to pass from this one, back to the handsome European settlement of large clean houses, of which a most imposing row stretch along the embankment of the fine crescent-shaped harbour.

Arriving by sea at Hong Kong, by contrast, she found a 'lovely city . . . its beauty, so suddenly revealed, left me mute with delight . . . this Rocky Isle, whose great city bears the name of England's Queen, and from whose crowning peak floats the Union Jack'. With her travelling companion, Miss Shervington, Gordon-Cumming disembarked from their sampan and went straight for breakfast at the principal hotel with Colonel Shervington, Miss S's father, and then straight to the cathedral for 'a nice hearty service'. Gordon-Cumming was delighted with the perfect winter climate and the prospect of some agreeable hobnobbing with the colonial elite: 'I have begun to feel myself quite at home in this British isle of Hong Kong.'

Constance Gordon-Cumming was born in 1837 at Altyre, Morayshire, daughter of the second baronet Sir William Gordon-Cumming. She was educated privately and it was after spending a year with her married sister in India in 1867 that her interest in travel was awakened. As she lacked neither funds nor social connections, her travels were always characterized by visits to, or stays with, the right people. She visited Ceylon, Fiji and the South Seas, which produced *A Lady's Cruise in a French Man-of-War in the South Seas* (1882), and later went to California and China, described in *Wanderings in China* (1886).

Christmas Day 1878 was rather more colourful than usual in Hong Kong for, in the middle of the night, a huge fire started (a small English general dealer's shop was later found saturated in kerosene) and, with firefighters on leave and Chinese New Year firecrackers exploding, the scene was both dangerous as the fire spread, and very striking: 'I never could have conceived a scene so awful and yet so wonderfully beautiful . . . I positively again and again found myself forgetting its horror in the ecstasy of its beauty! It really felt as if we were sitting luxuriously in the dress circle watching some wondrous panoramic play, with amazingly realistic scenic effects!' The next day, after the fire had raged for seventeen hours and destroyed four hundred houses over ten acres, thousands were left homeless though without abandoning 'a curiously suspicious and by no means flattering feeling towards such kindly Britons as wish to help them'.

Gordon-Cumming moved on from Hong Kong to catch the New Year's Ball at Government House in Guangzhou (Canton), arriving in a steamer heavily armed against pirates. After being borne in a chair by coolies from the dock to the foreign settlement, she immediately connected with the inhabitants of its 'palatial houses' and praised this expat heaven: 'Here is transplanted an English social life so completely fulfilling all English requirements, that the majority of the inhabitants rarely enter the city!' But although she frequented the races, sketched and mingled with the best society, Gordon-Cumming also opened her eyes to something that was for her 'a totally new experience in the annals of travel', the daily life of the city: 'What really fascinates the eye and bewilders the mind is simply the common street-life, which, from morning till night, as you move slowly through the streets, presents a succession of pictures, each of intense interest and novelty.' This 'life' made it 'an effort to turn aside from these to see any recognised "sight"'. Such sights included temples and shops with their striking signs: 'a satin skull-cap or a conical straw hat denote a hatter, a shoe for a shoemaker'. She went walking with Dr Chalmers of the London Mission: 'really to enjoy such an expedition, one must go quietly on foot, with all powers of observation on the alert, never knowing what strange novelty will entail'.

After staying in Guangzhou until the middle of February, Gordon-Cumming took the *Namoa* to Fuzhou (Foo-Chow) and other places along the South China coast, including Pagoda Island, where the foreigners lived because it was a treaty port and where the right sort of people could be mixed with: 'Nowhere in all the East have I found a pleasanter and more genial community than on this green isle, where English and Scotch, German and American residents combine to form such a kindly cheery society. What with pleasant visits by day, and dinner-parties and private theatricals in the evenings, I think I must already have made acquaintance with a very large portion of the community, mercantile, diplomatic, and missionary.' But again she found time to observe the other side of life, including a report of a horrible sight (which she did not herself witness) on the bridge from the island to Foo-Chow:

Not long ago a wretched thief, having been condemned to die of starvation as a mild sort of punishment for stealing part of a head-dress belonging to the wife of a wealthy mandarin, was here exposed in an upright cage with only his head protruding, and so nicely calculated as to height that he literally hung by his head, only his toes touching the ground. On his cage was fastened a paper recounting his crime and sentence; and idle crowds gathered round to read it, and to watch his lingering hours of torture, slowly dying beneath the fierce blazing sun which beat so pitilessly on his shaven head. Women and children, to whom pity or horror were apparently alike unknown, stood staring curiously at the poor wretch, till merciful death came to his relief.

In the company of Mrs Delano, the wife of the American consul, Gordon-Cumming went in a houseboat on the River Min – 'sight-seeing and sketching being our sole objects' – visiting a Buddhist monastery where her opera glasses performed their usual magic of charming the unsophisticated monks with their novelty. Fascinated though she was by everything she saw, there was plenty to criticize, such as 'the frightfully discordant sounds of Chinese music', the 'queer lodgings' and dubious food. She heard of a traveller who had allegedly been served up cold rice fried in lamp oil. Back in Foo-Chow American missionaries introduced her to foot-binding and traditional medicine ('quackery'), all of which excited her scorn: 'Truly it must be conceded that these are very odd people!' She was borne around the city on a chair with two American Presbyterian missionaries, Mr and Mrs C. C. Baldwin, who told her that the American Methodist Episcopal Church had made three thousand converts. One of these was a rich philan-thropist, Mr Ahok, who gave a dinner party at his home on the island of Nantai to introduce her to every kind of Chinese dish, including bird's nest soup. Many Victorian travellers seem to have taken against missionaries but Gordon-Cumming showered them with praise.

At Foo-Chow she was invited to the home of another very wealthy mandarin and borne there on wicker chairs: 'Our host, robed in rich dark-blue satin, came to receive us in the outer court, where, after many bows and much shaking of our own hands, pressing together our clenched fists, we left our chairs and our coolies, and then passed the kitchen, and crossed another court when we reached the great reception-hall.' Here everyone was nibbling melon seeds. 'In this respect the whole race are like squirrels.' Rather than a meal they were offered 'sweetmeats and small cakes', then, after the mandarin had shown them his expensive piles of ladies' dresses and recounted how much he paid for them, they bade farewell and were out once more into the 'filthy streets'.

At the end of April 1879 Gordon-Cumming set off by steamer to see Shanghai once more, contrasting it unfavourably with the beauty of Foo-Chow. Once again she headed for the Foreign Settlement, which was divided into three districts, English, French and American: 'There is a solid, business-like look of wealth about this great gas-lighted river-frontage of palaces which makes it a genuine relief to the artistic eye to find that it may look down, even from these luxurious verandahs, on some items of purely native interest.' She took a rickshaw around the regulation sights but found that 'the native city of Shanghai may claim the palm for dirt and bad smells in excess of those of any other city I have yet explored'. She looked into some temples, 'but I confess that I here find heathenism shorn of all its usual interests. The picturesque elements are utterly wanting, and filth is rampant'.

More striking was the consecration of the new Roman Catholic Bishop of Hong Kong in the Cathedral in the suburb of Tongkadoo. Allegedly eighty thousand of the city's 310,000 inhabitants were Catholic and the Cathedral was packed with two thousand people. After witnessing its ceremonial Gordon-Cumming was 'inclined to wish that the poverty of our own Missions did not necessitate such exceedingly ugly simplicity as that of the very bare chapels which are the best that can be provided by the majority of the native converts'. She seems to have spent some time visiting religious orphanages and native monasteries but her sympathies with Chinese culture do not seem to have been engaged. At a church service at the city of Ningpo she reflected: 'In the course of long wanderings, I have heard our beautiful liturgy recited in many strange tongues, to me unknown, but this was my first experience of it in Chinese – to my ear the most uncouth of all.' On a subsequent visit to some temples her patience wore thinner: 'Truly wearisome to the blunt Anglo-Saxon is the necessity for conforming with the elaborate civility enjoined by Chinese etiquette.'

'Satiated' with temple visiting, Gordon-Cumming embarked on the *Shun-Lee* for Beijing in the company of Mr and Mrs Pirkis of the British Legation there. Alas, at Beijing: 'Everything seemed alike hideous, and I have as yet seen no town to compare with this for dirt, dust, heat, and bad smells.' On the rough journey by cart from the port of Beijing to the city an even more horrifying assault on her senses took place. The party found itself stuck behind the funeral of a man dead for two months in an ill-sealed coffin which gave off an awful stench: 'These people certainly can have no sense of smell; that is proved at every turn.' On entering the city gate she looked on 'the dreariest wilderness of dirt and dust that you can possibly conceive' and quickly took refuge behind the three-acre site of the British Legation enclosed by high walls.

The next day the mandatory sightseeing began. She visited a 'dismally dreary' examination hall in the University and a blind school run by a one-armed Scot called Murray, who offered to be her guide to the outside of the Forbidden City. She set up her sketching materials at dawn, which resulted in crowds of curious passers-by gathering to see the weird stranger: 'This foreign peculiarity, of possessing hair which is not black, adds immensely to the interest of inspecting foreigners.' Although she achieved mastery in the use of chopsticks, her antipathy towards the Chinese and their culture remained intact.

And so, on 20 June, she embarked on a steamer to Che-Foo – 'by no means sorry to have seen the last of Peking', though she did concede that she would 'not on any account have missed seeing it' – then took another boat for Nagasaki, destined to rejoin her accumulated letters from home and her 'green paradise'.

After returning to Britain Gordon-Cumming made plans for a

new trip to California, invited by the famed Civil War commander General Ulysses S. Grant and his wife, and visited Hawaii, the subject of her last book. In retirement she passed her time exhibiting sketches and watercolours of her travels and performing good works (including supporting the worthy William Hill Murray in his efforts with the blind in China). She died in Perthshire on 4 September 1924.

## 23

## *A Land of Topsy-Turvydom: Lewis Wingfield*

Afar more enchanted Chinese traveller than Constance Gordon-Cumming – and one who went on to explore Japan also – was the Honourable Lewis Strange Wingfield. Born into the Irish aristocracy at Powerscourt Castle in County Wicklow in 1842 and educated at Eton and Bonn University, Wingfield was a dilettantish actor, writer and artist famous for his eccentricities such as attending the Derby dressed as a 'nigger minstrel', lodging in workhouses and spending time as an attendant at a lunatic asylum. His first book, *Under the Palms of Algeria and Tunis*, appeared in 1868, the year of his marriage, and he later fought on the German side in the Franco-Prussian War and was in Paris during the 1870 siege, writing articles on these events for the *Daily Telegraph*. Having studied art in Paris, he turned his hand to painting and exhibited at the Royal Academy. He decorated the family seat at Powerscourt with his series of paintings on the poems of Tom Moore. He returned to the theatre in the 1880s and was a costume and stage designer involved in several Shakespearean revivals. In 1887 he settled in 14 Montague Place, Bloomsbury, where his house was stocked with trophies from his travels.

Wingfield's *Wanderings of a Globe-Trotter in the Far East* (1889) begins in pleasant indolence on board a boat in the Malacca Strait where all that can be heard is the creaking of the *punkah* ropes in the saloon and the listless motions of a group of European whist players. Only two daily inconveniences mar his pleasure: the swabbing of decks and the thin coating of coal dust on all parts of the ship from the furnace:

And yet, in spite of annoying petty drawbacks, which when out of sight are soon out of mind, what is there more entrancing than landing for the first time on a new shore? It is the nearest thing to the wildly unorthodox proceedings of Fairyland, which are incompatible with our absurdly undeveloped and chrysalis existence. You have long had a sketch pictured on your mental retina of India, China, what not – the which sketch has been made a more or less accurate one by the conning of 'travellers' tales' and the examining of photographs. But what a delightful and bewildering series of new visions it is that assails your eye on setting foot ashore; one for which no photograph and no description can have prepared you . . . As we grow old we become *blasé* – it is an inevitable condition of incomplete mortality – but the first landing in a new country produces sensations which must stir the languid blood of the most world-worn.

Having sailed through Ceylon, Penang and Singapore (where 'the pallid, weary Briton in white line and pith helmet' puts in an appearance), Wingfield eventually steamed into Hong Kong: 'The first impression of China is that it is even more surprising than one expected, for it is a land of topsy-turvydom. Everything is done from an opposite standpoint to that which obtains with us.' Greeted by a gaggle of rickshaw drivers and sampan rowers, he came ashore, where a P&O agent warned him not to attempt this at night for 'on more than one occasion he had heard screams at night wafted across the water'. Shrewdly perceiving the mutual distrust which governed relations between Chinese and European in the 1880s, he observed of the first Chinese he met: 'Their manners are suave and ceremonious, covered with a veneer of extreme politeness, under which is but ill-concealed a contempt for the white barbarian.' Although, like Gordon-Cumming, he was mobbed wherever he went, he could see beneath the veneer: 'They are perforce civil, but they dislike you, and take no pains to conceal their antipathy. They are benignantly tolerant of a lower order of animal whose comic ways, like those of chimpanzees are worthy of casual study . . . you are followed by an obbligato of hoots and grimaces from a derisive posse of ragamuffins.'

Wingfield was in search of more hedonistic 'sights' than the interior of mission stations and, after a visit to an opium den with a guide called Ah-Cum, he set off with two 'sampan girls' called Sue and Bet, who, 'displaying a good deal of shapely limb', took him to a place of entertainment in the harbour called the Flowery Boats – a dozen barges moored together on which boards were erected. He was not immediately impressed: 'How strange a gathering! What a dull and solemn way of seeking amusement!' What he saw was 'a *posse* of fat and stolid Chinamen, with round spectacles like owls and gorgeously broidered robes, lying or sitting on divans, dining or taking tea in company of splendid houris, who rose and fled into adjacent ambush at sight of a barbarian, to the evident chagrin of their entertainers.' This entertainment was very far from *louche*.

> In some of the little rooms a strangely painted female, muffled in heavy robes, with face raddled red and white, and towers of gewgaws in her stiffly pomaded hair, was gyrating slowly; in others instrumental music and singing – such singing! took the place of dancing. There was no horseplay or undue familiarity. Nothing could have been more grimly proper, for Golden Youth was phlegmatic, sleepy from opium-smoking; sad and supremely bored.

An 'elderly Lothario' made a half-hearted attempt to heighten the atmosphere by serving tea and summoning from behind a curtain a dancer: 'The performer whirls slowly round like a somnolent teetotum, waving wide-spread arms, and chanting nasally in melancholic cadence.' Wingfield made his excuses and left.

The next day Ah-Cum started to guide him around Hong Kong and show him the exotic marvels, the highlight of which was the trial and execution of some pirates. Wingfield was shown the horrifying prison full of starving, tortured prisoners and the courtroom where each prisoner, under torture, was required to confess guilt.

Later he witnessed their execution in a little lane where the seven guilty pirates were lined up: 'A flash of a short two-handed sword. The head, swung by the pigtail, was dropped into a basket, and so on until all were headless; and then the baskets were laid at the feet of the officials . . . The rapidity of the transaction took one's breath away.'

From Hong Kong, Wingfield coasted northwards, stopping at the small ports open to foreign trade and commiserating with 'such of our unlucky countrymen as are compelled to vegetate in the far East'. These expatriate British were described as 'a small knot of Europeans clustering together for mutual protection against a vast population that loathes them'. They had 'no means of amusement, and no female society to cheer them'. At Foo-Chow he felt the local people were hostile but he also noted how the Europeans chose to dwell apart in shady bungalows on a little island overlooking 'the vast Chinese city'. In their enclave these were 'a cheery and hospitable set, but are fain to admit that in matters of amusement and relaxation there is much to be desired . . . Isolated on their island, they do not mix with the Chinese at all, except in matters of business.' In the evening they 'congregate at a cosy clubhouse for exchange of small gossip before dinner. Billiards, whisky pegs well iced and an undercurrent of light raillery. One marvels as one listens at the barren narrowness of such a life. The veriest trivialities grow into importance, like the spider in the prisoner's cell.' When each went home afterwards in his chair the bearers' paper lanterns lit up the night: 'Twinkling glowworm lights of all colours bob rapidly hither and thither, and vanish one by one. It is like a bit of fairyland. Then comes dinner and whist, and much yawning, and an early bed.'

Readily perceiving the shortcomings of the expatriate existence, Wingfield had nonetheless equal reservations about the attitudes of the Chinese. Like Gordon-Cumming, he noticed the bad smells, but it was the Chinese contempt for the foreigner that struck him most forcibly. On a visit to the Yuen-Foo Monastery he was sketching a temple on the river bank when some coolies came past and immediately thrust their hands out: 'The Chinee is always wanting money, and looks on the wandering globe-trotter as a well-filled money-bag sent by a beneficent deity for his especial benefit.' When he declined in this instance the men gave chase, so he was forced to run to the boat, where he was hauled back in for safety. 'No likee Inglees gentleman,' a crewman laconically informed him.

A brief respite in the monastery ('the usual altars and sleeping Buddhas, drums and bells, and pots with smouldering joss-sticks') was followed by more hostile pursuit by local villagers: 'What a lovely land, inhabited by how objectionable a people! Squalid, foully dirty, fierce and brutal, eaten up with overweening conceit. They are the only nation in the world; all other races are too mean for their serious consideration.' The only positive sign was the hospital set up by Murray and backed by local progressive merchants as an alternative to the 'farce' of indigenous medicine, in which 'superstition and incantation rub shoulders with outlandish nostrums'. This was undoubtedly 'the most promising sign for the future which I had yet seen in the Middle Kingdom' but he later discovered it had been destroyed by an arsonist.

On arrival at Shanghai Wingfield was unimpressed by its adulterated character: 'It is sham European, made up of shreds and patches stolen from other towns – possesses no individuality of its own.' It may have had a 'fine wide river frontage – a Bund or quay' but 'you did not undertake a pilgrimage of so many thousand miles for so feeble an imitation of Europe'. He looked with disbelief at broughams with servants in livery and 'British "bobbies" in cloth tunics and helmets' and noted: 'The fashionable drive is along the Bubbling Well Road, a suburb with trim gardens on each side, which instantly suggests the Edgbaston of Birmingham.' In short this 'prim and ostentatious Christian settlement' stood in sharp contrast with the 'venerable Chinese city which lies behind' – in spite of its stinking sewers and the condemned man left to starve to death in a cage.

Wingfield sailed on to Soo-Chow – 'the Paris of China' – and thence by a China Merchants' Company steamer north across the

Yellow Sea, up the Pei-Ho River to Tientsin. As usual he was the only passenger and was able to reflect – perhaps without the comforting expat voice at his elbow – on the difference in tempo and philosophy of the European and the Chinese: 'We of the West fume and fret and strain, to die early in the throes of abortive effort or to join the crowds that fill the lunatic asylums. The Chinese plod quietly on in the grooves which their ancestors found good.' From Tientsin, after a long and gruelling ride, he arrived at Beijing and the hospitality of the British Legation. Perhaps because so much of the celestial capital was closed to the foreigner, he was not enthusiastic about the city but he was required to 'do' it: 'If it were not for duties, the world would be bearable enough; but what one "ought to do" is always cropping up, and even in travel it is invariably disagreeable. I had barely recovered from the effects of that awful ride, and was revelling luxuriously in the fleshpots of the British Legation, when my host remarked sternly one morning at breakfast, "You must go to the Great Wall!" . . . Another awful ride, then – one that would spread over a week!'

Rising at dawn each day to avoid the great heat, he reached the Great Wall and was not impressed by the reward for his effort: 'I scrambled over the rubbish and loose bricks to the top of the gate, with a numbing sense of disappointment. This the much-vaunted Wall! . . . It is not more than eight feet wide at the summit, with an absurd parapet on either side which looks as if a jerry-builder had erected it.' But he allowed himself to lean on the parapet, where after some time 'the feeling of disillusion waned' and he decided: 'The Great Wall is a wonder, after all, as a monument of human patience.'

After a night in a nomads' stinking tent he pressed on to another walled city, Yshang-Ping-Dshou, to see the tombs of the Ming emperors: 'The intense stillness of this wild, remote and solitary spot, with its enchanted court and sleeping monarchs, alone, among the savage hills, oppressed the nerves. In spite of one's nineteenth-century common sense, one could not help picturing a waking. When the great king slumbering yonder should deign to rise, his marble following would surely quicken into life, prompt to do his bidding.' Afterwards he returned to Beijing and took a boat destined for Nagasaki. Unfortunately, this boat, captained by a drunken Dane, caught fire and the order was given to abandon ship (but many of the opium-soaked passengers were burnt alive). Not all could fit in the rescue boat and Wingfield watched in horror as someone clung to the side:

> One of the crew unwound the small frail fingers and shook off the hand, and, leaning over, I could see a woman sink – a child in one arm tight clasped – in the clear water, her face turned upward as she went, with bubbles round her head, down, down, turning greener and greener, fainter and more faint, till she melted out of sight . . . I never forgot, and never shall, and see again in dreams sometimes, the imploring face of that pallid, mute, drowning Chinese woman, pitifully staring upward, surrounded by its aureole of bubbles, as it slowly sank down into the green.

On his arrival in Nagasaki Bay at dawn on a summer morning on the *Hiroshima Maru*, 'everything came fresh upon the eye as a pleasant change' from China, but he tried to come to a balanced judgement:

> One misses (thankfully) the greasy offal, the infinitely varied dirt and shocking smells of the last few months; but one also misses the quaintly different gilt and painted signs that hang in such numbers, or stand erect on pedestals in a Chinese street, the curled up eaves and brilliant tracery of tiles. A Japanese street is dull and dismal always, monotonously brown and dark, the only ornamentation a blue or chocolate awning, bearing the cognizance of a local magnate.

Overall, Japan seemed more compact, more tranquil, more attractive – until he reached Kobé, where 'one comes thumping down again to the prosaic earth', for this was a treaty port with a Bund or quay like Shanghai and a hotel with 'billiard tables and Bourbon whisky and cocktails'. Wingfield ironically registered one of the oldest traveller's reflexes, the sense of dismay and regret at what his kind has done to a place and from which he wishes to dissociate himself: 'The grip of Europe is on Kobé. The things in the shops are horribly ugly. The ricksha-men gabble broken English, and try to cheat you, since you are not accustomed to the coinage. Selfishness gushes over the soul. Oh that, when Japan was opened, it had been to one alone – one's self the privileged foreigner!'

The first chapter of the Japanese volume of Wingfield's *Wanderings* is entitled 'Disillusion'. He wanted the country to fulfil its assigned role for the Westerner as a place of beautiful perfection, but, quite apart from the raging cholera epidemic into which he had walked, he found the country was 'degenerating rapidly' under the pressure of European contact. Japanese art was being ruined by the manufacture of cheap lacquerware for foreigners and ugliness was everywhere: 'Picturesque? No. Each day social Japan approaches more nearly to the drab dead level of European red-taped routine.' Men were wearing 'ill-made clothes of European cut' and women were 'rapidly assuming a dreadful something which they are pleased to consider the perfection of Western taste'. Worse, there were dresses made of that frightful Victorian fabric, bombazine. 'Good Gracious! And this is an age of progress! Bombazine! We shall behold them presently reclining on horse-hair sofas, before a curtain of red moreen.'

The old Japan seemed to be crumbling and the demon was Europeanization. While Wingfield was there 'the death-knell of native costume' was sounded by a new Tokyo theatre which announced that 'no person was to be admitted within the precincts on any pretence who was not wearing European clothes'. Many clothes were being imported from Germany: 'Grim bonnets and ghastly tea-gowns, and gruesome evening gear, were stored in the hold of some Vanderdecken ship.'

After this Wingfield's lost illusions coloured everything he saw.

The landscapes started to strike him as all alike. He disliked the Japanese houses, whose paper walls created a constant din of shouting, the clatter of wooden clogs and the noise of communal bathing. 'The Japanese,' he lamented, 'are at this moment a melancholy spectacle, for they are a rudderless ship, drifting they know not whither . . . For the moment all that is English is good – Pears' soap, Reckitt's blue, Colman's mustard, Epp's cocoa.' Wingfield felt that the temples were crumbling and decayed because money was being spent instead on armaments and he lambasted 'certain recent travellers' who had glossed over this dark side of the picture of contemporary Japan 'with a varnish of mendacious humbug'.

When he moved on to Tokyo the same disappointment met him. He found the city 'quite curiously insignificant and ugly for the capital of an important kingdom. The streets are so uniformly drab and unornamental, the houses are so low and mean, the streets are so similar and withal so tortuous and meandering, that the stranger dares not explore alone.' After buying a few craft items and visiting some prisons because prison reform was a personal interest of his, Wingfield soon moved on to Nikkō, reflecting that the fact that there was nothing to see in the capital had its benefits to the traveller worn down by the obligation to see all the sights: 'For this one ought to be grateful, I suppose, since in India one is driven mad by the necessity of tomb-hunting.'

Along the road to Nikkō Wingfield did succumb, as all other travellers did, to the natural beauty, and he was entertained at one point by a village wrestling match: 'The entertainment proved to be unexciting . . . Eye fixed on eye, they prowled, made feints of attack, rose to solace themselves with water, then, crouching again, as it were, with lashing tails, made a sudden rush and gripped. Swaying to and fro and grunting wheezily, they tried to bear each other down, by force of superior weight chiefly, keeping up the movement till the audience, excited to a proper pitch, flung coins into the arena.'

He spent four weeks in the grounds of a temple near Nikkō until the damp and insects finally proved too much: 'I made up my mind suddenly one evening that the watching of insects is not the destiny of man, and that it behoved me to move ere I was quite mouldy.'

Wingfield was a traveller in the Kinglake or Curzon mould, an easygoing, genial observer who was frank about his blasphemous rejection of one in particular of the articles of the serious explorer's faith: that discomfort is good for the soul. He was all too aware that the track before him had already been beaten by the intrepid Isabella Bird but he was determined, as he finally swapped horseback for the *kuruma* for the remainder of his journey, to travel in reasonable comfort, having had, in his army days, quite enough of roughing it:

> Now, although in the course of years I have trotted nearly all over the globe, I have never arrived at travelling 'lightly,' because I hold a firm and unalterable conviction that if you are to be made too uncomfortable, it would be better to stop at home. Miss Bird, I believe, wandered about Japan with little else but a raincoat and a book – certainly with only one packhorse [we have seen above that this is not actually true] – and I have ever looked on her achievements with veneration mingled with awe . . . She was content with native fare. Rather than face anything of the kind, I would much rather have stayed in London . . . But why be more miserable than is necessary?

One cannot imagine David Livingstone framing such a question. So Wingfield provided himself with five rickshaws, one for himself and one for his man, Otto, 'the three others for baggage transport, the which consisted of a folding-bed, a *batterie de cuisine*, a goodly store of whisky, biscuits, potted meats, jams, pickles, books, clothes, sketching materials, dry plates, and a camera. Miss Bird, I fear, will never look on me with any expression other than one of soul-harrowing contempt!' In fact, having snapped up some pieces of ancient armour along the way, he acquired three more rickshaws in which to carry the spoils. This find may have been the one famously exhibited at his Bloomsbury home, a mounted Japanese soldier in full armour. The caravan covered nearly forty miles every twelve hours. He journeyed over the plains beyond Ikao to reach Sawatari, another 'Alpine village', where he at last found a paradisal setting.

He stayed in a large square room reached by a ladder and looking out on to a magnificent panorama of hills: 'This residence in mid-air was to be my home, and, even for Japan, it was a new and astonishing experience.' When he woke the following morning the fourth wall of his room had been removed and replaced by a mountain landscape:

> I made up my mind then and there that it was the most delightful experience which I had ever enjoyed in my life. The sun was rising behind the house, touching the magnificent range with colours from a fairy palette, merging from purple to pink and blue and gold; far down below was a dense forest of conifers; an eagle was majestically skimming across the opalescent sky, and the bright crystalline air was wafted in on me, fresh and sweet and crisp, with such a gentle tingle in it, as one who had been panting in the vaporous atmosphere of the torrid plains was well fitted to appreciate.

This was the high point of Wingfield's visit to Japan. He went on into the mountains to see the spa of Kusatsu, 'where is carried on the most violent form of water-cure in the Far East', a 'cure' so severe some of the patients died. The chemical smells were nauseous and, after half an hour strolling about the hot springs, his gold watch and chain had turned black. Then it was on to Kyoto ('as dull and decayed now as an English cathedral town'), where his trip came to an end and he made plans to move on to Manila and the Philippines: 'The foreigner grows very tired of Japan and its numerous discomforts, after the novelty of strange dress and customs has worn off . . . Both in Nippon and in the northern isle of Yezo I had received much kindness; I had seen many interesting things, had enjoyed myself sometimes amazingly, had learned much, and yet I was not sorry to say adieu.'

Wingfield's last journey was to Australia. His health improved there, but he died in November 1891 at his Bloomsbury home and was buried in Kensal Green Cemetery. His biographer memorably described him as 'slim and delicate-looking with a thin and feminine but musical voice'.

## 24

## Standing by China: Alicia Little

'It was in the merry month of May, 1887, that I first landed in China,' wrote Alicia ('Mrs Archibald') Little, 'but from the first there was nothing merry about China.' She arrived with her new husband, Archibald Little, who also wrote books about their Chinese travels, such as *Through the Yangtse Gorges*, and was involved in the tea trade. They lived in China until 1907 and Alicia Little's commitment to the country went further than the usual traveller's passing acquaintance. In 1895 she founded the Natural Foot Society, the Pu Tsan Tsu Hui, to stamp out foot-binding, a movement that won the support of the Empress Dowager. She also championed education for women and was one of several women responsible for founding the first high school for girls, in Shanghai. 'With all the nations contending who is to have its bones to pick,' she wrote at the conclusion of *Intimate China* (1899), 'it is necessary that some nation or nation should in the first instance stand by China.'

Born in Madeira in 1845, Alicia Bewicke was the youngest child of a Leicestershire landowner, Calverley Bewicke, and was educated at home. In her twenties and thirties she wrote novels such as *Miss Standish* (1883), about an unmarried feminist with a profound concern for human rights, and *Mother Darling* (1885), written in defence of the Women's Property Act. She married the businessman and sinologist Archibald Little in 1886 and they went to live in the west of China at Chungking (Chongqing).

The title of Little's book promised a more inward picture of

China, based on long residence, one more probing than the usual traveller's series of snapshots. On that cold, windy May morning of her arrival in Shanghai the winds of change were also blowing. 'Everyone knows what Shanghai is like,' she declared. The British public had been treated to endless descriptions of the fine European houses and the department stores but she sensed change in the air. Increasingly prosperous Chinese were elbowing Europeans off the pavements: 'Their silken garments, their arched mouths, the coldness of their icy stare, has not been duly depicted . . . With their long nails, their musk-scented garments, their ivory opium-pipes, and delicate arrangements of colours, they cannot be without sensibilities. Do they feel that the Gaul is at the gates, and that the China of their childhood is passing away?' Little set herself the task of helping the English reader see the China of this people's childhood, descriptively and anecdotally, rather than with 'facts and columns of statistics'. Deferring in characteristic Victorian fashion to the authority of male texts such as those of her husband and Sir John Davis, she hoped 'to make the reader see China and the Chinese as I have seen them in their homes and at their dinner parties, and living long, oh! such long summer days among them, and yet wearier dark days of winter'.

Little's first great disappointment when she arrived was that China seemed to consist of 'brown mud' and was generally 'not at all like the willow-pattern plate'. She and her husband travelled six hundred miles up the River Yangtze under 'leaden skies' to the city of Hankow, where she had her first real encounter with 'horrible sights, and still more horrible smells' but she immediately tried – in a way quite untypical of the travel writing of her contemporaries – to put what she saw in a more pertinent context: 'But I fancy those, who talk in this way, can know very little of the East End of London, and nothing of the South of France or Italian towns.'

She crossed the Yangtze from Hankow to visit a missionary at the city of Wuchang, where she experienced 'one of the most exciting moments of all my life in China' when, after listening to the nightwatchman crying the hours and clacking his pieces of bamboo together to warn evil-doers to keep off, she suddenly realized 'with a choking sense of emotion' that the gates had been shut 'and I was within there with a whole cityful of Chinese so hostile to foreigners, and especially to foreign women, that it had not been thought safe to let me walk through them to the missionary's house. Even the curtain of my sedan-chair had been drawn down, so that I might not be seen by any one.'

On the trip through the gorges she herself was the object of much attention: 'The people are greatly interested in seeing a European woman. The women flock round, and beg me to take off my gloves and my hat, that they may see how my hair is done, and the colour of my hands. Then some old woman is sure to squeeze my feet, to see if there is really a foot filling up all those big boots: for of course, all the women here have small feet.' Progress was slow against the current of the river, at one mile an hour, but the voyage was 'like a dream of childhood realised, a dream inspired by many readings of Sinbad's marvellous travels'.

Little's narrative is a series of impressions and excursions rather than the sequential account of a single trip, with the result that different journeys mingle and sometimes (as in the case of the nocturnal drama of Wuchang) the end is omitted. One springtime journey by land was from Ichang to Chungking, where, at a lonely inn, the villagers' curiosity was rather troublesome. They climbed up ladders to look down on the Littles through gaps in the roof of their dwelling. Alicia went out into the moonlight to remonstrate with them: 'On which a man stepped forward as spokesman. "We are nothing but mountain people," he said, "and anything like you we have never seen before! So we do just want to look."' Moved by the reasonableness of this, she answered their questions, 'on which they laughed merrily, quite delighted'. But they did not retreat from the rafters so that, unlike her husband, who undressed by candle-light, she had to go to bed in the dark, reflecting: 'Certainly, a man has great advantages in travelling.'

A little later on this trip at Lichuan Little's coolies advised her to pretend to be a man because men and women were not allowed to share the same room when travelling. Sometimes on the road they were pelted with mud 'simply out of hatred to foreigners' but generally the people were, as she dryly put it, 'what we call in China very civil; in any other country it would be outrageously insolent and ill-mannered'. At Chungking she was warned that it was impossible for 'an English lady' to walk the streets but she insisted on doing so 'with my sedan-chair, of course, following behind to show I had some claim to respectability'. Within minutes two or three hundred men and boys were on her tail. They would overtake her and then turn round 'to stare into one's face in the most insulting and annoying manner'. Eventually she was forced to take refuge in her chair. For all her instinctive sympathy, therefore, Little had to confess the general difficulty of living in China: 'Whether it is their expressionlessness, their want of sympathy, or the whole character of their civilisation being so different from ours, very few Europeans can spend more than a year amongst Chinese without suffering from it.'

This sense of a harshness in the culture returned when she began to contemplate the practice of foot-binding and the 'hideous goat-like feet' much admired by Chinese men: 'Chinese civilisation being very ancient and conservative, abuses there go on increasing, and become exceptionally exaggerated. The Chinese are also as a nation curiously callous to suffering either in themselves or others, not taking pleasure in the infliction of it, as is the case with some highly strung natures, but strangely indifferent to it.' She was interested in the position of women generally, noting that while Chinese women always dutifully rose when a man entered the room 'they in nowise convey the impression that they are accustomed to consider themselves at the service or pleasure of men'. Little was convinced that reforms (of a kind that as a progressive Victorian woman she would later advocate on platforms at home, speaking on women's suffrage and family issues) would in the end make a difference: 'The women of China give me the idea that, if once set upon their feet again, they will become a great power in the land . . . and it is at least noteworthy that, since the Chinese have taken to mutilating the feet of their women, there has not been one man whom they reckon great born among them: so true it is that any injury to the women of a nation always reacts upon the men with redoubled force.'

One group who backed her stand on foot-binding was the missionaries. Little was sympathetic to their efforts and found the general prejudice against them 'one of the most amusing things in China'. She noted how the missionaries kept on coming: 'till China promises fair to be the best spiritually seen after country outside Christendom. Yet no missionary ever comes to the Europeans, whose spirituality seems to have withered for want of exercise.' But she wished for more sensitivity towards the Chinese: 'Why should we insist upon the Chinese swallowing our ugly clothes and ugly houses before they receive our beautiful gospel of glad tidings, I never can understand.' The pleasant tartness of Little's observations comes out in her view of the Chinese *literati*: 'They seem to me very much like the young men of other nations, except that they are more easily amused and amuse me less . . . I have no doubt, however, they are not really quite as nice as they seem to be. Perhaps, however, that is true of all young men.'

She met some more young men, ordinands at a Buddhist monastery, and submitted to their curiosity: 'They were apparently especially taken by my gloves, and would feel my hand gloved and feel my hand ungloved, and generally *hang around*.' The monks were canny enough and when the Littles visited the sacred mountain of Omi to escape the heat of Chungking in 1892 the chief priest of the monastery served them a twelve-course lunch and expatiated on his tourist-funded plans for restoration. Alicia thought that the sixteen-day journey would put visitors off 'till there are steamers running to Chungking, and Cook has organised through-tickets. But the chief priest thinks if he could only do these rooms up many foreigners would come, and all give him many taels, and then the temples could all be restored.'

That summer she travelled to Chinese Tibet and claimed that this 'had never fallen to the lot of any European woman before'. After six days on a pony from Omi Shan, including passage of a three-hundred-foot chain bridge over the River Tung, she encountered her first Tibetans: 'Everyone looked at us and smiled. Could anything be more different from the reception we were accustomed to in a Chinese city?' Her camera, which she took with her everywhere, was an object of great interest, though the monks refused to let her take a picture for fear that their souls would be stolen away.

Little's narrative ends with a description of Beijing in which she concurs with other travellers about its lack of metropolitan glamour. In fairness, many of its sights were closed to the foreigner, which meant that a building such as the British Legation, a grand old Chinese palace, had to stand in as the finest sight. 'Peking,' she observed, 'is probably the only large city in the whole world where no arrangements whatever are made for sanitation and even common decency. The result is alike startling and disgusting to the traveller.' Moreover: 'Even the passing foreigner must feel at Peking that it is not the throbbing heart of a great country as London is, as Paris is; but the remains of the magnificent camp of a nomad race, that has settled down, and built in stone after the fashion in which in its wanderings it used to build in wood.'

Little returned to England in 1907 after eleven years in China. She had been honoured in China for her work for women by being made Vice President of the International Women's Conference in Shanghai in 1900. On her return she became a popular public speaker on women's issues and continued to travel and engage in humanitarian work after her husband died in 1908. She herself survived until 1926, dying in Kensington on 31 July of that year.

# 25

## *A Digression on Orientalism*

A term already used several times above, 'Orientalism', meaning rather more than just the study of Eastern culture, established itself firmly in contemporary academic discourse with the publication in 1978 of Edward Said's *Orientalism*, a controversial study which argued that Orientalism was a powerful creation of European ideology, a way for writers, philosophers and colonial administrators to deal with – the ubiquitous term of art used in universities for several decades now – 'the Other'.

Far from acquiring disinterested knowledge, Said argued, Western Orientalists were moulding the study of the East in ways that served the interests of Western imperialism. Knowledge was a form of power and control, prescribing the ways in which these countries were seen, making them submissible to the colonial will. It was the intellectual equivalent of colonial map-making: filling in, with appropriate tints, the 'blank spaces' on the map in the interests of the West rather than those of the East, which already considered that it occupied those spaces. As an actively political Palestinian, Said was both used to controversy and destined to provoke reaction, not least from the outraged in the traditional academy.

This new politically charged understanding of Orientalism remains an intensely contested intellectual and ideological space. Robert Irwin, in *For Lust of Knowing: The Orientalists and Their Enemies* (2006), has written a lively attempt to rebut Said, whom he accuses of having written 'a work of malignant charlatanry'. The jury is still out on whether he has succeeded in trouncing Said, but he has certainly remedied one of the principal defects of the latter's work, its lack of historical specificity.

In the present work the word 'Orientalism' has generally been used a little more loosely to describe the overall Western perspective on the East, a cluster of often contradictory and deeply ambivalent attitudes ranging from the 'racist' to the benign and the empathetic. A recent academic collection of Victorian travel writing was prefaced by an ideological health warning: 'Our commentaries attempt to provide context and interpretation of texts, which will free us, we hope, from any charges of complicity with the imperial ambitions, explicit or implicit, of some of the writers we reprint.' The present work, unable to reach such elevated moral heights, simply assumes that the reader will make his or her own judgement about particular culpabilities.

Victorian writers and readers had a very definite perspective on the East which created an expectation that certain points of reference would be automatically present in any given text. 'I used to wish the Arabian tales were true,' wrote John Henry Newman in his *Apologia Pro Vita Sua* (1864), 'my imagination ran on unknown influences, on magical powers, and talismans'. Similar passages can be found in the works of Carlyle and Ruskin. Lane's translation of *The Arabian Nights*, for example, went rapidly through four editions after it was published in 1839 and according to one writer on the subject, Thomas Assad, in his *Three Victorian Travellers: Burton, Blunt and Doughty*, there was between about 1852 and 1913 'a very impressive bibliography of English scholarship in Arabic language and literature . . . The result was the growth of a more accurate awareness of Eastern culture, an awareness which coincided with a more earnest political interest in the Middle East.'

A figure such as Doughty is representative here. His knowledge of Arabic language and culture was extensive yet, as noted above, his sympathy for the Muslim faith, a central part of the culture of the region, was severely limited. Burton, too, was a scholarly Orientalist, with much more sympathy for Islam, but also no stranger to prejudice or, on occasion, outright racism. He was also regularly employed by the military authorities to acquire knowledge about the regions in which he travelled in order to facilitate more effective colonial administration. The idea that scholarly under-standing of countries and imperial rule of them could be separated – that anyone would think of wanting to separate them – would not have occurred to a man like Richard Burton. In a Dedication to his account of his travels in Brazil, Burton praised the Foreign Secretary, Lord Stanley, for acting 'upon the belief that the welfare of his own country is advanced by the advancement of all other nations'.

This imperial idea of Progress drove most Victorian travellers in some shape or form even when – as in the case of Wilfrid Scawen Blunt or Mrs Archibald Little – particular progressive agendas were being pursued. As the historian G. M. Young put it in his classic *Victorian England: Portrait of an Age* (1936), 'as it seemed to those who recalled the sordid and sullen past, England [in the 1850s] was renewing her youth, at Lucknow and Inkerman, with Livingstone in the African desert, with Burton on the road to Mecca'.

Let us give the last word to David Hogarth, writing in his *A Wandering Scholar in the Levant* (1896):

> These nations of the East are in their childhood, but it is their second childhood . . . It is a commonplace to regard the Eastern nations as children, to whom we are schoolmasters. India is to be taught Western methods, Egypt set in the path of our own development, Turkey regenerated in our image. Vanity of all vanities! here is the sheerest alchemy! It is *we* that are the children of these fathers; we have learned of them, but we shall surpass and outlive them, and our development is not just what theirs has been, even as development of a second generation is never quite like that of the first. When we speak of educating India or Egypt we are the modern son who proposes to bring his father up to date. We are dominant in those lands for the sake not of their but our own development,

and in order to use them as our own 'stepping stones to higher things'. It is possibly not amiss for own moral nature that we should hug an altruistic illusion at home, and we find little difficulty in doing so; but it is less easy abroad; no one who has been long in Egypt appears ever to talk about the 'political education' of the Egyptians.

# PART FIVE

# AFRICA

## 26

### Civilization's Cloak: Mansfield Parkyns in Abyssinia

For the Victorians, Africa – that vast, too often undifferentiated, Dark Continent – was often realized imaginatively as a place of darkness awaiting the light of Western civilization. Its inhabitants, even more so than the indigenous people of Asia or the Middle East, were repeatedly defined in European texts as 'savages'. Both polarities (light/darkness, civilized/savage) have already been encountered many times but the intensity of these antitheses was heightened in writing about Africa. This conception is rightly indicted by the historians Roland Oliver and J. D. Fage as 'a parochial European idea' but it was deeply entrenched.

Not all nineteenth-century British travellers in Africa, however, were blind to the long history of this continent where civilization began. The most interesting early-Victorian African traveller, in the 1840s, Mansfield Parkyns, admitted that he was unhappy with the description of the Abyssinians as savages: 'They were formerly a great nation, and, judging from the more ancient accounts of them, in a pretty advanced state of civilisation.' Parkyns's attitudes to the native population on show in his *Life in Abyssinia* (1853) were not, by modern standards, always enlightened, and more typical was his comment that the 'British Lion' behaved more like a donkey when trying to deal politically with less 'civilized' societies: 'He sends embassies and consuls, and makes treaties, and goes through all the formulae of state diplomacy with a half-naked nigger who, in solemn council with his ministers, would find unutterable amusement in letting off a box of lucifers – First Lord of the Treasury vying with Lord Chancellor who should have "next go".' But these verbally shocking passages are balanced by entirely contradictory evidence of a real gift of empathy with the people he travelled among.

Parkyns was born in 1823 into a family of Nottinghamshire landowners with aristocratic connections and educated at Uppingham School and Trinity College, Cambridge, though he left the university in 1840 after what he later described darkly as 'a scrape'. Two years later he set off on his travels, which lasted nine years and took him across Europe, Asia Minor, Abyssinia – where he spent three years – other parts of East Africa and Egypt.

Like so many Victorian travellers, as we have seen, Parkyns was anxious to disclaim any literary pretensions for his book about Abyssinia. 'I do not pretend to be learned in book-making,' he wrote. 'To my mind, style and beauty of composition belong rather to the poet or novelist than to one whose only pretension is to detail in a rough way certain incidents and experiences of a rough life.' He went on to suggest that: 'A book of travels should be either a scientific work or an entertaining one. Mine has, I fear, but little to recommend it in either of these particulars. If it has a merit, it is that *I believe most of it* to be true. What I have described has been almost entirely what I have myself witnessed, *or heard related on the spot.*' He did concede, however, that: 'In some few cases, I may have fallen into a common error, that of putting down as customs, incidents which I may have seen, but which, in reality, may happen scarcely once in a hundred years.'

His real claim to originality, he believed, was to have entered 'more particularly into the customs of the people I have visited than has hitherto been done. A tolerably long residence among them, and the fact of my having identified myself with the natives, perhaps more than any of my predecessors, not only in habits, but also in feelings, would lead me to hope that I may be enabled to do this with some correctness.' This is an early example of what would become a common claim among modern British travellers to an authenticity derived from a special inwardness with the people among whom they travelled. Parkyns certainly travelled in regions of Abyssinia and the Sudan never before described 'in any book of travels' and largely unknown to Europeans.

Parkyns was also a collector of birds and on one occasion had 1200 specimens shipped home in native cases made of bamboo and hide on a German brig, but they were dumped in a warehouse near the custom house for nearly four years, at the end of which, when he opened them up, all the best and brightest – Abyssinian rollers, parrots and emerald cuckoos – had been pilfered. A second collection was sent to Aden, half of which (including 'some very rare and beautiful monkeys') was eaten by rats and the rest lost in transit. A third collection from Nubia and the White Nile did arrive safely and consisted of about six hundred birds and 'about a ton of weight of nigger arms and implements'.

The secret of his success as a traveller, Parkyns believed, was his great austerity:

I have eaten of almost every living thing that walketh, flieth or creepeth – lion, leopard, wolf, cat, hawk, crocodile, snake, lizard, locust &c.; and I should be sorry to say what dirty messes I have at times been obliged to put up with . . . From a child I never knew a good dinner from a bad one, so long as there was plenty; and this is a taste, or rather want of taste, almost essential to a traveller . . . He who is blessed with a hardy frame, an easy, pliant temper, and an appetite which may be satisfied without luxuries, may travel all his life, and scarcely meet with more dangers or hardships than proportionally would occur to any other man of opposite disposition in England . . . To sum up, avoid all bad localities; follow as much as possible the native customs with regard to food; but, above all things, be abstemious in every respect.

Parkyns's tour began by passing through Switzerland, Milan, Venice, Trieste, the Ionian islands, Greece and Smyrna. He apologized that these destinations by the early 1850s had become 'part of the ordinary annual tour of our migrating countrymen. Nor is Constantinople any longer a place of curiosity.' At a hotel in Smyrna he met a Cambridge man, Richard Monckton Milnes MP, with whom he travelled to Alexandria to see the Nile. Hiring a donkey at Alexandria, where he stayed at Rey's hotel, Parkyns revealed again his shrewd and ironic understanding of the laws of travel: 'I addressed a boy, beginning my conversation (as all Englishmen are *supposed* to do) with a strongish expletive, and continuing my inquiry in very bad English, as all Englishmen do, in the idea, I suppose, that, because the natives speak a broken language, they will digest it better if broken up ready for their use.'

The two friends took an Egyptian Transit Company track-boat along the Nile to Atfé and thence a steamer to Cairo and the comforts of the Shepheard Hotel, where Parkyns spent most of his time ill in bed until he was ready to leave for a two-month tour of the Nile with Milnes. When Milnes then had to return to Parliament, Parkyns set off for Suez. Already he felt that British travel writing had done the Nile to death and he forbore to offer any description of this trip.

On his return to Cairo he armed himself for the main trip with:

a double-barrelled gun, a small single rifle carrying an ounce ball, a pair of double pistols, and a large bowie knife – the firearms all by Westley Richards. My knife was sent to me as a present, and 'warranted to chop off a tiger's head at a blow'. Truly it was a most formidable weapon; a blade fourteen inches long, more than two broad, and nearly half an inch thick . . . the large knife was not handy for skinning, butchering, or eating with; nor was it adapted for cutting lodge poles or firewood, and could therefore count only as a defensive or offensive weapon.

He also took along with him 'by way of presents to the chiefs whose territories I might visit, some pieces of white muslin for turbans, twenty or thirty yards of red cloth, three brace of common pistols, a dozen light cavalry sword-blades, and four common Turkey rugs'.

Finally, on the evening of 5 March 1843, Parkyns left his inn, seated on a jackass ('the cab of Egypt'), because an Arab boat bound for Jeddah was rumoured to be ready to sail. The fresh air of the desert rushing on his face, he produced another mocking observation on the art of travel: 'It was nearly dark; and thus leaving, as I was, for a long period, all civilization, friends, comforts, &c., had I been a poet I should no doubt have managed a neat poem in several cantos; or had I been a "tourist", three pages of very feeling matter; but being neither, I filled my pipe afresh, and changed my donkey for a dromedary that was waiting for me.' The dromedary, attended by an Arab camel man, proceeded at three and a half miles an hour and jolted and swung horribly. At this time the desert road between Suez and Cairo was divided into eight stages by seven stations, the even numbers of which were refreshment houses and the odd numbers merely stables.

On the second night Parkyns arrived at station number four, 'kept by a blooming young English woman – a most unexpected plant in the middle of the barren desert'. Parkyns listened to her tale, which was that she had married a Copt who boasted that he was an aspiring naval architect but who turned out, once she had married him, to be nothing more than a jobbing carpenter. They had soon parted company. Parkyns drew the moral that decent English girls should avoid being taken in by 'strange, foreign-looking people, with queer manners' for: 'She was really pretty, and apparently of respectable origin, for she played the piano . . . I mention these circumstances in the history of our unfortunate countrywoman as a warning to others of her sex to be cautious how they are led away by long beards, foreign manners, and foreign titles.'

The following morning, after a good meal and a few bottles of porter provided by his hostess the night before, Parkyns was sick on mounting his camel. His baggage servant, Said, was convinced that the young woman was in love with his master and had poisoned him when he tried to leave. On arrival at Suez an unfortunate wait of a fortnight was necessary: 'Nowhere I should think, could there be found a more dreary, uninteresting spot than Suez, surrounded as it is on three sides by the desert, and on the fourth by the neck of the Red Sea, which at low water becomes a flat of damp sand, without even a single tree, shrub, or other vestige of green herb, to relieve the eye from the glare of the yellow sand.'

Parkyns eventually got away from Suez on an Arab boat bound for Jeddah. Turks, Greeks, Armenians, Bedouins, Egyptians and up to a hundred other races crowded on to the vessel. Parkyns squeezed himself into a tiny space six feet by three among bales and boxes underneath the mizzen mast and, exploiting his gift for making friends easily, he started to learn enough Arabic from his companions to be able to dispense with an interpreter. The voyage took twenty-three days, during which a fire broke out. He refused the captain's request to throw overboard at this point the iron-bound deal box of 'Pigou and Wilks's best' gunpowder which he was using as a seat.

During the voyage he tucked into a meal of sea turtle: 'At the time of my first voyage to Jeddah this sort of communism in feeding was rather extraordinary to me; but since that time I have for years been in the constant habit of "dipping my finger in the dish" with niggers and think even now that that mode of eating is far more convenient, and, as it is practised in the East, quite as cleanly as the use of knives and forks.' Surveying his new friends, he observed: 'The Arabs in general are easily managed. They are at first disposed to be troublesome in their curiosity, and occasionally rather insolent; but if they see that the traveller is inclined to make himself agreeable and to bear with them, they are always ready to meet him more than half way.'

Parkyns was glad, however, to get ashore at Jeddah and billet himself for a fortnight at the home of the British consul, A. C. Ogilvy. He found it a tolerably attractive spot and no more full of 'bazaars, mosques, dates, flies and filth' than any other place in the region but he doubted the value of local people adopting Western manners: 'The adoption, for instance, of tight trousers and a buttoned-up frock coat in the East is as ridiculous as wearing a negro's clothing would be in England.' From Jeddah he caught a fast sailing boat to Souàkin and, attending to an Englishman dying there of fever, he reflected that he too might die on African soil, 'such being the lot of most of those whom science, curiosity, or a wandering taste lures under the fatal branches of that most deadly of all uppas-trees, "African discovery"'. Moving on to Massàwa, he was coolly received by the Governor because of his by now scruffy appearance. Parkyns didn't care. Freedom of dress and the simple life, as far as he was concerned, conduced to good health:

From the day I left Suez (March 25, 1843) till about the same time in the year 1846, I never wore any article of European dress, nor indeed ever slept on a bed of any sort, – not even a mattress; the utmost extent of luxury which I enjoyed, even when all but dying of a pestilential fever that kept me five months on my beam-ends at Khartoum, was a coverlid under a rug . . . for more than three years (that is till I reached Khartoum) I wore no covering to my head, except a little butter, when I could get it; nor to my feet, except the horny sole which a few months' rough usage placed under them. During the whole of this time I never had a headache, though exposed to the sun at all hours of the day, and was never foot-sore, though I walked constantly in the roughest imaginable places.

After a few weeks' shooting game at Ailat he set off for Kiaquor with a local man as guide, a Negro servant called Abdallah rom Sennaar, and an Abyssinian boy. All they took with them was a small bag of flour, half a pint of honey in a drinking horn, a change of clothes, ammunition and arms. Abandoning his sandals and going barefoot, Parkyns lived off bread and water which he considered the ideal diet for a hot country, and the essential pipe: 'a traveller's pipe is his substitute for food and medicine, the sole companion that can render him calm and patient under suffering, a great preventive against all sorts of infection, and highly useful where malaria is to be feared'. His wanderings now took him through a landscape ravaged by civil war and where the nightly accommodation was very rough: 'A miserable shed, carpeted with cow dung. Here, and often while in these countries, did I yearn for one of the neat, comfortable tenements assigned to cattle in England; but I may truly assert that for several years I have not slept in half so good a dwelling as most of those occupied by our horned dependants.'

Encountering some Anglo-German missionaries on the way to Adoua, the capital of Tigray, Parkyns reflected on their singular lack of success in conversion and that fact that the local people were 'naturally offended at the intrusion of persons whose avowed object is to uproot the religion they have received from their ancestors, and which is as dear and sacred to them as our own is to us'. Had the missionaries shown a little more cultural sensitivity, he believed, they might have had more success. He met some local men who had accepted the gift of a Bible then sold it the same evening for a jar of beer. Bibles were no use at all to an illiterate population, Parkyns pointed out, and what was needed was more proper education – at the end of which Abyssinia, 'once civilized, might be the starting point for civilizing a large part of Eastern Africa'.

After Adoua, 'the capital of one of the most powerful kingdoms of Aethiopia' but in reality nothing more than 'a large straggling village of huts', he set off for Mount Haramat, having now adopted the Abyssinian dress permanently. Not yet skilled at wearing the costume, he was mocked by the local people: 'Besides which, our straight hair, not yet long enough to be tressed, was plastered back with butter, and the faces of those of our party who were encased in a thin skin, which I am happy to say never was my fate, were as red as a fresh capsicum.'

Parkyns was dismissive of the advertised dangers of travelling in remote places and pushed on at the end of September 1843 into Addy Abo, a province on the northern frontier of Tigray, 'then so little known as not to be placed on any map'. The only two Europeans ever to have been to this region had died but his curiosity was aroused. During this trip he reflected on the moral value of hardship to the traveller: 'How little are the gifts of Nature appreciated by those who, living in the midst of luxury, are accustomed only to wish for a thing in order to obtain it! . . . leave for a time your lives of luxury, shoulder your rifle, and take a few months' experience of hardship in a hot climate . . . You will devour a half-burned piece of gazelle, and find it more palatable than the cuisine of the greatest gourmand in Paris.' He also revealed the secret of his success in remote countries: avoid imitating the noisy, demanding petulance of the European traveller and practise instead the quiet manners of the indigenous people:

On my arrival at a village I have always found it the better plan to do as native travellers would – wait under a tree till some one asks me in. This is generally soon done, though a little patience is sometimes needed. People often gather round you to look at you, and occasionally make rather personal remarks, though generally they are very civil. Only answer their questions good-naturedly, and take pleasure in making yourself agreeable, which you will find will become a habit, and you will be welcome everywhere.

For four years Parkyns walked barefoot in Abyssinia and thought highly of the practice: 'Oh, what a good law it would be that should forbid the use of shoes or stockings all over the world! . . . The shape of our feet is very different from what Nature intended it to be.' This was part of a wider philosophy of travel worked out by Parkyns in these years, not unknown in the English travelling tradition, and consisting in a celebration of primitivism and an indictment of what Bruce Chatwin used to call 'the sins of settlement':

> That a man brought up in the midst of civilisation and refinement should presume to look back on the time he passed among savages, without society, without even a book of any sort to refresh his memory, as one of the happiest periods of his life, would to many be equivalent to acknowledging himself possessed of a coarse and unintellectual mind. The beauties of Nature are little known, still less appreciated in Europe . . . Civilization and crime go hand in hand . . . even the most refined person, who has tasted the sweets of savage life, will always look back with longing to them . . . as a man who knows how little happiness depends on luxury, and how much it depends on the feeling that what he sees is, and is not merely an appearance, – that his actions will be judged by the motives which actuated them, not by conventionalities, – that his friends will be friends of heart, not of face, – and that his enemies will show their enmity openly before him, not secretly and behind his back.

So intimate did Parkyns become with the local people that the local prince in a district called Rohabaita offered him the government of the province if he wanted it. He was treated as a chief and 'felt myself one of them', entering 'with the greatest sympathy and zeal into all their proceedings'. At feasts, he claimed, no one enjoyed the dance and song more than he did and even though he did not get much to eat: 'I never felt lighter in my life or more free from the many ills that vex humanity, than during this long period of my semi-starvation. Wounds of all kinds healed on me like magic, and I never knew what it was to feel lazy or fatigued.' His time was passed on hunting expeditions: 'It is a most independent life. My dress on these occasions consisted of a short kilt of nicely tanned antelope's hide, a piece of coarse cotton cloth wrapped around my waist by day as a belt and used as a covering at night, and a small wild cat's or jackal's skin thrown over my shoulder.' Parkyns was not the first nor would he be the last travelling Englishman to go native in this way, discovering the bracing austerities of the elective primitive.

After nine months in this northern region Parkyns returned in June 1844 to Adoua to spend the rainy season there and study manners and customs, a study in which he had been preceded here by the great eighteenth-century British African traveller James Bruce, whose account of his Abyssinian travels had been published in 1792. Parkyns refined at length his idea of travel, its cultural impact and the shortcomings of understanding which proceeded from a Eurocentric scale of values:

It is a difficult task for any man to form a just opinion of the character of a nation through whose country he may have passed, or among whom he may have sojourned only for a short space of time. Travellers are far too apt to attribute to an entire population traits which they may have observed in the townspeople, or even in their immediate followers. Such an estimate is evidently unfair: the servants usually chosen by foreigners, in all parts of the world, are of a stamp peculiar to themselves, and often but poor samples even of the class to which they nominally belong . . .

Wherever travellers, no matter of what nation they be, are in the habit of passing, they spoil the people with whom they come into contact; or rather perhaps it is, that the people who volunteer their services to them are usually of not a very high grade. The newly-arrived tourist, from ignorance of the language, localities, and prices of the country, naturally applies to his interpreter to ascertain where he may best purchase anything that he may need; the servant as naturally directs him to the shops of those tradesmen from whom he anticipates the highest percentage – thus our friend gets among a bad set of tradesmen. And so on . . .

There are errors, too, into which the readers of travels may fall as well as the writer: such as attributing to character what may belong only to custom; as, for instance, natural cruelty to a people on account of certain of their habits in war being cruel; immorality to those who allow a plurality of wives; or who, like our Abyssinian friends, seldom marry at all, preferring a sort of concubinage; and thievishness to a Bedouin, because he always waylays a caravan. But this is nearly invariably wrong . . .

We are too apt also to compare the manners of other nations with our own, and to judge of the people accordingly . . . I don't believe that there exists a nation, however high in the scale of civilization, that can pick a hole in the character of the lowest, without being in danger of finding one nearly, if not quite, as big in its own. The vices of the savage are, like his person, very much exposed to view. Our own nakedness is not less unseemly than his, but is carefully concealed under that convenient cloak which we call 'civilization', but which he, in his ignorance, poor fellow, might, on some occasions, be led to look upon as hypocrisy.

At the end of this period of 'a most agreeable life on a very limited income' which was 'the only period of my life in which I ever felt myself a great man', Parkyns returned to the capital to prepare for another journey westwards to the Sudan:

like all happy moments, those years passed over quickly, and now appear to me more like a dream than anything else. I had no annoyances of any kind; was fortunate enough to leave the country without, I believe, a single personal enemy; and beyond having received a lance through my clothes, between my right arm and my side, when endeavouring to separate some combatants who had got drunk at a wedding – and, on another occasion, having been rather badly hurt with a blow on the back from a club or stone – I may say that neither my life, limbs, nor health, were ever in danger. Meanwhile, as I have before hinted, I was living without any means; my supplies and letters having been unaccountably detained on the way, so that from the time of my leaving Cairo, two years and a quarter before, I was in the dark about Europe and European goings-on.

Parkyns made his preparations – which were 'soon made when a man travels, as I do, with next to nothing in the baggage department' – and he set off at the end of June 1845, not the best time, as the rains were beginning, but his resources were running out. With bandaged eyes as a result of an attack of ophthalmia, he saw little on the first stage of his journey west but he was also frustrated by the difficulties of conveying such a scene to the English reader who could not begin to imagine it: 'What I mean is, that a description of things so totally different from what we are accustomed to, as everything in those remote countries is, cannot help losing its African feeling and becoming Anglicized, first by an English description, secondly and mainly by passing through the English imagination of the reader. This is the least that can happen to the best of books.' Such a concern with the problems of 'representation' would earn him warm approval from any present-day academic expert on 'postcolonial literature'.

Parkyns undertook this journey across the Sudan with a hard-up German called Yakoub, who, at the very outset, was almost swept away to his death by a swollen river. Parkyns himself lost in the turbulent waters a talisman that had been with him throughout his whole stay in Abyssinia: 'I may truly say that I can date the commencement of all the troubles, illnesses, and other human miseries which have hitherto fallen to my share from the day it left me; for up to that time, beyond the ordinary complaints of childhood and many a sound and well-deserved whipping at school, I had led a life of sunshine.' During the next three or four years in Africa, as if to confirm this, he had a succession of the very worst tropical fevers.

But when he eventually reached Cairo the talisman miraculously turned up in his luggage: it had not been lost at all. It took the form of 'a withered bouquet wrapped up in a bit of paper, a date on which proved it to have been worn by me about the time of my first appearance in the glorious, manly, and picturesque costume of a swallow-tailed dress-coat'. Parkyns had it 'neatly wrapped in a waxed cloth, and afterwards cased in leather by an Abyssinian saddler, so that it made a very respectable-looking amulet'. He always claimed it was a relic of a saint and he treated it as a link with the world on which he had turned his back: these

> withered roses . . . formed the last link, as it were, the only memorial that connected me with the life I had been brought up to. They had a curious power of representing England and English customs to me in different lights according as was best for the state of mind in which I happened to be at the moment. At times, when, lost in the excitement of a savage life, and dazzled by the splendour of a tropical climate, I might have almost wished to forget that there was such a place as home, they would remind me of friends and scenes I had left behind, paint civilization in her brightest colours, and even so far 'humbug' me as to persuade me that a drizzly November day was only a foil to set off the brightness of an English fireside.

For all his wanderings, Parkyns retained a vivid sense of a world on which he knew he could not in reality turn his back: 'Europe in general, but perhaps England in particular, has customs which, to a stranger, or even to a native who, like myself, has the power of closing an English mind's eye and opening a nigger one whenever he pleases, appear as wonderful and unaccountable as any that I have described or that could be found among the most barbarous nations in the world.'

His journey west continued through the province of Waldabba, across the swollen River Zarrima, the table-land of Walkait, where 'we passed some small villages, the inhabitants of which were in a delightful state of primitive simplicity, whole populations turning out to see a white man for the first time in their lives, and willingly exchanging any little necessaries we required for a few needles or glass beads'. The local populations were convinced that Parkyns was a spy and almost certainly a Turk and eventually he was arrested. He disarmed the soldiers, however, by his usual chaffing charm: 'Let this be a warning to hot-headed travellers.' The local governor of the frontier province, now that Parkyns had metamorphosed from spy to important celebrity, lent him three camels and sent him to visit a local chief called Nimr ('The Leopard'). The excursion provoked yet another diatribe from Parkyns on the inferiority of English civilization for a man of his stamp. He confessed to 'a decided preference for green trees over smoky chimneys – to loving fine scenery, and not caring for the contemplation of the last Paris fashions in Hyde Park etc etc . . .' One of the pleasures of a hard life was 'the enjoyment of exuberant animal spirits not dependent on temporary excitement, but the offspring of abstemious habits, combined with plenty of air and exercise'.

When he reached Nimr's territory the chief fed him and asked why he had come. It is the eternal and usually unanswerable question for travellers but Parkyns's answer is as good as any: 'I told him the truth that it was pure curiosity; that I was a man who, from boyhood, had wandered in various parts of the world for the sake of seeing all that was worth seeing, and gaining experience.'

Getting steadily nearer to Khartoum, Parkyns arrived at the River Seytit, where he reflected on his relationship to the indigenous people among whom he had lived and moved for so long: 'When I first began travelling in Africa I had just the same dislike of seeing a crowd of people squatted around me, and watching my every movement, that most young travellers experience . . . But after a time, perceiving that this was not at all the way to become acquainted with the people, I adopted a diametrically opposite line of conduct.' He spent three days at Soufi then set off for Cattàrif, encountering some Bedouin. He enjoyed sleeping out with them in the desert: 'But seriously, I've seen a good many different races of men, and tried their modes of life, and my firm conviction is that no civilized man enjoys half the happiness, either of mind or body, that falls to the lot of the desert Arab.' In all, Parkyns spent a year with the nomad Kababish tribe in the Sudan.

At Abou Kharraz Parkyns took a river boat to Khartoum, where he arrived quite without funds: 'I spent my time in the market-place and coffee-houses, preferring the society of the rude Turkish soldiers to the cold politeness of the Europeans, sleeping with them on the benches of the coffee-shops, dining, like them, on a bit of bread and some cheese or a few radishes, and thus passed my time not at all uncomfortably.' He had planned to send from Khartoum to Egypt for some money but waited three weeks before getting round to this important task, 'being rather of a careless and easily-satisfied disposition'.

For Parkyns this was the end of his journey and he reflected: 'I was treated inhospitably by no one during all my travels, excepting by Europeans, who had nothing against me but my apparent poverty.' He closed his long book with the words: 'During nine years of travel I met with companions of every colour, station, and religion; but never picked up with one who gave me a moment's cause to quarrel with him, or from whom I parted otherwise than with regret.'

Parkyns's account does not reveal the remarkable story of his marriage in 1843 to a local woman called Tures, from a village in Addi Harisho, a remote region of Abyssinia. She bore him a son called John who eventually died in 1916 in Eritrea. When Parkyns returned to England he did not bring his new family with him. He left Cairo, after a stay of several months, for home in 1849. He was taken up on his return by the Royal Geographical Society, who treated him as an authority on that great issue, the source of the Nile. The following year he was off again to Constantinople as assistant secretary to the British Embassy in the city, a posting that did not work, perhaps owing to his incapacity for subordination. He now wrote up his Abyssinian travels, which were published in 1853. Too carefree and anti-heroic for popular taste, the book retained a deserved reputation among RGS members, on whose council 'Abyssinia Parkyns' served in 1854.

By the autumn of that same year, however, Parkyns was newly married to the daughter of Sir Richard Bethell QC and embarking on the life of a Nottinghamshire squire. He subsequently became the father of eight daughters. His travelling days were over and new hobbies such as woodcarving took over. In order to earn a living for his large family he served for twenty years, between 1864 and 1884, as comptroller of the bankruptcy court in London. Ten years after his retirement from that post he died on 12 January 1894. He was buried in his local church at Woodborough in Nottinghamshire. Francis Galton, who once visited Parkyns in his mud hut at Khartoum, judged that he was 'the traveller most gifted with natural advantages for that career'.

## 27

## The White Man: Richard Burton in East Africa

We left Captain Richard Burton flushed with the triumph of his secret penetration of the holy city of Mecca. In November 1853 he was in Cairo, his leave expired, and his heart set on the conquest of another forbidden city, Harar, a centre of religious worship and an important slave-trading base in Somalia. Not merely had no European ever entered Harar, its inhabitants believed that should an infidel ever succeed in doing so their city would fall. Burton put up to his military superiors a proposal to mount an expedition to Somalia with the intention of travelling inland to Harar. He would then make a survey of the coast around Berbera before travelling south-east across the Somali peninsula as far as Zanzibar.

The expedition was enthusiastically backed by the Bombay military council and a party, including John Hanning Speke, with whom Burton was later to be entangled in rivalry and controversy, gathered at Aden on 1 October 1854. The plan, however, was scuppered there by the Aden political resident, Colonel James Outram, because he feared it was dangerous and likely to foment conflict. Burton was contemptuous of the 'timid colony' at Aden and observed with his customary macho swagger: 'The Anglo-Saxon spirit suffers, it has been observed, from confinement within any but wooden walls, and the European degenerates rapidly, as do his bull-dogs, his game-cocks, and other pugnacious animals, in the hot, enervating climates of the East.' He had, however, little option but to agree to limit the expedition to coastal areas but retained the prize of Harar for himself, sailing from Aden on the *Sahalat* on 29 October 1854.

Burton was happily in disguise again as 'an Arab merchant' performing the pilgrimage and he was clear that this region of East Africa, 'previously known only by the vague reports of native travellers', was a worthy object of his attention:

The land of the Somal was still a *terra incognita*. Harar, moreover, had never been visited, and few are the cities of the world which, in the present age, when men hurry about the earth, have not opened their gates to European adventure. The ancient metropolis of a once mighty race, the only permanent settlement in Eastern Africa, the reported seat of Moslem learning, a walled city of stone houses, possessing its independent chief, its peculiar population, its unknown language, and its own coinage, the emporium of the coffee trade, the head-quarters of slavery, the birth-place of the Kat plant, and the great manufactory of cotton-cloths, amply, it appeared, deserved the trouble of exploration.

Burton arrived on the Somali coast at Zayla on 3 January 1855 in bellicose mood. Not for him the gentle empathy of Mansfield Parkyns. He quickly concluded that the natives of this coast had 'lapsed into barbarism', though they did appear to contain 'material for moral regeneration', in contrast with the Arabs, who were 'a race untameable as the wolf' and expert at shaking off foreign dominion. The British flag had been fired on in southern Arabia and Burton objected to peaceful strategies in response: 'By a just, wholesome, and unsparing severity we may inspire the Bedouin with fear instead of contempt.' He derided the idea of peaceful administration and argued that colonies are retained only by an aggressive policy: 'The facts of history prove nothing more conclusively than this: a race either progresses or retrogrades, either increases or diminishes: the children of Time, like their sire, cannot stand still.'

Settled in Zayla, however, Burton began to calm down and, unlike Doughty, was soothed by the sound of the evening *muezzin:* 'The well-known sounds of El Islam returned from memory. Again the melodious chant of the Muezzin, – no evening bell can compare with it for solemnity and beauty.' Twenty-six days of 'sleep, and pipes, and coffee' ensued and even the distasteful spectacle of British society at Aden began to recede from his memory. Burton's pugnacious prejudice and distaste for being boxed in by colonial rituals came out in a highly characteristic tirade written on his arrival at Zayla:

Fresh from Aden, with its dull routine of meaningless parades and tiresome courts martial, where society is broken by ridiculous distinctions of staff-men and regimental-men, Madras-men and Bombay-men, 'European' officers, and 'black' officers; where literature is confined to acquiring the art of explaining yourself in the jargons of half-naked savages; where the business of life is comprised in ignoble official squabbles, dislikes, disapprobations, and 'references to superior authority;' where social intercourse is crushed by 'gup', gossip, and the scandal of small colonial circles; where – pleasant predicament for those who really love women's society! – it is scarcely possible to address fair dame, preserving at the same time her reputation and your own, and if seen with her twice, all 'camp' will swear it is an 'affair'; where, briefly, the march of mind is at a dead halt, and the march of matter is in double quick time to the hospital or sick-quarters. Then the fatal struggle for Name, and the painful necessity of doing the most with the smallest materials for a reputation!

With some relief Burton ventured out into the streets of Zayla to test the efficacy of his new disguise as a Turkish merchant. He quickly found that it was not working when the local people began to shriek: 'The White Man! run away, run away or we shall be eaten!' Burton reflected that he should have provided himself with a bottle of walnut juice, for 'a white colour is decidedly too conspicuous in this part of the East'. On an excursion he met a party of local girls who mocked his colour and claimed to have exposed him as an infidel but the men who were with them 'declared me to be a Shaykh of Shaykhs, and translated to the prettiest of the party an impromptu proposal of marriage. She showed but little coyness, and stated her price to be an Audulli or necklace, a couple of Tobes, – she asked one too many – a few handfuls of beads, and a small present for her papa.'

On 27 November 1854, after days of 'African indolence, petty intrigue, and interminable suspicion', Burton set off along the coast in a southerly direction for Harar. He had been growing most impatient: 'Travellers are an irritable genus: I stormed and fretted at the delays to show earnestness of purpose.' One earnest was to treat the 'Orientals' very firmly and to be 'on extreme terms' with them, for: 'In East Africa especially, English phlegm, shyness, or pride, will bar every heart and raise every hand against you.' The caravan was led by the guide Raghe and consisted of his man Eesa, two women cooks and four camels. They carried a box of beads, trinkets 'mosaic-gold earrings, necklaces, watches, and similar nick-nacks'. In addition Burton's party carried 300 pounds of rice, dates, salt, clarified butter, tea, coffee, sugar, a box of biscuits 'in case of famine', halva, turmeric, and a heavy box of ammunition 'sufficient for a three months' sporting tour'. He also had three attendants in 'the pink of Somali fashion. Their frizzled wigs are radiant with grease; their Tobes are splendidly white, with borders dazzlingly red; their new shields are covered with canvass cloth; and their two spears, poised over the right shoulder, are freshly scraped, oiled, blackened, and polished.'

Not to be left behind, Burton himself was mounted on 'a fine white mule . . . a double-barrelled gun lies across my lap; and a rude pair of holsters . . . contain my Colt's six-shooters'. He travelled due south along the 'hard, stoneless, and alluvial plain' that bordered the coast, alternately dry and boggy and 'bristling with salsolaceous vegetation familiar to the Arab voyager' before turning inland into 'the Ghauts, that threshold of the Aethopian highlands'.

Burton soon spotted along the way at Jiyaf 'a really pretty face'. In spite of the inevitable speculations biographers have made about Burton's sexuality, fuelled by his interest in erotic Arab literature, and by a famous overblown reference by his friend, the poet Swinburne, to 'that lost love of Burton's, the beloved and blue object of his Central African affections, whose caudal charms and simious seductions were too strong for the narrow laws of Levitical or Mosaic prudery which would confine the jewel of man to the lotus of a merely human female by the most odious and unnatural of priestly restrictions', Burton's literary persona at any rate projected a red-blooded heterosexual male wholly unreconstructed. He was plainly smitten with this Ethiopian beauty: 'Her skin was a warm, rich nut-brown, an especial charm in these regions, and her movements had that grace which suggests perfect symmetry of limb . . . As a tribute to her prettiness I gave her some cloth, tobacco, and a bit of salt, which was rapidly becoming valuable: her husband stood by, and although the preference was marked, he displayed neither anger nor jealousy.'

The journey, however, insisted that Burton abandon her and, towards the end of December, he started to cross the Marar Prairie for the final stretch to Harar, joining a caravan of 'four or five half-starved camels' and about fifty donkeys. His health was not good, probably as a result of drinking the impure water of the coast, the dry season yielding little in the way of fresh water. On 3 January 1855 he arrived at Harar, where he was made to wait half an hour at the gate of the city, then, after being admitted, there was a further wait underneath a tree before his party were told to remove their shoes and go into the presence of the Amir 'or, as he styles himself, the Sultan Ahmed bin Sultan Abibakr'.

The Amir presided in a dark room with whitewashed walls: 'His appearance was that of a little Indian Rajah, an etiolated youth twenty-four or twenty-five years old, plain and thin-bearded, with a yellow complexion, wrinkled brows and protruding eyes. His dress was a flowing robe of crimson cloth, edged with snowy fur, and a narrow white turban tightly twisted round a tall conical cap of red velvet, like the old Turkish headgear of our painters.' Burton greeted the Amir (but declined to kiss his hand) and, when asked his business, he handed over a letter (probably composed by himself), which was put to one side. Burton then took the decision, in spite of all the pains he had taken to perfect a disguise, to come out as an Englishman, judging it safer in the circumstances than being taken for a Turk. He told the Amir, in fluent Arabic, that he had come from Aden bearing the British Governor's compliments 'and that we had entered Harar to see the light of H.H.'s countenance'. Fortunately for Burton, the Amir accepted the compliments and smiled graciously. He was offered accommodation in the Amir's second palace and introduced to his Wazir, who was also informed by Burton that it was the wish of the British to re-establish friendly relations and commercial intercourse with Harar. Burton then returned home: 'worn out by fatigue and profoundly impressed with the *poésie* of our position. I was under the roof of a bigoted prince whose least word was death; amongst a people who detest foreigners; the only European that had ever passed over their inhospitable threshold, and the fated instrument of their future downfall.'

Burton's subsequent stay in Harar was short. The air, he said, reminded him of Tuscany and the peculiar dialect of the eight thousand inhabitants was 'unintelligible to any save the citizens'. The appearance of these citizens was 'highly unprepossessing'. He claimed not to have seen a single handsome face among the men: 'their features are coarse and debauched; many of them squint, others have lost an eye by small-pox, and they are disfigured by scrofula and other diseases'. In these circumstances the women 'appear beautiful by contrast with their lords' but 'the female voice is harsh and screaming, especially when heard after the delicate organs of the Somal'. Moreover: 'They are extremely bigoted, especially against Christians.' After making some ethnological and historical observations even Burton could not pad out his account much further and, after ten days, he was allowed to leave on Saturday 13 June.

Rising before dawn, he found his poor health suddenly vanished: 'So potent a drug is joy!' He made his way through 'uniform and uninteresting scenery' back to the coast, where, on 5 February, he caught a ramshackle craft along the coast to Berbera and there met his fellow officers, including Speke, whose mission had not been a success. The sense – shared by Burton's readers – that the trip was an anticlimax depressed the traveller. It had turned out to be a pale shadow of his Meccan adventure.

## 28

*Heathenism: Livingstone's Missionary Travels*

The most famous of all Victorian travellers – his fame not unrelated to the apocryphal jungle greeting of Henry Morton Stanley: 'Dr Livingstone, I presume?' that fuelled a thousand jokes and cartoon sketches – David Livingstone formerly enjoyed a reputation that today looks increasingly uncertain. This is not a matter of hostile debunking, rather a matter of a calm assessment of what he actually achieved in relation to his self-proclaimed goals. Livingstone was a missionary and this gave him an off-the-peg sense of high moral purpose not even sought by an easygoing traveller like Mansfield Parkyns. He demanded to be taken seriously and at his own estimation, with the result that questions are inevitable.

Livingstone's biographer Tim Jeal has pointed out that he 'failed in conventional missionary terms, making but a single convert, a chief, who subsequently lapsed', that the two missions that went to Africa at his behest 'ended in fiasco and heavy loss of life largely through his own fault', that 'a series of geographical miscalculations destroyed his government-sponsored Zambezi expedition' and that 'another series of errors in basic mapping and calculating, on his last journey, made him suppose himself on the upper Nile when he was in fact on the upper Congo'. In addition his wife became an alcoholic after spending years alone and 'his eldest son distanced himself from his father to the extent of changing his surname'. Yet, in spite of this catalogue of failures and character defects, Jeal insists: 'Livingstone remained a very great man whose overall achievement was unique.'

Whether or not one can go as far as this, his name is certainly pivotal in the history of European exploration of Africa. And a man cannot fairly be penalized merely for being humourless. Livingstone's first book, *Missionary Travels and Researches in South Africa* (1857), should more accurately have been entitled *Trade Promotion Travels*, for it was as much about opening up the continent to trade as saving souls – though Livingstone saw these as two sides of the same coin. Praising in his Preface the Astronomer Royal at the Cape, Thomas Maclear, for being one of those who rendered 'the pathway of the world safe to mariners, and the dark places of the earth open to Christians', Livingstone claimed that most of his book was taken up with

> a detail of the efforts made to open up a new field north of the Bechuana country to the sympathies of Christendom. The prospects there disclosed are fairer than I anticipated, and the capabilities of the new region lead me to hope, that, by the production of the raw materials of our manufactures, African and English interests will become more closely linked than heretofore – that both countries will be eventually benefited – and that the cause of freedom throughout the world will in some measure be promoted.

This ambitious prospectus immediately marked Livingstone out from the run of travellers and explorers, whose goals varied from the merely hedonistic to the diligently scientific but were generally working on a more specifically defined canvas.

Another distinctive feature of Livingstone's first book was its placing of the hero centre stage. Most of the travellers we have encountered so far introduced their personal histories into the narrative only fitfully, preferring the isolated comic or self-deprecatory fragment, the sporadically anecdotal or the ebullient Burtonian smoke-screen persona to extended passages of autobiography. What we learn about them from their travel narratives is largely *en passant.* Livingstone, by contrast, began his book with a long – and undoubtedly fascinating – 'personal sketch' of his own life and origins. Readers were being given the measure of the heroic figure who had come before them: 'Our great-grandfather fell at the battle of Culloden, fighting for the old line of kings,' the reader learns on the first page. In fact the Livingstones were displaced crofters driven to work in Glasgow's cotton mills, the explorer's grandfather having settled at Blantyre on the Clyde, eight miles from Glasgow. They were intensely religious people of a nonconformist cast and Livingstone's father, Neil, an itinerant tea salesman, teetotaller and distributor of tracts, eventually returned to the mill. David was born in Blantyre in a one-room tenement in Shuttle Row owned by the Blantyre Works. His true heroism lay in overcoming his crushing early poverty and managing, against all the odds, to educate himself.

At the age of ten he went to work in the mill as a 'piecer', responsible for repairing broken threads on the machines, and worked from six in the morning, 'with intervals for breakfast and dinner', till eight at night, six days a week. In spite of his exhaustion he attended an evening school, whose teacher was subsidized by the mill, from eight until ten at night, and with his first week's wages bought Ruddiman's *Rudiments of Latin.* He taught himself to read and write and continued to study at home until midnight or later 'if my mother did not interfere by snatching the books out of my hands'. Livingstone read everything he could get his hands on except novels. 'Scientific works and books of travel were my especial delight.' Neil Livingstone strongly disapproved of science as 'inimical to religion' and his son rebelled openly when forced to read William Wilberforce's *Practical Christianity*.

Although he professed to dislike religious reading, Livingstone was nonetheless deeply religious and progressed from an inherited strict Calvinism of the elect to a more forgiving version which allowed for salvation through good works. Once he had seen the light:

> The change was like what it may be supposed would take place were it possible to cure a case of 'colour blindness'. The fullness with which the pardon of all our guilt is offered in God's book drew forth feelings of affectionate love to Him who bought us with His blood, which in some measure has influenced my conduct ever since . . . In the glow of love which Christianity inspires, I soon resolved to devote my life to the alleviation of human misery. I felt that to be a pioneer of Christianity in China might lead to the material benefit of some portions of that immense empire; and therefore set myself to obtain a medical education, in order to be qualified for that enterprise.

To this end he went out with his brothers into the Lanarkshire countryside with *Culpeper's Herbal* in his hand, on rare moments of leisure, but most of his learning was achieved against the seemingly impossible obstacle of factory life: 'My reading in the factory was carried on by placing the book on a portion of the spinning jenny, so that I could catch sentence after sentence as I passed at my work; I thus kept up a pretty constant study undisturbed by the roar of machinery. To this part of my education I owe my power of completely abstracting my mind from surrounding noises, so as to read and write with perfect comfort amidst the play of children or the dancing and songs of savages.'

At the age of nineteen Livingstone was promoted to cotton spinner, which was hard work for one of slender build but it paid better and he was able to support himself while attending medical and

Greek classes in Glasgow during the winter and divinity lectures in the summer. As with many self-made men, there was a flinty self-satisfaction about those early trials which had robbed him of any boyish and adolescent joy and which made him in later life hard and opinionated. He claimed that he wouldn't have wanted anything other than this 'hardy training' and boasted: 'I never received a farthing from anyone.' He admired the sterling qualities of the Scottish poor and their interest in 'public questions' but he reassured his readers that education had not turned them into dangerous radicals and that they had a proper respect for the gentry: 'The mass of the working people of Scotland have read history, and are no levellers . . . While foreigners imagine that we want the spirit to overturn aristocracy, we in truth hate those stupid revolutions which sweep away time-honoured institutions, dear alike to rich and poor.'

Eventually, through working part-time at the mill, Livingstone managed to complete his medical studies, at Anderson's College, Glasgow, with all the inadequacies of medical knowledge at that time, and planned to go to China as it seemed a great field for the missionary. Greatly influenced by the work of medical missionaries, Livingstone was drawn to apply to the London Missionary Society (LMS), 'but it was not without a pang that I offered myself,' he noted characteristically, 'for it was not agreeable to one accustomed to work his own way to become in a measure dependent on others'. In fact he became very dependent because the LMS kept him waiting interminably. The terms in which he expressed his desire for China were significant: 'I felt that to be a pioneer of Christianity in China might lead to the material benefit of some portions of that immense empire; and therefore set myself to obtain a medical education, in order to be qualified for that enterprise.' But, unfortunately for Livingstone, China was just then being drawn into the Opium Wars and it became out of the question.

After a year spent studying theology and classics at the hands of a clergyman at Chipping Ongar in Essex, and further medical training in London, Livingstone was growing impatient to get into the field. He took his final medical examinations in Glasgow in 1840, becoming a Licentiate of the Faculty of Physicians and Surgeons in November, and was ordained in the same month in the Congregationalist Albion Chapel in London. The Society initially wanted to send Livingstone to the West Indies but he preferred South Africa, especially after meeting a well-known missionary, Robert Moffatt, while Moffatt was on leave in London from the LMS station at Kuruman, north of the Orange River. On 8 December 1840 Livingstone sailed to South Africa via Rio de Janeiro, where he had to put in because of gales, arriving at Cape Town three months later on 15 March 1841. After three weeks in Cape Town, where he learned about some rather un-Christian rivalries between missionaries, he set off for Algoa Bay, then travelled inland northwards by ox cart to the Kuruman mission station in the Bechuana country, seven hundred miles from Cape Town.

Kuruman was something of a disappointment to Livingstone. Much had been reported of it but in actuality it was a small place and progress in converting the heathen had been vestigial. Established thirty years previously by Moffatt, the station was a pleasant oasis of gardens growing European vegetables and fruit trees. It was beautiful but it was also emphatically not indigenous: 'The pleasantness of the place is enhanced by the contrast it presents to the surrounding scenery, and the fact that it owes all its beauty to the manual labour of the missionaries.' It was also in a troubled place where the Boer farmers were hostile to the missionaries.

Livingstone was to spend sixteen years from 1840 to 1856 'in medical and missionary labours in Africa' and had so much to do at certain times that he claimed to have less time than when he had been a cotton spinner: 'The want of time for self-improvement was the only regret I experienced during my African career.' Always anxious to make his own way, in a famous phrase he declared: 'I would never build on another man's foundation. I shall preach the gospel beyond every other man's line of things.'

He wanted to push farther north from Kuruman into more promising territory. But his first five years were involved mostly in what he called 'preparatory labours', including a six-month stint at Lepelolé, where he taught himself the native language 'and gained by this ordeal an insight into the habits, ways of thinking, laws, and language of the Bakwains, which has proved of incalculable advantage in my intercourse with them ever since'. Livingstone began by showing some real understanding of the local tribal people and realized that much of what the missionaries sought to do was in direct conflict with the cherished values and way of life of the native population.

At the end of 1843 Moffatt and his family returned to Kuruman, prompting Livingstone to persuade the LMS to send him north. He established a new mission station at Mabotsa and married Moffatt's elder daughter, Mary, who had been born in South Africa and who, as Livingstone put it, 'endured more than some who have written large books of travels'. Helping the local people to fight off marauding lions, Livingstone was involved in an incident recorded in an engraving in his book. He fired at one of the lions, which fell apparently dead but it revived and sprang on him: 'He caught me by the shoulder, and we both came to the ground together. Growling horribly, he shook me as a terrier does a rat. The shock produced a stupor similar to that which seems to be felt by a mouse after the first gripe of the cat. It caused a dreaminess, in which there was no sense of pain nor feeling of terror, though I was quite conscious of all that was happening.' After his rescue he found eleven teeth marks on his right upper arm, which suppurated and which, together with the splintered left arm, hampered, but did not deter, him in the active work ahead.

Between 1845 and 1859 Livingstone worked at Chonuane and then Kolobeng, aided only by his wife and two native teachers. It was a hard life, with water shortages and little material comfort. Livingstone became very skilled at a range of practical tasks and his wife learned how to make soap so that they were a typical missionary family in Central Africa: 'the husband to be a jack-of-all-trades without doors, and the wife a maid-of-all-work within'. As regards missionary advance, however, progress remained slow. The local people, desperate for rain, had noticed a certain connection 'between the presence of "God's Word" in their town and these successive droughts, they looked with no good will at the church-bell'. Worse still, the tribes who did not gather to pray with the missionaries were observed to receive the rain denied to the would-be faithful.

All this persuaded Livingstone that the field of missionary endeavour needed to be widened. This theme had been with him since he attended a meeting in London in 1840 at Exeter Hall organized by the Society for the Extinction of the Slave Trade and for the Civilization of Africa at which the speaker, Thomas Fowell Buxton (rather better known for instigating the disastrous Niger Expedition, launched at the same meeting), had said that the only way to defeat the slave trade was for Africans to develop their own produce. Promoting commerce would end mental isolation and foster a sense of social mutuality between the tribes:

> Sending the Gospel to the heathen must include much more than is implied in the usual picture of a missionary, which is that of a man going about with a Bible under his arm ... By commerce we may not only put a stop to the slave-trade, but introduce the negro family into the body corporate of nations, no one member of which can suffer without the others suffering with it ... Neither civilization nor Christianity can be promoted alone. In fact, they are inseparable.

Such enlightened ideas were not shared by the Boers, who continued to practise slavery, telling Livingstone, with breathtaking racial arrogance, that the indigenous people were forced to work for them 'in consideration of allowing them to live in our country'. The Boers, Livingstone believed, had become 'as degraded as the black, whom the stupid prejudice against colour leads them to detest'. He also pointed out that the native population had 'never engaged in offensive war with Europeans', ideas which resulted in attacks on the station by Boers who destroyed his library and smashed his stock of medicines.

Exploration was much more satisfying than missionary work, and Livingstone claimed to have discovered, during a trip with William Cotton Oswell and a man called Murray in July 1849, Lake Ngami: 'for the first time this sheet of water was beheld by Europeans'. This brought Livingstone a prize of twenty-five guineas from the RGS, his report not leading them to realize it had been a joint endeavour. It was actually the River Botletle that interested Livingstone more, tantalized as he was by the great prize of European travel in nineteenth-century Africa: the penetration of the 'interior'.

He made several subsequent trips, one with his wife and children and the chief Sechele, his sole convert, in search of the elusive river route to the east coast. He met the Kololo chief, Sebituane, 'of a tall and wiry form, an olive or coffee-and-milk complexion, and slightly bald', whose son succeeded him as chief and gave Livingstone and Oswell 'perfect liberty' to travel north, where they 'discovered' the Zambezi on 4 August 1851, a river 'not previously known to exist'. As the first white men ever seen in the region, 'we were visited by prodigious numbers'.

It became increasingly clear to Livingstone that the aggressive Boers would continue to frustrate missionary activity at Kolobeng, where his family was also prone to disease, so he sent them back to England 'while I returned to explore the country in search of a healthy district that might prove a centre of civilization, and open up the interior by a path to either the east or west coast'.

At the start of June 1852, having seen off his family, Livingstone set off in the direction of Quelimane in East Africa: 'I proceeded in the usual conveyance of the country, the heavy lumbering Cape waggon drawn by ten oxen, and was accompanied by two Christian Bechuanas from Kuruman – than whom I never saw better servants – by two Bakwain men, and two young girls, who, having come as nurses with our children to the Cape, were returning to their home at Kolobeng.' In fact he was detained at Kuruman by a broken wheel and the plan to go north was abandoned as unsafe because of conflict between the Boers and the Bakwains and it was not until November 1853 that he managed to organize another trip up the Zambezi to Luanda.

Livingstone's early tolerance of African diversity began to evaporate during these travels and he found the Bakalahari, for example, sunk in 'degradation' from 'centuries of barbarism and the hard struggle for the necessaries of life'. He recorded that they burst into laughter at the spectacle of missionaries kneeling in prayer: 'Nearly all their thoughts are directed to the supply of their bodily wants.' Livingstone, by contrast, drew attention to his higher moral tone: 'During the eleven years I had been in the country, though we always made present to the chiefs whom we visited, I invariably refused to take donations of ivory in return, from an idea that a religious instructor degraded himself by accepting gifts from those whose spiritual welfare he professed to seek.' He actually had an annual salary of only £100, which barely allowed him to feed and clothe his family, so it was fortunate that money had no value in these regions and barter was the usual way.

When he fell ill in May 1853 he was subjected to a native remedy which involved being put in a steam bath 'and smoked like a red herring over green twigs' but he felt that stern moral fibre was a better medicine: 'He who is low-spirited will die sooner than the man who is not of a melancholic nature.' More practical help came from his association with Sekeletu, son and successor of the chief, Sebituane, who helped him furnish another expedition up the Zambezi at the end of 1853, reaching the River Kwango eventually on 4 April 1854, ostensibly to find a site for a missionary settlement but really in search of east–west trade routes.

On the previous trip Livingstone's tolerance had again been under strain: 'During a nine weeks' tour I had been in closer contact with heathens than I had ever been before; yet to endure the dancing, roaring, and singing, the jesting, grumbling, quarrelling, and murderings of these children of nature, was the severest penance I had yet undergone in the course of my missionary duties. I thence derived a more intense disgust of paganism than I had hitherto felt, and formed a greatly elevated opinion of the effects of missions in the south, among tribes which are reported to have been as savage as the Makololo.' But the Makololo had wanted to trade with the coast and he was convinced that 'no permanent elevation of a people can be effected without commerce'.

On the new journey Livingstone was weakened by fever at the outset: 'But I had always believed that, if we serve God at all, it ought to be done in a manly way, and I was determined to "succeed or perish" in the attempt to open up this part of Africa.' He had twenty-seven men, three muskets, a double-barrelled, smooth-bore rifle for himself, twenty pounds of beads, a few biscuits, a few pounds of tea and sugar and twenty pounds of coffee:

> One small tin canister, about fifteen inches square, was filled with spare shirts, trowsers, and shoes, to be used when we reached civilised life; another of the same size was stored with medicines; a third with books; and a fourth box contained a magic lantern which we found of much service. The sextant and other instruments were carried apart. A bag contained the clothes we expected to wear out in the journey, which, with a small gipsy tent, just sufficient to sleep in, a sheepskin mantle as a blanket, and a horse-rug as a bed, completed my equipment. I had always found that the art of successful travel consisted in taking as few 'impedimenta' as possible.

Along the way, Livingstone found time to preach, sometimes attracting crowds of up to six hundred under the outspreading camel-thorn tree, and the magic lantern went down very well as a means of popular instruction but by the end of 1853 'a feeling of want wakened in my soul' at the difficulty of converting any of these people permanently. By early April 1854 Livingstone had reached Cassange, the farthest inland station of the Portuguese in West Africa, 'in a somewhat forlorn state as to clothing'. His fellow Europeans fed him and lodged him but they were suspicious: 'They evidently looked upon me as an agent of the English Government, engaged in some new movement for the suppression of slavery.

They could not divine what a "missionario" had to do with observations of latitude and longitude.'

On 31 May Livingstone arrived at Luanda and welcomed the hospitality of Edmund Gabriel, the local British commissioner for the suppression of the slave trade: 'Never shall I forget the luxuriant pleasure I enjoyed in feeling myself again on a good English couch, after six months' sleeping on the ground.' He was not well, however, and he did not move on from Luanda until September, when he set off for the return journey. On the way he crossed the River Lotembawa and saw the watershed at Lake Dilolo: 'I now for the first time apprehended the true form of the river systems and continent . . . I was now standing on the central ridge that divided these two systems [Congo and Zambezi] . . . I was not then aware that anyone else had discovered the elevated trough form of the centre of Africa.' He also offered medical help and while removing on one occasion the tumour on the forearm of a young woman one of the small arteries squirted some blood in his eye and she said: 'You were a friend before, now you are a blood-relation; whenever you pass this way, send me word, that I may cook for you.' It was one of those rare human touches in Livingstone's narrative.

Eventually, after nearly a year, Livingstone arrived back at Linyanti, where Sekeletu was so impressed that he helped him to fit out another expedition, which set off for the Zambezi in November, his aim being to find a water route now to the east coast and to sell the chief's ivory, proceeding along the north bank of the Zambezi on 3 November, when the cooling rains finally began. There was in fact a terrible thunderstorm which left Livingstone ill-prepared in the cold, damp night. Sekeletu offered him his blanket, leaving himself uncovered. The missionary was impressed and made the remarkable comment: 'I was much affected by this little act of genuine kindness. If such men must perish by the advance of civilization, as certain races of animals do before others, it is a pity. God grant that ere this time comes they may receive that gospel which is a solace for the soul in death!'

After Sesheke the expedition came to the giant waterfalls of

Mosi-oa-Tunya, known locally as, in Livingstone's translation, 'the waters that thunder' or 'smoke sounds there': 'Being persuaded that Mr Oswell and myself were the very first Europeans who ever visited the Zambesi in the heart of the country, I decided to use the same liberty as the Makololo had done, and named them the "Falls of Victoria" – the only English name I have affixed to any part of the country.' Livingstone was overwhelmed by the beauty of the falls even though nothing was visible except a dense white cloud 'which, at the time we visited the spot, had two bright rainbows on it'. The Makololo worshipped their deity here but 'not aware of His true character, they had no admiration of the beautiful and good in their bosoms'. The next day Livingstone returned and planted some peach and apricot stones and coffee seeds brought with him from the west coast. When the garden was thus prepared he cut his initials on a tree and added the date, 1855: 'This was the only instance in which I indulged this piece of vanity.'

On 20 November Sekeletu left Livingstone with over a hundred men to take his ivory tusks to the coast and the latter pressed on to reach the Portuguese settlement at Tete at the start of March. The Commandant of the Portuguese fort at Tete 'did everything in his power to restore my emaciated condition' and, after resting for a couple of weeks, Livingstone left Tete on 22 March and reached the port of Quelimane on 20 May 1856, 'very nearly four years since I started from Cape Town'. He had not heard from his family for three years (they were surviving in England largely from handouts from the LMS), their letters having with one exception failed to reach him. He waited six weeks at this 'unhealthy spot' until HMS *Frolic* arrived and offered him a passage to Mauritius, leaving in rough seas. After recovering on Mauritius from an enlarged spleen, Livingstone came up the Red Sea in November, then embarked on the P&O steamer *Candia* for home, arriving at Southampton on 12 December 1856, after eleven years away, 'once more in dear old England'.

Intending to stay only a month or two, Livingstone was immediately sucked into the RGS celebrity machine, awarded its annual gold medal at a special meeting three days after his arrival and offered a reception the next day chaired by Lord Shaftesbury. In addition a book deal was done with John Murray on the recommendation of Sir Roderick Murchison, President of the RGS, who also persuaded the Foreign Secretary, Lord Clarendon, to employ Livingstone as a consul in Central Africa. Meanwhile there were speaking tours and appearances throughout 1857 and the publication of his book cemented his fame, the first edition of 12,000 being sold out even before publication. The £100-a-year missionary earned £8500 from the book, its story of early hardship earning the admiration of Dickens. By the beginning of 1858 Livingstone was an established national hero and elected a Fellow of the Royal Society. In February he had an audience with Queen Victoria. Money was raised by public subscription to enable more heroic African journeys to be undertaken (£2000 was raised in Glasgow alone) and Parliament approved a grant of £5000 in December.

The expedition was to assess the prospects for trade up the Zambezi and the only conceivable leader was Livingstone.

Head Dresses of Wanyamwezı.

## 29

## *Lake Regions: Richard Burton in Central Africa*

After his brief pilgrimage to Harar, Richard Burton did what distinguished Victorian travellers normally did on return to London: he read a paper on his travels to the Royal Geographical Society on 11 June 1855 and subsequently, like Livingstone, received the Society's gold medal. The British public, however, was more interested at that time in the Crimean War. Burton volunteered for service in Constantinople but returned four months later having seen little action. Back in London he set himself the task of relaunching his plan to explore the source of the Nile – one of the great and enduring themes of Victorian exploration. He decided, accurately, that the great river flowed out of those Central African lakes which no European had yet seen and the existence of which was not even certain. The expedition was backed by the Expeditionary Committee of the RGS and the Foreign Office granted a sum of £1000. Burton's employers, the East India Company, gave him two years' paid leave to undertake it. As the expedition's leader, Burton invited his friend John Speke to join him and the two men sailed for Zanzibar, arriving on 20 December 1856.

With his customary bluster, Burton introduced his account of the expedition, *The Lake Regions of Central Africa* (1860), subtitled *A Picture of Exploration*, with the confession that he had wanted to mix his serious geographical and ethnological content with 'a narrative of occurrences and an exposition of the more popular and picturesque points of view which their subject offers'. On being informed of this plan his publisher, Longman, was unhappy with Burton's wish to write an exclusively 'light work', as he put it – a rare case of an author being persuaded *not* to dumb down a little. In a revealing insight into the growing seriousness of the Victorian readership of travel narratives, Longman decided that 'the public appetite required the addition of stronger meat'. Burton announced that he had complied: 'I have drawn two portraits of the same object, and mingled the gay with the graver details of travel, so as to produce an antipathetic cento.' But the bit was still between his teeth and, with an allusion to the RGS guide for serious travellers discussed above, he declared:

> Modern 'hints to travellers' direct the explorer and missionary to eschew theory and opinion. We are told somewhat peremptorily that it is our duty to gather actualities not inferences – to see and not to think, in fact, to confine ourselves to transmitting the rough material collected by us, that it may be worked into shape by the professionally learned at home. But why may not the observer be allowed a voice concerning his own observations, if at least his mind be sane and his stock of collateral knowledge be respectable?

It seems a fair point. Burton was well aware of the inevitable sub-
jectivity of travel writing: 'I have not attempted to avoid intruding
matters of a private and personal nature upon the reader; it would
have been impossible to avoid egotism in a purely egotistical narrative.' He should perhaps have left it there but in his Preface he
insisted, in his robust, pugnacious style, on taking a swipe at his colleague, Speke, with whom he had seriously fallen out on this trip. It
was partly a matter of rivalry, namely that Speke was taking too
much credit for what had been discovered, and also the contempt of
a proficient linguist for the inability of his colleague, as he saw it, to
understand sometimes what was being told to him through the
mediation of interpreters.

After his Harar episode Burton had returned to Berbera in April
1855 to join Speke and others in a march inland to seek the source
of the White Nile but, encamped outside the town, they had been
attacked and one of the party had been killed. 'The enemy
swarmed like hornets,' Burton wrote in an earlier account, 'with
shouts and screams intending to terrify, and proving that overwhelming odds were against us: it was by no means easy to avoid
in the shades of night the jabbing of javelins, and the long heavy
daggers thrown at our legs from under and through the opening of
the tent.' Speke was seriously wounded in the attack but Burton
was now 'indignant' at Speke's claiming of credit for the latest discoveries. He used his Preface to demolish his former friend: 'I
could not expect much from his assistance; he was not a linguist –
French and Arabic being equally unknown to him – nor a man of
science nor an accurate astronomical observer ... During the
exploration he acted in a subordinate capacity; and as may be
imagined amongst a party of Arabs, Baloch and Africans, whose
languages he ignored, he was unfit for any other but a subordinate
capacity.'

Perhaps as a way of justifying this extraordinary public attack,
Burton concluded by making a declaration of his travel-writing
principles, a warts-and-all ethic which he believed guaranteed
authenticity. There is no reason to think he was being disingenuous

but the modern reader will be aware both that Burton will have suppressed much to suit Victorian taste and that his own personality, for all its vivacious surface loquacity, was concealed and oblique. We do not really know him:

> It has been my duty to draw a Dutch picture, a cabaret-piece which could not be stripped of its ordonnance, its boors, its pipes, and its pots. I have shirked nothing of the unpleasant task, – of recording processes and not only results; I have entered into the recitals of the maladies, the weary squabbles, and the vast variety of petty troubles, without which the *coup d'oeil* of African adventure would be more like a Greek Saint in effigy – all lights and no shade – than the chapter of accidents which it now is.

The book, it must be said, also contains Burton's usual copious and shapeless cascade of information. After all these grand preliminaries, the actual narrative of Burton's search for the great lakes is in one sense a disappointment. They 'discovered' Lake Tanganyika, of course, and Lake Victoria (this Speke found on his own and pronounced, correctly as it turned out but hardly at the time with convincing verification, to be the source of the Nile), but from Burton's point of view this very long two-volume narrative describes in effect a journey to a lake where he fails actually to see the thing for which he went.

Burton and Speke left England in September 1856 and on 2 December they sailed from Bombay to Zanzibar Island. After a preliminary attempt in early January they set off again for Zanzibar on 16 June 1857 on the eighteen-gun, teak-built corvette *Artémise*, bidding farewell to Bombay's harbour's 'whitewashed mosques and houses of the Arabs, the cadjan-huts, the cocoa-grown coasts, and the ruddy hills striped with long lines of clove'. On board were the members of the expedition: Burton and Speke, two half-caste Goanese, two 'Negro gun-carriers', an Indian guide called Mubarak Mombai and his brother Muinyi Mabruki, and eight Baloch mercenary guards. Burton's idea of the mission was 'to form an expedition primarily for the purpose of ascertaining the limits of the "Sea of Ujiji, or Unyamwezi Lake", and secondarily, to determine the exportable produce of the interior, and the ethnography of its tribes'. He added sardonically: 'In these days every explorer of Central Africa is supposed to have set out in quest of the coy sources of the White Nile, and when he returns without them, his exploration, whatever may have been its value, is determined to be a failure.'

The excitement of finding himself on new ground once the expedition reached the mainland at Kaole, and the peculiarity of the scenery diverted Burton's 'melancholy forebodings'. He was principally interested, as always, in ethnography and customs and manners, finding the actual landscape rather monotonous ('the rocks and trees resemble one another'). In a rather sweeping dismissal of this part of Africa he announced:

> Eastern and central inter-tropical Africa also lacks antiquarian and historic interest, it has few traditions, no annals, and no ruins, the hoary remains of past splendour so dear to the traveller and to the reader of travels. It contains not a single useful or ornamental work, a canal or a dam is, and has ever been, beyond the narrow bounds of its civilisation. It wants even the scenes of barbaric pomp and savage grandeur with which the student of occidental Africa is familiar. But its ethnography has novelties: it exposes strange manners and customs, its Fetichism is in itself a wonder, its commerce deserves attention, and its social state is full of mournful interest.

And, in the way he showed himself dazzled by the white man's beads: 'The African preserves the instincts of infancy in the higher races.' This was hardly the open mind of a scientific, unprejudiced observer.

On 7 August the expedition left Zungonmero, heading east for the Usagara Mountains with a massive party of one hundred bearers for what was intended to be a two-year expedition. They encountered the usual sweaty hardships and troubles from porters, one of whom deserted with some valuable equipment (later recovered). 'The African traveller's fitness for the task of exploration,' Burton reflected, 'depends more upon his faculty of chafing under delays and kicking against the pricks, than upon his power of displaying the patience of a Griselda or a Job.' After 134 days of marching over six hundred miles they reached 'Kazeh, the principal Bandari of Eastern Unyamwezi, and the capital village of the Omani merchants' – Tabora in present-day Tanzania.

They next crossed the River Malagarazi and journeyed on for the rest of the year, conscious in many places that Livingstone had preceded them, until, on 13 February 1858, they glimpsed Lake Tanganyika at Ujiji: 'the whole scene suddenly burst upon my view, filling me with admiration, wonder, and delight'. It must have been a remarkable moment but, in spite of quoting Dante, Burton's powers of description, in common with those of most other African explorers, were not up to it. Generalized rapture took the place of vivid, particular detail: 'Nothing, in sooth, could be more picturesque than this first view of the Tanganyika Lake, as it lay in the lap of the mountains, basking in the gorgeous tropical sunshine.' Stale epithets follow, among them: 'snowy foam', 'ribbon of glistening yellow sand' and 'pearly mist'. But it was a welcome contrast with the 'silent and spectral mangrove-creeks' of the East African seaboard and the 'melancholy, monotonous experience of desert and jungle scenery, tawny rock and sun-parched plain or rank herbage and flats of black mire'. After all these months: 'Forgetting toils, dangers, and the doubt-fulness of return, I felt willing to endure double what I had endured.'

What Burton had to endure in the Lake Regions was extreme humidity which destroyed books and rendered writing illegible from stains and black mildew. The cold, damp climate was not good for his health or Speke's: 'All energy seemed to have abandoned us. I lay for a fortnight upon the earth, too blind to read or write, except with long intervals, too weak to ride, and too ill to converse.' Partly as a result of this poor health, they returned to Tabora on 26 May after having explored by canoe the northern part of the lake. Burton had been suffering from ulceration of the tongue which prevented him speaking to the local people and effectively halted any further inquiries: 'It is characteristic of African travel that the explorer may be arrested at the very bourne of his journey, on the very threshold of success, by a single stage, as effectually as if all the waves of the Atlantic or the sands of Arabia lay between.'

After the last spectacle of sunrise over Lake Tanganyika the return journey by the northerly route was dull and they arrived back on 20 June, having covered 265 miles in twenty-six days. Burton was not up to travelling and devoted his time to preparations and to ethnological study, in particular collecting 'specimens of the multitudinous dialects into which the great South African family here divides itself'. On 10 July he let Speke set off on his own to ascertain the truth of a rumoured large lake to the north. When Speke returned on 25 August Burton received a shock: 'We had scarcely, however, breakfasted before he announced to me the startling fact, that he had discovered the sources of the White Nile.' It was Lake Nyanza or Lake Victoria, the true source of the Nile as it turned out, but Burton remained sceptical: 'The fortunate discoverer's conviction was strong; his reasons were weak . . . and probably his sources of the Nile grew in his mind as his Mountains of the Moon had grown under his hand.' Burton was convinced that Speke's total ignorance of Arabic was responsible for misunderstandings: 'there is not a shade of proof *pro* . . . What tended at the time to make me the more sceptical was the substantial incorrectness of the geographical and other details brought back by my companion. This was natural enough [because of the need to translate through several different languages]. During such a journey to and fro words must be liable to severe accidents.' Although he agreed not to discuss it any further,

Speke was determined to claim credit as the man who discovered the source of the Nile. It was to develop into a major controversy, fanned in part by those who enjoyed the spectacle. In the short term, Speke now fell ill and Burton had to look after him on the return journey to the coast.

On the way there was plenty of opportunity for Burton to do what he liked best: expound racial generalizations. 'The East African is, like other barbarians, a strange mixture of good and evil,' he noted:

> As a rule, the civilised or highest type of man owns the sway of intellect, of reason; the semi-civilised – as are still the great nations of the East – are guided by sentiment and propensity in a degree incomprehensible to more advanced races; and the barbarian is the slave of impulse, passion and instinct, faintly modified by sentiment, but ignorant of intellectual discipline . . . He partakes largely of the worst characteristics of the lower Oriental types – stagnation of mind, indolence of body, moral deficiency, superstition, and childish passion . . . In dealing with the East African the traveller cannot do better than to follow the advice of Bacon – 'Use savages justly and graciously, with sufficient guard nevertheless.' They must be held as foes; and the prudent stranger will never put himself in their power, especially where life is concerned.

There was a great deal more in the same vein.

On 3 February 1859 Burton and Speke reached the coast and sailed to Zanzibar Island: 'The excitement of travel was succeeded by an utter depression of mind and body: even the labour of talking was too great, and I took refuge from society in a course of French novel *à vingt sous la pièce.*' Unwilling to leave while so much remained to be done, Burton was nevertheless forced to return on a clipper-built ship, the *Dragon of Salem,* to Aden, 'the coal-hole of the East', and on medical advice he started the return journey to England.

When Burton finally arrived in London, on 21 May 1859, he found that Speke, who had preceded him, had already given a paper to the RGS claiming most of the credit for the discovery, and proposing another expedition to Africa. Speke received lavish funding for this and set off with Captain James Augustus Grant to consolidate his reputation at Burton's expense.

## 30

### *A Sportsman: William Baldwin the Hunter*

Killing animals and birds was an important activity for the Victorian traveller, especially in Africa, though from time to time even a macho figure like Richard Burton would protest at the folly of killing just for sport rather than to provide food. One of the most dedicated African hunters was the Lancastrian William Charles Baldwin (1827–1903), about whom little is known except that he went on seven major hunting expeditions, the last one covering two thousand miles. He arrived in Natal at the end of 1851 stimulated to hunt big game by the stirring tales of hunting adventures written by Constance Gordon-Cumming, who had mounted an exhibition in London not long before. Baldwin was longing to meet the legendary animal killer 'Elephant White'. Baldwin's book *African Hunting* (1863) was derived from notes scribbled in the field: 'sometimes in ink, but often in pencil, gunpowder, tea, &c., in Kaffir kraals or wagon bottoms'.

In so far as he was aware of his own motives Baldwin claimed that 'the love of sport, dogs and horses was innate in me'. At the age of six he had joined the local harriers, mounted on a pony, and after leaving school he was placed in a large merchant's office belonging to 'an ex-MP' with, as he put it, 'a view of being fitted for going abroad'. After some time at the office stool it was agreed with the firm's junior partner that 'quill-driving was not my particular vocation, nor a three-legged stool the exact amount of range to which I was willing to restrict myself through the sunniest part of life'. So Baldwin quit his job and went ostensibly to learn farming in the West Highlands but in reality to hunt and fish. These were the happiest years of his life. But he was searching for 'a land of greater liberty' and decided that the wide open spaces of South Africa and Natal province in particular were the ticket. He stocked up with guns and saddles and hounds (though all the latter died on the ninety-two-day voyage) and took a boat to Natal, arriving in December 1851.

The introduction to the great elephant hunter was successfully achieved ('my dogs proved sufficient introduction to a brother sportsman') and he was soon off on his first hunting trip to kill hippopotami in St Lucia Bay. It was, however, 'the unhealthy season' and only two of the nine hunters returned alive, 'enervated and prostrated after months of insensibility in Kaffir kraals'. The expedition had set off with three wagons, seven 'white men' and 'lots of Kaffirs' to cross the River Tugela, which formed the boundary of the Cape Colony. On 7 January 1852 Baldwin killed a hippo calf and found it tasted very good, 'something like veal'. Then the first elephant presented itself and the white men gave chase, eventually killing it. Baldwin's journal that night recorded: 'Got back tired, at night, to a supper of elephant's heart, very tender and good;

and breakfasted on the foot baked in a large hole, very glutinous and not unlike brawn.'

The next week there was 'capital sport' shooting duck at the mouth of the River Umlilas and Baldwin 'bagged as many as I could hang round my waist-belt', though when he waded into the river to reach the wagons as the sun was going down he was spotted by a crocodile, escaping whose attentions resulted in the loss of his gun in the water. The travelling was tough because of the constant threat of fever which killed several of his companions and the depredations of mosquitoes which they tried to repel by burning flares of elephant dung. Baldwin's black servant Inyati ('Buffalo') nursed him back to health during one of these fevers and was regarded by him as 'a magnificent specimen of a savage'. By the time they returned to Durban Baldwin weighed under six stone.

The next venture was to join Elephant White at his 96,000-acre farm at Inanda, twenty-two miles from Durban and nine miles from the sea. Baldwin settled near here in a wattle-and-daub house he had built himself and existed alone – 'I can hardly call it living' – for over two years, selling to the local people cattle which White traded in Zulu country and brought or sent out to him. 'It was a horrid, weary, solitary, monotonous life,' Baldwin reflected and it gave him 'such a wholesome dread of the like ever again occurring, that I took to the wandering gypsy-life I have ever since led'.

On 15 July 1853 Baldwin set off with White in two wagons. At one point on their journey he was thrown off the wagon and fell beneath the wheel. Two of the 'Hottentot' women ministered to him, slicing off his trousers and rubbing turpentine and oil into the swelling on his leg for the next twelve hours, allowing him to deliver one of his rather qualified compliments: 'Their beautifully formed, delicate, diminutive hands, ankles, wrists and feet, a marked feature in all Hottentots, presented a singular contrast to their repulsive monkey-like faces.' As soon as he was better there were eland and buffalo to kill and only one sticky human encounter with a local chief, Panda, who took offence at White's decision to push on with his hunting instead of waiting for an audience with him. White was furious when the chief's men pursued them and forced them to return in order to pay the due homage and, in Baldwin's view, the tough elephant hunter 'would have infinitely preferred shooting half a dozen and being spitted himself, to the disgrace to white men of having to obey a Kaffir; but it was all brought on by his own obstinacy'.

In spite of the occasional hardships of this form of travelling life, Baldwin wouldn't have wished for any other sort of life: 'It is miserable enough at times, but altogether it is a roving, careless, wandering life that has charms for me. We do just what we like, and wear what is most convenient. When on foot, a blue and white shirt and a stout pair of gaiters, with the addition of a cap and shoes, are all that I burden my body with.' His contemporary readers would have relished these vicarious accounts of escaping the dress codes and formalities of stuffy mid-Victorian England. Travel writers, then and now, knowingly provided escapist fantasies for a grounded readership at home. In 1866 the traveller Winwood Reade described, in a characteristic travel-writing trope, being stuck in a dull job in a cholera hospital in Southampton, and dreaming of what possibilities opened out once one was launched on Southampton Water:

> Who has not been tempted at least once in his life to give up our rapid but monotonous railway-life for the excitements of savage solitude? As a nation we are the slaves of civilisation, with its groove-life of fixed habits, single purposes, and domestic ties; but we have inherited the nomade instinct from our ancestors . . . When a great traveller enters a London drawing-room there are more rustling of flowers, and whispering behind fans, than welcome the novelist or even the poet.

This passage could have been written by Bruce Chatwin in the 1990s. It also alludes to the celebrity status of the Victorian traveller in the second half of the nineteenth century. Reade was later to produce in his *The African Sketchbook* (1873) a 'Map of African

Literature' on which, instead of place names and rivers, prominence was given to the names of travellers who had created their legends in Africa. The largest letters were reserved, all the way from west to east of southern Central Africa, for Livingstone.

The rambling structure of Baldwin's book was probably an accurate reflection of his episodic pursuit of wildebeest, quagga, koodoo and waterbuck, as well as the more well-known creatures such as the giraffe ('the meat is really tender and good'). When his ink ran out he would mix tea and gunpowder as a substitute for ink to write his journal but there was often little else to distract him and the days could be lonely: 'The long nights were dreary with nothing but "Blaine's Field Sports" and a few old "Family Heralds" to read; but, though I should like companions in the evening, I should always prefer to shoot alone.' At first he found the Boers, who had been so antagonistic to Livingstone, 'first-rate pioneers in a new land', seeing them also as a 'primitive, hospitable, good-hearted set' while conceding that they were 'at least half a century behind the rest of the civilised world here'. But eventually, starved of reading matter and mental stimulation (he knew 'by heart' a copy of *Blackwood's Magazine* he had got hold of), Baldwin concluded that the Boers were 'hardly one remove from the Kaffirs . . . never read a book of any sort or description in their lives, are perfectly ignorant of what every child in England knows . . . How they get through life is a mystery.' On Christmas Day 1857 Baldwin ate 'a bit of rhinoceros, cold, and so fat as to make the strongest stomach bilious' and reflected on the wide, open spaces unimaginable back in 'crowded England'.

Eventually Baldwin couldn't ignore the wars going on around him and he was taken prisoner in the Transvaal, accused of smuggling gunpowder to the local tribes. He was soon released, minus his powder and ammunition. Undeterred, he set off again across 'the deserts of South Africa . . . with three Kaffirs, two Hottentots, a driver and after rider, a wagon, eighteen oxen, a cow and calf, five horses and seven dogs, with guns, powder and lead, beads, wire, and supplies of tea, coffee, meal &c., for a twelvemonth at least'.

Baldwin was philosophical. He had come to escape the boredom of a sedentary office life and to find whatever adventures came along and was content. In the spring of 1858, in spite of admitting that 'elephant hunting is the very hardest life a man can chalk out for himself', he reflected:

I believe I have almost every other requisite [than the wagon breaking down and leaving him alone in the desert] for exploring the continent – health, strength, a constitution well inured to the climate, a constant supply of good spirits, a knack of gaining the good will of the Kaffirs, natives, and Hottentots, who will go anywhere and do anything for me, as I always lend a hand at anything, and study their comfort as well as my own. I have no ties of kindred or friends here to make me wish myself amongst them. I never weary with vain regrets, but always make myself happy, and endeavour to make the best of everything, and interest myself in the journey throughout . . . if health is permitted me, I can go wherever my restless fancy and my love of excitement and adventure may lead me, and if the Kaffirs don't turn me back, or, worse still, make an end of me, it will be a hard matter if I don't make a good hunt . . . Now for a cup of tea.

All that remained was to glimpse 'the great Falls of the Zambesi' made famous by Livingstone and on 4 August 1860 he found that they 'far exceed all I have been led to expect'. He heard the roar ten miles off and saw the great volumes of spray 'ascending like a great white cloud, over which shines an eternal rainbow'. It was the most magnificent sight he had ever beheld: 'It is as if streams of brimstone fire were ascending high into the clouds . . . No words can express their grandeur.'

On 8 August Baldwin cut his initials on a tree on the island above the Falls just below Livingstone's 'as being the second European who has reached the Falls, and the first from the East Coast'. Baldwin met Livingstone and his party: 'I spent the evening with him, and gained great information about his recent discoveries. He has gone on to Sesheke.' Tantalizingly, he gave nothing away about his conversations with Livingstone. A little later he reached Letloche, where he met two Englishmen, one of whom lent him a copy of Livingstone's book with its account of the Falls. Baldwin was surprised at Livingstone's description: 'He has much underrated their magnitude . . . I am confident I have not overrated the river at 2,000 yards wide.' Baldwin also reflected: 'The discovery of the Falls was made in 1855, and from that time to this (1860), with the exception of Livingstone's party, no European but myself has found his way thither.'

After this encounter Baldwin made his way back to Durban. From there he sailed to England, taking with him 'some very fine ivory', the residue of his diligent elephant hunting brought by wagon to the coast.

31

*Naked Africa: Speke and the Source of the Nile*

The 1859 expedition to East Africa of John Hanning Speke had
a simple aim: to ascertain the truth of his claims to have discovered, when in the Lake Regions with Richard Burton, the source
of the Nile, a discovery for which he already claimed full credit at
Burton's expense. It is immediately obvious from the opening pages
of Speke's *Journal of the Discovery of the Source of the Nile* (1863) that
he had a very pronounced view of the African and the role of the
colonial powers. 'If my account should not entirely harmonise with
preconceived notions as to primitive races, I cannot help it,' he
began:

I profess accurately to describe naked Africa – Africa in those places where it has not received the slightest impulse, whether for good or for evil, from European civilisation. If the picture be a dark one, we should, when contemplating these sons of Noah, try and carry our mind back to that time when our poor elder brother Ham was cursed by his father, and condemned to be the slave of both Shem and Japheth; for as they were then, so they appear to be now – a strikingly existing proof of the Holy Scriptures.

Speke's interesting blend of racial prejudice and religious deter-minism made him insist that 'unlike Europeans and Asians, the Africans were excluded from God's dispensation'. The result was that Africans had 'no idea of an overruling Providence or a future state; they therefore trust to luck and to charms, and think only of self-preservation in this world'. It is the fault of the white man not to have instructed those who 'whilst they are sinning, know not what they are doing'. Looking on the bright side, however, he saw some hope:

To say a negro is incapable of instruction, is a mere absurdity; for those few boys who have been educated in our schools have proved themselves even quicker than our own at learning; whilst, among themselves, the deepness of their cunning and their power of repartee are quite surprising, and are especially shown in their proficiency for telling lies most appropriately in preference to truth, and with an off-handed manner that makes them most amusing.

Speke judged the African ('the true curly-head, pouch-mouthed negro') to be too lazy to avoid famine by laying in supplies for the wet season and his real problem was 'want of a strong, protecting government'. His patriarchal society was run by chiefs and grey-beards ruled by magicians, 'as did the old popes of Europe'. In short:

How the negro has lived so many ages without advancing seems marvellous, when all countries surrounding Africa are so forward in comparison; and judging from the progressive state of the world, one is led to suppose that the African must soon either step out from his darkness, or be superseded by a being superior to himself. Could a government be formed for them like ours in India, they would be saved; but without it, I fear there is very little chance; for at present the African neither can help himself nor will he be helped about by others, because his country is in such a constant state of turmoil he has too much anxiety on hand looking out for his food to think of anything else . . . Laziness is inherent in these men, for which reason, although extremely powerful, they will not work unless compelled to do so. Having no God, in the Christian sense of the term, to fear or worship, they have no love for truth, honour, or honesty. Controlled by no government, nor yet by home ties, they have no reason to think of or look to the future.

With this bracing picture of its people, Speke set off for Africa from Portsmouth on 27 April 1859 on the brand-new steam frigate *Forte*.

Victorian travellers in Africa were far more likely to be explorers proper. The real thing. The mildly amused dilettantism of a Curzon, a Kinglake, a Lear seems out of place in the steamy heat and disease-ridden, dark spaces of the African interior. African travel was a serious business and it was the stage on which some of the great dramas of British exploration were acted out. Many of the major nineteenth-century expeditions of discovery were coordinated by the Royal Geographical Society so that, as its historian, Ian Cameron, claims, 'hardly a corner of the continent escaped the probing of its expeditions'. Burton, Speke, Baker, Livingstone and Stanley are among the roll-call of heroic names. African explorers (to the occasional chagrin of serious contemporary scientists) were the superstars and celebrities, some of whom were not above showing off before the public or even enhancing their narratives to emphasize their heroism. They needed, however, to be tough and determined and courageous to attempt these journeys into uncharted territory, for Africa, at the start of the Victorian period, was a largely unknown continent.

As the later 'scramble for Africa' would prove, European nations eyed the potential resources and riches of this continent with great interest. Exploration was intimately bound up with trade. But African travellers were also hunters, missionaries (significantly that was Livingstone's official *métier*) or opponents of slavery. Interestingly, these three themes came to a focus in the personality of the famous President of the RGS, Sir Roderick Murchison, who was a 'sportsman' (i.e. hunter), devout Christian and sincere opponent of slavery.

Of all the great themes of Victorian travel in Africa none could displace the search for the source of the Nile, a symbolic quest that dwarfed all others and defeated so many – and about which little more was known in the 1830s than Ptolemy or Herodotus knew. But exploration also 'discovered', named and mapped all the major mountain ranges, lakes and rivers in Africa during this period. The youthful Conrad's blank spaces on the map were filled by the century's end. The greater seriousness of African exploration is confirmed by the fact that some of its findings – geographical, historical, anthropological – are still drawn on by scholars.

John Hanning Speke was born on 4 May 1827 near Bideford in Devon, the son of a soldier and landowner. Educated at Barnstaple Grammar School and in London, he was accepted at the age of seventeen for a commission in the Indian Army, joining the 46th Native Bengal Infantry. Bored by military life he diverted himself with hunting, especially in Tibet, and amassing trophies which were sent home. After ten years he joined Burton's expedition to the Somali coast but his role in this expedition – exploring the area south of Bunder Gori – was not a success, partly as a result of his lack of experience and competence in languages. In the attack in April 1855 referred to above, Speke was badly injured and captured. Burton's insinuation that Speke lacked courage may have been the start of the falling-out between the two men. Like Burton, he went to the Crimea in 1855 and soon afterwards joined Burton's expedition to the Lakes.

As well as the rivalry over the claim to have discovered the source of the Nile there were additional tensions between the scholar and linguist, Burton, and Speke, whose education and intellectual powers were much less evident and who was certainly treated with contempt by Burton. But now in 1859 Speke was in charge, with the words of Sir Roderick Murchison, President of the RGS, ringing in his ears: 'Speke, we must send you there again.' He was accompanied by J. A. Grant, 'an old friend and brother sportsman in India'.

Speke arrived at the Cape on 4 July to stay with the Governor, Sir George Grey, a former explorer himself, and on the 16th they sailed again on the steam corvette *Brisk* for Zanzibar, bagging some turtle eggs on the way from a coral island called Europa. On arrival at Zanzibar preparations for the trip were put in hand: 'The Hottentots, the mules, and the baggage having been landed, our preparatory work began in earnest. It consisted in proving the sextants; rating the watches; examining the compasses and boiling thermometers; making tents and packsaddles; ordering supplies of beads, cloth, and brass wire; and collecting servants and porters.' While all this was going on Speke went off hunting and bagged a couple of hippopotami. On 21 July another twenty-two-gun corvette, the *Secundrah Shah*, belonging to Sheikh Said, took them to Bagamyo and then, on 2 October, the expedition mustered at Ugéni. The large caravan consisted of nearly two hundred people, including two former slaves called Bombay and Baraka, who were vital as interpreters. There were also: '1 corporal and 9 privates, Hottentots – 1 jemadar and 25 privates, Beluchs – 1 Arab Cafila Bashi and 75 freed slaves – 1 kirangozi, or leader, and 100 negro porters – 12 mules untrained, 3 donkeys, and 22 goats.' Ten of the thirty-six men given by the Sultan of Zanzibar ran away on the first day of the expedition because they feared the white men were cannibals whose sole aim in taking them into the interior was to eat them. It was an impressive sight as they moved off:

The kirangozi, with a load on his shoulder, led the way, flag in hand, followed by the pagazis [bearers] carrying spears or bows and arrows in their hands, and bearing their share of the baggage in the shape either of bolster-shaped loads of cloth and beads covered with matting, each tied into the fork of a three-pronged stick, or else coils of brass or copper wire tied in even weights to each end of sticks which they laid on the shoulder; then helter-skelter came the Wanguana, carrying carbines in their hands, and boxes, bundles, tents, cooking-pots – all the miscellaneous property – on their heads; next the Hottentots, dragging the refractory mules laden with ammunition-boxes, but very lightly, to save the animals for the future; and, finally, Sheikh Said and the Beluch escort; while the goats, sick women, and stragglers brought up the rear.

Speke's first task was to map the country and he made regular determinations of altitude, sketched and collected geological and zoological specimens. As they moved into the uplands the people seemed very poor and frightened of travellers, which again pro-voked Speke to prescribe strong government for them, for 'without it, the slave trade will wipe them off the face of the earth'. The game was a terrible provocation to Speke which 'as often hap-pened, made me wish I had come on a shooting rather than on a long exploring expedition'. One day they managed to shoot a giraffe and on another: 'Grant and myself went out pot-hunting and brought home a bag consisting of one striped eland, one saltiana antelope, four guinea-fowl, four ringdoves, and one par-tridge – a welcome supply, considering we were quite out of flesh.' Later, 'after shooting six guinea-fowl, [we] turned in for the night'. Killing a rhinoceros, however, Speke was taken aback by the energy with which the servants weighed in: 'A more savage, filthy, dis-gusting but at the same time grotesque, scene than that which followed can hardly be conceived. All fell to work armed with swords, spears, knives, and hatchets – cutting and slashing, thump-ing and bawling, fighting and tearing, tumbling and wrestling up to their knees in filth and blood in the middle of the carcass.' Nonetheless he shot a few more antelopes for the pot and confessed: 'always eager to shoot something, either for science or the pot, I killed a bicornis rhinoceros, at a distance of five paces only, with my small 40-gauge Lancaster, as the beast stood quietly feeding in the bush'.

The journey was a difficult one. Local rulers demanded copious amounts of passing tribute or 'hongo', porters deserted *en masse*, taking, eventually, half the expedition's property with them, the severe famine raised the cost of food and there were complicated negotiations with local chiefs and Arab traders for supplies. In addition Speke developed a bad cough and could not sleep properly. His health was bad throughout July and August but towards the end of September he began to recover 'so much so, that I began shooting small birds for specimens'. The resumption of killing, however, did not always gratify Speke and he seems to have had some awareness of the unnecessariness of it all: 'Small antelopes occasionally sprang up from the grass. I shot a florikan for the pot; and as I had never before seen white rhinoceros, killed one now; though, as no one would eat him, I felt sorry rather than otherwise for what I had done.'

Climbing now to five thousand feet among the Weranhanje hills, in a region Speke called 'the great turn-point of the Central African watershed', he visited at Karagwe the local king, Rumanika, who greatly impressed him with his quick and enquiring mind. Rumanika was utterly amazed that men with so many means should expend it on travelling when they could simply sit and enjoy their wealth. Why on earth did they do it?

'Oh no,' was the reply; 'we have had our fill of the luxuries of life; eating, drinking, or sleeping have no charms for us now; we are above trade, therefore require no profits, and seek for enjoyment the run of the world. To observe and admire the beauties of creation are worth much more than beads to us. But what led us this way we have told you before; it was to see your majesty in particular, and the great kings of Africa – and at the same time to open another road to the north, whereby the best manufactures of Europe would find their way to Karagué, and you would get so many more guests.'

Rumanika was an important ruler and he was concerned about Speke's motives for being in the region. This resulted in his being detained until January 1862. When he moved on it was to the court of Mutesa, the ruler of Buganda, where he presented himself at the palace behind a Union Jack, bearing the usual tribute of gifts but resolved not to observe local custom by seating himself on the floor: 'I felt that if I did not stand up for my social position at once, I should be treated with contempt during the remainder of my visit, and thus lose the vantage-ground I had assumed of appearing rather as a prince than a trader, for the purpose of better gaining the confidence of the king.'

When Speke finally met the twenty-five-year-old ruler he found the whole business rather 'theatrical' but he went down well with a ruler who demanded to see his umbrella opened and shut and who was well pleased with his gifts. Speke was less happy with the court intrigues into which he was being drawn: 'The farce continued, and how to manage these haughty capricious blacks puzzled my brains considerably; but I felt that if I did not stand up now, no one would ever be treated better hereafter.' Finally Mutesa asked Speke what he wanted and Speke replied: 'To open the country to the north, that an uninterrupted line of commerce might exist between England and this country by means of the Nile.' This indicated what 'the source of the Nile' was really about: trade routes. But Speke was pleased that, spurred by resentment at the rival power of Rumanika, Mutesa was anxious to be seen to be able in his own right to grant something to Speke: 'The moment of triumph had come at last, and suddenly the road was granted!'

The party was escorted to the point where the Nile flowed out of Lake Victoria, reaching it on 28 July 1862: 'we arrived at the extreme end of the journey, the farthest point ever visited by the expedition on the same parallel of latitude as king Mtésa's palace, and just forty miles east of it.' The falls at this point were:

> by far the most interesting sight I had seen in Africa . . . it was a sight that attracted one to it for hours – the roar of the waters, the thousands of passenger-fish, leaping at the falls with all their might; the Wasoga and Waganda fishermen coming out in boats and taking post on all the rocks with rod and hook, hippopotami and crocodiles lying sleepily on the water, the ferry at work above the falls, and cattle driven down to drink at the margin of the lake, – made, in all, with the nature of the country – small hills, grassy-topped, with trees in folds, and gardens on the lower slopes, – as interesting a picture as one could wish to see.

Speke reflected: 'The expedition had now performed its functions. I saw that old father Nile without any doubt rises in the Victoria N'yanza, and, as I had foretold, that lake is the great source of the holy river which cradled the first expounder of our religious belief.' He sketched what he saw and proceeded to perform the rites of renaming that were a mandatory part of the protocols of European exploration: 'I now christened the "stones" Ripon Falls, after the nobleman who presided over the Royal Geographical Society when my expedition was got up; and the arm of water from which the Nile issued, Napoleon Channel, in token of respect to the French Geographical Society, for the honour they had done me, just before leaving England, in presenting me with their gold medal for the discovery of the Victoria N'yanza.'

Speke next made his first voyage on the Nile in five boats bound together, each of five planks, with the aim of visiting Kamrasi's palace at Bunyoro but he was soon warned off this enterprise because of threats of war in the region. Grant, whose ulcerated leg meant that he had been sent back north, was unable to be present to verify the discovery, which did not help Speke's aim of proving everything beyond doubt and Speke's account closes with a vague sense of anticlimax for the reader.

The expedition returned in February 1863 to Gondokoro, where Speke caught up with letters from home, including one from Sir Roderick Murchison in which he learned that he had been awarded the Founder's Medal for his discovery of Lake Victoria. They then moved on to Cairo, where Speke put up at the Shepheard Hotel, had all his servants photographed (an engraving of 'Speke's Faithfuls' records the scene) and 'indulged them at the public concerts, tableaux vivants, etc'. The celebrations culminated in a visit to the Viceroy in his palace.

Speke's return to London began as a triumph and he was mobbed but soon the shine began to wear off. On its publication in December 1863 his *Journal* did not sell as well as might have been expected – it is an often tedious and rambling volume and of no special literary merit – and Burton began to question the discovery claims of his former associate. Publishing his findings from William Blackwood rather than the RGS, who had financed the expedition, made Murchison cool and probably cost Speke his gong. Murchison also arranged for a debate in September 1864 with Burton on the Nile question, which some have seen as a deliberately malicious act.

On 15 September, the day before the debate was due to take place, Speke went shooting partridge at Neston Park, his uncle's estate at Corsham in Wiltshire. Climbing over a wall, he accidentally shot himself dead. The suggestion that this might have been the suicide of a man who could not be sure that he would survive inquiry the next day into his claims has never wholly been discounted. It would be twelve years before Henry Morton Stanley and others confirmed that Speke was right about Lake Victoria being the source of the Nile but it was too late to dispel the cloud that lingered and still seems to linger over his reputation.

## 32

### *Barbarous Practices: Richard Burton in Dahomey*

After his return from the Lake Regions of East Africa, Richard Burton soon set sail again for North America, in April 1860. He travelled across the Rocky Mountains to California and also visited Salt Lake City, where he reported in detail on Mormonism. After visiting San Francisco he returned to England at the end of the year via the Isthmus of Panama. On 22 January 1861 Burton married Isabel Arundell and felt the need to apply for a consular post to support himself and his new wife, hoping that Damascus would be recognized as the best place to exploit his knowledge and skills. But the Foreign Office sent him to Fernando Po, a small island off the West

African coast – in his words 'the very abomination of desolation'.
Actually Burton grew to appreciate the colonial languor of his position at Fernando Po, which, as he watched the toiling black workers,
was 'the counterpart of a landowner's existence in the Southern
States'. The previous incumbent of this rather lawless spot had left
under a cloud. Burton did what travelling he could during this
period and managed to write *Wanderings in West Africa* (1863) and
*Abeokuta and the Cameroons Mountains* (1863) as well as some volumes that would be published more than a decade later.

From Fernando Po he was entrusted with a mission to visit
Gelele, King of Dahomey, as part of diplomatic moves to make the
end of the slave trade permanent. This was also at the time a very
important trading coast for palm oil, ivory and cotton, and the
European powers wanted stability and order to replace the traditional chaos in order to protect their profits. But, above all,
Dahomey was associated in the mind of the Victorian public with
lurid tales of human sacrifice. The *Saturday Review* in July 1863
claimed that the King had recently sacrificed two thousand people
on a whim but Burton was sceptical and set himself the goal of
showing the kingdom 'in its true lights'. He arrived on 8 December
1863, having been preceded in August by a collection of presents
which did not include, to Gelele's chagrin, the English carriage and
horses he had requested. He did receive, however, as the cargo ship's
docket itemized: 'One forty feet circular crimson silk Damask Tent
with Pole complete (contained in two boxes). One richly embossed
silver Pipe with amber mouth-piece, in morocco case. Two richly
embossed silver Belts with Lion and Crane in raised relief, in
morocco cases. One Coat of Mail and Gauntlets. (Contained in one
deal case, addressed to Captain Burton, H.B.M.'s Consul for the
Bight of Biafra, West Coast of Africa).'

Burton landed on the Dahomean coast from the naval vessel
*Antelope* with an escort of twenty men led by a Kruman carrying the
flag of St George attached to a boarding pike and with the five
white men slung on hammocks suspended from bamboo poles.
They were greeted by a plump fetish-priest and an unwholesome

smell that spoke to Burton of fever and dysentery. Soldiers and chiefs arrived with drums and musical instruments, all of whom had their 'Fetishes or charms – birds' claws and small wooden dolls smeared red as though with blood'. There was much dancing and singing as the white men made their way through the market to the English fort, where toasts of sherry, gin and rum were given to their hosts. After five hours of this they were allowed to retire but the following morning the King's men were back to present them with a goat, a pig, a pair of fowls and forty yams. Burton spent the next three days exploring Whydah (Ouidah in modern Benin), finding it 'a ruined place, everything showing decay, and during the last three years it has changed much for the worse . . . The place is temporarily ruined, and dull as dull can be.'

On 13 December Burton, in a procession of more than a hundred people, set off for the interior and the court of Gelele. On the way he paused to receive the hospitality of various dignitaries, exchange gifts and watch tribal dances. At Hen-vi he saw the so-called Amazons: 'The four soldieresses were armed with muskets, and habited in tunics and white calottes, with two blue patches, meant for crocodiles . . . Two of the women dancers were of abnormal size, nearly six feet tall, and of proportional breadth, whilst generally the men were smooth, full-breasted, round-limbed, and effeminate-looking.' Although Burton had arrived with his customary prejudices in full working order, he was prepared to concede that the slave trade explained much: 'The aspect of the country confirms the general impression that the Dahomans were, for negroes, an industrious race, till demoralised by slave hunts and by long predatory wars.'

When Burton's party reached Kana in the vicinity of Gelele's palace at Agbome (Abomey) they were greeted by outriding courtiers bearing the King's canes carved with 'chameleons, parrots, and monkeys half-swallowed by snakes, the whole ornamented with thin plates of beaten dollars' and they duly prepared for 'the penance of reception'. When they finally entered the royal gate they were forced to remove their swords and close their umbrellas. The

King appeared and turned out to be 'in the full vigour of life, from forty to forty-five, before the days of increasing belly and decreasing leg . . . His person is athletic, upwards of six feet high, lithe, agile, thin flanked and broad shouldered, with muscular limbs, well turned wrists and neat ankles, but a distinctly cucumber-shaped shin . . . His nails are allowed to attain mandarin-length . . . white strong and sound teeth.' His nose was turned up: 'this mean and hideous concave is the African substitute for the beautiful, the sympathetic, and the noble convexity of the Caucasian'. He dressed simply and on this occasion he wore a short cylindrical straw cap, with a ribbon of purple velvet round the middle. His throne was an earth bench three feet high 'strewed with the red, blue, and striped cotton cloths made in the palace' and there was an 'intense personal veneration' from the wives, attendants and other hangers-on.

Gelele came forward and shook Burton's hand and asked after the health of the sovereign 'and the people of England, which he and his naturally suppose to be a little larger and a much richer Dahome surrounded by water'. The stools on which Burton and his party sat were placed before the throne under a gorgeous tent-canopy and there was singing and dancing until sunset. Burton conceded that the court showed that the Dahomeans possessed what he called 'the ceremonial faculty' but, outside the court, displays offered to them were 'wretched . . . the real negro grotesqueness, like bad perspective, injures the whole picture'.

Burton was given rather 'dire' lodgings at Abomey for two months and proceeded to learn the local language, Fon. On 22 December the King, having returned now to his capital, demanded to inspect his presents and was not impressed. The only part of the tent that he liked was the gingerbread lion on the pole's top and the pipe was of no interest to him. The belts were a disappointment to the royal party – they had expected bracelets – and they rejected the excuses given that the carriage and horses would not have survived the sea journey from England. 'Africans are offended if their wishes are not exactly consulted, and they mulishly look upon any such small oversight as an intended slight,' Burton decided.

Burton claimed that the stories of human sacrifice, canoes paddling in human blood and so on had been invented by slave traders to deter the English from visiting the King and he advised his readers to exercise a little self-reflection before condemning these barbaric rites:

We can hardly find fault with putting criminals to death, when, in the Year of Grace 1864, we hung four murderers upon the same gibbet before 100,000 gaping souls at Liverpool . . . and when our last Christian king but one killed a starving mother of seventeen, with an infant at her breast, for lifting a yard of linen from a shop counter. A Dahoman visiting England but a few years ago would have witnessed customs almost quite as curious as those which raise our bile now.

But he did not deny that perhaps five hundred were beheaded each year and he personally witnessed corpses dangling from gallows and a row of twelve severed heads. He believed that the King was powerless to abolish human sacrifice (the so called 'So-sin Customs') even if he wanted to, and the attempt by outsiders to interfere in the practice 'will cause more secrecy and more decorum in the practice; but the remedy must come from the people themselves'. And a remedy was needed because the kingdom was in decline: 'Thus Dahome steadily loses *prestige*. Weakened by traditional policy, by a continual issue of blood, and by the arbitrary measures of her king, and demoralised by an export slave trade, by close connection with Europeans, and by frequent failure, this breed of black Spartans is rapidly falling into decay.'

Burton, the first European to penetrate seriously into the kingdom, discovered two things not mentioned by previous travellers: the double kingship (where Gelele's city rule was paired with Addo-Kpon, King of the Bush) and the precedence given to women. He was compelled to join in a dance with Addo-Kpon accompanied by a 'Reverend' who was in the party and who rendered some Wesleyan hymns. The King of the Bush was hugely impressed: 'It required some strength of mind to prevent holding oneself a manner of prodigy; the people evidently thought the power of dancing, of using a sword, of learning enough to understand them in a month, of writing down everything seen so as to recall it to their memories, and of sketching objects so that even they could recognise them, to be an avatar of intellect.' He stressed how important it was to try to understand the Dahomean religion in order to understand the culture: 'I cannot but admire the incuriousness of so many travellers who have visited Dahome and have described its Customs without an attempt to master, or at least to explain, the faith that underlines them.' Were the King, for example, to refuse to scatter the graves of his ancestors with human blood it 'would be as if a European monarch were forcibly to abolish prayers for the dead'. Burton industriously catalogued the varieties of fetishism and reflected on attempts by missionaries to end the practice: 'But all who know how deeply rooted is fetishism in the negro brain, will despair of the nineteenth succeeding better than the sixteenth century. In our modern day the good work has begun here with the curse of sectarian theology upon it: Catholics and Protestants working against one another in the same field.'

Such genuine attempts by Burton to offer knowledge and understanding were undermined by his dogged racism, in particular his long-standing obsession with the inferiority of the Negro, who was, for him, 'an awful example of the corruption of man when left to himself'. His discourse on 'The Negro's Place in Nature' derives much of its offensiveness from its source in the contemporary phenomenon of 'scientific racism' to which Burton was drawn. He had read his paper on this topic to the Anthropological Society of London, where these ideas were debated. Burton warmly commended Dr James Hunt, founder of the Society, for his good work:

for having so graphically shown the great gulf, moral and physical, separating the black from the white races of men, and for having placed in so striking a light the physiological cause of the difference – namely, the arrested physical development of the negro. There is hardly a traveller, however unobservant, who has not remarked the peculiar and precocious intelligence of the African's childhood, his 'turning stupid' as the general phrase is, about the age of puberty, and the rapid declension of his mental powers in old age, – a process reminding us of the simiad. It is pleasant to see anatomically discovered facts harmonising with, and accounting for, the provisionary theories of those who register merely what they have observed.

Burton claimed that this nonsense was the product of ten years of travel and of comparisons with 'the Western Asiatics, amongst whom I have lived eight years, for the most part like one of themselves'. He believed that, now that slavery had been abolished, any positive ideas about the Negroes derived from sympathy for their plight would be reversed and that travel and increased contact with them would strengthen the backlash against the abolitionists' sympathy, putting back in fashion 'my conviction of the innate and enduring inferiority of a race which has had so many an opportunity of acquiring civilization, but which has ever deliberately rejected improvement'. Calling on phrenology to aid him, he expounded his racist theories at length, concluding: 'The negro has never invented an alphabet, a musical scale, or any other element of knowledge . . . His painting and statuary are, like his person, ungraceful and grotesque . . . he mentally remains a child, and is never capable of a generalisation.' There was only one solution: 'The removal of the negro from Africa is like sending a boy to school; it is his only chance of improvement, of learning that there is something more in life than drumming and dancing, talking and singing, drinking and killing.' He rejected imposed solutions in a characteristic preference for non-intervention, which was the odd counterpart of his militant racism: 'Nations are poor judges of one another; each looks upon itself as an exemplar to the world, and vents its philanthropy by forcing its infallible system or systems upon its neighbour.' Burton's only hope for the African, he said, was the spread of Islam southwards.

After six weeks at the court Burton was growing impatient at his failure to deliver the formal message of Her Majesty's Government to King Gelele. On 13 February 1864 he was finally summoned to the palace but kept for two hours waiting outside in the sun. When allowed eventually to speak he said that the British Government was determined to stop the traffic in slaves and to reduce human sacrifice: 'In enlarging upon these last two paragraphs, I felt a sense of hopelessness with which the reader of these pages will, perhaps, sympathise; it was like talking to the winds.' Gelele replied 'in rambling style' that the slave trade was an ancestral custom and, moreover, the modern trade had been established by white men 'to whom he would sell all they wanted'. The alternative to selling slaves was to kill them, 'which England, perhaps, would like even less'. England was a friend and the King of England (*sic*) and he were now 'like one finger'. Gelele shook hands with Burton and told him he was a good man but warned that he was 'too angry'. The mission was a total failure.

On Monday 15 February 1864, after fifty-six days in Abomey, Burton and his men moved off: 'We felt some natural elation, although setting out upon what was fated to be the most comfortless march which I had made in Africa.' It was a hard journey with difficult servants and a lack of water and food but on 18 February they arrived back at Ouidah, spent a few quiet days at the French mission, then boarded HMS *Jaseur* on 26 February, relieved to be away from Gelele's kingdom.

In August 1864 Burton returned to England, where the Speke controversy awaited his attention.

View of Quillimane and of the Pioneer.

## 33

### *The Garden of Eden: Livingstone on the Zambezi*

On 10 March 1858 the national hero David Livingstone and his brother Charles set sail from Birkenhead in 'Her Majesty's Colonial Steamer *Pearl*' for the Zambezi on a well-financed and government-backed expedition with the same dual ambition as before: 'Our first object was to explore the Zambesi, its mouths and tributaries, with a view to their being used as highways for commerce and Christianity to pass into the vast interior of Africa.' In his Preface to *Narrative of an Expedition to the Zambesi and its Tributaries; and of the Discovery of the Lakes Shirwa and Nyassa, 1858–1864* (1865) Livingstone announced his ambition to give an account of 'tracts of country previously unexplored, with their river systems, natural productions, and capabilities' but also to highlight 'the misery entailed by the slave-trade in its inland phases'. Just as 'commerce and Christianity' were mutually dependent, so the solution to the slave trade lay in a combination of trade and tracts, backed by British naval strength. Livingstone wished to replicate what he judged to be the success on the west coast of Africa of a system 'combining the repressive efforts of H.M. cruisers with lawful trade and Christian Missions – the moral results of which have been so gratifying'.

There was a problem, however, with the Portuguese, who controlled much of the coast. This 'unwarranted assumption of power' according to Livingstone prevented the local people entering into proper commercial relations with the colonial powers and perpetuated their 'barbarism'. He did not believe the claim of the Portuguese to be opposed to slavery and decided: 'This Portuguese pretence to dominion is the curse of the negro race on the East Coast of Africa.' By contrast, he hoped that his mission would cause 'the great and fertile continent of Africa to be no longer kept wantonly sealed, but made available as the scene of European enterprise, and will enable its people to take a place among the nations of the earth, thus securing the happiness and prosperity of tribes now sunk in barbarism or debased by slavery; and above all, I cherish the hope that it may lead to the introduction of the blessings of the Gospel'.

Livingstone was aware that the great prize of the discovery of the source of the Nile had been won by others, and he praised the achievement of Speke and Grant as something 'which every Englishman must feel an honest pride in knowing was accomplished by our gallant countrymen'. He made clear that his plan to explore the rivers and pass along the northern end of Lake Nyasa and round the southern end of Lake Tanganyika 'to ascertain the watershed of that part of Africa' was done with 'no wish to unsettle what with so much toil and danger was accomplished by Speke and Grant, but rather to confirm their illustrious discoveries'. But, in a possible criticism of the occasional celebrity antics of the great explorers performing in London for the RGS, he added: 'In our exploration the chief object in view was not to discover objects of nine days' wonder, to gaze and be gazed at by barbarians; but to note the climate, the natural productions, the local diseases, the natives and their relation to the rest of the world; all of which were observed with that peculiar interest which, as regards the future, the first white man cannot but feel in *a continent whose history is only just beginning* [italics added].' This striking phrase illustrates the characteristic standpoint of the great Victorian explorers, that of the white man, with his gaze, bringing a continent into being.

The *Pearl* reached Cape Town in May and Livingstone prepared for the first phase of his exploration of the Zambezi and its tributaries, 'with a view to their being used as highways for commerce and Christianity to pass into the vast interior of Africa'. He had brought with him from England, in three prefabricated sections, a small steam launch which was now screwed together and christened the *Ma Robert* after Mary Livingstone's African nickname. Mrs Livingstone accompanied her husband with her youngest son, Oswell.

Livingstone frequently alluded to his difficulties in writing and his lack of literary accomplishment and it is true that his writing was seldom distinguished by real feats of vivid description, but as he began his river voyage inland along the Kongone (one of four branches of the Zambezi flowing into the sea) he allowed himself a little lyrical outburst:

When a native of the temperate north first lands in the tropics, his feelings and emotions resemble in some respects those which the First Man may have had on his entrance into the Garden of Eden. He has set foot in a new world, another state of existence is before him; everything he sees, every sound that falls upon the ear, has all the freshness and charm of novelty. The trees and the plants are new, the flowers and the fruits, the beasts, the birds, and the insects are curious and strange; the very sky itself is new, glowing with colours, or sparkling with constellations, never seen in northern climes.

But the *Ma Robert* was less than Edenic. Because the boat had been designed in a hurry, its badly constructed furnaces consumed a 'frightful' amount of wood, and Livingstone realized that boats or even canoes would have been just as effective with half the toil and expense. He had brought with him, in addition to members of his family, physician and botanist John Kirk, artist Thomas Baines and geologist Richard Thornton, but he was a stubborn man and the latter two were dismissed during that first summer and his steamship commander, Norman Bedingfield, resigned. Livingstone ended 1858 defeated by the Quebrasa cataracts, which he refused initially to admit were obstacles to navigation.

At Christmas, in reflective mood, he pondered the cultural contrasts of black and white races, concluding that 'we must smile at the heaps of nonsense which have been written about the negro intellect . . . A complaint as to the poverty of the language is often only a sure proof of the scanty attainments of the complainant . . . a couple of centuries back, the ancestors of common people in England – probably our own great-great-grandfathers – were as unenlightened as the Africans are now.' Livingstone, though he could happily employ on occasion the prejudicial language that was the European norm in Africa, never shared Burton's hostile contempt for the black experience.

In January 1859 Livingstone began to explore the River Shiré and by April he had discovered Lake Shirwa: 'a considerable body of bitter water, containing leeches, fish, crocodiles, and hippopotami.' A little before noon on 16 September 1859 the party discovered Lake Nyasa and reflected with satisfaction: 'The regular publication of our letters by the Royal Geographical Society we felt to be an inestimable benefit. It fixed the date of, and perpetuated every discovery.' Exploration was a competitive business.

Livingstone learned in early 1860 that the government was

prepared to extend his expedition for another three years. He was also joined by new parties of missionaries. But he quarrelled even with his son Charles and the *Ma Robert*, sardonically nicknamed the *Asthmatic*, hit another sandbank on 21 December and filled with water overnight so that 'all that was visible of the worn-out craft next day was about six feet of her two masts. Most of the property we had on board was saved; and we spent the Christmas of 1860 encamped on the island of Chimba.'

The following month a new ship, the *Pioneer*, arrived from England and Livingstone and his party set off to explore the River Rovuma, getting enmeshed with local slave traders in the process, then decided to explore Lake Nyasa looking for an outlet to the Rovuma. At the end of 1861 they were back on the Zambezi and heading for the coast, where they took delivery of the twenty-four sections of a new iron steamer, *Lady Nyassa*, together with more missionaries. It took four months to put the boat together at Shupanga and during this time Mary Livingstone caught malarial fever and died on 27 April 1862: 'her eyes were closed in the sleep of death . . . A coffin was made during the night, a grave was dug next day under the branches of the great Baobab-tree, and with sympathizing hearts the little band of his countrymen assisted the bereaved husband in burying his dead.'

Two months later the *Nyassa* was successfully launched but tensions increased between Livingstone and Kirk after the Zambezi was found to be too low and Kirk grew frustrated at his companion's stubborn insistence on forcing the sailing boats they employed instead through all the shallows. 'Dr L. is out of his mind,' Kirk later wrote in his *Zambesi Journal*, 'he is a most unsafe leader.' Livingstone himself, however, liked to paint himself as a tolerant figure. Following a dispute between some of his boatmen, happily resolved, he reflected:

In travelling it is best to enjoy the little simple incidents of this kind which, at most, exemplify the tendencies woven into the being of the whole human family. It is a pity to hear that some of our countrymen rudely interfere in what really does no harm. Blows even have been inflicted under the silly assumption that the negro is this, that, and the other thing, and not, like other men, a curious mixture of good and evil, wisdom and folly, cleverness and stupidity . . . Let us fancy the effect on an English village if a black man came to it, and a white servant complained that he had been maltreated by him on the way. We have felt heartily ashamed sometimes on discovering how causelessly we have been angry. No doubt the natives are at times as perversely stupid as servants at home can be when they like; but our conduct must often appear to the native mind as a mixture of silliness and insanity.

At the start of 1863 the *Lady Nyassa* and the *Pioneer* set off once more on to the Shiré, where, to their horror, the Livingstone party saw corpses floating on the river, slaughtered by slave raiders. They pressed on to reach the cataracts in April but in July they received a letter from London recalling the expedition. While waiting for the waters to rise sufficiently for them to make the return journey Livingstone decided to investigate the slave trade to the north-west. Eventually, in February 1864, he returned to the coast, where he sailed the *Lady Nyassa* to Zanzibar from Mozambique. From Zanzibar the boat was sailed to Bombay to be sold.

Although Livingstone judged his expedition a success, his reception when he returned to London in July 1864 was considerably less rapturous than that which followed his 1850s triumph. The general view was that the expedition had been expensive in proportion to its achievements. Only about eighteen months of the six and a half years had been spent actually travelling and many explorers and missionaries had died. Nor had the slave trade ceased.

Livingstone now devoted his time to writing up his travels, drawing on his son's journals, but he was still tempted by the prize of African discoveries that would rival those of men like Burton and Speke. He began to raise funds from the RGS and the government and started to prepare for what would be his final journey.

# 34

## *Missionary Enterprise: Anna Hinderer in Yoruba Country*

Intimate accounts of the European experience in Africa – day-to-day human encounters on a personal level – are far rarer than might be expected given the volume of writing that exists. Sometimes it was a sense of racial difference or a failure of cultural empathy that prevented explorers, travellers and missionaries from sparing time from the narrative of their heroic deeds to notice the people around them – which makes the account of the missionary Anna Hinderer so refreshing. Her *Seventeen Years in the Yoruba Country* (1872) was put together after her death from her journal, letters and other papers (from which the male editor had removed her political observations on the causes and solutions of the tribal wars because they 'would have served no useful purpose').

Anna Martin was born at Hempnall in Norfolk in March 1827. Her mother died when Anna was five, leaving her with some early memories of sitting sewing on a low, broad window seat by her mother's sickbed. For every ten stitches she was rewarded with a strawberry. She would read improving texts to her mother and was allowed into her room only twice a day. This sense of loss was connected to her religious experience. Anna was, in her own words, 'pining after something beyond this world, but could not yet grasp it'. In 1839 her merchant father sent her to live with her grandfather and aunt at Lowestoft, where she soon asked to be allowed to conduct a Sunday school: 'I was seeking for something solid; I felt the want of something to make me happy, something this world could not give.' There she got to know the Reverend Francis and Mrs

Cunningham (the sister of the Quaker philanthropist Elizabeth Fry) and eventually went to live with them at the vicarage and was very happy. She visited the poor, started a Sunday class for 'ragged and neglected children' which grew to two hundred pupils, and she also ran a class for boys at the workhouse.

On 14 October 1852 Anna married the Reverend David Hinderer from Schorndorf, in Württemberg, Germany, who had been working for the Church Missionary Society (CMS) in the Yoruba country and was briefly back in England on CMS business. She 'rejoiced in the thought of living and dying for Africa' and was determined to go out with him: 'though so much of my work at home was of a missionary character, yet I felt that to heathen lands I was to go'. The worst pang was leaving Reverend Cunningham, 'this beloved father and friend'.

Anna Hinderer went out to Africa with the mind-set natural to an ardent young Christian woman of the mid-Victorian period: 'The gradual suppression of the slave trade opened the way, in 1843, for the preaching of the Gospel to the inhabitants of this country, whose religion is a system of idolatry . . . Their religion is laden with foolish and cruel superstitions.' The expansion of Christianity overseas throughout the Victorian period was massive and missionaries were at the centre of this movement, which was boosted by the arrival of practising Christians as administrators, traders and soldiers who established their own churches in the countries in which they settled. The evangelical societies founded at the end of the eighteenth century – the London Missionary Society, the Baptist Missionary Society and the Anglican Church Missionary Society were the most prominent – grew throughout the nineteenth century, with the result that by 1900 around ten thousand missionaries were active across the world. It is possible to see this as part of the 'civilizing', that is to say, imperialist, project, but there were often tensions between the aims of missionaries and colonial powers, their common purposes not always apparent, and in extreme instances missionaries could side with the native populations against the colonial rulers.

Sometimes, as Livingstone discovered in South Africa, missionaries could find themselves in local armed conflict with white settlers who held very different views from them of the natives and their lands. Many travellers, as has already been seen, were in two minds about the activities of missionaries, articulating concerns about the imposition of alien values on indigenous peoples or simply expressing scepticism about the efficiency of missionary activity. A good example is Mansfield Parkyns in Abyssinia, who agreed that missionaries were 'doubtless composed of some of the most charitable and well-meaning men in the land . . . still I should fear that the success attending their missions, and the benefit derived from their exertions, are comparatively small in proportion to the outlay of property and lives, the expectations of the societies, the reports they receive, and the actual mischief done where good was intended'.

Generally missionary activity was helped by imperial expansion. The growing awareness and knowledge of other countries at the metropolitan centre throughout the Victorian period – fuelled by some of the travellers' accounts discussed here and publications such as the Church Missionary Society's *Intelligencer* – created interest and sympathy with missionary positions among the British public. And it must be stressed that there were positive gains, in schooling, literacy skills and other useful knowledge, which many local populations did value.

David Hinderer had been a pioneering missionary in what is now modern Nigeria, seeking new 'openings for missionary enterprise' and being, in 1851, the first white man to enter the city of Ibadan. He claimed that the chiefs welcomed the prospect of Christian teachers of their people, one of them saying: 'Now we have got a white man, we must hold him very tight.' Hinderer's reason for being back in London had been to marshal more spiritual arms for the struggle against the rival, Islam, because 'the Mohammedans . . . had embittered the minds of the people against Christianity'.

On 6 December 1852 the Hinderers set sail from Plymouth in

terrible weather on the *Propontis* with a Mr Kefer, a recent graduate of the CMS College at Islington, north London, and a party of good people including the new Bishop of Sierra Leone, but, regrettably for Anna, also on board was 'a sad and godless collection' of colonial officials. On Christmas Eve 1852 she delightedly set eyes for the first time on the shores of Africa. They dropped off the Bishop at Sierra Leone and sailed on for the Yoruba country, landing at Lagos on 5 January 1853.

Anna immediately fell victim to fever and was not ready to move on until the end of the month, when they set off up the River Ogun in canoes: 'There was much to enjoy; the scenery was magnificent; such banks, foliage, flowers, scented shrubs, exquisite little birds – red, purple, orange, yellow, green – besides plenty of chattering monkeys and parrots.' Her observations were clear and simple yet also very vivid. They stopped the first night at a little town, where they pitched their tents in a small market-place. 'Hundreds of people sat round to look at us, and clapped their hands and shouted to see us eat.' On subsequent nights they camped on river banks and lit fires to keep off the wild animals: 'Still there were many things that made a queer noise all night.' They left the canoes at Abomiga, then Anna was put in a hammock and transported to the house at Abeokuta which was to be their missionary base.

The house had been abandoned by missionaries who had gone back to England and was 'not very inviting in its appearance'. White ants had eaten holes in the floor and walls and there were spiders 'as large as the palm of your hand'. It was a far cry from a comfortable Victorian vicarage in Suffolk. The next day was Sunday, with prayers at six in the morning followed by school at nine. Anna cried to hear the hymns and think of the Sunday school back home. A four-year-old girl noticed this: 'As I walked home she still clung to me, and then put her little black hand into mine, and ran away. The next day she saw me, and looked up saying "Missis no cry to-day, Missis cry no more."'

Illness dogged Anna's first months at Abeokuta but after

recovering she tried, unsuccessfully at first, to engage the small children: 'heathen children run away in the most ludicrous manner, as if I were a serpent . . . Poor little things, such slavish fear. One quite sees the effect of slavery through everything, their countenances speak it.' At the end of February a harmonium arrived, a present from Mrs Cunningham, who was told of the first singing class: 'I only longed for the power of painting, to give you some idea of the scene – the black beaming faces.' The great war-chief Ogubonna tried to play but couldn't, observing: 'it is only white people who can do anything great, and only the "Iya" (mother, as they call me) who can make wood and ivory speak, with her fingers.' The people praised Anna's rosy cheeks but: 'I would give all the colour I possess to be able to talk a little Yoruba, and tell them of something else.'

In March David Hinderer set off for Ibadan on mission business and Anna was rather alone, studying the language: 'I am looked upon as somebody wonderful, being so much stronger than any white woman has been who has been here.' She played ball with the children and struggled to overcome their fear, which was palpable: 'never having seen a white woman, and, as slaves, having a horror of white people'. Anna's simple Christianity reflected an equally sim-plistic view of black people. She referred to them as 'these poor but affectionate and well-meaning people, who, though black enough their skins may be, have never-dying souls, which need to be led to the Saviour, to be washed clean in the blood of the Lamb'. This did not prevent her from easily making friends of the people: 'Their black skin makes no difference to me; to have them come to me, to see them pleased, makes me quite happy.' She took them for walks and they came to listen to the magically ticking clock and look at pictures and rummage in her work-basket. She wrote very touch-ingly and directly about her interactions with the local people.

On 25 April 1853 the Hinderers left Abeokuta for Ibadan to attack, as Anna put it, 'in the name of the Lord of Hosts, this stronghold of sin and Satan'. She was carried in a hammock whose 'cradle-like motion' comforted her on the long journey, during which they started to run out of water. On arriving at Ibadan they were surrounded by an excitable, voluble crowd chanting: 'The white man is come!' and greeting them with cries of 'Alafia, alafia. Peace, peace.'

For the next year the Hinderers lived in a thirty-foot-long dwelling with 'dismal bare mud walls, mud floor, and thatched roof', divided into three rooms for themselves and the other two missionaries, but they were happy for 'a great, a holy work commenced'. The church was a shed covered in palm leaves. The people were affectionate, especially the children, and one day when Anna did not appear because of illness a tearful small boy went around saying he could not 'find Missis all day'. Ill-health continued to be a problem for her and in July she nearly died but she persisted in teaching the gospel in the Yoruba Testament: 'We have very pleasant Sunday evenings over the Noah's ark, or Mrs Buxton's beautiful Scripture pictures.' But Kefer began to report that he had been ordered away when preaching in public, being told: 'We will not have you white men, you are the world's spoilers.' Anna confessed during a period of depression: 'one is apt to get flat, and cold, and heartless sometimes, and to go down, down'. The school was slow to grow: 'people are afraid to send their children; they think "book" will make them cowards'.

Eventually the missionaries built themselves a new mission house at Ibadan, of which Anna wrote: 'it is water-tight! has a good-sized sitting and bed room, white-washed walls, and a good iron roof; comfortable piazzas, and all very airy, and as cool as anything can be in Africa, which was my principal desire'. But they took care to remind themselves that 'this is not our home, but a tent pitched for the day'. Bale, the head chief of the district, paid a visit and was 'extremely amused to see himself in the looking-glass'. Anna rejoiced in her boys' talk of Jesus: 'I thought it was worth while to come to Africa, only to hear this from little lips which, such a short time ago, were taught senseless words over wood, and stone, and charms.' And so they persisted, even after Kefer died of yellow fever and was buried in the churchyard.

In August 1855 the Hinderers held their first Christian wedding but the converted had to face the fact that they were, by the rest of the people, 'looked down upon as contemptible, and are called book-followers, forsakers of their forefathers, and despisers of their gods, who have given them strength, power, and everything'. Nevertheless eight of the children living with Anna were baptised, dressed in white, 'with an earnest desire in my heart that they might be possessors of the robe made white in the blood of the Lamb'. Clearly there was persecution of some of the converts with young women being beaten and tortured by their families.

In May 1856, after an attack of the fever that had killed Kefer, David Hinderer decided to return to England and Anna joined him on the Lagos mail: 'homeward bound, though I think I then felt that I was rather leaving home'. She was ill for the whole voyage to Plymouth and the captain, handing her up the landing steps, told her: 'a few more voyages must kill you.' She admitted: 'I am not the strong person I was before I went to poor Africa.'

Back in England the Hinderers went around talking to small groups of missionary supporters about their experiences in Africa and in June they visited David's family in Württemberg but they decided to return to Africa and in January 1858 they were back in Ibadan to a rapturous welcome from 'the heathens'. They started to encourage the people to make an amnesty of their idols and soon had 'a large basketful' of them. A former slave dealer even arrived with his irons. By now they had twenty-nine communicants, thirty-nine candidates for baptism and twelve more in the queue: 'Thus the Lord's work is going on, and ought we not to be the more encouraged as it is truly hard ground to work upon?' David's health improved each time he set off on his own on missionary duties or trips to Sierra Leone and even Anna welcomed a short trip to Abeokuta for 'a little communion, and interchange of thought and words, with Europeans'.

During the life of the Yoruba mission there was disruption from the surrounding wars, which included struggles between Ibadan and its neighbours Ijaiye, Abeokuta and Ijebu after 1860, and until

1865 the Hinderers were cut off from the coast and fellow missionaries. In January 1860, with 'the barbarous king of Dahomey'
threatening war, Anna admitted that 'the anticipation of war
unstrings all my nerves'. When Ibadan offered a human sacrifice in
advance of the war with one of these neighbours her patience nearly
gave way: 'O the blindness, the darkness, the foolishness of heathenism, and in the midst of all this we are living; and when pressed
down under the thought of these and a thousand other sorrows and
horrors, we can hardly help asking sometimes, are we of any use in
such a country?'

Food shortages and cowrie shell inflation followed and the war
hampered the Hinderers' work, so that they made only one convert
in 1861. Anna sold her cloak and onions from her patch for cowrie
shells but, by the end of 1862, they had sold everything they had
for food. They were increasingly isolated and even David's great
work of translating *The Pilgrim's Progress* into Yoruba was threatened by a shortage of paper. Of this period Anna wrote: 'We are
not yet delivered, but kept and even comforted in our trial in a
land of captivity . . . We do get so cast down at times, we are so let
and hindered in our work, our hearts faint, and our hands hang
down. No materials for our schools, not even a Bible for each
child, and we have such hard work and toil in only just holding
things together.'

In April 1865 the Governor of Lagos sent an expedition to Ibadan
and Anna was rescued and carried in a hammock to the coast, arriving at Liverpool on 13 May. Two months later David joined her for
recuperation and rest but in November 1866 they were back in
Ibadan. By 1868, however, the couple began to realize that their missionary days were numbered. A hundred now worshipped in the
first church at Kudeti and they were trying to train native teachers
for the work and, in February 1869, Anna left, alone, on the mail for
England. She would never return.

Unwell himself, David joined his wife five months later. Anna,
after finding she had lost the sight of her right eye, was told by the
oculist that she would have gone blind had she remained in Africa.

In November they moved to Norfolk, where David became curate of Martham and where Anna died on 6 June 1870. 'So passed away,' wrote the editor of her journals, 'in her forty-fourth year, one whose health had been utterly ruined by the pestilential climate of Africa, the dangers of which she had encountered for the love of Christ.'

## 35

## *I Presume: Stanley's Quest for Livingstone*

On 16 October 1869 a telegram arrived at the hotel in Madrid of an ambitious young journalist called Henry Morton Stanley, sent by James Gordon Bennett Jr, manager of the *New York Herald*. It said simply: 'COME TO PARIS ON IMPORTANT BUSINESS.' Stanley, who could tell a good story, and whose fictional gifts extended to reinventing himself as an American journalist when in fact he was a Welshman called John Rowlands, told the best one of all about his encounter with Livingstone at Ujiji (see Chapter 29). It is extremely unlikely that what he purported to say to Livingstone was actually said but it was, as the Italians say, *ben trovato*.

But that October, if the tale is true, Stanley was on the train to Paris from Madrid by three the same afternoon. The next night he hammered on the door of Bennett's room at the Grand Hotel and was ordered to come in. He found the newspaper boss in bed.

'"Who are you?" he asked.

'"My name is Stanley," I answered.

'"Ah, yes! sit down; I have important business on hand for you."'

Bennett pulled on a *robe de chambre* and began to throw out a series of questions about David Livingstone, who was, famously by now, lost in the African jungle. Stanley confessed he knew nothing about the explorer or his whereabouts but Bennett said he could do what he liked 'BUT FIND LIVINGSTONE!' Stanley then asked if he had considered the cost. Burton and Speke's journey to Central Africa cost between £3000 and £5000 and Stanley doubted if it could be done for under £2500. Bennett immediately advanced £1000 and said there would be more but the priority was 'FIND LIVINGSTONE!' Bennett made up for what he lacked in knowledge about the realities of such an expedition with an enthusiasm for issuing instructions. He wanted a good journalistic return on his money.

Stanley was told to go to the Suez Canal and then up the Nile, report on an expedition that was just starting for Upper Egypt under the leadership of Samuel Baker ('describe as well as possible whatever is interesting for tourists'), go to Jerusalem to investigate the discoveries being made by Captain Warren, 'visit Constantinople, and find out about that trouble between the Khedive and the Sultan', visit the old Crimean battle grounds and then press on to the Caucasus, Caspian Sea, Persia, India and Baghdad, where he was to write about the Euphrates Valley railway. Bennett concluded this breathless briefing with the words: 'Then, when you have come to India, you can go after Livingstone. Probably you will hear by that time that Livingstone is on his way to Zanzibar; but if not, go into the interior and find him. If alive, get what news of his discoveries you can; and if he is dead, bring all possible proofs of his being dead. That is all. Good-night, and God be with you.'

So Stanley boarded the express train to Marseilles and in due course was pursuing his mission: 'I travelled over the Crimean battle-grounds with Kinglake's glorious books for reference in my hand ... I saw the Arabian traveller Palgrave at Trebizond ... I wrote my name on one of the Persepolitan monuments. In the month of August 1870, I arrived in India.' On 12 October 1870 he sailed from Bombay to Mauritius on the barque *Polly*, another ship took him to the Seychelles and then an American whaling vessel took him on to Zanzibar, where he arrived on 6 January 1871.

Stanley's narrative is racier than the norm of the Victorian travel narrative (digressions and portly padding time and again leaving the reader puzzling out where the writer is). He deliberately rejected the discursive diary or journal approach in favour of a swift journalistic narrative, 'and I think that in this manner I avoid the great fault of repetition for which some travellers have been severely criticised'. He also had the journalist's ability to take the measure of the gap between tradition and what he saw with his own eyes on the ground: 'One day's life at Zanzibar made me thoroughly conscious of my ignorance respecting African people and things in general. I imagined I had read Burton and Speke through, fairly well, and that consequently I had penetrated the meaning, the full importance and grandeur, of the work I was about to be engaged upon. But my estimates, for instance, based on book information, were simply ridiculous.'

Stanley was different also in his approach to the indigenous people and the Arab traders of Zanzibar. He found the latter had: 'a calm, resolute, defiant, independent air about them, which wins unconsciously one's respect'. Although he seemed to despise half-castes, he suggested – in direct contrast with the strident racism of Burton – that the 'white stranger' needed to learn at the outset: 'that negroes are men, like himself, though of a different colour; that they have passions and prejudices, likes and dislikes, sympathies and antipathies, tastes and feelings, in common with all human nature. The sooner he perceives this fact, and adapts himself accordingly, the easier will be his journey among the several races of the interior. The more plastic his nature, the more prosperous will be his travels.'

As he prepared to venture into the interior Stanley continued to regret that all that purple prose of the great travellers had not included some hard practical information and that Burton, Speke, Grant *et al.* had not troubled to write a chapter entitled 'How to get ready for an Expedition for Central Africa'. Endless 'geographical, ethnological and other information' existed but nothing about the nuts and bolts of organizing such an expedition: 'There was not one white man in Zanzibar who could tell how many *dotis* a day a force of one hundred men required to buy food for one day on the road.' By consulting an Arab ivory trader, Sheikh Hashid, Stanley got more information 'than I had obtained from three months' study of books upon Central Africa'.

Stanley packed plenty of cloth, beads and wire to use as currency, and rehired six of Speke's 'Faithfuls', including the famous Bombay, who was 'the captain of my soldiers to Ujiji'. Of his team, Stanley declared: 'They were an exceedingly fine-looking body of men, far more intelligent in appearance than I could ever have believed African barbarians could be.' He acquired two boats and stripped them of their boards with the plan of covering each with a double skin of tarred canvas. Reviewing his six tons of equipment, he wondered: 'How will it ever be possible to move all this inert mass across the wilderness stretching between the sea, and the great lakes of Africa?'

On 5 February 1871, after twenty-eight days of preparation at Zanzibar, Stanley was ready to set sail for Bagamoyo, twenty-five miles across the water on the mainland of Africa. Intending to move straight on, he was in fact soon bogged down at Bagamoyo because of problems recruiting enough men. He was anxious about the approach of the rainy season and had a canny sense that if Livingstone got wind of the idea that the *New York Herald* was on his trail he would disappear: 'for my impression was that he was a man who would try to put as much distance as possible between us, rather than make an effort to shorten it, and I should have my long journey for nothing'. It was not until 21 March, seventy-three days after arriving at Zanzibar, that Stanley – or 'Bwana Mkuba' (the big master), as the natives christened him – eventually moved off behind the American flag. It made quite a substantial presence:

Altogether the Expedition numbers on the day of departure three white men, twenty-three soldiers, four supernumeraries, four chiefs, and one hundred and fifty-three pagazis, twenty-seven donkeys, and one cart, conveying cloth, beads, and wire, boat-fixings, tents, cooking utensils and dishes, medicine, powder, small shot, musket-balls, and metallic cartridges; instruments and small necessaries, such as soap, sugar, tea, coffee, Liebig's extract of meat, pemmican, candles, &c., which make a total of

153 loads. The weapons of defence which the Expedition possesses consist of one double-barrel breech-loading gun, smooth bore; one American Winchester rifle, or 'sixteen-shooter;' one Henry rifle, or 'sixteen-shooter;' two Starr's breech-loaders, one Jocelyn breech-loader, one elephant rifle, carrying balls eight to the pound; two breech-loading revolvers, twenty-four muskets (flint locks) six single-barrelled pistols, one battle-axe, two swords, two daggers (Persian kummers, purchased at Shiraz by myself) one boar-spear, two American axes 4 lbs each, twenty-four hatchets, and twenty-four butcher-knives.

Stanley was ecstatic at being on the move at last ('the enthusiasm of youth still clung to me') and, as he moved into the interior, he began to get reports of Livingstone. At Muhalleh he met Salim bin Rashid, who reported that the explorer was 'looking old, with long grey moustaches and beard, just recovered from serious illness, looking very wan'. It was a tough and exhausting journey and Stanley nearly died of dysentery and fevers during which: 'The wonders of Africa that bodied themselves forth in the shape of flocks of zebras, giraffes, elands, or antelopes, galloping over the jungleless plain, had no charm for me.'

When he reached Unyanyembe on 22 June he was asked by the Governor about 'Haji Abdullah' and he replied that Richard Burton was now the British Consul at Damascus. Stanley was very much aware of his distinguished precursors in this landscape which he regarded as 'classic ground, since Capts. Burton, Speke and Grant years ago had visited it, and described it'. Unfortunately war had now broken out with the tribal leader Mirambo and Stanley's plan to proceed by boat across Lake Victoria and from there down the Nile had to be abandoned. He was frustrated by 'these stupid, slow-witted Arabs and their warnings and croakings' and suspected them of trying to keep him back to help in the war with Mirambo, but his resolution was firm 'never to give up the search until I find Livingstone alive, or find his dead body . . . only death can prevent me'.

By 20 September Stanley had had enough and he set off by the southern route with fifty-four men and boys 'on the apparently useless mission of seeking for the lost traveller, David Livingstone'. The party carried '1000 doti, or 4000 yds. of cloth, six bags of beads, four loads of ammunition, one tent, one bed and clothes, one box of medicine, sextant and books, two loads of tea, coffee and sugar, one load of flour and candles, one load of canned meats, sardines, and miscellaneous necessaries, and one load of cooking utensils'. They were constantly being attacked by fever and Stanley brandished a slave-chain for anyone who tried to desert: 'I told them I was the first white man who had taken a slave-chain with him on his travels.'

Rumours of sightings of Livingstone reached Stanley and he pressed on eagerly: 'God grant me patience, but I do wish there was a railroad, or, at least, horses in this country.' Each night, while he wrote up his diary in his circular tent from whose central pole the American flag fluttered, he told his servant to 'lay out my new flannel suit, to oil my boots, to chalk my helmet, and fold a new puggaree around it, that I may make as presentable an appearance as possible before the white man with the grey beard, and before the Arabs of Ujiji; for the clothes I have worn through jungle and forest are in tatters'.

On 10 November, 236 days after leaving Bagamoyo, Stanley finally caught sight of Lake Tanganyika, 'an immense broad sheet, a burnished bed of silver', and approached Ujiji, firing off a volley of shots. They soon met Livingstone's servant, Susi, who confirmed that his master was there: 'My heart beats fast, but I must not let my face betray my emotions, lest it shall detract from the dignity of a white man appearing under such extraordinary circumstances.' Walking down 'a living avenue of people', Stanley at last spotted Livingstone standing in a semicircle of Arabs: 'As I advanced slowly towards him I noticed he was pale, that he looked wearied and wan, that he had grey whiskers and moustache, that he wore a bluish cloth cap with a faded gold band on a red ground round it, and that he had on a red-sleeved waistcoat, and a pair of grey tweed trousers.' Stanley (our sole witness and orchestrator of this famous tale) then stepped deliberately towards Livingstone, took off his hat and said: 'Dr Livingstone, I presume?'

'Yes,' said he, with a kind and cordial smile, lifting his cap slightly.

'I thank God, Doctor, I have been permitted to see you.'

He answered, 'I feel thankful that I am here to welcome you.'

They adjourned to Livingstone's house with a thousand natives watching the scene of 'two white men meeting at Ujiji – one just come from Manyuema, in the west, the other from Unyanyembe, in the east'. Stanley completely forgot what they talked about, so distracted was he by his hero: 'I found myself gazing at him, conning the wonderful figure and face of the man at whose side I now sat in Central Africa.' Livingstone was handed a year-old bag of letters and he demanded to hear the world's news. Stanley told him that the Suez Canal had been opened, the Pacific railroad completed, Grant elected President of the United States, Isabella driven from the throne by a revolution in Spain, 'Napoleon's dynasty extinguished by the Prussian' and Schleswig-Holstein annexed. 'There was no need for exaggeration,' Stanley noted after delivering this bulletin, 'of any penny-a-line news, or of any sensationalism.'

Livingstone apparently showed a proper appreciation of the splendour of modern journalism and 'listened in wonder to one of the most exciting pages of history ever repeated'. But Stanley admitted that he had been too excited to get out his shorthand notebook so that although they talked a great deal he reported almost nothing of its substance. Livingstone was said to have declared twice: 'You have brought me new life.'

Champagne and silver goblets were called for and much-needed food offered. The next morning, having read all his letters, Livingstone returned to Stanley, who admitted that at first the great explorer had only been 'a great item for a daily newspaper, as much as other subjects in which the voracious news-loving public delight in' but now he was turning into a friend. Nothing in his journalistic missions to date had 'moved me so much' and he saw 'an overruling and kindly Providence' at work in all that had happened. He suggested to Livingstone that they should explore the northern head of Lake Tanganyika and the two men spent the next four months together, from 10 November 1871 to 14 March 1872.

During this time Stanley found that 'there is no guile, and what is apparent on the surface is the thing that is in him'. He reported the views of Livingstone's detractors and hinted at the fuller picture: 'I grant he is no angel.' He found Livingstone reserved but claimed he had a sense of humour and a retentive memory. 'Livingstone no doubt may be mistaken in some of his conclusions about certain points in the geography of Central Africa,' Stanley conceded, 'but he is not so dogmatic and positive a man as to refuse conviction.' The principal example of this just now was Livingstone's belief that he had discovered in the Lualaba the headwaters of the Nile and he wanted to press on in order to prove it, saying he needed only another five or six months. The opportunistic Stanley was impressed by both Livingstone's dedication and his indifference to exploiting his discoveries: 'Had he followed the example of ordinary explorers, he would have been running backwards and forwards to tell the news, instead of exploring; and he might have been able to write a volume upon the discovery of each lake, and earn much money thereby.' The two men cruised on Lake Tanganyika and then travelled together back to Unyanyembe to get stores from Zanzibar. On arrival they heard about the events of the Paris Commune, which provoked Stanley to the lament: 'Oh France! Oh Frenchmen! Such things are unknown even in the heart of barbarous Central Africa!'

If Stanley is to be believed, Livingstone returned his respect and appreciated the mission which had brought Stanley to him. From Ujiji he wrote to Stanley's boss, Gordon Bennett: 'I am as cold and non-demonstrative as we islanders are usually reputed to be; but your kindness made my frame thrill.' Stanley, however, had performed his mission. He had been ill repeatedly and was shocked by his own emaciated and greying appearance when he looked in a mirror in Zanzibar. The world demanded the great self-dramatizing newspaperman's skills (the Atlantic telegraph cables had just been laid) and it was time to move on. He finally bade farewell to Livingstone at Tabora on 14 March 1872: 'But though I may live half a century longer, I shall never forget that parting scene in Central Africa . . . I waved a handkerchief to him, as a final token of farewell, and he responded to it by lifting his cap.'

Livingstone resumed his explorations of the River Lualaba, searching still for the mystery of the Nile. His health was deteriorating and by April 1873 he had to be carried on a litter. He died on 30 April 1873 at the village of Chitambo in the Lake Regions, where his heart was buried. His body was preserved and taken to the coast, from where it was sent to England and laid to rest in the nave of Westminster Abbey. Stanley would be one of the pallbearers.

## 36

*Purposeless Curiosity: Amelia Edwards in Egypt*

The best journeys have about them an element of accident: the charms of the unintended. At the end of the summer of 1873 two ladies were sketching in central France but had been driven by persistent rain first into Italy and then to a stormy passage by boat on the *Simla* from Brindisi to Alexandria. On 29 November 1873 they reached Cairo and the refuge of the Shepheard Hotel. 'For in simple truth,' wrote Amelia Edwards with her characteristically sharp and realistic pen, 'we had had drifted hither by accident, with no excuse of health, or business, or any serious object whatever; and had just taken refuge in Egypt as one might turn aside into the

Burlington Arcade or the Passage des Panoramas – to get out of the rain.' So began the career of the pioneering Egyptologist Amelia Ann Blanford Edwards.

Born in London on 30 June 1831, Amelia Edwards was the only child of Thomas Edwards, an army officer, and Alicia, *née* Walpole, and was educated at home and by private tutors, displaying a precocious talent for writing, sketching and music. After breaking off an unsatisfactory engagement in 1853 she started to travel in Europe and to launch herself as a writer, her first novel appearing in 1864 (she would eventually publish nine), to be followed by biographies, anthologies of poetry and books of travels. In 1873 she set off with her friend Lucy Renshawe on the journey that would eventually land them in Cairo.

What distinguishes Amelia Edwards's account is its brisk realism, her awareness that she was travelling in the blossoming age of tourism and her sharp observation. In the great dining room of the Shepheard Hotel she observed nearly three hundred people daily, 'half of whom are Anglo-Indians homeward or outward bound, European residents, or visitors established in Cairo for the winter' and claimed to be able to distinguish immediately, as noted earlier, between 'a Cook's tourist and an independent traveller'. She was undoubtedly one of the latter but was interested in the other kind: 'Here are invalids in search of health; artists in search of subjects; sportsmen keen upon crocodiles; statesmen out for a holiday; special correspondents alert for gossip; collectors on the scent of papyri and mummies; men of science with only scientific ends in view; and the usual surplus of idlers who travel for the mere love of travel, or the satisfaction of purposeless curiosity.' The morning after her arrival she looked out of her window at the grey-green palms and noticed a veiled woman walking on the terraced roof in the midst of a cloud of pigeons: 'Nothing could be more simple than the scene and its accessories; nothing, at the same time, more Eastern, strange, and unreal.'

Edwards's first excursion was into the crowded bazaars of Cairo, where everything seemed to be 'a ready-made picture' and everyone looked 'as if they had been put there expressly to be painted'. This was her constant theme: the clash of vivid actuality and the sense that Egypt was suffused with an Orientalist glow and redolent of ancient mystery. In the *souks* 'Englishmen in palm-leaf hats and knickerbockers' rubbed up against 'figures that come and go like the actors in some Christmas piece of Oriental pageantry'. Symbolic of this conjunction of Oriental mystery and the grim purposiveness of the modern travel industry were, of course, the Pyramids, a mere half-hour's drive from the hotel: 'But it must be understood that we did not go to *see* the Pyramids. We went only to look at them . . . The first glimpse that most travellers now get of the Pyramids is from the window of the railway carriage as they come from Alexandria; and it is not impressive.'

But, on approaching the Great Pyramid from the desert, she *was* impressed by the way its 'unexpected bulk and majesty towers close above one's head, the effect is as sudden as it is overwhelming. It shuts out the sky and the horizon. It shuts out all the other Pyramids. It shuts out everything but the sense of awe and wonder.' She was determined to understand the Great Pyramid and to give it her sole attention – unlike the breathless tourists scurrying about her in an attempt to tick everything off: 'With such energy and despatch as the modern traveller uses, we might have been to the top, and seen the temple of the Sphinx, and done two or three of the principal tombs in the time.'

After visiting the decaying mosque of Sultan Hassan, where she was impressed by the 'profound and unaffected devotion' of the Muslim faithful, Edwards watched the departure of the two-thousand-strong Mecca Pilgrimage: 'A harmless, unsavoury, good-humoured, inoffensive throng, one glance at which was enough to put to flight all one's preconceived notions about Oriental gravity of demeanour!' Then she and Lucy, with three other travellers, set off on a boat, the *Philae*, a hundred feet long and twenty feet wide, with the high upper deck furnished with lounge chairs, tables and rugs, 'like a drawing room in the open air', to explore the Nile. Their first important stop was Memphis and

Edwards was as acutely aware as ever of the incongruous sight presented by the British tourist: 'we cut a sorry figure with our hideous palm-leaf hats, green veils, and white umbrellas'. Beneath her feet were scattered shards of pottery and bits of mummified corpse, for they were standing on 'violated graves'.

They descended into the Serapeum, or sepulchral temple, of the Sacred Bulls, which had been discovered only twenty years earlier, and read by candlelight the hieroglyphics on the sarcophagi. The gap between past and present was insistent: 'We have of course been dipping into Herodotus – everyone takes Herodotus up the Nile – and our heads are full of the ancient glories of this famous city.' But all that remained were 'a few huge rubbish-heaps, a dozen or so of broken statues, and a name!', which made it 'a disappointing place to see'. Nevertheless: 'Those melancholy mounds and that heron-haunted lake must be seen, if only that they may take their due place in the picture-gallery of one's memory.'

Partly because she could not bear to see the neglected condition of the very young children, Edwards tended to avoid going about the native towns when the boat stopped but she also had doubts about the value of rapid first impressions, the tourist's stock-in-trade: 'That I may so have lost an opportunity of now and then seeing more of the street-life of the people is very probable; but such outside glimpses are of little real value, and I at all events escaped the sight of much poverty, sickness and squalor.' She was, however, a little more ready to observe her fellow countrymen. On Christmas Day 1873, on board the *Philae*, she directed her forensic gaze on a honeymooning young couple: 'Of people who are struggling through that helpless phase of human life called the honeymoon, it is not fair to say more than that they are both young enough to make the situation interesting.' It was very hot on deck: 'Not, however, till the plum-pudding, blazing demoniacally, appeared upon the scene, did any of us succeed in believing that it was really Christmas Day.'

On board Edwards sketched, wrote letters, read the Egyptologists and 'worked hard at Egyptian dynasties . . . Such is our Noah's ark life, pleasant, peaceful, and patriarchal.' This kind of travel was a far cry from the fever-infested jungles of Central Africa. Arriving at the temple of Denderah, she was aware of the huge gap between this preparatory mugging-up and the reality of the direct encounter: 'We have been reading about these gods and emblems for weeks past – we have studied the plan of the Temple beforehand; yet now that we are actually here, our book knowledge goes for nothing, and we feel as hopelessly ignorant as if we had been suddenly landed in a new world.' Edwards' descriptions of the ruins are detailed and painstaking and she was methodical in her observations and the due order in which the sights should be seen. To 'put things in their right places' was 'a mental process which every traveller must perform for himself'.

At Luxor she saw, beyond the entrance to the temple: 'a smoky, filthy, intricate labyrinth of lanes and passages . . . Cocks crew, hens cackled, pigeons cooed, turkeys gobbled, children swarmed, women were baking and gossiping, and all the sordid routine of Arab life was going on, amid winding alleys that masked the colonnades and defaced the inscriptions of the Pharaohs.' And at Karnak, faced with 'the noblest architectural work ever designed and executed by human hands', the Hypostyle Hall of Seti I, she gave voice to the central dilemma of the travel writer: 'All admit their inability to describe it; yet all attempt the description.'

When a local sold her an ancient Egyptian coin which turned out to be a George IV farthing she delivered her verdict on the Arab: 'a singularly transparent piece of humanity, easily amused, easily deceived, easily angered, easily pacified . . . his good points outnumber his bad ones'. She defended her right to generalize in this way because she felt that this mode of travel by Nile boat in which 'one really sees the whole land of Egypt', rather than being segregated in the manner of European upper- and middle-class travel, by first-class compartments and grand hotels, enabled proper observation to be made: 'In Europe, and indeed in most parts of the East, one sees too little of the people to be able to form an opinion about them; but it is not so on the Nile. Cut off from hotels, railways, from Europeanised cities, you are brought into continual intercourse with natives.'

At Aswan Edwards did what was expected of her, the short journey from there to Philae forming 'part of every dragoman's programme, and figur[ing] as the crowning achievement of every Cook's tourist'. She was a dedicated traveller, however, and made copious drawings and sketches which adorn her hefty volume *A Thousand Miles Up the Nile* (1877). She understood how important it was to grasp the complexities of ancient Egyptian history and at the great temple of Abu Simbel, which she reached in the moonlight, she argued that the traveller, without a knowledge of Rameses the Great, was impoverished: 'Holding to the merest thread of explanation, he wanders from hall to hall, lacking altogether that potent charm of foregone association which no Murray can furnish.'

Edwards stayed for eighteen days at Abu Simbel: 'it was wonderful to wake every morning close under the steep bank, and, without lifting one's head from the pillow, to see that row of giant faces so close against the sky . . . Every morning I waked in time to witness that daily miracle.' She found the site 'a wonderful place to be alone in – a place in which the very darkness and silence are old, and in which Time himself seems to have fallen asleep'. It was so 'weird and awful . . . that I rarely ventured beyond the first hall when quite alone'.

On 16 February 1874 one of the party noticed a crack in some sculptures near the south buttress of the temple and they found the entrance to a tomb with a painted frieze and some bas-relief sculptures. The next day workmen were called in to further the excavation and afterwards the travellers left their names on the discovery: 'the only occasion upon which any of us left our names upon an Egyptian monument'. A letter was immediately dispatched to *The Times* to claim the discovery. But Edwards later discovered that not only had their names been effaced but the wall paintings were already being damaged by tourist attention and she was angry at the destructiveness unleashed by collectors and museums:

The most famous of all Victorian travellers: David Livingstone.
(Mary Evans/Rue des Archives)

'I saw that old father Nile without any doubt rises in the Victoria N'yanza': John Hanning Speke, July 1862.

The priority was 'FIND LIVINGSTONE!': Henry Morton Stanley.
(Mary Evans)

'It shuts out the sky and the horizon.' Amelia Edwards describes the Great Pyramid on an excursion from Cairo in 1873.
(National Portrait Gallery)

In Africa killing animals and birds was important to some Victorian travellers. Charles Baldwin was one of the most dedicated hunters.

An engraving of a charging elephant by Herbert Ward, traveller in the Congo Free State.

'It is none of my business to go up mountains. There's next to no fish on them in West Africa': avid collector of freshwater specimens, Mary Kingsley.
(Mary Evans)

Helen Caddick's husband carried in a hammock by native porters, central Africa.

A portrait of Charles Darwin before his fame as author of *The Origin of Species*.
(AKG Images)

Engraving of the *Beagle*, Darwin's ship for his five-year voyage of scientific discovery and exploration.

'The world is gradually acquiring a painful similarity': Henry Kirke, who spent twenty-five years in British Guiana, 1898.

Missionary to the central South Pacific Jonathan Williams takes delivery of idols in the South Seas.

'Let me ask him if it would not be an honourable achievement to be the first to place a foot in its centre.' Charles Sturt, explorer to Australia, 1849.
(National Portrait Gallery)

James Clark Ross, who in 1839 set off for the South Pole. The expedition lasted five years.
(National Portrait Gallery)

Francis McLintock's *Fox* trapped in ice, trying to find a North-West Passage through the polar sea, 1857.

'Sir John Franklin died on the 11th June 1847 and the total loss by deaths in the Expedition has been to this date 9 officers & 15 men': note discovered in polar ice by McLintock. Franklin and his crew had failed to return from their own attempt at the passage twelve years before.

Such is the fate of every Egyptian monument, great or small. The tourist carves it all over with names and dates, and in some instances with caricatures. The student of Egyptology, by taking wet paper 'squeezes', sponges away every vestige of the original colour. The 'collector' buys and carries off everything of value that he can get; and the Arab steals for him. The work of destruction, meanwhile, goes on apace. There is no one to prevent it; there is no one to discourage it. Every day, more inscriptions are mutilated – more tombs are rifled – more paintings and sculptures are defaced. The Louvre contains a full-length portrait of Seti I, cut out bodily from the walls of his sepulchre in the Valley of the Tombs of the Kings. The Museums of Berlin, of Turin, of Florence [she omits reference to the British Museum or her own *graffiti*], are rich in spoils which tell their own lamentable tale. When science leads the way, is it wonderful that ignorance should follow?

On her return journey back along the Nile, Edwards's appetite for temples remained 'insatiable' and she continued to work on her detailed ground plans and architectural drawings. Making a proper visit to Luxor on this return leg, she noted some travel statistics: 'In every twenty-five boats, one may fairly calculate upon an average of twelve English, nine American, two German, one Belgian, and one French.' At Luxor these boats came under siege from dealers and touts and locals who had dug up treasure to sell to the tourists: 'Some hundreds of families live in this grim way, spoiling the dead-and-gone Egyptians for a livelihood.' She actually witnessed the excavation of a mummy which looked 'startlingly human and pathetic lying at the bottom of its grave in the morning sunlight'. But once again Edwards was not averse to a little light hypocrisy: 'Life at Thebes is made up of incongruities. A morning among temples is followed by an afternoon of antiquity-hunting; and a day of meditation among tombs winds up with a dinner-party on board some friend's dahabeeyah, or a fantasia at the British Consulate.' She and Lucy did their 'fair share of antiquity-hunting' and she admitted: 'we enjoyed it nonetheless because it was illegal'.

Their last weeks on the Nile 'went by like one long, lazy summer's day' and, though Edwards's book ends rather abruptly, she and Lucy in fact went on to Syria and Constantinople. On her return to England she threw herself into the study of ancient Egypt and of hieroglyphics, wrote her book, which was well-received, and started to contribute articles on Egyptology and to make contacts with leading European scholars. She was also instrumental in the founding of the Egypt Exploration Fund, dedicated to promoting responsible scientific excavation, and she was elected honorary joint secretary in March 1882. For the next ten years until her death she worked tirelessly for the fund (which later became the Egypt Exploration Society) but also found time to be vice-president of the Society for the Promotion of Women's Suffrage. She lectured widely at home and in the United States. She died on 15 April 1892 at her home in Somerset after contracting a lung infection while supervising antiquities arriving at London docks from Egypt. Her library was left to University College London, where she had founded the first-ever chair of Egyptology, its first occupant being Flinders Petrie.

37

*A Wife in a Wheelbarrow: Annie Hore*
*at Lake Tanganyika*

Without question the Victorian travel book with the most
intriguing title of any so far considered is *To Lake
Tanganyika in a Bath Chair* (1886). Annie Boyle Hore's account of
her ninety-day, 830-mile trip from the sea to Ujiji and the Lake
offered itself – in a crowded library of 'travel and adventure' in
Central Africa – as a description of scenes 'for the first time witnessed and experienced by one of my own sex'.

Born in 1853, Annie B. Gibbon married in 1881 Edward Coode
Hore, a member of the Wesleyan Missionary Society living in

Bedford. In 1877 Edward Hore had been appointed scientific officer of a large expedition to Tanganyika which aimed to establish a mission station and a European commercial settlement. He spent three years surveying Lake Tanganyika 'before the work of missions and commerce commenced' less than a quarter of a century after its first discovery by Burton and Speke. Notwithstanding the resourcefulness called for by her African journey with her husband, Annie Hore began her narrative in the customary fashion by representing herself as 'a weak woman with a child in her arms'. She apologized if some of her remarks 'appear rather too advanced for one of so little experience' but reassured her readers that 'I have been posted up in such matters by my husband'. Edward had been frustrated by the failure to get bullock carts to work because of fatal attacks on the oxen by the tsetse fly and, as an alternative to carriage by porters, he was convinced that some form of wheeled conveyance could be used. At a public meeting of missionary supporters he declared that 'if he could succeed in getting no other vehicle, he would at least take his wife to Ujiji in a wheelbarrow'.

Before they left England in 1882 the Hores purchased a wicker bath chair made by the manufacturer Carter with a broad double wheel, adjustable as one or two wheels, and fitted with short poles for lifting the whole contraption over difficult places in the manner of a palanquin. Another of Edward's schemes was to send a steam launch in sections to be conveyed overland by a caravan of several hundred native porters.

On 17 May 1882 the couple and their three-month-old son Jack sailed from London to Zanzibar. The roughness of the voyage made Zanzibar seem even more attractive, presenting as it did: 'the most romantic ideal of Oriental landscape; white villas environed with cocoa-nuts, and the square white lines of the town, backed and studded with vivid greens, and pleasing forms of foliage'. They soon took an Arab dhow to the mainland at Saadani, then set off for Ndumi. 'As I stepped into the bath chair, which had many eager candidates for its conveyance, I felt I had at last commenced the African journey,' wrote Annie Hore. 'I could see nothing of the country or the people, only the dark forms of our own men and, dimly, the clumps of bushes and trees gliding by.'

They stayed in tents at night, and the next morning: 'I seemed to wake up suddenly in Central Africa.' It was an exciting change for Hore: 'Here you may see an almost naked savage drinking out of a tumbler, or the wildest native orgies carried on by the light of a paraffin lamp.' A donkey called Oliver was provided for her while the bath chair was deemed to be still in its experimental phase but after a bad attack of sunstroke held her back, and the season in consequence became too advanced, she was sent back to England from Mamboia, where she had been staying with missionaries. She experimented with the chair on the way back to the coast 'until I was obliged to confess that of all the means of conveyance I had tried, the bath chair was by far the most comfortable, except when in motion'.

At the end of July 1884 Hore was back at Zanzibar again and set off on 4 October for the mainland to try the new prototype. The Universities' Mission had helpfully offered the carcass of an old pram, 'which was turned into an excellent palanquin for Jack', and at Ndumi they began to prepare her chair:

> From a very long, stout bamboo the chair was suspended or slung by stout coir ropes; along the top of the bamboo was stretched a waterproof canvas awning, lined with white cotton and thick matting, and impervious alike to sun and rain, the cover extended down behind, and moveable sides could be secured up or down at pleasure; an apron of the same material covered the front of the chair. Sixteen picked men were told off for carrying the bath chair, and four in like manner for Jack's chair. The nature of the road permits only the passage of two men at a time, and in line, the others all kept close at hand, and each pair of men had only a short spell of the carrying at a time. The combination of the bamboo and the coir rope gave a pleasant springiness to the whole, and in this way I was carried right through to Ujiji in a less number of days, I believe, than achieved before by any European.

On 10 October 1884 the party moved off into the jungle. Young Jack, who was in the chair with his mother, noticing that a particularly muddy river crossing demanded all that the native bearers could put into it, 'suggested that I should tell the men to sing, as he had observed that that seemed to encourage them under any unusual exertion'. Hore pointed out that they were not 'luxurious travellers' on this trip and had no 'gilt tent-knobs, or fancy portmanteaus or canteens', just the basic necessities. When they reached the valley of the Mukondokwa she saw lying by the path some 'curious dark objects' which turned out to be the perfectly hardened and preserved bodies of dead slaves: 'I must discharge my conscience of this duty to solemnly remind and warn whoever in Christian and civilized lands may read this book, that inner Africa is as much as ever given over to all the horrors of the slave traffic, so often and so ably described.'

And so the journey continued, starting typically at dawn with an hour's halt at eight for breakfast, but the rains were becoming a problem. 'We are in the baby boat, Ma,' piped up Jack at one waterlogged point. They passed through swamps swarming with hippopotami and pelicans and other wild animals until they reached the richer Unyamwezi country at Tabora. The final phase of the journey ended on 7 January 1885, one of the hardest days, it turned out, of the whole trip because they had to cross the swollen River Luiche, the bearers thigh-deep in slimy black mud: 'All my bearers gathered round the chair, holding it at about the level of their heads, and thus entered the river. For a good part of the passage I could see nothing but the men's heads and hands, and wondered how they were not carried away by the stream; but I suppose the weight of Jack and myself in the chair, hard work as its carriage must have been, aided to bear up the whole party.'

After a rest on the other side of the river they crossed a ridge and followed some well-trodden paths 'and soon came in full sight of the lake in all its wide-spreading grandeur, while immediately before and below us, imbedded and dotted amongst a mass of deep-green oil palms, lay the settlement of Ujiji'. They professed themselves 'deeply thankful to God, who, through many perils and troubles, had enabled us to reach in safety at the end of our journey, which, achieved in ninety days from the coast, was, I think, notwithstanding its difficulties the quickest on record by any European'.

Hore's friends had told her in advance that her journey was 'utterly chimerical and ridiculous' but she had confounded them and, she believed, this was a turning point in African travel: 'the possibility, not only of solitary travellers, but of women and children penetrating Africa was demonstrated'. She looked with delight on 'the most beautiful lake in the world, giving easy access, by its coast-line of one thousand miles, to numerous tribes of Central African natives, as yet untouched by the hand of civilization'. The town of Ujiji, by contrast, was 'squalid and unwholesome' and scarred by its association with the hateful slave trade.

Hore was conscious of the debt she owed to her bearers and aware that sometimes she had been less than positive in her attitudes to the native Africans: 'Too often I could regard the natives only as savages opposing our passage, and seeking to hinder and rob, if not to molest us to a still more serious extent. But arrived at my destination, I regarded all natives with more gentle and serious interest, as the people I had come to live and work amongst; and their failings rather as further appeal for Christian and civilized help, than as cause for fear or estrangement.' She argued:

Here in Central Africa the various tribes, far behind the civilized world as they are in many ways, yet have their own distinct ideas of order, independence, and morals . . . All these things are seen to the best advantage when the natives have been untouched for some time by the foreign adventurers, whose advent, although enriching bold and influential individuals and parties, yet can only strike terror into the main part of the population, and effectually disturb the progress and welfare of ordinary native life.

The foreign adventurers I have alluded to are the Arab, Wamrima, and half-caste merchants and slavers, who are constantly streaming over these regions.

Slavery, she stated, persisted in the region and the Africans were crying out for a benevolent colonial power that would deliver them: 'The Africans are like a lot of passionate children, mauling one another with varied success, but lamentable impending consequences; who would, however, with scarce an exception, instinctively hail with joy the advent of the adult power, which should secure them (though perhaps not without present reproof to some) peace and happiness.'

Her husband, with whom she was now joined and who was Superintendent of the Marine Department of the Mission, was busy building on Lake Tanganyika an auxiliary steam vessel, the *Good News*. They set off on a small boat across the Lake, thirteen days after her arrival, to take a look at progress. It was 'a night to be remembered' for Hore, who was frightened at the motion of the boat on the vast lake: 'For a long time I lay and watched his dark figure, apparently swaying to and fro on the seat above, and now and then he would strike a match under a corner of the blanket, to consult the compass . . . That I was on the path of duty, I had and have decided, both before and since.' Her new path of duty, now that the bath chair was safely stowed away, was to live as a missionary's wife in a mud hut consisting of two rooms, respectively nine and sixteen feet by fifteen feet with holes in the walls which gave it 'rather the character of a cage'. She insisted on eating European food at the new mission in order to preserve her distance from the natives: 'It is not impossible for isolated representatives of civilization to be swamped in savagedom.' It was a 'hard, rough life' but she threw herself into it, starting a class for girls and building a school house.

She sent a final message back home to her readers: 'It is to be hoped that amongst the thousands in England, who long and wish for the emancipation of the African people, from the chains of depravity, ignorance and slavery, there are large numbers who see in Christian missions, a means to that end which goes to the root of the matter, by aiming at the purification of the blood, while other organizations are endeavouring to staunch the outward wound.'

Annie Hore closed her account with a picture of little Jack, who, recovered from his ordeal and his fevers, was 'almost himself again, and plays with the Waguha boys, whom he invites into the verandah to play with his toys'.

38

*People Die There: Herbert Ward in the Congo*

In his rooms in Sackville Street, in the West End of London, Henry Morton Stanley looked across at the young man who had come to him asking to be sent to Central Africa and asked why he entertained such a desire. 'People die there,' Stanley told his young visitor, Herbert Ward, gravely. Stanley had 'just completed his work of creating the Congo Free State', Ward later wrote, in the year before the Berlin Conference on West Africa of 1884–5, which triggered the European 'Scramble for Africa'.

As soon as he had Stanley's approval, Ward boarded a steamer at Liverpool and arrived at the mouth of the Congo in October 1884, eager for adventure. His account of his Congo travels, *Five Years with the Congo Cannibals* (1890), is prefaced by a romantic picture of a young man's passion for travel and excitement. Some of his words have already been quoted above as an epigraph to the present book. He confessed that 'my literary taste was confined to records of travel and adventure', eagerly devouring 'every book upon these subjects from Herodotus to Robinson Crusoe'. His father was less keen to learn that his son planned to travel and threatened at once to disinherit him. His father's lawyer added: 'Well, Mr Ward, if he was a son of mine, I would soon change his views with a horse-whip.' But Herbert was not dissuaded: 'One wintry morning shortly after this, in a typical London fog, amid the gruff voices of half-drunken sailors busy hauling ropes and heaving capstan bars, the English barque, "James Wishart", was extricated from the maze of docks, and I, with my hands deep down in my otherwise empty pockets, formed one of the little group of poor emigrants who were huddled together on the main deck.'

The ship was bound for Auckland: 'It was in this way that my life of travel and adventure commenced, and I faced the world a friend-less boy with a stout heart and strong arms as my only capital.' In New Zealand and later Australia Ward was willing to turn his hands to anything and was 'surprised at my own versatility. I was by turns a stock-rider, a circus-performer, and a miner.' This was, he con-cluded, 'a rough but wholesome apprenticeship'.

After four years in the antipodes Ward sailed back to England via San Francisco but was soon off again for Borneo as a cadet in the service of the British North Borneo Company He was sent imme-diately into 'the far interior of that wild and almost unknown country', where at first he lived for seven months surrounded by tribes of Dyak head-hunters and where he nearly died from mal-arial fever. The invalid was put on a ship to Japan but not before he had seen his friend Frank Hatton accidentally shoot himself while tracking an elephant. It was Hatton's father who rewarded Ward's account of his son's last moments with an introduction to Stanley.

Ward arrived in the Congo with not just an adventurous spirit but a knowledge of the three most popular local languages, which put him 'in a position to obtain information direct from the people'. His first tasks were the rather less swashbuckling ones of marshalling native porters at Vivi at the start of the cataract region, the principal depot on the river. After fifteen months of this he was appointed to command the station of the Bangalas, the most thickly populated district in the Congo State, but this lasted only six months until the Belgians took over and he was returned to his original post.

By the start of 1887 Ward was ready to go home but he heard of the famous Emin Pasha Relief Expedition under Stanley: 'My sole hope and desire was to be enlisted in the little band who were bound for far regions in Equatorial Africa, to carry relief to a brave and devoted man.' He dashed back to Lukunga, where he met Stanley 'attired in his famous African costume'. Stanley handed the impetuous youth a cigar from a silver case given to him by the Prince of Wales and agreed to take him on. Ward's venture into the Upper Congo was one, he reported, into the company of the 'savages of the interior'. He earned himself the nickname Mayala Mbemba, or 'The Wings of the Eagle', for the speed with which he travelled through the jungle en route from Matadi to Stanley Pool.

Six hundred miles into the Bolobo district Ward found himself among not necessarily the legendary cannibals but 'one of the most cruel races met with in this part of Central Africa', especially when dealing with their slaves. He seems to have been less aware of the white man's brutality in the Congo and had nothing but praise for Stanley's collaboration with the regime of King Leopold II in the Congo. Far from the region being an arid waste, impenetrable to the white man:

> Mr Stanley told the world another tale; and, moved by the story of the great explorer, and actuated by the highest motives of patriotism and a desire to benefit others beside his own countrymen – to give to the poor savages of the Congo the means of coming in contact with the enlightened influences of civilisation, as well as to find another outlet for the products and energies of the white man, His Majesty King Leopold II, of the

Belgians, commissioned Mr Stanley to return to the scene of his explorations at the head of a well-equipped expedition, and to undertake the work of founding stations along the course of the Congo, which should prove the means of opening up that great highway to the advance of commerce, and of winning the tribes along its banks to a condition of peaceful industry, and a desire to obtain the benefits they beheld the white man possessing in their midst.

Ward had been appointed to the Bangala station in the Congo Free State in 1886 and almost weekly, he claimed, 'some savage act of cannibalism would be brought to my notice'. One day a slave boy disappeared and the Bangala agent was told by the chief's sixteen-year-old son: 'That slave boy was very good eating – he was nice and fat.' When Ward crossed the River Congo to Mobunga to shoot elephant he created great excitement, 'for the natives had never before been visited by a white man'. The scene, however, had more of farce than dark horror about it: 'For several hours, until sunset, I was surrounded by numbers of inquisitive, foul smelling savages, whose black, beady eyes watched keenly my every move-ment.' He tried to sooth them by playing his musical box: 'It was advertised to play one tune, "Home, Sweet Home", but, in conse-quence of hard knocks and the damp and enervating influence of the African climate, the beautiful air was rendered almost indistin-guishable.'

On 3 April 1888 Ward left Stanley's fortified camp on the south bank of the Congo at the confluence of the River Lomami to carry dispatches to the coast about the expedition. He travelled with a rough crew of thirty men on two large war canoes bound together, facing a journey of several hundred miles through a thickly populated country of 'more or less hostile savages'. On board were fowls, a couple of goats and 'enormous bunches of green bananas and plantains, sweet potatoes, and an abundance of sour-smelling cassava root, which, when soaked, pounded, rolled in banana leaves and boiled, forms the staple food of most Central

African tribes'. Ominously, across the water, he heard war drums and yells of 'Niama', or 'Meat', from a dark mass of canoes drawn up across the river: 'All through the long night I kept watch, peering anxiously into the darkness. I knew not at what moment we might be attacked; the drums and horns sounded from all sides and sometimes the shrieking voices of the savages fell so keenly on the ear that my men thought that the foe was upon them.' Eventually he reached Bangala safely, then Stanley Pool and finally the coast.

When he had delivered his dispatch he returned to Stanley Pool and took a steam launch to Stanley Falls, where he stayed with some Arabs. One old Arab asked him: 'Would twenty thousand dollars be sufficient money for me to travel through Europe with, and see all these wonderful things you have told us of? And how should I find the road? For there must be many paths through the different countries of Europe.' Notwithstanding the hospitality of these Arabs, Ward concluded from all he had seen: 'The white man can never, as long as he may live in Africa, conquer his repugnance to the callous indifference to suffering that he meets with everywhere in Arab and Negro.'

After further adventures and encounters with hostile war canoes and the menacing sound of war drums behind the forest trees, Ward declared he had notched up 2500 miles of River Congo travel. On his next journey to the coast he received orders from the Emin Pasha Relief Committee to embark for London with his twelve Zanzibari men, who would then be rerouted to Zanzibar via the Suez Canal. They took a Dutch steamer, the *Afrikaan*, to Rotterdam, where they attracted some notice: 'It was Sunday when we arrived at the old city of Rotterdam, where the citizens, in their Sunday attire, crowded the quays to catch a glimpse of the strange group of Zanzibaris gathered on the forecastle of the African steamer.' Just before catching the London steamer, Ward acquired 'twelve suits of rough blue serge' for his men and later as they made their way up the Thames in fog and rain the blue dye ran and the men said they wanted to wash themselves in the river. At Blackwall they were put up in an 'emigrant's home' and a few days later a British steamer took them out again to Zanzibar.

It was 4 July 1889 when Ward finally bade farewell to his men: 'Standing on the jetty while the vessel was slowly moving out of the dock, I could not suppress a feeling of sadness, as, grouped on the deck, my Zanzibaris, waving their ragged turbans, shouted a last farewell, "Kwa heri! Kwa heri bwana wangu (good bye, my master, good bye!)."'

After his Congo experiences Ward lectured widely in Britain and the United States about Africa. In 1890 he married an American, Sarita Sanford, and three years later, at the age of thirty, he moved to Paris to train as an artist. On his return to England he was apprenticed to Seymour Lucas RA but in 1900 he moved into sculpture. He returned to Paris and settled there as a sculptor, winning medals at the Paris Salon and receiving in 1911 the *Légion d'honneur*. In the Great War he served on the Western front (where his son was killed) with the British Ambulance Committee and earned the *Croix de Guerre*. Ward died in 1919 and in 1927 his widow published a biography entitled *A Valiant Gentleman*.

## 39

## *The Deadliest Spot on Earth: Mary Kingsley in West Africa*

Humour of a peculiarly English kind – sometimes deflating, sometimes self-consciously trenchant and outspoken – has a long pedigree in British travel writing. We have already encountered the dry ironies of Robert Curzon and Alexander Kinglake, as well as various kinds of anti-heroic posture or intermittent rueful comedy. Mary Kingsley, in her classic *Travels in West Africa* (1897), is a particularly striking example of the robust and no-nonsense traveller prepared, through jokes against herself, to give short shrift to her own dignity.

Once she had decided to satisfy her desire to travel by focusing on West Africa, Kingsley set about remedying her complete absence of knowledge about where she was going by asking questions. The information, she reported, came back under the following headings:

The dangers of West Africa
The disagreeables of West Africa
The diseases of West Africa

The things you must take to West Africa

The things you find most handy in West Africa.

The worst possible things you can do in West Africa.

The only thing her friends could find to say was: 'That's where Sierra Leone is, the white man's grave, you know.' Moreover, it was a place where questionable relatives known as 'sad trials' disappeared from view. 'One lady however kindly remembered a case of a gentleman who had resided some few years at Fernando Po, but when he returned an aged wreck of forty he shook so violently with ague as to dislodge a chandelier, thereby destroying a valuable tea-service and flattening the silver teapot in its midst.' She was told by doctors that it was 'the deadliest spot on earth', the map of diseases being coloured black from above Sierra Leone to below the Congo. Dutifully looking up the missionary literature that she had been recommended to read she merely confirmed the diseases 'and various details of the distribution of cotton shirts over which I did not linger'. When at last she found someone who had actually been to West Africa he told her: 'When you have made up your mind to go to West Africa the very best thing you can do is to get it unmade again and go to Scotland instead; but if your intelligence is not strong enough to do so, abstain from exposing yourself to the direct rays of the sun, take 4 grains of quinine every day for a fortnight before you reach the Rivers, and get some introductions to the Wesleyans; they are the only people on the Coast who have got a hearse with feathers.'

Mary Henrietta Kingsley was not deterred and set off for Liverpool, albeit 'none the more cheerful for the matter-of-fact manner in which the steamboat agents had informed me that they did not issue return tickets by the West African lines of steamers'. Born in Islington, north London, on 13 October 1862, niece of the novelist Charles Kingsley, Mary had a quiet upbringing in nearby Highgate while her father, a physician who attached himself to rich patrons on world tours, was away, and she read a great deal instead of attending school. In her teenage years she nursed her parents in their debility in Cambridge, and lived a life she called 'an entirely domestic one in a University town', but after they both died in 1892 she moved back to London with her brother and prepared for the freedom of travel. In August 1893, having drawn up her will, she set off alone with 'a long, waterproof sack neatly closed at the top with a bar and handle. Into this I put blankets, boots, books, in fact anything that would not go into my portmanteau or black bag.'

The skipper of the Liverpool steamer was Captain Murray, whose thirty-year knowledge of the West African coast was immediately put at her disposal, knowledge which was far more useful than that likely to be contained in the Dahomean phrase book she had just read about in the *Daily Telegraph* and which contained such useful idioms as 'Help, I am drowning' and 'Why has not this man been buried?' She also took care (a most unusual thing for a Victorian traveller to do) to express her gratitude to 'the Africans themselves – to cultured men and women among them like Charles Owoo, Mbo, Sanga Glass, Jane Harrington and her sister at Gaboon, and to the bush natives'.

Kingsley was fascinated by the West African coast: 'the chances you have of returning from it are small, for it is a *Belle Dame sans merci*'. She believed that even those back home enamoured of 'the glorious joys of omnibuses, underground railways, and evening newspapers' would, once smitten, 'be found sneaking back apologetically to the Coast'. She wrote of Africa, 'with its great forests and rivers and its animistic-minded inhabitants', that she was 'more comfortable there than in England'. After this initial short trip of two weeks during which she went to Old Calabar (then in Niger Coast Protectorate and today in south-east Nigeria) collecting freshwater fish specimens, returning to Liverpool in December, she set off again on 23 December on the *Batanga*, after twenty-four hours' delay because of gales on the Mersey which held up even the mighty Cunard liner *Lucania* and forced the closure of the dock gates.

On arrival at Freetown in Sierra Leone on 9 January 1894 Kingsley called it 'the Liverpool of West Africa' and plunged into

a detailed description of the town. On the voyage she had confessed to her 'liability to become diffuse', which is a palpable
fault but common to most travel writers and endemic in a genre
that always tends towards the episodic, the digressive and glorifi-
cation of the accidental. She rambled along the Gold Coast and
approved the Wesleyan missions for educating the Africans ('so
strangely deficient in mechanical culture') in technology, though
this had its downside: 'Corrugated iron is my abomination.' She
went to 'a tea-party at a police station to meet a king' (a nice
example of English travel writer's bathos) and at Christianborg
met a rather gloomy government official who pointed to two
dug graves for any Europeans who might die – as indeed they did
at an alarming rate, though the true extent of European mortality was suppressed by the authorities. 'I shall go on telling you
stories and wasting your time,' Kingsley informed her readers
disarmingly.

This is precisely what she proceeded to do and the results are
intermittently charming, diffuse and somewhat random, though
she had a sort of mission to collect fish and insect specimens. She
went to Fernando Po, Lagos and the French Congo, noting how the
European traders had a power of 'living for a considerable time in
a district without taking any interest in it, keeping their whole
attention concentrated on the point of how long it will be before
their time comes to get out of it'.

Kingsley continued south to the River Ogowé (Ogooué in
modern Gabon), which she judged 'the greatest strictly equatorial
river in the world', and began guiltily to reproduce extracts from her
diary even though it was 'a form of literary crime'; but then 'no one
expects literature in a book of travel'. However, she rejected the idea
of a travel-writing genre in which she herself was the true subject: 'I
am not bent on discoursing on my psychological state, but on the
state of things in general in West Africa.' On the other hand she
confessed: 'I am not a geographer.' But she was someone who
attempted to get to know the people as well as the tropical landscape: 'As it is with the forest, so it is with the minds of the natives.

Unless you live among the natives, you never get to know them; if you do this you gradually get a light into the true state of their mind-forest. At first you see nothing but a confused stupidity and crime; but when you get to see – well! as in the other forest, – you see things worth seeing.'

She steamed up the Ogowé on the *Mové* collecting fish specimens and transferring later to 'a charming little stern wheel steamer', the *Eclaireur*, which took her as far as the mission station at Talagouga. The missionary's wife, Evangélique, had a small baby who rather disconcerted Kingsley: 'I am not a general admirer of babies of her age.' She was, however, an admirer of the local people, the Fans: 'They are sweet unsophisticated children of nature, these West African tribes.'

Kingsley soon wanted to press on to see the Ogowé rapids and dismissed the arguments of officials who said she should not risk the trip. She pointed out that a Frenchwoman had preceded her. But she had a husband, they said. Kingsley replied firmly: 'Neither the Royal Geographical Society's list in their "Hints to Travellers" nor Messrs. Silver, in their elaborate lists of articles necessary for a traveller in tropical climates [a reference to Silver & Co.'s handbooks], make mention of husbands.' All objections overcome, she set off in a canoe, though the water was frightening in places and she had to scramble up the bank and hang on to a rock wall 'in a manner more befitting an insect than an insect-hunter'. Her pencil was lost, her notebook a pulpy mass and her pockets full of fish but she managed it and returned to Talagouga in triumph.

Watching the local people in their canoes she was determined to experiment with paddling her own and managed to do so in a fifteen-foot boat. Later she started to take note of birds as well as fish, remembering the advice of a Cambridge scientist who had advised her before she left: 'Always take measurements, Miss Kingsley, and always take them from the adult male.'

At Ncovi she left her canoe behind and set off with some Fans on a land journey into the tropical forest and became more friendly with these people. When she went into a hut for a nap, however, she made a rather 'unpleasant discovery'. The distasteful smell from a sack in the corner turned out to come from its contents: 'a human hand, three big toes, four eyes, two ears, and other portions of the human frame. The hand was fresh, the others only so so, and shrivelled.' These were the left-overs from a Fan supper.

On this trip she fell into a game pit at the bottom of which was a set of wooden spikes. She was glad to have rejected advice to wear 'masculine garments', preferring instead the security of 'a good thick skirt'. Although she refused to pander to the public taste by retailing 'cannibal stories' she did point out that the Fans' cannibalism was no danger to white people 'except as regards the bother it gives one in preventing one's black companions from getting eaten'.

Kingsley's next excursion was along the River Rembwé in the company of a rather theatrical boatman called Obanjo ('but he liked it pronounced Captain Johnson'): 'He wore, when first we met, a huge sombrero hat, a spotless singlet, and a suit of clean, well-got-up dungaree [coarse calico], and an uncommonly picturesque, powerful figure he cut in them, with his finely moulded, well-knit form and good-looking face, full of expression always, but always with the keen, small eyes in it watching the effect his genial smiles and hearty laugh produced.' She spent some idyllic nights with Obanjo drifting along the river. Later she met an equally dignified native prince called Makaga, who 'appeared to me to be an English gentleman who had from some misfortune lost his trousers and been compelled to replace them with a highly ornamental table-cloth'.

About two-thirds of the way through her *Travels in West Africa* Kingsley changed tack from these discursive accounts of life with tribes 'in a state uninfluenced by European ideas and culture' in order to attempt a more systematic description of 'the African form of thought and the difficulty of studying it, because the studying of this thing is my chief motive for going to West Africa'. She was an ardent collector of information about

fetishism and had studied ('being a good Cambridge person')
the anthropological texts of Frazer, author of *The Golden Bough*.
Not that this was an easy business: 'Stalking the wild West
African idea is one of the most charming pursuits in the world.
Quite apart from the intellectual, it has a high sporting interest;
for its pursuit is as beset with difficulty and danger as grizzly
bear hunting, yet the climate in which you carry on this pursuit –
vile as it is – is warm, which to me is almost an essential of
existence.'

The goal, which she defined as gaining 'a true conception of the
savage's real idea', was worth pursuing if only to preserve the
indigenous people from the 'derision and contempt' of the missionaries. She praised the 'remarkable acuteness and a large share of
common sense' the Africans possessed, though she also referred to
their 'mind muddle'. She felt they were not good at picturesque
descriptions of scenery but she found them fertile sources of ethnological speculation: 'The African is usually great at dreams, and
has them very noisily; but he does not seem to me to attach
immense importance to them, certainly not so much as the Red
Indian does. I doubt whether there is much real ground for sup-
posing that from dreams came man's first conception of the spirit
world, and I think the origin of man's religious belief lies in man's
misfortunes.'

Before returning home Kingsley ascended 'the Great Peak of
Cameroons', at 13,760 feet one of the highest points in Africa.
'Now it is none of my business to go up mountains. There's next
to no fish on them in West Africa, and precious little good rank
fetish, as the population on them is sparse – the African, like
myself, abhorring cool air.' She described herself as 'the third
Englishman [*sic*] to ascend the peak and the first to have ascended
it from the south-east face'. The first Englishman had been
Richard Burton. Kingsley's was a thrilling ascent: 'Imagine a vast,
seemingly limitless cathedral with its countless columns covered,
nay, composed of the most exquisite dark-green, large-fronded
moss, with here and there a delicate fern embedded in it as an

extra decoration.' Unfortunately, on reaching the peak of Mount Cameroon she found it covered in rain and mist, which 'robbed me of my main object in coming here'.

Kingsley returned to Victoria and one evening was in reflective mood: 'as I sat on the verandah overlooking Victoria and the sea, in the dim soft light of the stars, with the fire-flies round me, and the lights of Victoria away below, and heard the soft rush of the Lukola River, and the sound of the sea-surf on the rocks, and the tom-tomming and singing of the natives, all matching and mingling together, "Why did I come to Africa?" thought I. Why! who would not come to its twin brother hell itself for all the beauty and charm of it!'

She landed back in England on 30 November 1895 with her collection of insects, shells, plants, reptiles and fish. Three of her sixty-five specimens of fish were new and were named after her. Because of the venturesome nature of her travels as a lone woman she was an instant celebrity, though she was obliged to write to the *Daily Telegraph* to disown the radical label of a New Woman. She had nothing but contempt for the 'androgynes' who campaigned for women to be admitted to male-dominated learned societies.

She lectured widely and her book appeared in January 1897. By June she had employed the services of a lecture agent, Gerald Christy. So busy had she become, especially as an advocate of economic initiatives that earned the interest of politicians and businessmen, that she had a breakdown in 1898. Although very much supportive of British trading interests, she also urged understanding of the colonies and was prepared to voice criticisms of colonial administration. In particular she claimed an ability to 'think in black' and she deplored the missionaries' attempts to Europeanize Africans and peddle to them a 'second hand rubbishy white culture'. In 1899 her second book, *West African Studies*, appeared and it contained an ambitious political blueprint for the region which suggested that an administration of European trading interests rather than ornamentalist 'pen-pushers and ostrich feathers' would better ensure the integrity of West African culture.

In 1900 Kingsley visited South Africa as a prelude to visiting the west coast again but, after volunteering to work in a hospital for Boer prisoners in Cape Town she caught typhoid and died. She was, as she had wanted to be, buried at sea.

40

*The Lady and the Savages: Helen Caddick
in Central Africa*

Like Mary Kingsley, Helen Caddick, author of *A White Woman in Central Africa* (1900), travelled alone. 'The warning with which every account of the journey [that I intended to make] concluded, namely, that I must not go alone,' she wrote, 'made me the more desirous to set out.'

Born in 1843 in West Bromwich to a Herefordshire landowning family, Helen Caddick travelled widely and her unpublished travel diaries are in the possession of Birmingham Central Library, though little else is known about her life until her death in 1927. She eventually became a Governor of Birmingham University. It was in January 1898 that she set out for Cape Town, travelling through

Bulawayo, 'the ruins of Zimbabwe', to Beira, where she decided, instead of going home, to press on to the Lake Regions.

'During the last few years,' Caddick wrote, 'Africa has been very much in the minds of people everywhere; especially has it been in the minds of the British people, therefore I hope it will be thought that no apology is necessary for my writing this brief account of a lady's journey from the mouth of the Zambesi to the great Lake Tanganyika, which divides German East Africa from the Congo Free State.' The journey had been 'undertaken through love of travel, and for the purposes of observation only', by which she meant that it was a 'lady's journey', and therefore presumably void of serious content. It was a journey which would amuse 'those who have neither time nor inclination to travel so far. Also, I should like them to know how kind and attentive the natives, who are spoken of as "savages", can be to a lady travelling absolutely alone with them.'

Caddick took the steamer the *Matabele* from Beira to Quelimane, north of the Zambezi, calling on the way at Chinde, a Portuguese concession to the British at one of the four mouths of the great river, and there she met the British Consul, who kept a splendid fish eagle in a cage as a sort of watchdog. Missing the African Lakes steamer from Chinde to Katunga upriver, she caught instead a missionary boat, the *Henry Henderson*, which, as the only paddle boat on the river and owned by missionaries, had been nick-named the *Pious Paddler*. True to her self-designated task of merely observing, she carefully noted the various kinds of African hairstyle glimpsed along the journey: 'Another very charming style was a sort of garden arrangement, in which little pathways were shaved, winding in and out in all directions among and around beds of hair.'

When she reached the Zambezi proper there were 'galumping' hippotami and crocodiles and exotic birds. She was upset by the passion of her fellow passengers for shooting everything that moved, particularly the birds, but when she objected she was informed that it was 'sport'. Scornfully, she reflected: 'Where the "sport" of the proceeding lay I could not discover, for there was nothing of skill about the shooting. It was just like firing into a poultry yard.' What made it worse was the fact that one of the sportsmen was at home in Britain a member of the Society for the Prevention of Cruelty to Animals. She spotted kingfishers, reed martins, fish eagles, African cuckoos, black and white ibis, divers, herons, saddle-billed storks, egrets and quantities of duck and guinea-fowl, but the carnage continued until she threatened to leave the boat at the next station if they did not stop.

Reluctantly the sportsmen laid down their guns. But Caddick was not finished, noting prophetically:

> Among the many practices of white men out here which tend to retard the civilising of the natives, this is a prominent one. The missionaries endeavour to impress them with a sense of the gentleness and tenderness of Christianity, and yet they see professing Christians indulge in wanton cruelty of this nature . . . In many parts of Africa the native fauna are fast disappearing, owing to the sporting proclivities of the white man. The tendency is to pass laws for their protection, when there is no longer any to protect.

In all other respects it was a pleasant cruise, lounging on a long cane chair on the upper deck of the *Pious Paddler*. She paused at Shipanga to visit the grave of Mrs Livingstone under a huge baobab tree and there were frequent stops at wooding stations for fuel. Once again her observations were sharp and pertinent: 'One is constantly hearing about the way the natives "spoil the timber" [by chopping down and clearing it] . . . nothing is ever said about the immense amount of timber *we* have felled for burning on our steamers. In Africa we always appear to consider the country ours and the natives the intruders.'

When the steamer entered the River Shiré the days were long, starting at five or six in the morning and tying up to the bank after sunset around seven in the evening. After six days on this river she came to a faded sign, only part of which could be read: 'Here commences B.C.A. [British Central Africa] territory and reaches to . . .' At the Chiromo station she was told that, apart from professional missionaries, she was the first 'lady' to have ventured this far. 'My hosts were much horrified at the idea of my going alone to Lake Tanganyika, and many and terrible were the consequences they foretold.' She seemed, however, to have avoided fever and to have taken very little quinine. In 'B.C.A.' from June to November she 'never once was stopped by illness, or had to give up any expedition I had planned'. She put this down to healthy living and opined that Europeans in Africa should take more care of their health and not do things detrimental to it: 'Directors of companies at home might give more care and thought to the comfort and health of their agents and clerks out there; but their chief care seems to be about their dividends.' Another evil they could address was whisky drinking.

Arriving at Katunga, Caddick praised the 'musical sound' of the place names: 'Therefore it seems a pity that so many English and Scotch names are now being substituted when they have no meaning out there, and do not commemorate any special deed, whether religious, civil or military.' In her seemingly innocent way she was building an indictment of the colonial presence. Because of the falls and rapids beyond this point she set off the next morning by land with twelve native bearers taking turns to carry her in a machila, 'which is really a hammock made of strong sailcloth and slung on a bamboo pole'. Two men bore it at each end and two more shouldered the luggage. In her hammock she had curtains and pillows and, when she tumbled out at the first attempt to clamber into it, the bearers were hugely amused: 'The men who were carrying me were a happy lot, and sang and shouted at the tops of their voices. The words of their songs were generally improvised about the "Ulendo" (the journey), and the person they were carrying, and all the extraordinary things he or she had done or said.'

On arriving at Blantyre, which belonged to the African Lakes

Company, three thousand feet above the sea, she was not entirely happy with Livingstone's 'Scotch' settlement where 'nearly everyone's name begins with Mac'. Witnessing the activities of missionaries, she urged respect for the native culture in similar terms to Mary Kingsley: 'All this instruction makes them very useful servants for us; but I sometimes wondered how much is honestly and solely for the good of the natives. We are certainly creating in the native a desire, and even greed, for money, and with that a wish for finery and clothing such as they had not before, and that certainly is not for their good.' She actually believed they were better with a loincloth and without hats and boots. Also a decline in native industries had been permitted even though 'native iron and copperwork were excellent'. Weaving and bead work were dying out. 'Architecturally, we are not improving the look of the country. Red brick houses are certainly not pretty; while the Wankonde huts at the north end of Lake Nyasa are most picturesque and beautifully clean and neat.'

As ever, Caddick's conclusion was plainly and vigorously put:

We English are an odd mixture, we send out large sums for missions, and then permit and encourage such a show in London as 'Savage Africa', which must thoroughly demoralise the natives, and undo years of patient work . . . It surely will be counted one of the disgraces of the nineteenth century that such a show was permitted and supported . . . The great hold we have over the natives in Africa is on account of the respect, and almost awe, they have for the white man, and their belief in his superiority; but such shows must lessen their respect for us, and do incalculable harm.

Caddick spent some time on lake steamers exploring the vast expanses of water, sharing a tiny cabin on Lake Nyasa with cockroaches that 'ran races over my bunk and nibbled my hair'. At Karonga the African Lakes Company's agent was amused to hear that a 'tourist' had arrived but quite appalled when she announced her intention to hire men to take her, alone, to Lake Tanganyika. She was worried by her inability to speak the men's language so she hired a boy as interpreter. Unfortunately his missionary education had left him speaking in Biblical idiom. When she summoned him to her tent he would announce: 'It is I; behold I am come.' For the journey she packed tinned meat, rice, marmalade, jam tins of biscuits, cocoa, tea and for barter 'calico, both blue and white, beads in great variety, and salt, for money is not used or wanted'. Her party, when boy, cook, washer-up and 'capitao' were added, swelled to twenty-five men. Six days later she arrived at Mwenzo mission station: 'I thoroughly enjoyed seeing a lady again, and having a "real good talk", as for nearly a week I had not had an opportunity of communicating my thoughts to anyone.'

At Fife she hired twenty-two new 'boys' but soon found that these were 'even madder than the last ones', constantly singing and dancing. After a stay at Mbala she descended to Lake Tanganyika and the Kituta African Lakes Station and was delighted with its beauty. Unfortunately the steamer *Good News* was out of action and no native boats were available to take her to Ujiji. She amused herself instead by walking around the shore of Lake Tanganyika collecting shells, but she was followed everywhere by villagers and children: 'I tried hard not to mind them, for I knew how queer I must seem to them; and I thought of how we Britishers, in much the same way, mob any special hero or heroine.'

After five days at Kituta Caddick started her return journey, bartering along the way for a hat made of the skin of a zebra's head and a stool belonging to a chief. Boys passed with letters carried in a split bamboo stick 'which they offer to any European they meet, in case the letter should be for him'. Of all the Victorian travellers in Africa, Helen Caddick seems the one who took the most spontaneous and natural pleasure in the company of the ordinary local people.

Her final journey was to the north of Lake Nyasa, where the missionaries marvelled at her intrepid feats of solitary travel. Her 'boys' always seemed pleased when she enjoyed the view 'and they always pointed out what they thought interesting'. At one village a hundred men were dancing, oiled and with tufts of feathers in their hair: 'The singing was wonderful, sometimes very wild, sometimes very musical, and occasionally reminded me of some of Wagner's choruses.' At Makarere, 'one of the most beautiful places I have seen', she stayed at the mission and made various excursions: 'At the mission station there was one little white boy, the son of the missionary. He was about four years old, and it was the prettiest sight possible to see him marching along attended by five or six little black boys, his most devoted admirers, who patiently followed him wherever he went, and were only too delighted when he permitted them to do anything for him.'

Her final visit was to the missionary Dr Law at Kondowe. He had been a missionary for twenty-five years: 'He understands the natives, and they thoroughly respect and trust him – which is what the natives should always be able to do to the white man.' By the time she reached Chiromo on the return journey she calculated that she had travelled a thousand miles by machila.

At Chinde Caddick caught a steamer to Mozambique, then transferred to a larger German steamer bound for Zanzibar. From there she travelled to Mombasa and passed through the Suez Canal to sail on to Marseilles, completing the rest of the journey overland. She reached England just before Christmas 1898 'feeling that I had had a glorious time, and had gone through most interesting experiences'.

## 41

## *A Digression on the Camel (and the Elephant)*

In those passages of *Mandeville's Travels* that describe the African kingdom of the legendary Prester John the medieval taste for exotic marvels from strange countries is fully gratified: 'In that country be many white elephants without number and of unicorns and of lions of many manners; and many of such beasts that I have told you before and of many other hideous beasts without number.' Strange and alarming fauna have always been among the stock-in-trade of the travel writer and even in the age of steam the elephant and the camel held their own. They were both symbols of the exoticism of foreign places and sources of – frequently comic – anecdote.

In his account of his travels in the India province of Sind, Richard Burton gave his readers some advice on how to mount a dromedary: 'If you startle him at first when mounting him, he is very apt to get into a habit of converting his squatting into a standing position, with a suddenness by no means pleasant.' His first ride was on a baggage camel: 'After considerable difficulty in getting on the roaring, yelling beast, it became palpably necessary to draw my sword and prick his nose each time it crept round disagreeably near my boot. Finding his efforts to bite me unavailing, he changed tactics, and made a point of dashing under every low thorn tree, as close to the trunk as possible, in the hope of rubbing his rider off.' In passages like this the dumb beast acquires some of the characteristics of the hostile human inhabitant encountered by the traveller, one more perplexing or antagonistic Other.

On his journey from Suez to Gaza, Alexander Kinglake observed the behaviour of the desert camel and the way in which there was nearly always a leading camel accustomed to making the others set off. But when such a leader was not available there was trouble:

> If you force your beast forward for a moment, he will contrive to wheel and draw back, at the same time looking at one of the other camels with an expression and gesture exactly equivalent to 'après vous'. The responsibility of finding the way is evidently assumed very unwillingly. After some time, however, it becomes understood that one of the beasts has reluctantly consented to take the lead, and he accordingly advances for that purpose . . . When once the leadership is established, you cannot by any persuasion, and scarcely even by blows, induce a junior camel to walk one single step in advance of the chosen guide.

'The camel has his virtues,' Amelia Edwards agreed, 'but they do not lie upon the surface.' She found the temper of the camel 'abominable' and considered the various objections to it as a means of transport:

> It is unpleasant, in the first place, to ride an animal which not only objects to being ridden, but cherishes a strong personal antipathy to his rider . . . You know that he hates you, from the moment you first walk round him, wondering where and how to begin the ascent of his hump. He does not, in fact, hesitate to tell you so in the roundest terms. He swears freely while you are taking your seat; snarls if you but move in the saddle; and stares you angrily in the face, if you attempt to turn his head in any direction save that which he himself prefers. Should you persevere, he tries to bite your feet. If biting your feet does not answer, he lies down.

In addition to his rough behaviour towards humans, the pace of the camel was another trial. There were four types of movement, Edwards went on:

a short walk, like the rolling of a small boat in a chopping sea; a long walk which dislocates every bone in your body; a trot that reduces you to imbecility; and a gallop that is sudden death. One tries in vain to imagine a crime for which the *peine forte et dure* of sixteen hours on camel-back would not be a full and sufficient expiation. It is a punishment to which one would not willingly be the means of condemning any human being – not even a reviewer.

The first confrontation with the camel, in fact became a stock scene in the Victorian travel narrative. Here is the Reverend Porter in Damascus:

> I had often heard that the first mounting of a dromedary formed a kind of era in a man's life, and I confess that, when I saw mine with open mouth, growling savagely, and struggling to free itself from the grasp of the driver, I felt a little trepidation. No sooner had I leaped into the saddle than the brute, giving a sharp lurch backwards, and a heavy one forward, and then another backwards, gained its feet and ran a few yards at a smart trot; it then wheeled about, and suddenly, by a similar but reversed series of lurches, was again upon the ground. A second time it went through this pantomime, and was preparing for a third, when its driver seized and pinioned it by placing his foot upon its knee . . . it was with no little anxiety I looked forward to a ride of nearly two hundred miles on such an animal. The pace was dreadful when it trotted; and then the sittings-down and risings-up and sudden jerks had almost dislocated my spine. In walking, however, when I became a little accustomed to the rocking motion, I found the pace easy, and even pleasant.

A further indignity was in store when he was forced to dismount clumsily in a village to the amusement of small boys who burst into laughter when 'the small dimensions of my nether garments became visible'.

Charles Doughty, whose description of the camel as a 'great shuffle-footed beast' is inimitable, noted how the camel of the nomads never slept: 'the weary brute may stretch down his long neck upon the ground, closing awhile his great liquid eyes; but after a space he will right again the great languid carcase and fall to chawing'.

The elephant generally got a better character reference from travellers, lacking the snappish aggression of the shuffle-footed beast, but the advice of Francis Galton in *The Art of Travel* was to exercise some charm: 'They are an expensive and delicate, but excellent beast of burden, in rainy tropical countries. The traveller should make friends with the one he regularly rides, by giving it a piece of sugar-cane or banana before mounting.'

There was a sense in which an elephant, because of its great bulk, gave the rider some special elevated dignity. When William Sleeman was unable to ride a horse after an injury he chose an elephant instead 'that I might see as much as possible of the country over which we were passing. The pace of an elephant is about that of a good walker, and I had generally some of the landholders and cultivators riding or walking by my side to talk with.'

Unfortunately the elephant was attractive to the big game hunter. In Central Africa, Herbert Ward shot an elephant and was not prepared for the result: 'The scene that followed was wild and disgusting, as the men hacked and gashed the still warm, steaming flesh, heaving it in reeking lumps to their women, who were eagerly crowding around, quarreling and fighting with one another like hungry dogs. Now and then a bigger lump of meat than usual would be thrown among them, and they would all rush forward and literally tear it to pieces in their wild greed.'

One that was denied its 'piece of sugar-cane or banana'.

# PART SIX
# THE AMERICAS

## 42

*A Scientific Person: Darwin on the* Beagle

On 27 December 1831 HMS *Beagle*, a ten-gun brig, sailed out of Devonport (having twice been driven back by heavy south-westerly gales) under the command of Captain Fitzroy with the aim of completing a survey of Patagonia and Tierra del Fuego started in the previous decade, and of some Pacific islands. Fitzroy had wanted to have a scientist on board and was pleased to accept the recommendation of a Cambridge botany professor, the Reverend John Stevens Henslow, that he take one of his promising young students, Charles Darwin.

Darwin was born in 1809 in Shrewsbury and brought up after

his mother's early death by his father, a well-off local physician, and three elder sisters. Educated at Shrewsbury School, he went on to Edinburgh University to study medicine. He soon developed an interest in natural history but eventually left Edinburgh in April 1827 without a degree. His father sent him to Cambridge to read for a degree in preparation for becoming a Church of England vicar, and there Darwin resumed his researches in natural history, attending Henslow's lectures on botany. He took his BA in January 1831 and, after reading Alexander von Humboldt's *Personal Narrative* of his voyage to the tropics, was planning a trip to Tenerife when Henslow's letter arrived offering him the chance to voyage on the *Beagle*. The voyage would last five years and, as Darwin later wrote in his *Autobiography*, it 'determined my whole career'.

On 16 January 1832 the *Beagle* anchored at Porto Praya in St Jago, the chief island of the Cape Verde archipelago and a place that seemed to Darwin rather bleak and desolate, volcanic and treeless: 'The island would generally be considered as very uninteresting; but to any one accustomed only to an English landscape, the novel aspect of an utterly sterile land possesses a grandeur which more vegetation might spoil.' The first wildlife Darwin spotted was a kingfisher 'which tamely sits on the branches of the castor-oil plant, and thence darts on grasshoppers and lizards'. He threw himself into his scientific duties, collecting samples of dust and geological specimens, but also, during one excursion, noticed the less inanimate fauna: 'On our return we overtook a party of about twenty young black girls, dressed in excellent taste; their black skins and snow-white linen being set off by coloured turbans and large shawls.' He also examined marine animals such as the sea slug and octopus by wading into the sea.

The next port of call was Salvador, in the state of Bahia, on the Brazilian coast, where Darwin had a delightful day of exploration and was in his element: 'Delight itself, however, is a weak term to express the feelings of a naturalist who, for the first time, has wandered by himself in a Brazilian forest . . . To a person fond of natural history, such a day as this brings with it a deeper pleasure than he can ever hope to experience again.' Darwin's keen scientific mind is everywhere noticeable, constantly asking questions and interrogating the evidence of other authorities. The *Beagle* frequently stayed put for long periods along its voyage and Darwin made some extended land journeys.

At Rio de Janeiro he went on such a trip, collecting insects in the forests but also showing that he was not indifferent to the human species. Seeing a Negro cringe because he thought he was just about to be struck by a white man, he noted: 'This man had been trained to a degradation lower than the slavery of the most helpless animal.' Darwin hated slavery and it was the cause of some strong words between him and his captain.

Generally, however, Darwin was overwhelmed as a naturalist with what was being presented to him: 'In England any person fond of natural history enjoys in his walks a great advantage, by always having something to attract his attention; but in these fertile climates, teeming with life, the attractions are so numerous, that he is scarcely able to walk at all.' He was particularly interested in invertebrate animals and found a dozen different species of terrestrial Planariae. The grandeur and magnificence of the tropical landscape awed the young Englishman: 'At this elevation the landscape attains its most brilliant tint; and every form, every shade, so completely surpasses in magnificence all that the European has ever beheld in his own country, that he knows not how to express his feelings.' But always he was attending to the detail of his researches rather than yielding to the usual purple of the traveller's rapture: 'A person, on first entering a tropical forest, is astonished at the labours of the ants . . .'

The *Beagle* sailed next for Montevideo and Buenos Aires. Darwin stayed for ten weeks at Maldonado on the northern bank of the Plata and made a 'nearly perfect collection of the animals, birds, and reptiles'. On an excursion he made to the River Polanco the local people were intrigued by his pocket compass, which created 'unbounded astonishment'. He also had with him some 'promethean matches', which he ignited by biting them: 'It was thought so wonderful that a man should strike fire with his teeth, that it was usual to collect the whole family to see it.' Darwin noted: 'I am writing as if I had been among the inhabitants of Central Africa.' He was conscious of the available traditions of writing about native populations but he himself rarely indulged in those passages about 'savages' or 'uncivilized races' of a kind now wearily familiar.

At Maldonado he collected 'several quadrupeds, eighty kinds of birds, and many reptiles, including nine species of snakes' before sailing on to Rio on 24 July. On one excursion with an English merchant they caught an armadillo 'which, although a most excellent dish when roasted in its shell, did not make a very substantial breakfast and dinner for two hungry men'.

At Bahía Blanca the ship left Darwin to make his way by land to Buenos Aires. He heard rumours of wars between General Rosas, whom he met, and the 'wild Indians' and he very much regretted what was happening on the continent:

> The warfare is too bloody to last; the Christians killing every Indian, and the Indians doing the same by the Christians. It is melancholy to trace how the Indians have given way before the Spanish invaders . . . Not only have whole tribes been exterminated, but the remaining Indians have become more barbarous: instead of living in large villages, and being employed in the arts of fishing, as well as of the chase, they now wander about the open plains, without home or fixed occupation.

Travelling inland on this four-hundred-mile ride to Buenos Aires was thus dangerous, and at a *posta* the owner looked him up and down until he saw his passport with its designation 'El Naturalista Don Carlos' and his respect and civility became 'as unbounded as his suspicions had been before. What a naturalist might be, neither he nor his countrymen, I suspect, had any idea; but probably my title lost nothing of its value from that cause.' Later, in October, at Las Conchas, Darwin was briefly imprisoned until he mentioned his association with General Rosas. He was glad to get away on a packet bound for Montevideo.

At the end of the year the *Beagle* arrived at Port Desire on the coast of Patagonia, where the zoology was 'as unlimited as its Flora'. Darwin was always interested to make wider connections from his detailed naturalist's observations: 'It is impossible to reflect on the changed state of the American continent without the deepest astonishment. Formerly it must have swarmed with great monsters: now we find mere pigmies.' Another passage on the extinction of species from 'causes generally quite inappreciable by us' suggests the stirrings of his great theory.

On reaching Tierra del Fuego Darwin finally succumbed to the 'savage' riff when met by the local people: 'It was without exception the most curious and interesting spectacle I ever beheld: I could not have believed how wide was the difference between savage and civilized man: it is greater than between a wild and domesticated animal, inasmuch as in man there is a greater power of improvement.' Nonetheless he appreciated their 'keener senses' and made the effort to communicate with the local people.

Darwin visited Chile, the island of Chiloe and the Chonos Islands, with his interest in the human as ever measuring up to his scientific inquiries: 'A strong desire is always felt to ascertain whether any human being has previously visited an unfrequented spot. A bit of wood with a nail in it, is picked up and studied as if it were covered with hieroglyphics.' One of the most interesting things he witnessed, he said, was an earthquake on Chiloe on 20 February 1835: 'I happened to be on shore, and was lying down in the wood to rest myself. It came on suddenly, and lasted two minutes, but the time appeared much longer . . . There was no difficulty in standing upright, but the motion made me almost giddy: it was something like the movement of a vessel in a little cross-ripple, or still more like that felt by a person skating over thin ice, which bends under the weight of his body.'

Darwin was particularly entranced by the Galápagos Archipelago. Not long after landing, as he was walking along: 'I met two large tortoises, each of which must have weighed at least two hundred pounds.' They 'seemed to my fancy like some ante-diluvian animals'. Darwin thought the archipelago 'a little world within itself', full of so many 'aboriginal creations'. He found twenty-six land birds to be found nowhere else and three of the eleven kinds of wader and water bird were new species, but it was the reptiles which were the most striking feature of the Galápagos: 'Some grow to an immense size: Mr Lawson, an Englishman, and vice-governor of the colony, told us that he had seen several so large, that it required six or eight men to lift them from the ground; and that some had afforded as much as two hundred pounds of meat . . . I frequently got on their backs, and then giving a few raps on the hinder parts of their shells, they would rise up and walk away; – but I found it very difficult to keep my balance.'

Darwin split open the stomachs of various lizards to see what they had been eating, recorded fifteen new species of fish and noted that of the 185 species of flowering plants a hundred were new ones unique to the Galápagos: 'We see that a vast majority of all the land animals, and that more than half the flowering plants, are aboriginal productions.' In addition the most remarkable feature of the islands was that 'the different islands to a considerable extent are inhabited by a different set of beings'. Of the thirty-eight species of plant unique to the Galápagos, thirty were found only on James Island.

Like so many travellers, Darwin was greeted in Tahiti by 'laughing merry faces' and was immediately attracted to the inhabitants: 'There is a mildness in the expression of their countenances which at once banishes the idea of a savage; and an intelligence which shows that they are advancing in civilization.' He admired the graceful tattoos of the men: 'The simile may be a fanciful one, but I thought the body of a man thus ornamented was like the trunk of a noble tree embraced by a delicate creeper.' Pressing into the interior of the island, he encountered missionaries and came to their defence against those who 'expect the missionaries to effect that which the Apostles themselves failed to do'.

Late in December 1835 the *Beagle* saw New Zealand in the distance. They had nearly crossed the Pacific: 'It is necessary to sail over this great ocean to comprehend its immensity . . . Accustomed to look at maps drawn on a small scale, where dots, shading, and names are crowded together, we do not rightly judge how infinitely small the proportion of dry land is to the water of this vast expanse.' Darwin was a scientist but in passages like these he showed he had the imagination of an artist: 'These Antipodes call to one's mind old recollections of childish doubt and wonder. Only the other day I looked forward to this airy barrier as a definite point in our voyage homewards; but now I find it, and all such resting places for the imagination, are like shadows, which a man moving onwards cannot catch.'

Shortly after Christmas – having been nearly four years now away from home – Darwin quit New Zealand, glad to leave behind its human element ('the greater part of the English are the very refuse of society') and to head for Australia, where they arrived on 12 January 1836. After anchoring in Sydney Cove and taking a walk Darwin was overcome by a patriotic fit: 'In the evening I walked through the town, and returned full of admiration at the whole scene. It is a most magnificent testimony to the power of the British nation . . . My first feeling was to congratulate myself that I was born an Englishman.' He hired a man and two horses to take him to Bathurst, 120 miles into the interior, and greatly admired the first group of Aboriginal people that he saw, who appeared 'far from being such utterly degraded beings as they have usually been represented'. They gave him much food for thought: 'It is very curious thus to see in the midst of a civilized people, a set of harmless savages wandering about without knowing where they shall sleep at night, and gaining their livelihood by hunting in the woods.' He noted, however: 'Wherever the European has trod, death seems to pursue the aboriginal . . . The varieties of man seem to act on each other in the same way as different species of animals – the stronger always extirpating the weaker.' Once again the evolution theory seemed to be making a ghostly tread through his observations, as when he hinted at 'some more mysterious agency generally at work' in these 'extirpations'. He went kangaroo hunting but none turned up: 'It may be long before these animals are altogether exterminated, but their doom is fixed.'

In Australia he seemed rather more interested in social than natural history and was generally 'disappointed in the state of society'. In fact: 'My opinion is such, that nothing but rather sharp necessity should compel me to emigrate.' But perhaps Darwin's disillusion was in part the product of being away from home for so long.

After Australia he visited Tasmania, the Cocos Islands, Mauritius, Cape Town, St Helena and Ascension. On St Helena he stayed within a stone's throw of Napoleon's tomb and enjoyed his 'rambles among the rocks and mountains'. After leaving Brazil in August 1836 he thanked God that he would never again visit a slave country: 'To this day, if I hear a distant scream, it recalls with painful vividness my feelings when, passing a house near Pernambuco, I heard the most pitiable moans, and could not but suspect that some poor slave was being tortured, yet knew that I was as powerless as a child even to remonstrate.'

After six days in the Azores Darwin returned to England on board the *Beagle*, reaching Falmouth on 2 October 1836, 'having lived on board the good little vessel nearly five years'. At the end of his *Journal of Researches into the Natural History & Geology of the Countries Visited During the Voyage Round the World of H.M.S. 'Beagle'* (1839) Darwin offered 'a short retrospect of the advantages and disadvantages, the pains and pleasures, of our circumnavigation of the world'. He tried to draw up a balance sheet of the credits and debits of travel and decided that it was only the thought of some long-term 'harvest' that made it worthwhile: 'No doubt it is a high satisfaction to behold various countries and the many races of mankind, but the pleasures gained at the time do not counterbalance the evils.' He listed some of the deprivations of travel: 'the want of room, of seclusion, of rest; the jading feeling of constant hurry; the privation of small luxuries, the loss of domestic society, and even of music and other pleasures of the imagination'. But he also admitted that, compared with the time of Captain Cook, modern navigation was swifter and easier and 'the whole western shores of America are thrown open, and Australia has become the capital of a rising continent'. Being at sea, however, could be a bore: 'A tedious waste, a desert of water, as the Arabian calls it.' Storms at sea could be picturesque when viewed from the shore but for those at sea 'the feelings partake more of horror than of wild delight'.

On the positive side there was much beauty to be seen, though, as with music, the keenest appreciation was enjoyed by those who could read it: 'Hence, a traveller should be a botanist, for in all views plants form the chief embellishment.' The most impressive sights he saw were 'the primeval forests undefaced by the hand of man', for 'no one can stand in these solitudes unmoved, and not feel there is more in man than the mere breath of his body'. Darwin was intrigued by the way the apparently drear and bleak wastes of Patagonia continued to haunt his memory: 'it must be partly owing to the free scope given to the imagination'. The most astonishing thing seen by a traveller was 'the first sight in his native haunt of a barbarian, – of man in his lowest and most savage state. One's mind hurries back over past centuries, and then asks, Could our progenitors have been men like these?'

There was also the pleasure of living in the open air 'with the sky for a roof and the ground for a table' and the pleasure of discovery: 'The map of the world ceases to be a blank; it becomes a picture full of the most varied and animated figures.' The progress of exploration and discovery was also very encouraging, Darwin felt: 'The march of improvement, consequent on the introduction of Christianity throughout the South Sea, probably stands by itself in the records of history.' The sight of distant British colonies was another cause of self-satisfaction: 'To hoist the British flag seems to draw with it as a certain consequence, wealth, prosperity, and civilisation.'

After his voyage Darwin did not travel again but in the years to come, during which he formulated and defended his great theory of evolution, he would draw constantly on the experience of this five-year voyage of discovery and scientific observation.

# 43

## *Civilization's Verge: Isabella Bird and Clara Bromley in North America*

Isabella Bird has already been encountered in Japan (see Chapter 21) but one of her earliest journeys was to the United States, in 1854, a trip which resulted in *The Englishwoman in America* (1856). Never was a travel book better titled, for its pleasure is in the encounter – or collision – between the very model of an English Victorian lady traveller – robust, forthright, jaunty, outspoken – and the reality of expanding America in the mid-nineteenth century. Isabella Bird, it should be pointed out, was Isabella Bird and there was no one quite like her. She actually considered that her impressions of the United States were more favourable than those of previous English travellers because she had 'taken out many excellent introductions, which afforded me greater facilities of seeing the best society in the States than are usually possessed by those who travel merely to see the country'. In short, she was well-connected.

In accordance with her travel philosophy already observed in Japan, Bird was keen to get off the 'beaten track' but also to give 'a faithful picture of what I saw and heard' in contrast with 'the disposition which leads travellers to seize and dwell upon the ludicrous points which continually present themselves'. She was also keenly aware of the force of domestic prejudice towards Americans: 'We know that they are famous for smoking, spitting, "gouging", and bowie-knives – for monster hotels, steamboat explosions, railway collisions, and repudiated debts. It is believed also that this nation is renowned for keeping three millions of Africans in slavery – for wooden nutmegs, paper money, and "filibuster" expeditions – for carrying out nationally and individually the maxim

"That they may take who have the power.

And they may keep who can.'"

She claimed, rather self-servingly, that Americans were more sensitive to criticism than was John Bull, who had the faculty of laughing at himself.

At eight o'clock one Saturday morning in early 1854 Bird and her friends found themselves on the landing stage at Liverpool ready for her to board a steam tender called the *Satellite*. Huddled together on this 'like a flock of sheep', the 168 passengers chugged out into the Mersey to board the 1850-ton Cunard paddle-steamer *Canada*: 'The summer sun shone brightly – the waves of the Mersey were crisp and foam-capped.' Unfortunately Bird had to share her stateroom for the next 'nine days and five hours' with a nightmare companion, a drunken Englishwoman who lived in New York. The whining Brit made her prefer the boasting of Americans about their country to 'the abusive manner in which an Englishman accustoms himself to speak of the glorious country to which he appears to feel it a disgrace to belong'.

After arriving at Cunard's Wharf in Halifax, Nova Scotia, she took a coach for the twenty-hour journey to Picton, then a boat to Charlotte Town, 'the garden of British America'. She had to spend the next six weeks on Prince Edward Island because cholera was raging. Naturally she glided into all the parties at Government House during this interval, which ended when she sailed on the *Lady Le Marchant* to Shediac in New Brunswick, where she was asked whether Queen Victoria was a 'tall grand lady'. With characteristic English patrician deflation, Bird replied that the Queen 'dressed very simply on ordinary occasions; had never, I believed, worn the crown since her coronation, and was very little above my height'.

Bird pressed on through New England by train, noting as she went the high speed with which people consumed their meals in American hotels, but also the comfort of rail travel: 'We must be well aware that in many parts of England it would be difficult for a lady to travel unattended in a second-class, impossible in a third-class carriage; yet I travelled several thousand miles in America, frequently alone, from the house of one friend to another's, and never met with anything approaching to incivility.'

At Boston she noted the Emigrants' Car on the train in which Irish and other races were herded: 'I once got into one by mistake, and was almost sickened by the smell of tobacco, spirits, dirty fustian, and old leather, which assailed my olfactory organs.' As she rattled along the rails she threw out her opinions on such things as *Uncle Tom's Cabin* and the question of slavery, which was 'no less morally than politically wrong. That it is a political mistake is plainly evidenced by the retarded development and apparent decay of the Southern States, as compared with the ceaseless material progress of the North and West.' At one point, challenged by fellow passengers as to her reasons for travelling, she replied: 'Health and pleasure.' Sometimes they thought she was a New Englander: 'I was glad to be taken for an American, as it gave me a better opportunity of seeing things as they really are.'

On the long train journey south to Mississippi Bird recorded how deferential people were towards a 'lady' and noted the obsession with temperance and the ubiquity of jugs of iced water. Chicago was 'a wonderful place, and tells more forcibly of the astonishing energy and progress of the Americans than anything I saw . . . the city has sprung up rapidly, and is supplied with all the accessories of a high state of civilisation'. She admired its 'wide, airy streets' which presented 'an extraordinary spectacle. Everything reminds that one is standing on the very verge of western civilisation.' She was also bowled over by the American male: 'It is impossible to give an idea of the "western men" to any one who has not seen one at least as a specimen. They are men before whom the Indians melt away as grass before the scythe. They shoot them down on the smallest provocation, and speak of "head of Indian," as we do in England of head of game.'

Everywhere she went Bird marvelled at the speed of travel, trains sometimes reaching sixty-seven miles an hour: 'We dashed through woods, across prairies, and over bridges without parapets, at a uniform rate of progress.' Even in what she thought of as the provincial backwaters there was much to gratify her: 'I spent two days most agreeably at Detroit, in a very refined and intellectual circle, perfectly free from those mannerisms which I had expected to find in a place so distant from the coast.'

On a steamer to Buffalo, however, she found the saloon rather disfigured by spittoons and: 'I saw only one person whom I liked to speak to, among my three hundred fellow-voyagers.' Four of these in the 'ladies' cabin' were Negresses who had recently purchased their freedom and they provoked some vintage Birdisms: 'These blacks were really lady-like and intelligent, and so agreeable and *naive* that, although they chattered to me till two in the morning, I was not the least tired of them . . . Their black faces and wooly hair contrasted most ludicrously with the white pillow-case.' She considered that: 'Providence, which has not endowed the negro with intellectual powers of the highest order, has given him an amount of *heart* and enthusiasm to which we are strangers.'

During a gale when her fellow passengers were seasick, Bird had to deal with one of the more horrifying experiences of her trip: picking up and nursing a screaming infant, something she had never done in her life before. She managed for an hour, against all odds, to pacify the 'poor little black thing' with its 'monkey face': 'It was so awfully ugly, so much like a black ape, and so little like the young of the human species, that I was obliged while I held it to avert my eyes from it, lest in a sudden fit of foolish prejudice and disgust I should let it fall.'

After crossing Lake Ontario in the *Peerless* Bird arrived at Toronto with a 'thrill of pleasure' at seeing the English flag. She was told that Toronto was 'the most English place to be met with outside of England' and once again she approved the signs everywhere of rapid material progress, though not, alas, improved courtesy: 'The manners of the emigrants who settle in Canada are far from prepossessing. Wherever I heard torrents of slang and abuse of

England; wherever I noticed brutality of manner, unaccompanied by respect to ladies, I always found upon inquiry that the delinquent had newly arrived from the old country.' And there was the servant problem: 'The great annoyance of which people complain in this pleasant land is the difficulty of obtaining domestic servants, and the extraordinary specimens of humanity who go out in this capacity. It is difficult to obtain any, and those that are procured are solely Irish Roman Catholics, who think it a hardship to wear shoes, and speak of their master as the "*boss*".'

As noted in Chapter 8, Bird visited the Niagara Falls, where she was appalled by the tacky tourist spectacle: 'We passed through the town bearing the names of Niagara Falls and Manchester, an agglomeration of tea-gardens, curiosity-shops, and monster hotels, with domes of shining tin.' But in spite of the cheap souvenirs and the herding, the sight was a magnificent one and she felt that 'one wish of my life had been granted in seeing Niagara'.

Her next port of call was Montreal, an 'extraordinary place' but one which again roused her vigorous anti-Catholic prejudice on account of its multiplicity of 'Romish' churches. It was less brash and modern than the other cities she had seen: 'It was a most curious and startling change from the wooden erections, wide streets, and the impress of novelty which pervaded everything I had seen in the New World, to the old stone edifices, lofty houses, narrow streets, and tin roofs of the city of Montreal.' But rather than go into detail she brusquely declared: 'There are some very fine public buildings and banks; but as I am not writing a guide-book, I will not dilate upon their merits.'

At Quebec, too, she felt that the town 'has been so often described, that I may well pass on to other subjects'. The latter included lots of parties, increased in frequency because the Viceroy, Lord Elgin, was celebrating the end of his period of office. Bird quickly sniffed out the places of the elite which turned out to centre on the ramparts and the suburb of St Louis: 'The little world in the upper part of the city is probably the most brilliant to be found anywhere in so small a compass.' But she also visited, at the opposite end of the scale, the quarter of St Roch with its 'hideous houses, and hideous men . . . and . . . their still more repulsive progeny'. Of course: 'The same state of things exists in a far greater degree in our large towns at home.'

As she prepared to leave for Montreal again, Bird reflected on her new-found perception of the essence of North America:

> An entire revolution had been effected in my way of looking at things since I had landed on the shores of the New World. I had ceased to look for vestiges of the past, or for relics of ancient magnificence, and, in place of these, I now contemplated vast resources in a state of progressive and almost feverish development, and, having become accustomed to a general absence of the picturesque, had learned to look at the practical and the utilitarian with a high degree of interest and pleasure.

New York, however, tested her new tolerance, being: 'the western receptacle not only of the traveller and the energetic merchant, but of the destitute, the friendless, the vagabond, and in short all the outpourings of Europe, who here form a conglomerate mass of evil, making America responsible for their vices and their crimes'. It was undoubtedly a 'handsome' city and she approved of the replacement of the old wooden houses by brick and brownstone but she also noted the political corruption, crime and poverty, and visited some schools for the poor. Unfortunately some of these poor were Catholics, so her sympathy evaporated: 'The goods and chattels of the Irish appeared to consist principally of numerous red-haired, unruly children, and ragged-looking bundles tied round with rope.' After a visit to the poor quarter Bird thought that they were well off compared with the old world's urban poor: 'But with abundant employment . . . there is no excuse for the squalid wretchedness in which a considerable number of persons have chosen to sink themselves.' And the 'Irish Roman Catholics' were the worst examples. Her final verdict was: 'A strange dreamy resemblance to Liverpool pervades the whole.'

Bird's last city after leaving New York ('the amount of oysters eaten in New York surprised me') was Boston, which she found to lack the restless, provisional quality of the other cities: 'Stately, substantial, and handsome, it looks as if it had been begun and completed in a day.' She arranged to meet the poet Longfellow ('It would be out of place here to criticise his poetry') and found that he was 'extremely courteous to strangers' (though no doubt fascinated by the formidable Mrs Bird). He took her around the University at Cambridge, Massachusetts.

Bird left Boston for Liverpool on the *America* in December sleet and wind, only sorry 'not to return in a clipper' because 'there is something so exhilarating in the motion of a sailing-vessel'. She ended her book with a rhetorical flourish about other lands having their 'charms' but none that could compare to the return to English soil: 'thanking God for the religion and the liberty which have made this weather-beaten island in a northern sea to be the light and glory of the world'.

The year before Bird set off for the United States another, more energetic, English traveller left Southampton with her friend, Eleanor, for a 20,000-mile trip over ten months to North and South America. Little is known about Clara Fitzroy Bromley (*née* Paley), the author of *A Woman's Wanderings in the Western World* (1861), who set off on 17 July 1853, coming ashore on the Azores after seven days' sailing. This was the first time in her life that she had set foot '*not on European ground*' and immediately she had exactly the same traumatic experience as Bird: the alarmed encounter of a childless woman with a young baby who also happened to be black: 'I could scarcely have imagined anything so hideous as a black baby, and I don't know which was worst, one I saw about six months old, in *white* swaddling clothes, or another just able to toddle alone, and who, instead of being a rosy, dimpled little cherub, as might be expected, was as black as ink, and, moreover, stark naked.'

Changing vessels for a steamer to Havana, where on arrival she was immediately taken with the graceful evening *passeggiata*, Bromley attended the theatre in the company of a general and visited the grave of Columbus. On the next ship for the United States there was a degree of social alarm in the beautiful crimson and gold-decorated saloon when their fellow passengers turned out to be 'not of the choicest description' and 'very much out of place'. Stopping at Key West to take on board some turtles, Bromley was moved by their fate: 'Poor things! it is melancholy to see them flapping and floundering about the deck, awaiting their fate and their turn to be converted into soup!' There is an amusing freshness and naivety about some of her observations delivered from the point of view of a very English mid-Victorian young woman. The ashes and cinders blowing back from the engine on their train from Wilmington to Richmond, Virginia, meant: 'We looked like a set of sweeps before reaching our journey's end.'

The two travellers were not impressed by the landscape and the 'ludicrous' place names – Warsaw, for instance, 'consists of exactly four houses'. At Wilmington they spotted a railway notice saying: 'Gents and ladies 75 cents, children and slaves 35 cents.' Bromley interpreted American patriotic pride differently from Bird: 'They are quite the most conceited people possible . . . And yet, until the Americans cure themselves of some of their personal habits, to which it would be disagreeable more particularly to allude, I think they can scarcely be suffered to class themselves among civilised nations, and certainly not among civilised society.'

Arriving in Washington, they put up at Brown's Hotel on Pennsylvania Avenue, where they were pleased with the cheapness and abundance of American food and Bromley developed an amusing line in mimicry of the 'Yankee twang'. A rapid train took them on to Baltimore but they decided that there was really not much to see: 'I can quite appreciate the feeling of some traveller I have read of, who on arriving I forget where, thanked heaven there was nothing to be seen. In a hurried journey one gets sadly tired of lionising.' The next stop was Philadelphia, which she decided would make her 'expire with *ennui*' if she had to spend a week there. She disliked the 'extreme regularity' of American cities and such things as the indecent haste of hotel guests to rush and stuff their plates when the dinner gong sounded: 'There is much in the domestic manners and customs in this country to which I find it impossible to reconcile myself. When will the people learn that they may be free and independent yet at the same time neither coarse nor vulgar.'

At last New York met with Bromley's approval: 'I must frankly allow that the first view of New York far surpasses in splendour any town in the world I have yet seen, and of those the number is not small . . . I can scarcely imagine anything more beautiful than the view which burst upon us as we gradually approached the entrance to the harbour.' This was by far the best town she had visited in the US, and Broadway ('so written to death by travellers of every kind') was most striking. She visited the Italian opera and Christy's Minstrels, where she saw 'a set of apparently black men, numbering from twelve to fourteen persons, who impersonate the "darkies"'. She particularly liked their rendering of 'My Old Kentucky Home'.

Like Bird, Bromley 'did' the Niagara Falls, dressed in 'a pair of drawers and stockings of flannel, then a pair of trousers and a dress of bloomer fashion, descending only to the knees made of india-rubber, and lastly, a covering for the head of an indescribable shape, something between a quakeress's bonnet and a helmet'. She later watched a slave who had escaped by swimming to the Canadian shore: 'I have not the slightest doubt he deserved to be caught; still my sympathies are always with the hunted and not with the hunters, under any circumstances.' Unlike Bird (a distant relative of William Wilberforce), she merely made an unsuccessful bid to 'wade through' Harriet Beecher Stowe. She herself crossed to Canada and stayed at Russell's Hotel in Quebec, where Bird would stay the following year. Canada greatly impressed her, partly for the fluttering English flag, but partly for the demeanour of the citizens: 'The people are so gentle, civil, and above all, so polished in manner. They combine a good deal of the *old French* school of thorough politeness with our natural characteristic of frankness, *without* rudeness.'

After New York, Bromley sailed to Mexico, where she refused to watch a bullfight '*unless* I could make sure of seeing some of the men killed who so cruelly torture the bulls, and, far worse still, their helpless and courageous horses'. She visited silver mines and went to a ball where everyone was encrusted with diamonds and where she saw President Antonio Santa Anna, 'a sallow-complexioned, care-worn-looking man'.

In Cuba she was sympathetic to the resistance to 'the secret machinations and insidious agents of the United States, always at work to sow the seeds of revolt' and partied with the British Consul and his wife and went to the opera. The Captain-General at Havana plainly took a shine to her and presented her with a fan and two gazelles – which died within two weeks of leaving by sea for England.

Bromley visited the Windward Islands, Martinique (where they were mistakenly assumed to be the party of the new archbishop, 'so over the carpets and under the arches we walked, and thus made our triumphal *entrée* into St Pierre') and Barbados, where there were 'dinners, rides, balls, picnics etc' and where she stayed in a little yellow cottage in and out of whose windows humming-birds flew. She was amused, in the way Miss Bromley was amused, by the black population: 'The way they set about doing everything is so perfectly ludicrous, I could not help fancying them a lot of baboons got up as a travestie on men and women.' Later there was a 'coloured ball' given by soldiers of the West Indian Regiment: 'I cannot yet familiarise myself to the sight of black *ladies* (as they are very tenacious of being called) in delicate-coloured ball-dresses.'

She continued south into Panama and the Peruvian capital, Lima, where an English soprano at the opera house sang Rosina to an almost exclusively British audience of expatriate merchants, then on to Puerto Rico and Jamaica, where she was put up in the Governor's mountain residence and entertained at Government House before preparing to sail back to England at midnight on 20 April 1854. Clara Bromley might be brought as a witness in any tribunal of inquiry into whether or not travel broadens the mind.

44

*Rude and Uncompromising:*
*Richard Burton in Brazil*

Nothing about Richard Burton or his wife Isabel was ordinary but the Preface to his *Explorations of the Highlands of Brazil* (1869) was odd indeed. Written by Isabel, who had been given the job of editing his narrative of a five-month trip between June and November 1867, it protests 'vehemently against his religious and moral sentiments which belie a good and chivalrous life'. What Isabel found difficult was her husband's 'misrepresentation' of the Catholic Church, to which she belonged, and his seeming to endorse 'that unnatural and repulsive law, Polygamy, which the

Author is careful not to practise himself, but from a high moral pedestal he preached to the ignorant as a means of population in young countries'. Her protest over, Isabel allowed his text to stand.

After the debacle of the Nile Controversy involving himself and Speke, and the latter's death in 1864, Burton had been sent to the British Consulate in Santos, Brazil, though he soon established himself at the healthier spot of São Paulo, where he spent 'eighteen dull months'. The book was the product of a period of leave. Burton felt that Brazil was less well known than Central Africa yet it had everything 'that man can desire' and was 'the youngest of empires and the only monarchy in the New World'. Noting that the abolition of slavery had created 'a want of black hands' in Brazil, he advocated emigration from Britain. He scorned what he believed was the waste of money on trying to suppress slavery in Africa when 900,000 'paupers or persons in receipt of relief' were idle at home and where 'overcrowding produces the horrors of the Black Country'. Even 'vacation tourists' would find that Brazil was only ten days' sea voyage from Europe.

This was the first of Burton's books to be written with a very strong sense of the new mass-tourism phenomenon, which contrasted with his old-fashioned style of travel across over two thousand miles, more than half of it by raft. He even seemed to predict the age of cheap, long-haul flights: 'Our journey has a something of general interest; in a few years it will have its Handbook and form a section of the Nineteenth Century "Grand Tour". And I venture to predict that many of those now living will be whirled over the land at hurricane speed, covering sixty miles per hour, where our painful "pede-locomotion" wasted nearly a week. Perhaps they may fly – *Quem sabe?*

Burton's goals were to visit the headwaters of the Rio de São Francisco and float down its whole length and to inspect the diamond mines of Brazil. On Wednesday 12 June 1867 he left the 'somewhat drowsy, and do-little Capital' of São Paulo with Isabel on a little steamer, the *Petropolis*, to Mauá Landing Place, where they transferred to a 'shaky, creaky little plank-jetty leading to the railway

carriages'. The Mauá Railway climbed up to the start of the mari-
time mountain range, then they transferred for the third phase of
the journey to a mule carriage. They ascended 'under giants of the
virgin forest . . . Everywhere the soft rush and plash, and the silvery
tinkle and murmur of falling water, make music in our ears . . . The
white road glistens in the sun as if powdered with silver.' The
summit of the pass was the Alto da Serra, 2900 feet above sea level:
'Here you stand, enchanted by the glories of the view.' Then they
descended to the Hotel Inglez at Petropolis.

On 15 June they set off again on a top-heavy mail coach loaded
with seventeen passengers and twenty-eight bags of mail to Juiz de
Fóra. Burton everywhere saw confirmation of his view that Brazil
was an up-and-coming country and he outlined his belief that
polygamy was necessary in this 'poorly-peopled country'. He also
offered his views on slavery, which, given his tendency to endorse
local custom and to question the white man's attempts to uproot it
(that odd accompaniment to his bouts of enthusiastic racism), he
was reluctant to criticize: 'Without slavery how could the Antilles
and the Southern States of the American Union have been cleared
of jungle? White men could not, and free black men would not
have done it.'

Burton and Isabel went next to the Golden Lake or Alagôa
Dourada, where they were invited to lay the first chain of a new railway being built there. They also had a bibulous Midsummer's Day
with some expatriates before pressing on into the highlands. One of
Burton's many digressions was an ironic packet of advice for anyone
who would wish to be a 'comfortable traveller':

Let every thought be duly subordinate to self. Let no weak regard
for sex or age deter you from taking, or at least trying to take, the
strongest beast, the best room, the superior cut, the last glass of
sherry. When riding lead the way, monopolise the path, and
bump up against all who approach you – they will probably steer
clear for the future. If a companion choose a horse, a saddle, or
a bridle, endeavour to abstract it – he had evidently some reason

for the choice. In the morning take care of No. 1; muffle your head, wrap up your throat, stuff your boots with cotton. As the sun rises gradually unshell yourself – 'good people are scarce' – open your umbrella and suck oranges, not omitting all the little contrivances of refection which your ingenuity will suggest. Never go to a hotel if there be a private house within a league, and above all things keep the accounts. Finally, if you invite a man to dine, score up his liquor on the wall, staring him 'in the face', so shall or may it deter him from the other bottle. And thus your trip will cost you 123 milreis, when your friend is minus 750 milreis a head.

Burton visited the gold mine at Morro Velho, descending in a bucket with a rough wooden seat: 'We were advised by the pitmen not to look downwards, as the glimmer of sparks and light-points moving about in the mighty obscure below, causes giddiness and sea-sickness.' At the bottom he and Isabel went through 'a timber avenue of monstrous grandeur' and were 'habited in brown-holland trowsers, belted blouses, and miner's caps'. The mine's height and width (1134 feet and 108 feet) were 'unparalleled in the annals of mining' and Burton compared it to Dante's *Inferno*:

Here dark bodies, gleaming with beaded heat-drops, hung by chains in what seemed frightful positions; there they swung like Leotard from place to place; there they swarmed up loose ropes like the Troglodytes; there they moved over scaffolds, which, even to look up at, would make a nervous temperament dizzy . . . the effect will remain upon the mental retina as long as our brains do their duty . . . At the end of two hours we left this cathedral's cavern of thick-ribbed gold, and we were safely got like ore to grass.

Dazzled by Brazil's mineral wealth, Burton was less enchanted with its social arrangements. On the one hand: 'It may be said with truth that as a field for the white man no country equals the Brazil,' but on the other: 'There is only really one kind of class distinction, between free and slave, black and white . . . Hence here, as in the United States, we observe the unnecessary insolence with which the prolétaire from Europe delights to assert his independence. I have been addressed by a runaway English seaman whom I had never seen, simply thus, "Burtin", &c., &c.' He claimed that hard work got results in this country, basing that claim on three years' experience 'during which I have studied every phase of society between the palace and the cottage'. Unfortunately the freed black slave had done 'incalculable injury' to 'the higher race which admitted him . . . chiefly by prepossessing it against all labour . . . Where blacks work all work becomes servile, consequently the people has no "bold peasantry, its country's pride".' Burton maintained that there was an 'exceptionally humane treatment of the slave in Brazil'.

Beautiful as the lush tropical forest landscape of the highlands was, it was a 'monotonous beauty, primitive and savage' and Burton admitted that he hankered after the human element in all this:

The truth is, we want humanity; we want a little ugliness to speak plain English, by way of relief. Anthropos and his works are to the land he holds, what life is to the body; without them Nature lies a corpse or in a swoon . . . I cannot but hold that green is the most monotonous of colours, and that in a warm, damp climate its effect is a peculiar depression. In the desert of rock and clay there is a vitality and a vivacity of brain which we never experience in India or in Zanzibar.

This longing was satisfied by visiting more Dantesque mines where the slaves 'directed by white overseers – streamed with perspiration, and merrily sang their wild song and chorus, keeping time with the strokes of hammer and drill'.

Another branch of the human race, encountered on the return to Morro Velho, Southerners from the United States, was less welcome to Burton's always vivid prejudices: 'The first impression made by our Transatlantic cousins – speaking only of the farmer and little educated class – is peculiar and unpleasant. In them the bristly individuality of the Briton appears to have grown rank . . . they are untaught but ready to teach everything . . . This is not an agreeable account of the pioneers now leading the great Anglo-American movement in the Brazil.'

On Wednesday 7 August 1867 the second phase of Burton's trip began at Sabará. He had now covered five hundred miles:

> Here, however, ends the excursionist portion, much of which, I have said before, will soon form a section of the nineteenth century Grand Tour. But what now comes is not yet exactly a pleasure trip down the Thames or up the Rhine: there are hot suns, drenching rains, and angry winds to be endured; there is before us a certain amount of hardship, privation, and fatigue, with just enough of risk to enliven the passage; and, finally, there are nearly 1300 miles to be covered by the craziest of crafts, caulked with Sabará clay.

Burton's first glimpse of the raft that would take him as far as the Great Rapids was not very encouraging: 'I never saw such an old Noah's Ark, with its standing awning, a floating gipsy "pál", some seven feet high and twenty-two long, and pitched like a tent upon two hollowed logs. The river must indeed be safe, if this article can get down without accident.' The raft consisted of two or three canoes over thirty-three feet long lashed together to make a vessel six feet wide. Burton slept at the front in a cotton tent which contained a tall deal writing desk which, like his awning, caught the wind. There was a galley at the rear and a crew of three, his personal 'boy' Agostinho and a dog called Negra. There were two further passengers.

As he drifted down the river Burton noted everywhere the signs of change and development: 'this desert stream will presently become a highway of nations, an artery supplying the life-blood of commerce to the world'. In fact he became quite infatuated with the idea of the new country:

We are taught to dwell far too much upon what has been; upon the first canti of the grand Epos of Humanity; we are too indifferent about what is to be, in the days when the whole poem shall be unfolded. Rightly understood, there is nothing more interesting than travel in these New Worlds. They are emphatically the Lands of Promise, the 'expression of the Infinite', and the scenes where the dead Past shall be buried in the presence of that nobler state to which we must now look in the far Future.

Meeting some local women selling chickens he found their traditional mode of existence colourless and pointless: 'I prefer real, hearty barbarism to such torpid semi-civilization.'

By the middle of September Burton had reached the Rio de São Francisco and he was off again: 'With a flush of joy I found myself upon the bosom of this glorious stream of the future, whose dimensions hereabouts average 700 feet. I had seen nothing that could be compared with it since my visit to the African Congo.' He was convinced that Brazil's waterways had been underexploited, as had those in British India. Railways had been preferred. For him 'the various modes of communication have been performed in the reverse order of their merit'. As he drifted down the river, changing crews from time to time and languidly inspecting the scene, Burton grew out of sorts, especially at 'God-forgotten' São Romao, where: 'The Sao Romanese did not affect me pleasantly. I did not see a single white skin amongst them.' The problem was that these rural places had 'a barbarous uniformity . . . After a day or two's halt in these hot-beds of indolence, I begin to feel like one of those who are raised there.'

When Burton finally reached the end of his river journey at Varzéa Redonda: 'I felt the calm which accompanies the successful end of a dubious undertaking.' He had still to see the rapids but he was articulating a feeling, far from unknown to experienced travellers, of disappointment or *tristesse* at the long-desired goal having been reached. On approaching the rapids he heard 'a deep hollow sound, soft withal, like the rumbling of a distant storm; but it seemed to come from below the earth, as if we trod upon it: after another mile the ground appeared to tremble at the eternal thunder . . . The general effect of the picture – and the same may be said of all great cataracts – is the "realized" idea of power, of power tremendous, inexorable, irresistible.' But for Burton 'what at first seemed grand and sublime at last had a feeling of awe too intense to be in any way enjoyable, and I left the place that the confusion and emotion might pass away . . . My task was done. I won its reward, and the strength passed away from me.'

And here, at last, we leave Richard Burton. His next posting was to Damascus, and it was one he enjoyed and felt was useful, but inevitably he made enemies and was accused at one point of anti-Semitism by the local Jewish moneylenders. He was recalled in August 1871 and kept unemployed by the Foreign Office for a year, during which he wrote a book published posthumously as *The Jew, the Gypsy, and El Islam* (1898) which would not have helped to scotch suspicions about his attitude towards the Jews. In the summer of 1872 he explored for sulphur in Iceland, an expedition which resulted in another book, *Ultima Thule, or, A Summer in Iceland* (1875), and during which he learned that he had been offered the consulship at Trieste. After arriving there in October 1872 he did not have enough to do officially but it was an ideal place to write and translate. His interests in poetry, sexology and erotic literature continued to expand and he continued to take periods of leave for further travel.

But it was Burton's translation of *The Arabian Nights* that made his reputation and his fortune, for he earned 16,000 guineas from it, telling his wife: 'I have struggled for forty-seven years, distinguishing myself honourably in every way that I possibly could. I never had a compliment, nor a "thank you", nor a single farthing. I translate a doubtful book in my old age, and I immediately make sixteen thousand guineas. Now that I know the tastes of England, we need never be without money.'

In 1886 Captain Richard Burton finally became Sir Richard Burton and he pressed on with his translation of *The Perfumed Garden*, which he hoped would be 'the crown of my life' but, one day short of completing it, at the Consulate at Trieste, he died on 20 October 1890.

45

## Three South Americans: Hill in Peru, Dance in Venezuela and Kirke in British Guiana

Almost nothing is known about 'S. S. Hill', not even what lies behind those initials, and there is a suspicion that he could even have used a *nom de plume*. His two-volume *Travels in Peru and Mexico* (1860), however, is interesting as a portrait of a mid-Victorian Englishman abroad with all his prejudices and presuppositions intact.

Hill arrived in Valparaíso during an earthquake but nothing could disturb the rather plodding nature of his narrative. At his hotel, 'where everything was arranged in the European continental style, including a tolerable *table d'hôte*, he met 'a polite French gentleman' who had been ruined by the ending of slavery on his estate in Guadeloupe and was off to dig for gold in California. After a visit to the English church and the Protestant cemetery, Hill decided that Valparaíso had too many foreign residents to furnish the necessary exoticism and so set off for Santiago in a horse-drawn *valuchi* with a French companion: 'We were unacquainted with the mode of travelling; knew nothing of the customs, and no more of the language of the good people with whom we were about to mingle, than what we had learned from books.'

Obviously well connected, Hill made his first call in the capital on the President of the Republic, Señor Don Manuel Bulnes Prieto, which provoked the rather back-handed observation that 'in one or two houses where I visited of an evening, I experienced a degree of politeness and hospitality towards strangers, which most travellers in Spain will agree with me, is not common among the race from which the Chilians proceed'. Hill's next stop was Bolivia but unfortunately he arrived in the wake of a small revolution: 'Such is the manner of carrying on political affairs in this and most of the republics of South America.' Finding himself in a Catholic country, he made the required observation: 'We are apt in England to look upon the Romish religion as a very odd system of Christianity and very unsuited to the age in which we live.'

From Bolivia he travelled to Peru and as he climbed into the Andes he began to reflect on the glories of the Inca past: 'It is not possible to travel in Peru without having the mind constantly occupied with the consideration of what more concerns the ancient inhabitants than the present possessors of the country.' Hill had some appreciation of 'that partially civilised people whom the Spaniards found in possession of so large a portion of this continent', especially given the fact that their supplanters had been of the Romish persuasion. At Cuzco he reflected: 'We now look down upon the effects of the vices of the rulers of mankind ... What should be our thoughts when we look upon the scenes now beneath these hills, and remember that the people who once dwelt in this city were destroyed, or robbed and reduced to slavery by men professing to be of the religion which teaches peace and the good will of all men towards one another.' That religion, he discovered in the cloisters of the convent of Merced, could sanction a shocking mural of the Virgin suckling the Christ-child at her naked breast: 'I am not indeed sure whether the subjects of these paintings can be mentioned in such a manner as to be received by an English reader without experiencing such a feeling of disgust as it is as disagreeable to give as to entertain.'

The journey was pleasantly punctuated by meetings with a variety of expatriate Englishmen and women, especially the women, for whom he seems to have had a keen appreciation: 'Those Englishmen only who have been early in life deprived of the society of their countrywomen, can fully appreciate the pleasure of seeing fair English faces abroad, and meeting ladies with whom they may converse without the restraints prevalent in so many countries.' His travels took him to Lima, where he saw the tomb of Francisco Pizarro, whose acts 'strike us in this age with a degree of horror, which is at least a proof of the advance that has been made in civilization in Europe during the last three centuries, and in the better comprehension of the spirit of the religion we profess.' He predicted that the native Indians would regain control of their country. He was pleased also to meet more ladies: 'It is always agreeable for the rougher portion of the human race, to associate with the more delicate. We not only feel the pleasure which your society naturally affords us, but we imbibe your refinement, which tends to make us more just towards one another.'

Hill was particularly excited by four lovingly described young women of Lima to whose mother he expressed his impression 'that we had somehow or other got into the harem of some great Pacha in the eastern world'. Alas, the Latins were fond of bullfights: 'Our feelings may be best described by saying, that we experienced the utmost disgust at all we saw, mingled with pity for the noble animals especially that were killed by the bulls.'

He travelled on to Panama, where he was served by a 'naked girl' who provoked the reflection: 'the human form could never be represented perfect by the chisel, unless it were taken from a figure that had never worn clothes'. His next country was Jamaica, which offered another pleasure: 'To myself, the novelty of hearing my native accent, albeit not in its native purity, from the negroes of the working classes, was so agreeable that I felt as if I had arrived at a home long looked for, and at length attained.' The next country, however, provoked rather more disagreeable thoughts, as it was Cuba: 'We had just left an ancient colony of our own civilised and powerful country in the day of her prosperity, where all was discontent and decay; and we now saw flourishing commerce, riches and elegance, in the last remaining American colony of an European power in its state of decay.' Hill therefore moved on by a Spanish schooner to Veracruz in Mexico, where he stayed at the principal hotel, which allowed him to 'dine tolerably', but all was not well. 'What a frightful country,' his companion observed, 'for civilised man to inhabit.'

They caught an omnibus to Mexico City and visited some silver mines at Real del Monte, where the English owner had a comely wife: 'Here I must express my gratification at meeting an elegant English lady, in the very prime of life, and, I must add, of great beauty.' Unfortunately the rest of Mexico was not at the same level of pleasant civility: 'I do not believe there is in the world a country that has ever been civilised, now so deficient as the republic of Mexico in the two great essentials to prosperity and progress, tranquillity and security of property'. After three years of constant travelling it was time to return, especially when his mind turned towards 'the peaceful island of my birth, whose noble institutions become more and more dear to those who witness the insecurity of property and life prevailing in the countries through which I had lately travelled'.

On the steamer home Hill met Lady Emmeline Stuart Wortley, who asked him about his earlier travels in Siberia and showed an 'affable . . . lively disposition and many promising signs of beauty at a riper age'. He travelled back via Cadiz but was soon off again travelling in mainland Europe without having returned to England.

Hill concluded with a philosophical summation on the consequences of travel: 'When the civilised man and the savage are brought into peaceable contact, the savage contracts the vices of the civilised man more easily than his virtues, and the civilised man too often forgets his good manners, and relaxes in his former respect for decency and good morals.'

Venezuela was the destination of another traveller known only through his *Recollections of Four Years in Venezuela* (1876). Charles Daniel Dance originally had the idea of going to Venezuela as a cheaper option than California, where the gold rush was raging at the time. The companies founded to exploit the gold at Upata attracted what Dance called 'inexperienced and thoughtless young men, most of whom had scarcely ever travelled beyond the streets of a town, and whose previous occupations unfitted them for the exposure, fatigues, and self-denial required for a successful issue to the project'. He was one of those young men and he threw himself into the adventure with youthful enthusiasm: 'I purchased a double-barrelled gun, a large quantity of powder and shot, a pick-axe, cutlass, spade, a large blanket, and clothing for work, and had a dozen small bags made, to secure the gold when I got it.'

Two weeks before Dance was due to set off he met an older and wiser hand who had just come back from Upata and who told him that the plan was absurd. So Dance resolved to become a farmer in Venezuela, which was an 'Eden, a Paradise of abundance of real, substantial, inartificial wealth'. Another fortuitous meeting, in Trinidad, where he was cooling his heels, with Don Carlos Gerilleau, brother of the Minister of Finance, secured him fifty acres and the right number of peons to work it, and so he sailed to what the Spanish called the Costa Firma, the coast of Venezuela at La Ceiba: 'The yellow mud-flat was dotted with innumerable flamingoes . . . Above the mud-flat waved the low dark green mangrove bush . . . And away in the distance, its summit touching the clouds, the blue Sierra de San Juan.' Dance's first task was to clear his plot of land and put up his *ranchería*, aided by two Chaima Indians, Cristobal and Domingo, who sang to him and told him tales. He also met a man called M. Edmond, a failed meat exporter now running a plantation. At the end of a good meal Dance suggested that this older man's experience must be well worth hearing. 'Not at all,' he replied, 'only the common one of travellers, exposure, privation, fatigue.'

At night Dance heard tigers screaming and during the day he saw alligators, snakes hanging down from trees and the great South American eagle. He once went out with a revenue officer, Juan Pinado, an ex-smuggler now hunting down his own kind and who cooked Dance and himself breakfast of the brain of a stingray. However, eventually he became bored and took his family to Maturín, the party consisting of 'my wife and little daughter Ninine, myself, and our little African god-son Johnnie, a waif that had attached himself to me, – a street-gamin who had been accustomed to sleep under upturned boats, or under wharves, or in an empty barrel'. Dance found the city rich and abundant but it was a time of political turbulence ('The curse of Venezuela is her form of government') and when General Sotillo occupied Maturín he accused foreigners like Dance of abetting the insurgents. Dance now thought it prudent to lose himself in a larger city where there were more foreigners, so he prepared to travel to Bolívar on the Orinoco.

The party consisted of his family, a tall, thin Sambo guide, a Scot named McDonald and a German, Herr Wilhelm (both of these gentlemen turned out to be a bit of a handful), and two donkeys:

The order of our march was, first the guide's two donkeys, with provision for the road, knives, needles, cotton &c, – and our trunks. Then came our guide, with his fusil and little travelling bag. Next, my wife, on her favourite donkey, with his two panniers – one containing our little Ninine [the child died on this journey], and the other our little boy. I walked at their side. The rear was brought up by the donkey, with necessary travelling gear, followed by the two men.

They journeyed into the high plateau of the Llanos and Dance was forced to admit: 'There is a monotony in Llano travelling which embarrasses the describer; especially if he be writing from memory years after his travels.' He could have inserted some graphic inventions: 'But I am writing truthfully what passed within my own experience, and have neither talent nor ambition for a work of fiction.'

In the end Dance reached Bolívar, describing it as 'no mean object', and he found the money was easy there but his narrative rather peters out and eventually, revolution approaching the city, he decided to leave. His book, in its rather arbitrary ramblings and intermittent flashes of vivid incident or description, is characteristic of a certain kind of Victorian travel narrative: unpretentious, auto-biographical, full of youthful adventure and written with competence rather than panache. It is one of thousands.

Henry Kirke, author of *Twenty Five Years in British Guiana* (1898), spent 1872–97 in the colony. He witnessed rapid changes, not all, he felt, for the better:

Railways and steam vessels are now hurrying through vast territories only known twenty years ago to the fierce Carib or placid Arawak; gold diggers and diamond searchers are swarming up every great river and gloomy creek, and the whole face of the country is being rapidly changed. And with this change of circumstances the people have changed. Their old quaint manners and habits have disappeared; the old legends are vanishing; the people dress and talk as others; the electric light illuminates their houses; the tramcar patrols their streets; the silk chimney-pot of civilization is constantly in evidence; and they are as other men. The world is gradually acquiring a painful similarity; in a few hundred years every one will dress alike and speak the same language, and the human race will be reduced to one dull commonplace level of uniformity.

He described the capital, Georgetown, as 'the Venice of the West Indies' and his abiding memories of it were of heat and dampness: 'It is one of the hottest places in the world.' Unlike Dance, who merely recorded artlessly what he saw, Kirke was keen to analyse the colonial society in which he lived. Disdaining any scandalous gossip (and thereby indicating that it must exist), he conceded: 'It is true that in most colonies there are a few black sheep, who have been shipped thither by despairing friends and relations, after having failed to find them any satisfactory position in England; but the majority of the ruling caste are energetic men who, failing to find an opening for their talents in their native land, have pushed towards that Greater Britain beyond the seas, where there is still elbow-room for all who want to work.'

But the main difference, in Kirke's view, between British Guiana and Britain was the absence in the former of 'the leisured and liter-ary classes'. Certainly there were no artists, but this was simply a fact of colonial life: 'young and vigorous communities are too much occupied in providing for the necessities of life to have time for art studies, which must be sought amongst old and somewhat decaying civilizations'. The older colonists, in particular, were: 'ill-educated and prejudiced, rough-mannered men who had been nurtured in the evil days of slavery'. Nevertheless: 'One of the most touching incidents of colonial life is the universal use of the word "home" amongst all classes of the community, when speaking of England.'

Cricket was a universal passion and Georgetown Cricket Club had a fine pavilion and all the paraphernalia of a first-class ground: 'The turf is as good as that of an English county club, although sometimes, when it is most wanted, it is flooded with water and more suited for a regatta than a cricket match.' It was not just a white settler's sport: 'The black and coloured people are madly fond of cricket, every available open space of ground is full of them playing the game in one form or another. Little boys play on the sides of the streets with an empty kerosene oil tin for wickets, and the rib of a palm leaf for a bat.'

The colonial society had its 'characters', including some rather shady-sounding barristers, one of the latter being the legendary James Crosby, an energetic septuagenarian fond of dancing 'like a youngster'. At a croquet party at Government House Crosby dashed across the green to shake hands with a lady friend and 'tripped over a hoop, and fell into a box full of mallets, breaking one of his ribs'. In the absence of intellectual pursuits the expatriate community did a great deal of hunting and fishing, got very drunk and played practical jokes: 'I am afraid we were rather a wild lot on the coast in those days; and our pastors, whatever we may say about our masters, were, as a rule, of the sign-post order, pointing the way, but not troubling to go themselves.' The Reverend William Austin, rural Dean of Essequibo, once broke off his reading of the first lesson to address his old verger, Thomas, having spotted some goats (the church had a roof but no walls). The venerable Dean called out: 'Thomas, Thomas, why don't you drive that goat out of my waggon; don't you see it is eating the cushions?' The verger hobbled off to execute the commission and the Dean resumed the lesson.

But none of these diversions could cure what Kirke called 'the monotony of life in British Guiana' and he travelled whenever he could. In 1880 he took a boat trip up the River Pomeroon in a tent-boat with 'five black men as paddlers'. The latter, however, simply got drunk and had to be replaced by Indians. Slinging their hammocks in the bush, Kirke and his friends were wakened by 'the most infernal barking and roaring' which turned out to be 'a troop of howling baboons'. The next day, along the river: 'There was not much life to be seen, except some toucans, galdings [*sic*], cranes, kingfishers, and humming-birds, some of which we shot.' Eventually the boat, which had been caulked with mere mud and grass, sank.

Although Kirke had the usual prejudices ('The Indian is not a very amiable character; he is essentially selfish, grasping, improvident, and lazy. Black people are, as a rule, very improvident') he seems to have been a humane administrator, in spite of supervising many hangings. Given the 'simply appalling' levels of crime in the colony, he became also an advocate of floggings. He said, however, some things about the colonial presence which were not usual:

One of the principal causes of the extermination of native races before European civilization is the absurd practice of making these poor people wear clothes . . . when by the efforts of some well-meaning but misdirected missionary, they don clothes, they soon become victims of phthisis and pneumonia, their clothes getting wet through and drying on their bodies several times a day . . . It is a dangerous experiment to interfere with the immemorial customs and habits of an ancient race, and to preach to them doctrines strange and unnatural.

For the latter reason, Kirke was not keen on missionaries: 'I am no great believer in missionary enterprise; I am sure every honest Christian in the colony will confess that the attempt to convert the Hindoo and Mahommedan immigrants to Christianity has been an utter failure.'

He also had a sense of humour. He recalled a barrister in court insisting to a witness that what he was putting to the witness was true: 'Witness: "I no know dat." Counsel: "What do you mean, sir?" Witness: "I kiss book to talk true; you no kiss book, you hable for lie."'

Writing at the end of the century and of the Victorian era, Kirke had none of the ardent confidence of the early colonizers and missionaries. He seemed to see what was coming.

PART SEVEN

# AUSTRALASIA

## 46

*Missionary Exertions: Jonathan Williams in the Pacific*

'The Missionary enterprise,' declared the Pacific islands missionary Jonathan Williams, in the second year of Queen Victoria's reign, 'regards the whole globe as its sphere of operation.' Inspired by a Birmingham preacher whom he heard at the Moorfields Tabernacle in London in January 1814, Williams abandoned his apprenticeship to a City Road ironmonger two years later to become a missionary candidate for the London Missionary Society. He was moved by the idea of the heathen 'daily perishing for lack of knowledge' and was appointed to the mission centred on the Society Islands in the central South Pacific.

Williams believed that the missionary had 'much nobler work to perform' than any naturalist or geologist and claimed that in his time he had travelled 'a *hundred thousand miles*, and spent *eighteen years*, in promoting the spread of the Gospel'. He was sustained by a lofty conception of what the missionary enterprise entailed:

> It is founded upon the grand principles of Christian benevolence, made imperative by the command of the ascending Saviour, and has for its primary object to roll away from six hundred millions of the race of Adam the heavy curse which rests upon them; – to secure their elevation to the dignity of intelligent creatures and children of God; – to engage their thoughts in the contemplation, and to gladden their hearts with the prospects of immortality; – to make known 'the way of life' through the meritorious sufferings of the Redeemer; – in a word, 'to fill the whole earth with the glory of the Lord'.

Notwithstanding these high aims, Williams's *A Narrative of Missionary Enterprises in the South Sea Islands* (1838) offered itself as 'a simple and unadorned narrative of facts'. He made a fetish of accuracy, claiming that his book was like a plaster cast of 'the images and impressions' in his mind. Speaking of himself in the third person, he explained how he had: 'preserved the dialogues in which much of his knowledge was obtained, and has not spoken for the natives, but allowed them to speak for themselves . . . In a word, the Author has endeavoured to take his reader with him to each of the islands he has visited; to make him familiar with their chiefs and people; to show him what a missionary life is, and to awaken in his mind emotions similar to those which successively filled his own.' Like David Livingstone, Williams believed that missionary work was intimately bound up with the advance of 'civilization' and modern technological progress. At its most basic level, below the spiritual, missionary work was: 'an apparatus for overthrowing puerile, debasing, and cruel superstitions; for raising a large portion of our species in the scale of being; and for introducing amongst them the laws, order, the usages, the arts, and the comforts of civilized life'.

The dilemma for the missionary was to decide which particular tract of heathen darkness out of many should be chosen to be flooded with light and Williams quoted a magnificent oration from Dr Haweis, Rector of All Saints, Aldwinkle, Northamptonshire, delivered at that temple of evangelism the Surrey Chapel in London: 'The field before us is immense! O that we could enter at a thousand gates! – that every limb were a tongue, and every tongue a trumpet, to spread the joyful sound! Where so considerable a part of the habitable globe on very side calls for our efforts, and, like the man of Macedonia, cries, "Come over and help us," it is not a little difficult to decide at what part to begin.' In the event, of all the 'dark places of the earth' the LMS plumped pragmatically for the South Sea islands as presenting 'the fewest difficulties and the fairest prospects of success'. Its first efforts were in Tahiti and the Society Islands, where good work was done 'in transforming their barbarous, indolent, and idolatrous inhabitants into a comparatively civilized, industrious, and Christian people', but this was merely the launch pad for wider efforts. New Guinea, for example, was reported to be well stocked with 'several millions of immortal beings suffering all the terrific miseries of a barbarous state, and dying without a knowledge of God or the Gospel of his Son'. Ambitious claims to have already converted 300,000 were made by the LMS (after a sixteen-year initial period when no progress at all was achieved) and Williams wanted to be part of the action, 'an instrument in accelerating this great work'.

On 17 November 1816, newly married to Mary Chawner, Williams set sail from London on the *Harriet*, reaching the 'wild and romantic' Society Islands on 17 November 1817. He lost no time in learning the Tahitian language in which he preached (unable to pronounce his name, the local people settled for 'Variamu') and then in September 1818 he moved to establish a permanent mission station on Raiatea. He had particular success from here in converting the entire island of Rurutu, where one evening the people's rejected idols were 'publicly exhibited from the pulpit'. On Aitutaki he was greeted by people waving their European hats and spelling books, their idols abandoned. A service followed in the newly built chapel: 'It was indeed, a delightful sight to behold from 1500 to 2000 people, just emerged from heathenism, of the most uncultivated appearance, some with long beards, others decorated with gaudy ornaments, but all behaving with the greatest decorum, and attending, with glistening eyes and open mouth, to the wonderful fact that, "God so loved the world, as to give his only begotten Son".' On his previous visit, he reflected with satisfaction, these people had been eating one another.

He explained his missionary method: they would begin by teaching people the alphabet and the Lord's Prayer, then they would move on to confront the local traditional priest, exposing his shaky theology, then bring on, for theological support, the angels and the creation of the world: 'All this was new to the people; and the interest excited by the announcement appears to have been intense; for, if the slightest noise was made, there was a general cry of "Be still, be still, let us hear."' Encouraged, the teachers went on to describe the garden of Eden and the sacrifice on the Cross, on hearing which the people exclaimed 'with one accord, "Surely this is the truth; ours is all deceit"'.

It did not always go as smoothly as this, however, and many converts faced the wrath of their 'heathen countrymen', but sometimes it was done in a day and the heaped-up idols were burnt publicly. 'The simple-hearted inhabitants were much astonished at our appearance,' Williams noted, 'took hold of our hands, smelt us, turned up our sleeves, examined us most minutely, and being delighted with the whiteness of our skin, concluded that we must be very great chiefs.' He was struck by 'the impression made upon a barbarous people by their first intercourse with civilized man'. There was one brush with 'the licentiousness of heathenism' when one of the native chiefs decided to add to his tally of nineteen wives by bearing off one of the native teacher's wives, an act which caused the missionary's heart to recoil in 'horror and disgust from the contemplation of the deep moral degradation into which our race is sunk'. Generally, however, the work was triumphal: 'And as other warriors feel a pride in displaying trophies of the victories they win, we hung the rejected idols of Aitutaki to the yard-arms and other parts of the vessel, entered the harbour in triumph, sailed down to the settlement, and dropped anchor, amidst the shouts and congratulations of the people.'

Like Livingstone, Williams believed in the intimate connection between conversion and trade ('wherever the Missionary goes, new channels are cut for the stream of commerce') and he clashed repeatedly with the LMS directors over his desire to trade island products such as sugar cane and tobacco with Sydney. He even bought a boat with his own funds for the purpose but the scheme did not pay – though another boat, the *Messenger of Peace*, was built on Rarotonga in 1827 and used to spread the word. On the same island in 1830 disease was nearly wiping out the local population. Williams recognized that the source was the ships: 'the FIRST intercourse between Europeans and natives is, I think, invariably attended with the introduction of fever, dysentery, or some other disease which carries off numbers of the people . . . It is an affecting consideration, that civilized man should thus convey physical as well as moral contamination with him wherever he goes.' He did not push this argument to any more extreme logical conclusion. In fact he believed that, had missionaries been the first white men the local people had seen, all would have been well. The local people, however, did not always see it his way and on one occasion he conceded that the natives were saying that 'since the introduction of Christianity, they had been visited with a greater number of direful calamities than when they were heathens'.

Williams was very energetic and good with his hands, teaching building and carpentry skills to the people. He built himself a handsome house on Rarotonga, justifying his comparative luxury on the grounds that his job was to pull up the natives by example: 'for the Missionary does not go to barbarize himself, but to civilize the heathen. He ought not therefore to sink down to their standard, but to elevate them to his.' His continued stay among them led to an increase of sympathy. The 'savages' were eventually granted to be in many respects not 'below the European' – particularly in their humour, puns, proverbs and similes, ingenuity, good sense, eloquence and keen desire for instruction.

As he prepared to leave, Williams drew up a balance sheet of what had been achieved in the South Seas by the missionaries. First, the blessings brought by Christianity were not just spiritual in character, for 'civilization and commerce have invariably followed in her train' and the whole civilized world benefited from the exertions of missionaries because of the 'reflex influence of the Missionary enterprise upon home exertions' and, more particularly, from the commercial exports. 'From a barbarous people very little can be obtained' but once there was trade all would change. The Samoan islanders, who had nothing to export, would soon be taught to grow sugar and coconut oil, and supply provisions for ships. There were other benefits too: 'New fields of discovery have been opened, new regions explored, and wilds previously inaccessible to the traveller penetrated by the Missionary. In addition to this, languages before unknown have been mastered and reduced to a system; man has been presented under circumstances the most peculiar and interesting; and new facts have been added to his natural and moral history.'

When his account of his travels was published in 1837 Williams suggested to the directors of the LMS that they send copies to fifty members of the nobility with a letter asking for charitable donations, a strategy that worked. The book was a huge success, selling 38,000 copies and making Williams a celebrity. In 1838 he returned to the Pacific with his own ship, the *Camden,* and settled in Samoa as a base for carrying the work forward into the New Hebrides. On 20 November 1839 his party came ashore on Eromanga in the southern New Hebrides and were attacked. Fleeing back to the boat, Williams was clubbed to death in the water. It has been thought that he and his companion James Harris were then eaten.

## 47

## The Cause of Geography: Sturt in the Australian Desert

'Let any man lay the map of Australia before him, and regard the blank upon its surface,' wrote Charles Sturt, 'and then let me ask him if it would not be an honourable achievement to be the first to place a foot in its centre.' His *Narrative of an Expedition into Central Australia* (1849) is the record of an attempt to penetrate the Australian interior in the conviction that he would find an inland lake or watercourse.

Born in 1795 in Bengal, where his father was an East India Company judge, Sturt was sent back to relatives in England for his education and attended Harrow. Instead of going on to university he obtained a commission, and it was to accompany a detachment of his regiment in charge of convicts bound for New South Wales that he left England in December 1826. In November 1827 he was appointed to lead an expedition into the interior. A year later he set off and, though he found no pastoral land, he named the River Darling. On a later expedition in 1830 he named the River Murray but illness eventually forced him to return home. In 1834 he married and, with his wife, returned to Australia, trying unsuccessfully to farm. He was appointed in 1838 to the post of surveyor-general and then registrar-general and in January 1843 he was charged with leading an expedition to search for the inland sea.

In his account of the expedition Sturt explained how the goal had been in his mind through all the previous journeys:

I had adopted an impression, that this immense tract of land had formerly been an archipelago of islands, and that the apparently boundless plains into which I had descended on my former expeditions, were, or rather had been, the sea-beds of the channels, which at that time separated one island from the other; it was impossible, indeed, to traverse them as I had done, and not feel convinced that they had at one period or the other been covered by the waters of the sea . . . I therefore commenced my investigations, under an impression that . . . sooner or later I should be stopped by a large body of inland waters.

Sturt was disappointed and his career as an explorer is a record principally of failure. 'I am still of opinion that there is more than one sea in the interior of the Australian continent,' he concluded, adding rather lamely, 'but such may not be the case.'

On 10 August 1844, after a public breakfast given by 'the colonists', Sturt set out from Adelaide with two hundred sheep in lieu of salted meat (hoping thereby to avoid scurvy) and four hundredweight of bacon, led as far as Williorara by two Aboriginal guides, Camboli and Nadbuck: 'They were in truth two fine specimens of Australian aborigines, stern, impetuous, and determined, active, muscular, and energetic.' Sturt's deputy was James Poole and he had with him surgeon John Harris Browne, draughtsman McDougall Stuart and several others, including a storekeeper, a stockman, a bullock driver and sheep and horse handlers. The party was completed with eleven horses, three drays, thirty bullocks, four kangaroo dogs and two sheep dogs. They also carried a boat and boat carriage, a horse dray and a spring cart.

After turning the Great Bend of the Murray and pursuing an easterly course, Sturt noted: 'the natives generally, seemed to regard our progress with suspicion'. He was interested to witness a corroboree ('the natives think as much of them as we should do the finest play at Covent Garden') but he was in general wary: 'Although I was always disposed to be kind to the natives, I still felt it right to shew them that they were not to be unruly.' He believed they were 'strongly susceptible of kindness' and that his not being attacked was due to his good treatment of them. When he arrived at Laidley's Ponds on 10 October he noted: 'It was clear that the natives still remembered the first visit the Europeans had made to them, and its consequences, and that they were very well disposed to retaliate.' As it turned out, the Aborigines seem to have respected him, calling him 'Boocolo', a term generally given to a tribe's chief or elder, and Sturt admired the 'most pleasing' manners of the Cawndilla tribe: 'There was a polish in them, a freedom and grace that would have befitted a drawing-room.'

What really surprised him was the fact that the country after he left the Darling was not better inhabited: 'For however unfit for civilised man, it seemed a most desirable one for the savage, for there was no want of game of the larger kind, as emus and kangaroos, whilst in every tree and bush there was a nest of some kind or other, and a variety of vegetable productions of which these rude people are fond.'

On 27 January 1845 Sturt's party pitched their tents at Depot Glen for what he called a 'ruinous detention', forced upon them by a lack of water, which lasted until 17 July:

It became evident to me that we were locked up in the desolate and heated region, into which we had penetrated, as effectually as if we had wintered at the Pole. It was long indeed ere I could bring myself to believe that so great a misfortune had overtaken us, but so it was. Providence had, in its allwise purposes, guided us to the only spot, in that wide-spread desert, where our wants could have been permanently supplied, but had there stayed our further progress into a region that almost appears to be forbidden ground.

It was maddening to have got so far only to be blocked from further progress, perhaps even to face having to retreat: 'I had by severe exertion gained a most commanding position, the wide field of the interior lay like an open sea before me, and yet every sanguine hope

I had ever indulged appeared as if about to be extinguished.' To make matters worse they were attacked by scurvy and Sturt's deputy became ill and died on the very day they had decided to split the party, nine remaining and the rest, under Poole, returning to Adelaide.

Sturt's valiant nine pressed on north-westwards, reaching Lake Torrens and then entering a drier, more difficult country: 'My men were also beginning to feel the effects of constant exposure, of ceaseless journeying, and of poverty of food, for all we had was 5lbs of flour, and 2 oz. of tea per week.' This was supplemented by the odd pigeon or duck but scurvy returned and the going got tougher. Sturt's dilemma was clear: 'I felt that it required greater moral firmness to determine me to retrace my steps than to proceed onwards.' He was only 150 miles from the centre of the continent: 'If I had gained that spot my task would have been performed, my most earnest wish would have been gratified, but for some wise purpose this was denied to me.'

He remained possessed by the monomaniac goal he had set himself:

A veil hung over Central Australia that could neither be pierced or raised. Girt round about by deserts, it almost appeared as if Nature had intentionally closed it upon civilized man, that she might have one domain on the earth's wide field over which the savage might roam in freedom ... I had traced down almost every inland river of the continent, and had followed their courses for hundreds of miles, but, they had not led me to its central regions. I had run the Castlereagh, the Macquarie, the Lachlan, the Murrumbidgee, the Hume, the Darling, and the Murray down to their respective terminations, but beyond them I had not passed – yet – I looked upon Central Australia as a legitimate field, to explore which no man had a greater claim than myself, and the first wish of my heart was to close my services in the cause of Geography by dispelling the mists that hung over it.

Sturt pressed on to Eyre's Creek on the edge of the Simpson Desert but was driven back by the usual obstacles and his own failing health. The failure sparked some deep reflections on what it was he was trying to do:

Purposes of utility were amongst the first objects I had in view in my pursuit of geographical discovery; nor do I think that any country, however barren, can be explored without the attainment of some good end. Circumstances may yet arise to give a value to my recent labours, and my name may be remembered by after generations in Australia, as the first who tried to penetrate to its centre. If I failed in that great object, I have one consolation in the retrospect of my past services. My path amongst savage tribes has been a bloodless one, not but that I have often been placed in situations of risk and danger, when I might have been justified in shedding blood, but I trust I have ever made allowances for human timidity, and respected the customs and prejudices of the rudest people . . . Most assuredly in my intercourse with the savage, I have endeavoured to elevate the character of the white man. Justice and humanity have been my guides, but while I have the consolation to know that no European will follow my track into the Desert without experiencing kindness from its tenants, I have to regret that the progress of civilized man into an uncivilized region, is almost invariably attended with misfortune to its original inhabitants.

So hot was it in November 1845 that the thermometer reached 125 degrees Fahrenheit and then the bulb burst: 'a circumstance that I believe no traveller has ever before had to record. I cannot find language to convey to the reader's mind an idea of the intense and oppressive heat that prevailed.' Sturt had no choice but to turn back, disappointed of his inland sea, and he returned to Adelaide at the start of 1846 still insisting that the Aborigines ('an inoffensive and harmless race') should be more favourably regarded: 'It is true that all attempts to improve the social condition of the Australian native has failed, but where is the savage nation with which we have succeeded better? . . . All I can say is that they have submitted to our occupation of their country with a forbearance that commands our best sympathies.'

In May 1847 Sturt returned on leave to England, then came back to Australia as colonial secretary in 1849, the same year that his book was published, but failing health forced him to resign in December 1851. In 1853 he finally left Australia in order to return to Cheltenham, where he died on 16 June 1869. Although a popular Australian hero with many statues and streets named after him, he had little in terms of concrete, measurable achievement to point to as an explorer.

# PART EIGHT

# THE POLAR REGIONS

# 48

## *Ice: James Clark Ross in Antarctica*

O f all the images of travel and exploration, the heroic
Englishman (for it was a man's world on the ice in the
Victorian period) pressing on to plant his nation's flag on some
polar ice-cap remains one of the most romantic. There are no
records of any human sightings of the mainland of Antarctica before
1820 and it was not until the 1830s that major expeditions to the
South Pole – the North Pole attracted much less initial interest – got
under way. The most famous of these by a British explorer was that
of James Clark Ross from 1839 to 1843.

Born in Scotland in 1800, James Clark Ross entered the navy in
1812 and made his first Arctic voyage in 1818, searching for the elusive North-West Passage. On subsequent voyages he began to
develop a reputation as a scientific observer, naming Ross's gull and
being elected a member of the Linnean Society. He was the nephew
of the Arctic explorer John Ross and the two often sailed together.
He was on the voyage of the *Victory* which planted the British flag
on the north magnetic pole, or North Pole, on 1 June 1831. Ross
developed an interest in terrestrial magnetism and between 1835
and 1838 he carried out the first systematic magnetic survey of the
British Isles. It was to carry out similar magnetic observations that
Ross entered the Antarctic in 1839.

Backed by the British Association for the Advancement of
Science, and carrying a sheaf of very precise instructions from the
Lords Commissioners of the Admiralty, Ross sailed from
Gillingham on 25 September 1839 in command of the two ships, the

*Erebus* and the *Terror*. After a delay of five days caused by lack of wind at Margate Roads he was finally off the Lizard by 5 October: 'The last point of the coast of England seen by us, and from which therefore we took our departure. It is not easy to describe the joy and lightheartedness we all felt as we passed the entrance of the Channel, bounding before a favourable breeze over the blue waves of the ocean, fairly embarked in the enterprise we had all so long desired to commence, and freed from the anxious and tedious operations of our protracted but requisite preparation.'

On 3 December they crossed the equator, performing the rituals 'with as much amusement and good-natured fun as usual on such occasions'. Much of the voyage was taken up with painstaking scientific measurements but there were occasional observations of the wider scene. At Van Diemen's Land, governed by Sir John Franklin, they found the society of Hobart 'most perfectly English, and therefore most agreeable to visitors from the mother country' and noted with approval the arrival of a clergyman to sort out the colony's educational system, bearing the recommendation of Dr Arnold of Rugby. It was not until December 1840 that the expedition finally approached the ice:

> The fifteen months which had elapsed since we took our departure from England had in no degree diminished our eagerness for the southern voyage; and now that we had at length the prospect before us of entering upon those labours from which we all hoped the most remarkable and important results of our voyage might be fairly anticipated, joy and satisfaction beamed in every face . . . I felt that we had nothing to desire but the guidance and blessing of Almighty God throughout the arduous duties we were about to commence, and without which all human skill and courage must prove utterly unavailing.

On 27 December they saw their first icebergs and a profusion of whales, then seals and white petrel and penguins. The boat's progress was now greatly retarded by the ice.

Then, on 15 January 1841, they had a fine view of a chain of mountains: 'These were named after the eminent philosophers of the Royal Society and the British Association, at whose recommendation the government was induced to send forth this expedition.' An example was Mount Herschel. By 17 February Ross was only 160 miles from the South Pole and there was great satisfaction at having approached it some hundred miles nearer than his predecessors, but conditions frustrated any nearer approach. This provoked one of Ross's characteristic pious laments, which combined religious humility and scientific ambition in equal measure:

It was nevertheless painfully vexatious to behold at an easily accessible distance under other circumstances the range of mountains in which the pole is placed, and to feel how nearly that chief object of our undertaking had been accomplished: and but few can understand the deep feelings of regret with which I felt myself compelled to abandon the perhaps too ambitious hope I had so long cherished of being permitted to plant the flag of my country on both the magnetic poles of our globe; but the obstacles which presented themselves being of so insurmountable a character was some degree of consolation, as it left us no grounds for self-reproach, and as we bowed in humble acquiescence to the will of Him who had so defined the boundary of our researches, with grateful hearts we offered up our thanksgivings for the large measure of success which He had permitted to reward our exertions.

In March 1841 Ross glimpsed the Aurora Australis and then recrossed the Antarctic Circle, having been south of it for sixty-three days. A gale got up and the ship feared that it was being driven towards a dangerous chain of icebergs: 'Sublime and magnificent as such a scene must have appeared under different circumstances, to us it was awful, if not appalling. For eight hours we had been gradually drifting towards what to human eyes appeared inevitable destruction . . . the dreadful calamity that seemed to await us.' As the ship approached within half a mile of the icebergs:

> The roar of the surf, which extended each way as far as we could see, and the crashing of the ice, fell upon the ear with fearful distinctness, whilst the frequently averted eye as immediately returned to contemplate the awful destruction that threatened in one short hour to close the world and all its hopes and joys and sorrows upon us for ever. In this our deep distress we called upon the Lord and He heard our voices out of His temple, and our cry came before Him.

Mercifully, their prayers were heard and a gentle wind lifted them out of danger. On 4 April 1841 the two ships entered the bay of Van Diemen's Land, offering their cheers to the welcoming Governor's barge.

The success of this first season of Antarctic operations was followed by several months of repairing damage to the ships. By the end of June Ross had finished all the repairs and refitting and had loaded provisions and stores to last for three years. He made a few short local forays but, as he put it: 'The natives at the time of our visit were beginning to feel deeply, and to express in terms of severe bitterness, their great disappointment at the effects of the treaty of Waitangi . . . It could not escape the jealous vigilance of the chiefs that the numbers of Europeans were increasing so rapidly that they would soon outnumber themselves, and gain possession of all their lands.'

On New Year's Day 1842 the *Erebus* and the *Terror* were already 250 miles into the ice packs and celebrating the holiday with 'various amusing games on the ice' which culminated in a bizarre 'grand fancy ball, of a novel and original character, in which all the officers bore a part'. Things were less amusing for the many penguins they now began to spot: 'Several of them were caught and brought on board alive; indeed it was a very difficult matter to kill them, and a most cruel operation, until we resorted to hydrocyanic acid, of which a tablespoonful effectually accomplished the purpose in less than a minute. These enormous birds varied in weight from sixty to seventy-five pounds . . . They are remarkably stupid and allow you to approach them so near as to strike them on the head with a bludgeon.' Penguins were first discovered during Captain Cook's voyage but 'we were fortunate in bringing the first perfect specimens to England. Some of these were preserved entire in casks of strong pickle, that the physiologist and comparative anatomist might have an opportunity of thoroughly examining the structure of this wonderful creature.' Ross also had some seals captured: 'They are, however, not in sufficient numbers to induce our merchants to send to these regions after them.'

The main problem now facing the expedition was the encroaching ice. To break through an intervening belt of ice 'required some hours hard labour with poles and warps' and to make matters worse gales threw the ships against the ice, damaging their rudders: 'Hour passed away after hour without the least mitigation of the awful circumstances in which we were placed. Indeed, there seemed to be but little probability of our ships holding together much longer, so frequent and violent were the shocks they sustained.' The next day, however, the damage proved not to be as great as first feared: 'The shattered rudder being hoisted on board, the carpenters and their assistants were employed, setting it straight, cutting away the splinters, and replacing the parts that had been torn away, whilst the armourers at the forge were engaged making bolts and hoops to bind all firmly together, and, by the unceasing labour of the officers and artificers, the Erebus's rudder was ready for shipping again before midnight.' The rudder of the *Terror* was so completely destroyed that a spare one had to be fitted.

The problem now was a lack of wind to proceed but, as befitted the scrupulous piety of Ross, thanksgivings were offered to Him 'who had showed us the terrible things and wonders of the great deep, from which we might learn our own weakness, and His power and readiness to help all those that call upon and trust in Him'. It was so cold that ice formed by the freezing of a portion of each wave had to be chipped away from the bows: 'A small fish was found in the mass; it must have been dashed against the ship, and instantly frozen fast. It was carefully removed for the purpose of preservation, a sketch of it made, and its dimensions taken by Dr Robertson, but it was unfortunately seized upon and devoured by a cat.'

Once under way the ships made rapid progress eastwards and came at last into the South Atlantic, anchoring in the Falkland Islands, where they went ashore for fresh beef and vegetables. The Falklands Governor gave them permission to form a hunting party and twelve hundredweight of wild cattle meat was shipped. The ships were refitted by the end of July but they had to wait until the start of September to be able to resume magnetic observations.

On 8 September Ross sailed for his third season, hoping to make a series of magnetic experiments in the vicinity of Cape Horn. He stopped at Tierra del Fuego, where he found the local people 'the most abject and miserable race of human beings', a judgement he immediately qualified by conceding: 'They are admirable mimics, and were fond of the company of our people, singing and dancing with them.' Moreover, their conduct was 'peaceable and inoffensive, and their cheerfulness and good temper rendered their presence agreeable to us rather than otherwise'. Ross gave them knives, axes, saws, carpenter's tools, fishing lines and hooks and so on. He admitted that he couldn't understand their language and knew nothing of their religious ideas: 'but we may now hope that the day is not far distant when the blessings of civilisation and the joyful tidings of the Gospel may be extended to these most degraded of human beings'. This little vignette, its confusions and shifts of tone and sympathy, by turns receptively observant and stiffly judgemental, is a highly characteristic example of the way the Victorians represented and wrote about other races.

By February 1843, facing the prospect of the ships being frozen into the pack of ice, Ross abandoned any attempt to penetrate farther. On 4 April the expedition returned to Cape Point for the third time: 'From the arduous service in which it had been engaged, without a single individual of either of the ships on the sick list.'

They began their journey home and: 'The shores of Old England came into view at 5h20m A.M. on the 2nd September, and we anchored off Folkestone at midnight of the 4th. Next day immediately proceeded to the Admiralty.'

Like all the best expeditions, it had not actually succeeded in its goal of reaching the south magnetic pole but much valuable magnetic measurement had been completed (though there are differing views about the quality of his data). Ross was awarded the RGS gold medal and knighted in 1844 and after his marriage he lived quietly in Buckinghamshire, though he did lead the first expedition to search for Franklin, returning empty-handed in 1849. Ross died at Aston Abbots, Buckinghamshire, on 3 April 1862.

49

## *A Bold Adventure: Francis McLintock*
## *in Search of Franklin*

In the spring of 1845 the two ice-battered ships formerly captained by Sir James Ross, the *Erebus* and the *Terror*, set out from London under the command of Sir John Franklin on an official expedition to find a North-West Passage through the polar sea, that Victorian obsession that mirrored the desire to find the source of the Nile: the great goal of every explorer. Since Ross's expedition to Antarctica the ships had been specially strengthened and fitted with a small steam engine to work a screw. This ill-fated expedition to the Bering Strait would result in countless attempts, over twelve years, to find the lost mariners when they failed either to reach their goal or to return. It was the voyage of Francis Leopold McLintock in 1857 that finally solved the mystery.

Introducing McLintock's *The Voyage of the 'Fox' in Arctic Seas: A*

*Narrative of the Discovery of the Fate of Sir John Franklin and his Companions* (1859), the RGS President, Sir Roderick Murchison, called it 'a simple tale of how, in a little vessel of 170 tons burthen, he and his well-chosen companions have cleared up this great mystery'. The lost explorer's wife, Lady Franklin, had 'shown what a true-hearted English woman can accomplish' by commissioning McLintock after Lord Palmerston decided he could no longer justify the expense of further search expeditions. For Murchison, Franklin was – and he resorted to italics to emphasize his point – '*the first real discoverer of the North-West Passage*' and 'this great fact must therefore be inscribed upon the monument of Franklin'.

In spite of the boost provided by news in 1854 that a party of Eskimo had seen, in the spring of 1850, about forty white men dead from starvation at the mouth of the Great Fish River, the government would not back another voyage, so Lady Franklin financed the expedition herself and bought for £2000 the screw-yacht the *Fox*. McLintock eagerly accepted the commission to command it: 'I could not willingly resign to posterity, the honour of filling up even the small remaining blank upon our maps.' He supervised the refitting of the ship: 'the sharp stem to be cased in iron until it resembled a ponderous chisel set up edgeways'. He recruited a crew of twenty-five men, seventeen of whom had previous Arctic experience, and the deluge of offers from others, even from non-seamen, proved to him 'that the spirit of the country was favorable to us, and that the ardent love of hardy enterprise still lives amongst Englishmen, as of old'. It was a patriotic epic of a particular kind: the tiny band of courageous Britons strong with the minimum of means: 'An earnest desire to extend succor to any chance survivors of the ill-fated expedition . . . to rescue from oblivion their heroic deeds, seemed the natural promptings of every honest English heart.'

McLintock (who was actually an Irishman born in Dundalk) felt that 'the glorious mission entrusted to me was in reality a *great national duty* . . . amongst the noblest efforts in the cause of humanity any nation ever engaged in' but also made more striking by the modest means of a 'little vessel, containing but twenty-five souls . . .

The less the means, the more arduous I felt was the achievement.' Lady Franklin confirmed the picture by writing to commend his 'little band of heroes'.

The plucky band sailed on 1 July 1857 with ample provisions for a twenty-eight-day voyage, including: 'preserved vegetables, lemon-juice and pickles, for daily consumption, and preserved meats for every third day: also as much of Messrs Allsopp's stoutest ale as we could find room for'. The government offered ammunition and the Admiralty 6682 pounds of pemmican: 'It is composed of prime beef cut into thin slices and dried over a wood fire; then pounded up and mixed with about an equal weight of melted beef fat. The pemmican is then pressed into cases capable of containing 42lbs each.' The Admiralty also supplied ice-gear.

On 20 July the *Fox* reached Greenland, where they put off a sick crew member and met some Danish missionaries who had taught the Inuit to read and write: 'Have we English done more, or as much, for the aborigines in any of our numerous colonies, and especially for the Esquimaux within our own territories of Labrador and Hudson's Bay?'

By early August the ship was well into the ice in frozen Baffin Bay and on the 12th they saw the 'mighty glacier' of Melville Bay extending for forty to fifty miles. Each evening the men played rounders on the ice. The 'imprisonment' here, however, was frustrating and they were forced to kill seals in order to feed the dogs. There were 170 miles of frozen sea to cross in the Bay and they were making only nine miles a week against the ice, slowed down by ice-bergs. McLintock was bitterly disappointed and concluded: 'We are doomed to pass a long winter of absolute inutility, if not of idleness, in comparative peril and privation . . . One day is very like another; we have to battle stoutly with monotony.' Food was a problem, especially when a hole was dug in the ice to soak some salt meat and a shark helped itself to the offered morsel. They killed a bear to feed the dogs and measured their progress by watching two large icebergs that had drifted with them, their relative positions remaining nearly the same for a month.

On 5 November they burnt an effigy of Guy Fawkes on the ice and early in December they had to bury, by dropping the body through a hole cut in the ice, Scott, the engineer, who had fallen to his death down a hatch. During December they managed sixty-seven miles, directly down Baffin Bay towards the Atlantic. It was not until 12 April 1858 that they finally 'drifted ingloriously out of the Arctic regions' and at last reached the sea after 'our long, long winter and mysterious ice-drift' of 1194 miles in 242 days, 'the longest drift I know of'.

On 28 April the *Fox* anchored at Holsteinborg, Greenland, to refit and refresh the crew before setting out again on 8 May. 'Summer has suddenly burst on us!' McLintock exclaimed before making the perhaps redundant observation: 'There is nothing more uncertain than ice-navigation, dependent as it is upon winds, temperatures, and currents.' Throughout the summer they voyaged on (discovering a live mouse in a sealed cask of biscuit packed in Aberdeen in June 1857), then prepared travelling parties: 'In this way I trust we shall complete the Franklin search and the geographical discovery of Arctic America, both left unfinished by the former expeditions; and in so doing we can hardly fail to obtain some trace, some relic, or, it may be, important records of those whose mysterious fate it is our great object to discover.' Then winter quarters were established and another Christmas came and went. Although they seemed to be making little progress with their search for Franklin, all these travelling parties when on land were completing the discovery of the coastline of continental America, 120 miles being added to the charts.

On one land journey, during which they slept in their own igloos at night, McLintock met some Inuit who said that none of their people had seen 'the whites' but 'one man said he had seen their bones upon the island where they died, but some were buried. Petersen also understood him to say that the boat was crushed by the ice. Almost all of them had part of the plunder.' He spoke to various Inuit who claimed to have seen one of the ships sink and the other wrecked on shore at a place they called Oot-loo-lik, where they took wood from the wreck for their own use. They had seen the white men set off with a boat and added that in the following winter they found their bones. McLintock picked up further reports of the wreck and later he discovered a piece of preserved meat tin, scraps of copper and an iron hoop-bolt.

Shortly after midnight on 24 May a human skeleton with a frozen pocket-book, looking from his dress like a ship's steward, was found in a position that showed he had fallen face forward, confirming Inuit reports that 'they fell down and died as they walked along'. McLintock found a cairn, Simpson's Cairn, but nothing else: 'I cannot divest myself of the belief that *some record was left here* by the retreating crews, and perhaps some valuable documents . . . It was with a feeling of deep regret and much disappointment that I left this spot without finding some certain record of those martyrs to their country's fame.'

On 24 June 1859 McLintock reached Montreal Island, passing on foot through what he judged the only feasible North-West Passage: 'But all this is as nothing to the interest attached to the *Franklin records* picked up by Hobson, and now safe in my possession! We now know the fate of the "Erebus" and "Terror". The sole object of our voyage has at length been completed and we anxiously await the time when escape from these bleak regions will become practicable.' In his account he rather abruptly announces this momentous discovery without much in the way of preliminaries. It was made by his colleague Hobson, at Point Victory, on the north-west coast of King William's Land. A document, signed by 'John Franklin, commanding the Expedition', with the words 'All well' underlined and dated 28 May 1847, requested, in several languages, whoever found it 'to forward it to the Secretary of the Admiralty, London *with a note of the time and place at which it was found*. It was, wrote McLintock, 'a sad and touching relic of our lost friends', for written in ink around the edge of this paper was an update saying that the two ships had been deserted on 25 April 1848 and that Sir John Franklin had died on 11 June 1847. 'A sad tale was never told in fewer words.'

Their mission accomplished, and convinced that no more relics remained, the *Fox* began the homeward journey in August. They celebrated the last glimpse of an iceberg on 10 September and after 'two years' sojourn in the still waters of the frozen north' they arrived in the English Channel on 20 September, having made the passage from Greenland in only nineteen days.

PART NINE

# EUROPE, A CODA

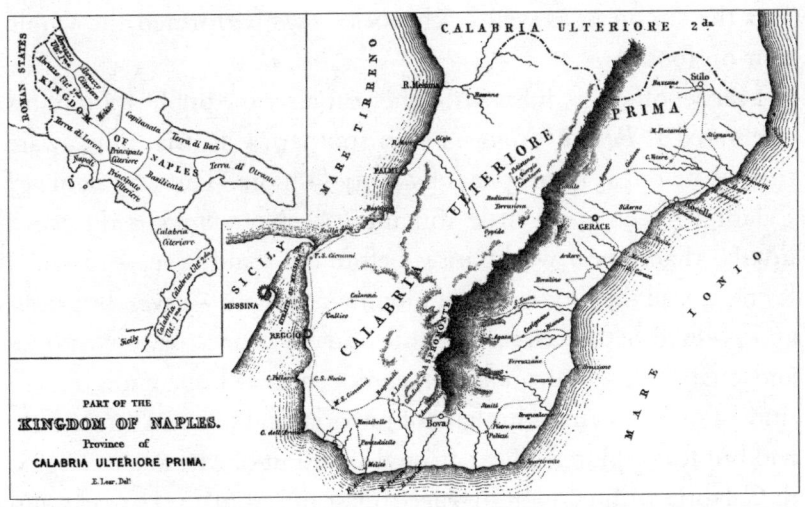

## 50

### *A Wanderer: Edward Lear in Italy and Albania*

This has been a book about the ventures of nineteenth-century Europeans into 'strange countries' far from home, but southern Europe itself was in many ways as wild and challenging a destination for the Victorian traveller as any selected by the men in pith helmets. For a token journey into Europe, therefore, it seems appropriate to choose to conclude with one of the most engaging and delightful of Victorian travellers, Edward Lear. He did not fraternize with alligators and hippopotami, nor was he borne by native bearers in a white hammock through the jungle, nor did he sway high on the back of a camel or elephant. He merely offered his *Journals of a Landscape Painter* as the record of an ordinary English traveller in pursuit of the picturesque. 'The mode of travel which I and my fellow-wanderer adopted while these journals were written,' he recorded of his Calabrian journey, 'was the simplest, as well as cheapest – we performed the whole tour on foot.'

Lear set off on 25 July 1847 – the year after the publication of his celebrated *A Book of Nonsense* – to southern Calabria, fully aware that, as he put it in his playfully witty fashion: 'The very name of Calabria has in it no little romance . . . No sooner is the word uttered than a new world arises before the mind's eye, – torrents, fastnesses, all the prodigality of mountain scenery, – caves, brigands, and pointed hats, – Mrs. Radcliffe and Salvator Rosa, – costumes and character, – horrors and magnificence without end.' Yet, in spite of these charms: 'this land of pictorial and poetical interest has had but few explorers'. Lear crossed the strait of Messina to Reggio di Calabria with enough luggage to last him four to six weeks and 'well supplied with letters to those persons in its chief city who would send us on our way through the interior'. Arriving at Reggio, he and his companion sailed through customs and quarantine because they bore, on ducal notepaper, 'an introductory letter to the Direttore, whose address we asked for in a judiciously elevated tone of voice'.

The following morning Lear left the Locanda Giordano: 'At sunrise I set out on an exploring expedition, and was soon dodging here and there to find the best views of Reggio amongst its endless cactus and aloe lanes, fig gardens, and orange groves. Reggio is indeed one vast garden, and doubtless one of the loveliest spots on earth.' As a painter, Lear was naturally keen to find good views and travelled with this uppermost in his mind: 'A man must be guided pretty much by hazard in arranging a tour through a country so little visited as this: the general rule of keeping near the mountains is perhaps the best, and if you hear of a town, or costume, or piece of antiquity anywise remarkable, to make a dash at it as inclination may devise, sometimes to be repaid for the trouble, – as often the contrary.'

The two friends hired a muleteer called Ciccio for six carlini a day but were facetiously disappointed that he did not wear a pointed brigand's hat, merely a Sicilian long blue cap. In the English fashion, much humour was derived from the (very basic) lodgings: 'I had warned my companion (hitherto untravelled in these regions) that he would probably meet with much simplicity, much cordiality, and heaps more dirt throughout Calabria.'

Like an English traveller of the previous century in search of the picturesque, Lear was drawn to the 'many scraps of Poussinesque landscape which I would fain have lingered to draw [had it not been raining]' or the 'picturesque peasants' at Condufiri who offered him pears as they passed. At the woods of Pietrapennata he exclaimed on cue: 'Claude and Salvator Rosa at every step!' Travelling was hard work and, at the end of the day, Lear and his companion simply wanted to sleep but their hosts would not let them and they were reduced to 'a state of torture and despair, in the protracted struggle between hunger, Morpheus, and civility'.

Southern Europe in the 1850s was still a very primitive place and the local people were as intrigued by strangers as any desert nomad or African tribesman: 'You might talk for ever; but you could not convince them you are not a political agent sent to spy out the nakedness of the land, and masking the intentions of your government under the thin veil of portraying scenes, in which they see no novelty, and take no delight.' On another occasion an old man announced to all that they were on a British government mission of reconnaissance: 'a conceit universally ridiculed by Englishmen, but not quite so absurd as it may seem, if we reflect that the conquest of many countries by others has been preceded by individual observation and research'. Already Lear was aware of the onward march of tourism and he knew that the peasant life he was sketching would not long remain 'unspoiled by high roads and the changes of all-fusing and assimilating civilisation'. Staying at a monastery at Santa Maria di Polsi, he found the experience 'the very antithesis of life in our own civilised and distant home'.

Lear's letters of introduction ensured that he did not restrict himself to colourful peasants in local costume. He met, on the coast at Bovalino, Count Garrolo, a voluble and putatively learned landowner, who 'bustled about like an armadillo in a cage' when showing them their room, and at Rocella he met Don Giuseppe Nanni, the lord of an old palazzo, who pitied the Englishmen for the absence of fruit in their country. Lear tentatively pointed out that there were gooseberries and greengages but their existence in England was hotly denied by the count. Staying with another well-bred family at Stignagno, they watched a scene that must have been a gift for the author of *A Book of Nonsense*. A toddler climbed on to the dining table and immediately tumbled over into a dish of macaroni: 'One sees in valentines cupids on beds of roses, or on birds' nests but a slightly-clothed Calabrese infant sitting in the midst of a hot dish of macaroni appears to me a perfectly novel idea.'

As Lear pushed deeper into the Calabrian countryside he guessed that he was the first stranger to have penetrated some of the little towns, with the result that he was sometimes followed around by up to a hundred people 'but ever with the utmost good feeling and propriety'. The delightful sketches which accompany his text convey this sense of rugged isolation and dramatic mountain scenery. Lear scorned the Cook's tourist who would be seeing none of this: 'How undeniable is the simplicity of those who think they have "done" Calabria, by travelling in a carriage from Naples to Reggio! All the beautiful incidents of pastoral or mountain life, all the romance of a wandering artist's existence, is carefully banished from your high-road tourist's journey; and the best he can boast of is an extended view from some elevated point of road.' Suggestive of the gulf between Lear's enterprising travel and the reading pleasures of the mid-Victorian domestic travelling public was a publisher's advertisement at the back of his book. It was for Bentley's Shilling Railway Library, which offered the following titles to while away the traveller's time: *Broad Grins from China, Notes on Noses (with illustrations)* and *The Comic English Grammar*.

At the 'strange rock-town' of Pentedatilo he found that 'the whole population bristled on wall and window' to glimpse 'Mr Lear'. The few women who caught sight of him 'screamed aloud on seeing me, and rushed back to their rocky fastnesses'. Unfortunately, however,

Lear's trip was cut short by news of the outbreak of revolution: 'Distress and anxiety, stagnation and terror, have taken the place of activity, prosperity, security and peace'. He had no choice but to return to Naples. On 5 September 1847 a steamer arrived from Malta and at six in the evening they sailed: 'Gloom, gloom over-shadows the memory of a tour so agreeably begun, and which should have extended yet through two provinces.' At Naples, though Italy generally was 'in too unsettled a state to admit of pros-perous artistic tours', he made some local excursions but most of the scenery 'wanted the romance of Calabria'.

The following summer Lear travelled in 'Turkey in Europe', Albania and Greece, which resulted in *Journals of a Landscape Painter in Albania, Illyria &c* (1851). He pointed out that Albania was 'a country within sight of Italy less known than the interior of America'. Although much of the area had been written about by previous travellers such as Leake and Hobhouse, 'the Author believes himself to be the only Englishman who has published any account; and scanty and slight as his may be, it is something in these days to be able to add the smallest mite of novelty to the trav-ellers' world of information and interest'. Reviewing what the guidebooks advised, especially Murray's *Hand-book for Travellers in the Ionian Islands, Greece, Turkey &c* (1845), he concluded: 'Arms, and ammunition, fine raiment, presents for natives, are all non-sense; simplicity should be your aim.' Lear had been ill and had spent six weeks recuperating in the British Embassy at Constan-tinople but was ready to leave on 9 September 1848 for Thessalonika on an Austrian paddle steamer, the *Ferdinando*, 'crammed with Turks, Jews, Greeks, Bulgarians, wedged together with a density, compared to which a Gravesend steamer is emptiness: a section of a fig-drum, or of a herring-barrel is the only apt simile for this extraordinary crowd of recumbent human beings'.

Lear's vivid pictorial sense brings many of his descriptions alive. On arrival at Thessalonika he noted the extraordinary range of colours in the Muslim women's dress: 'The polychromatic hareem arose, and moved like a bed of tulips in a breeze.' The large Jewish population of the city seem to have had the monopoly of porterage and they waded out into the water fighting for the privilege of carrying his luggage: 'From yells and pullings, to and fro, the scene changed in a few moments to a real fight, and the whole community fell to the most furious hair-pulling, turban-clenching, and robe-tearing, till the luggage was forgotten, and all the party was involved in one terrific combat.' Then the police arrived and beat them with whips and sticks so that the tender-hearted Lear was 'not unvexed at being the indirect cause of so much strife'.

A cholera epidemic at Thessalonika and a cordon sanitaire imposed by the monks of Mount Athos left Lear with no choice but to abandon his planned trip to Greece and instead take the north-western road through Macedonia to Illyrian Albania by the ancient Via Egnatia. He reckoned he had a good servant and that the mountain air would do him good: 'As for the risk run by thus rushing into strange places, and among unknown people, when a man has walked all over the wildest parts of Italy, he does not prognosticate danger.' In fact he was impressed by Ottoman courtesy. When he stepped on a Turkish man's pipe-bowl and broke it, the man replied: 'The breaking such a pipe-bowl would indeed, under ordinary circumstances, be disagreeable; but in a friend every action has its charm!' Lear was also reassured by Giorgio, his 'dragoman, cook, valet, interpreter and guide', a Smyrnan Greek who spoke ten languages: 'In countenance my attendant is somewhat like one of those strange faces, lion or griffin, which we see on door-knockers or urn handles, and a grim twist of his under-jaw gives an idea that it would not be safe to try his temper too much.'

As in Calabria, Lear's sketching attracted much local attention: 'Their shouts of laughter, as I represented the houses, were electrifying.' Soon the crowds (and the ferocious dogs) made it nearly impossible for him to work and he began to have difficulties with officials but the beauty drew him on: 'Such sublime scenery obliterated from memory all annoyances of travel.' Those annoyances included being pelted with missiles by women and children in the street and being cursed by a shepherd as Shaitan, or the Devil.

As Lear penetrated deeper into the northern Albanian country-side the hostility grew: 'The greater part of the mob put their fingers into their mouths and whistled furiously, after the manner of butcher-boys in England.' Later they would say: 'The Frank is a Russian, and he is sent by the Sultan to write us all down before he sells us to the Russian Emperor.' On arrival at 'wretched and dis-gusting' Tirana he was prevented by 'a mad or fanatic dervish' from sketching any of the mosques but there was the consolation of being put up in the palace of Ali Bey. This dignitary loosed on him ten servants 'who stood in much expectation, till, finding I was about to take off my shoes, they made a rush at me as the Jews did at Saloniki'. In the evening he was required to imitate, for the Bey's enlightenment, the sound made by a railway train and a steamship.

Lear now started to turn south and visited the plain of Berat, where an official defended him against the mob as he sketched, though when bored this Kawas, or guard, handed over his stick to: 'A young pickle of a boy, who took infinite delight in using his tem-porary dignity to the utmost, greatly to the disgust of his elders, who durst not complain.' He decided that the region of Khimara was 'the most romantic as well as the most novel of my own (or any-body else's) Albanian wanderings'. In particular the region around Dukadhes was 'one of the most secluded in Europe'. It was perfectly picturesque: 'Let a painter visit Acroceraunia – until he does so, he will not be aware of the grandest phase of savage, yet classic, pic-turesqueness – whether Illyrian or Epirote – men or mountains.' Lear was rather put out, however, to discover that women here seemed to be used as beasts of burden: '"Heavens!" said I, surprised out of my wonted philosophy of travel, which ought not to exclaim at anything, "how can you make your women such slaves?"' They replied matter-of-factly that the women were not completely satis-factory but there was a shortage of mules.

At the regional capital, named Khimara like the region itself, Lear was told that he was only the second Englishman to have vis-ited there ('no great wonder considering the nature of the country') and he threw himself into sketching wild pelicans, which he had seen before only in the menagerie of Lord Derby at Knowsley in Liverpool. The news of the Emperor's flight from Vienna excited his hosts into denunciations of everyone, including the English, but Lear, a very English traveller who considered it bad manners to raise anything to do with politics, requested 'earnestly that we might henceforth talk about pelicans, or red mullet, or whatever they pleased, so that we eschewed politics'.

When Lear finally left Albania and reached Epirus the food improved and he discovered: 'Turkeys and tongues, walnuts and good wine, with other pleasant solidities and frivolities quite out of character with Albanian travel.' The light-hearted maker of limericks and nonsense verses entertained himself with some village children at a place he called Episkop'. Seeing him pick some watercress to go with his bread and cheese, the children emerged with all sorts of comic contributions to the crazy foreigner's lunch, such as thistles and a fat grasshopper: 'The whole scene was acted amid shouts of laughter, in which I joined as loudly as any. We parted amazingly good friends, and the wits of Episkop' will long remember the Frank who fed on weeds out of the water.' At Ioannina, after so many rough and verminous lodgings, he stayed in spacious and clean rooms at the British Consulate: 'After the khans and horrors of Upper Albania, the spacious and clean rooms at the Vice-consulate were delightful to repose in; and newspapers, letters, joined with all kinds of comfort, suddenly and amply atoned for by-gone toils and disagreeables.'

The following spring, after winter in Cairo and Mount Sinai, Lear returned to Greece with another Greek dragoman, picked up at Patras, Andrea Vrindisi, who boasted of knowing ten languages. After a stay with the Lord High Commissioner at Corfu he and Vrindisi sailed to Arta, turning over in their minds some of this region's turbulent recent history. Every bit of scenery recalled: 'the struggles of the heroic people who so lately as forty years back were exterminated or banished by their tyrant enemy. Every turn in the pass I am about to enter has been distinguished by some stratagem or slaughter: every line in the annals of the last Suliote war is written in characters of blood.' He returned to Ioannina, where he took a boat on its lake and sketched the 'mournful ruins' of Ali Pasha's palace, largely ignored by the local population. He then crossed the Pindus mountains into Thessaly and the Albanian border guards were satisfied with his official-looking documentation, unaware that it was 'a bill of Mrs. Dunford's Hotel at Malta'.

He pressed on to see the monasteries of the Meteora (seen in Chapter 11 through the eyes of Robert Curzon) but as a result of an injury he could not actually climb up and visit any of the monasteries: 'I do not think I ever saw any scene so startling and incredible; such vast sheer perpendicular pyramids, standing out of the earth, with the tiny houses of the village clustering at the roots . . . more picturesque than I expected them to be . . . an artist should stay here for a month. No pen or pencil can do justice to the scenery of Meteora.'

The Meteora seems to have been the high point of this Greek tour. Rain and cloud subsequently obscured Mount Olympus and the Vale of Tempe ('of all the places in Greece that which I had most desired to see') was actually a disappointment in part because the poets had generated an impossible expectation of its beauty. Now destined to be driven back by rain – fatal for a landscape painter – Lear had experienced one of the iron laws of travel (though one that is not always unwelcome): the provisional invariably displaces the planned.

On 9 June 1849, on a Maltese steamer, the *Antelope*, Edward Lear, the irrepressible wanderer, sailed home through the Ionian Channel 'for the ninth time'.

A poem, it has been said, is never finished, merely abandoned. The same can be said of a journey, where endings often return upon beginnings, and the fiction of a linear narrative, a logical progress from A to B, masks the reality that travelling, at its best, is beautifully purposeless, random, a sequence (if we are lucky) of unplanned accidents and unexpected encounters. The Victorians travelled for many purposes, some of which (scientific, imperial, commercial) were more dedicated to profitable outcomes than others. But they also travelled for a sense of adventure, to see what would happen next, what would appear over the next hill or round the next bend in the river. They travelled because the lure of place is enduring, the human disposition to wander universal. They travelled, that is to say, like us and if their 'attitudes' sometimes cause us to emit a censorious tut-tut, we can be sure that we, in our turn, will be tut-tutted by travelling generations to come.

# BIBLIOGRAPHY

Achebe, Chinua, 'An Image of Africa: Racism in Conrad's *Heart of Darkness*', *Massachusetts Review*, 18 (4), Winter 1975

Adams, W. H. Davenport, *Celebrated Women Travellers of the Nineteenth Century*, 1883

Allan, M., *Palgrave of Arabia: The Life of William Gifford Palgrave, 1826–88*, 1972

Allen, Benedict, *The Faber Book of Exploration*, 2002

Anderson, Monica, *Women and the Politics of Travel 1870–1914*, 2006

Assad, Thomas J., *Three Victorian Travellers: Burton, Blunt, Doughty*, 1964

Baker, William (ed.), *Nineteenth-Century Travels, Explorations and Empires: Writings from the Era of Imperial Consolidation 1835–1910. Volume 2: North America*, 2003

Baker, William (ed.), *Nineteenth-Century Travels, Explorations and Empires: Writings from the Era of Imperial Consolidation 1835–1910. Volume 5: Middle East*, 2004

Baldwin, William Charles, *African Hunting: from Natal to the Zambesi including Lake Ngami, the Kalahari Desert & from 1852 to 1860*, 1863

Barr, Pat, *The Deer Cry Pavilion: A Story of Westerners in Japan 1868–1905*, 1968

Barr, Pat, *A Curious Life for a Lady: The Story of Isabella Bird, Traveller Extraordinary*, 1970

Bates, Henry Walter, *The Naturalist on the River Amazon*, 1863

Beeching, Jack (ed.), *Richard Hakluyt: The Principal Navigations, Voyages, Traffiques and Discoveries of the English Nation*, 1972

Ben-Arieh, Y., *The Rediscovery of the Holy Land in the Nineteenth Century*, 1979

Bird, Isabella, *The Englishwoman in America*, 1856

Bird, Isabella L., *Unbeaten Tracks in Japan: An Account of Travels in the*

*Interior including Visits to the Aborigines of Yezo and the Shrines of Nikkō and Isé*, 1880

Birkett, Dea, *Spinsters Abroad: Victorian Lady Explorers*, 1989

Birkett, Dea, *Mary Kingsley: Imperial Adventuress*, 1992

Blunt, Wilfrid Scawen, *India under Ripon: A Private Diary, Continued from his 'Secret History of the English Occupation of Egypt'*, 1909

Brendon, Piers, *Thomas Cook: 150 Years of Popular Tourism*, 1991

Brodie, Fawn, *The Devil Drives: A Life of Sir Richard Burton*, 1967

Bromley, Clara, *A Woman's Wanderings in the Western World: A Series of Letters Addressed to Sir Fitzroy Kelly MP by His Daughter, Mrs Bromley*, 1861

Brown, Charles Barrington, *Canoe and Camp Life in British Guiana*, 1876

Browne, Janet, *Charles Darwin: Voyaging. Volume 1 of a Biography*, 1995

Burke, Thomas, *Travel in England: From Pilgrim and Pack-horse to Car and Plane*, 1942

Burnes, Alexander, *Travels into Bokhara Being the Account of a Journey from India to Cabool, Tartary, and Persia; also, Narrative of a Voyage on the Indus from the Sea to Lahore with Presents from the King of Great Britain*, 1834

Burton, Anthony and Pip, *The Green Bag Travellers*, 1978

Burton, Isabel, *The Inner Life of Syria, Palestine, and the Holy Land from My Private Journal*, 1875

Burton, Richard, *Sindh, and the Races that Inhabit the Valley of the Indus with Notices of the Topography and History of the Province*, 1851

Burton, Richard, *Scinde; or The Unhappy Valley*, 2 vols., 1851

Burton, Richard, *Falconry in the Valley of the Indus*, 1852

Burton, Richard, *A Complete System of Bayonet Exercise*, 1853

Burton, Richard, *Personal Narrative of a Pilgrimage to El-Medinah and Meccah*, 1855

Burton, Richard, *First Footsteps in East Africa or An Exploration of Harar*, 1856

Burton, Richard, *The Lake Regions of Central Africa: A Picture of Exploration*, 1860

Burton, Richard, *A Mission to Gelele, King of Dahome: with Notices of the So-called 'Amazons', the Grand Customs, the Yearly Customs, the Human Sacrifices, the Present State of the Slave Trade, and the Negro's Place in Nature*, 2 vols., 1864

Burton, Richard, *Explorations of the Highlands of the Brazil; with a Full Account of the Gold and Diamond Mines. Also, Canoeing down 1500 Miles of the Great River Sao Francisco, from Sabara to the Sea*, 1869

Burton, Richard, *Sir Richard Burton's Travels in Arabia and Africa: Four Lectures from a Huntington Library Manuscript*, ed. John Hayman, 1990

Buzard, James, *The Beaten Track: European Tourism, Literature and the Ways to Culture, 1800–1918*, 1993

Caddick, Helen, *A White Woman in Central Africa*, 1900

Cameron, Ian, *To the Farthest Ends of the Earth: 150 Years of World Exploration: The History of the Royal Geographical Society 1830–1980*, 1980

Cameron, Verney Lovett, *Across Africa*, 2 vols., 1877

Cannadine, David, *Ornamentalism: How the British Saw Their Empire*, 2001

Clark, Steve (ed.), *Travel Writing and Empire: Postcolonial Theory in Transit*, 1999

Conrad, Joseph, *Heart of Darkness*, 1917

Conrad, Joseph, 'Geography and Some Explorers', in *Last Essays*, 1926

Cook, Thomas, *Letters from the Sea and from Foreign Lands Descriptive of a Tour Round the World with an Appendix Containing Announcements of Annual Tours Around the World &c*, 1873

Cook, Thomas, *The Tourist's Guide: A Hand Book of The Trip From Leicester, Nottingham, and Derby to Liverpool and the Coast of North Wales*, 1845

Coopland, R. M., *A Lady's Escape from Gwalior and Life in the Fort of Agra during the Mutinies of 1857*, 1859

Cordiviola, Alfredo, *Richard Burton: A Traveller in Brazil, 1865–1868*, 2001

Crone, G. R., *The Explorers: An Anthology of Discovery*, 1962

Cumming, Constance F. Gordon, *Wanderings in China*, 1886

Cumming, D., *The Gentleman Savage: The Life of Mansfield Parkyns, 1823–1894*, 1987

Curzon, Robert, *Visits to Monasteries in the Levant*, 1849

Dalrymple, William, *White Mughals: Love and Betrayal in Eighteenth-Century India*, 2002

Dalrymple, William, *The Last Mughal: The Fall of a Dynasty, Delhi, 1857*, 2006

Dance, Charles Daniel, *Recollections of Four Years in Venezuela*, 1876

Darwin, Charles, *Journal of Researches into the Geology and Natural History of the Various Countries Visited by H.M.S. Beagle under the Command of Captain Fitzroy, R.N. from 1832 to 1836*, 1839

Darwin, Charles, *Voyage of the Beagle*, edited with an introduction by Janet Browne and Michael Neve, 1989

Desmond, Adrian, and Moore, James, *Darwin,* 1991

Dixon, William Hepworth, *The Holy Land,* 1865

Dodge, E. S., *The Polar Rosses,* 1973

Doughty, Charles Montagu, *Passages from Arabia Deserta: Selected by Edward Garnett,* 1931

Doughty, Charles Montagu, *Wanderings in Arabia: Being an Abridgement of 'Travels in Arabia Deserta',* 2 vols., 1908

Doughty, Charles, *Travels in Arabia Deserta,* 1888

Driver, Felix, *Geography Militant: Cultures of Exploration and Empire,* 2001

Dunbar, Janet, *Golden Interlude: The Edens in India, 1836–1842,* 1955

Dunbar, Janet, *Tigers, Durbars and Kings: Fanny Eden's Indian Journals, 1837–1838,* 1988

Eden, Emily, *Letters from India Edited by Her Niece,* 1872

Eden, Emily, *Up The Country: Letters Written to Her Sister from The Upper Provinces of India,* with an introduction and notes by Edward Thompson, 1930

Edwards, Amelia B., *A Thousand Miles up the Nile,* 2 vols., 1877

Eisner, Robert, *Travelers to an Antique Land: The History and Literature of Travel to Greece,* 1993

Foran, F. W., *African Odyssey: The Life of Verney Lovett-Cameron,* 1937

Franey, Laura E., *Victorian Travel Writing and Imperial Violence: British Writing on Africa, 1855–1902,* 2003

Fraser, Ian H. C., *The Heir of Parham,* 1986

Fulford, Tim, and Kitson, Peter (eds.), *Travels, Explorations and Empires: Writings from the Era of Imperial Expansion 1770–1835,* 2001

Galton, Francis, *The Art of Travel or Shifts and Contrivances Available in Wild Countries,* 1855

Ghose, Indira (ed.), *Memsahibs Abroad: Writings by Women Travellers in Nineteenth Century India,* 1998

Ghose, Indira, *Women Travellers in Colonial India: The Power of the Female Gaze,* 1998

Ghose, Indira (ed.), *Travels, Explorations and Empires: Writings from the Era of Imperial Expansion 1770–1835. Volume 6: India,* 2001

Ghose, Indira (ed.), *Nineteenth-Century Travels, Explorations, and Empires: Writings from the Era of Imperial Consolidation 1835–1910. Volume 3: India,* 2003

Groves, C. P., *The Planting of Christianity in Africa,* 1954

Gutch, J., *Beyond the Reefs: The Life of John Williams, Missionary,* 1974

Haddon, Alfred C., *Head Hunters Black, White and Brown,* 1901

Hakluyt, Richard, *Voyages and Discoveries: The Principal Navigations,*

*Voyages, Traffiques and Discoveries of the English Nation*, edited, abridged and introduced by Jack Beeching, 1972

Hanbury-Tenison, Robin, *The Oxford Book of Exploration*, 1993

Herschel, Sir John F. W., *A Manual of Scientific Enquiry; Prepared for the Use of Her Majesty's Navy: and Adapted for Travellers in General*, 1849

Hibbert, Christopher, *Africa Explored: Europeans in the Dark Continent, 1769–1889*, 1982

Hill, S. S., *Travels in Peru and Mexico*, 2 vols., 1860

Hinderer, Anna, *Seventeen Years in the Yoruba Country*, 1872

Hogarth, David G., *A Wandering Scholar in the Levant*, 1896

Hore, Annie B., *To Lake Tanganyika in a Bath Chair*, 1886

Jackson, J. R., *What to Observe; or The Traveller's Remembrancer*, 1841

Jeal, Tim, *Livingstone*, 1973, 2nd edn., 2001

Jeal, Tim, *Stanley: The Impossible Life of Africa's Greatest Explorer*, 2007

Judd, Dennis, *The Victorian Empire, 1837–1901*, 1970

Judd, Dennis, *The Lion and the Tiger: The Rise and Fall of the British Raj, 1600–1947*, 2004

Kennedy, Dane, *The Highly Civilised Man: Richard Burton and the Victorian World*, 2005

Keynes, Richard Darwin, *The Beagle Record: Selections from the Original Pictorial Records and Written Accounts of the Voyage of H.M.S. Beagle*, 1979

Kinglake, Alexander, *Eothen, or Traces of Travel Brought Home from the East*, 1845

Kingsley, Mary H., *Travels in West Africa: Congo Français, Corisco and Cameroons*, 1897

Kingston, William H. G., and Frith, Henry, *Great African Travellers from Mungo Park to Livingstone, Stanley, and Cameron*, 1885

Kipling, Rudyard, *Kim*, edited with an introduction and notes by Edward Said, 1987

Kirke, Henry, *Twenty-Five Years in British Guiana*, 1898

Kitson, Peter J. (ed.), *Nineteenth-Century Travels, Explorations and Empires: Writings from the Era of Imperial Consolidation 1835–1910. Volume 1: North and South Poles*, 2003

Langley, M., *Sturt of the Murray*, 1969

Lear, Edward, *Journals of a Landscape Painter in Albania, Illyria &c*, 1851

Lear, Edward, *Journals of a Landscape Painter in Southern Calabria*, 1852

Libersohn, Harry, *The Travelers' World: Europe to the Pacific*, 2006

Little, Mrs Archibald, *Intimate China: The Chinese as I Have Seen Them*, 1899

Livingstone, David, *Missionary Travels and Researches in South Africa; including a Sketch of Sixteen Years' Residence in the Interior of Africa*, 1857

Livingstone, David and Charles, *Narrative of an Expedition to the Zambesi and its Tributaries; and of the Discovery of the Lakes Shirwar and Nyassa, 1858–64*, 1865

Longford, Elizabeth, *A Pilgrimage of Passion: The Life of Wilfrid Scawen Blunt*, 1979

Lovell, Mary S., *A Rage to Live: A Biography of Richard and Isabel Burton*, 1998

Lunt, James, *Bokhara Burnes*, 1969

McClintock, Captain F. L., *The Voyage of the 'Fox' in the Arctic Seas: A Narrative of the Discovery of the Fate of Sir John Franklin and His Companions*, 1859

Mackenzie, John, *David Livingstone and the Victorian Encounter with Africa*, National Portrait Gallery, 1996

McLynn, Frank, *Hearts of Darkness: The European Exploration of Africa*, 1992

Madden, R. R., *Travels in Turkey, Egypt, Nubia, and Palestine in 1824, 1825, 1826, and 1827*, 2 vols., 1829

Maitland, A., *Speke*, 1971

Mandeville, Sir John, *Mandeville's Travels*, ed. M. C. Seymour, 1968

Mansfield, Peter, *The Arabs*, 1976

Melman, B., *Women's Orients: English Women and the Middle East, 1718–1918*, 1995

Middleton, Dorothy, *Victorian Lady Travellers*, 1965

Moon, H. P., *Henry Walter Bates, FRS, 1825–1892: Explorer, Scientist and Darwinian*, 1976

Morgan, Marjorie, *National Identities and Travel in Victorian Britain*, 2001

Mounsey, Augustus H., *A Journey Through the Caucasus and the Interior of Persia*, 1872

Murray, John (pub.), *A Hand-Book for Travellers on the Continent: Being a Guide through Holland, Belgium, Prussia, and Northern Germany and along the Rhine from Holland to Switzerland . . .*, 1836

Nash, Geoffrey, *From Empire to Orient: Travellers to the Middle East 1830–1926*, 2006

National Portrait Gallery, *David Livingstone and the Victorian Encounter with Africa*, 1996

Nowrojee, Jehangeer, and Merwanjee, Hirjeebhoy, *Journal of a Residence of Two Years and a Half in Great Britain*, 1841

Oliphant, Laurence, *The Land of Gilead with Excursions in the Lebanon*, 1880

Oliver, Roland, and Fage, J. T., *A Short History of Africa*, 6th edn., 1988

Ousby, Ian, *The Englishman's England: Taste, Travel and the Rise of Tourism*, 1990

Palgrave, William Gifford, *Narrative of a Year's Journey through Central and Eastern Arabia (1862–63)*, 1865

Pardoe, Julia, *The City of the Sultan; and Domestic Manners of the Turks*, 2 vols., 1837

Parks, Fanny, *Wanderings of a Pilgrim in Search of the Picturesque during Four-and-Twenty Years in the East; with Revelations of Life in the Zenana*, 1850

Parkyns, Mansfield, *Life in Abyssinia: Being Notes Collected during Three Years' Residence and Travels in that Country*, 2 vols., 1853, 1868

Polo, Marco, *The Travels*, trans. Ronald Latham, 1958

Porter, Andrew (ed.), *The Oxford History of the British Empire: The Nineteenth Century*, 1999

Porter, Rev. J. L., *Five Years in Damascus: including an Account of the History, Topography, and Antiquities of that City with Travels and Researches in Palmyra, Lebanon, and the Hauran*, 1855

Pratt, Mary Louise, *Imperial Eyes: Travel Writing and Transculturation*, 1992

Ramsay, Mrs W., *Everyday Life in Turkey*, 1897

Rees, Joan, *Writings on the Nile: Harriet Martineau, Florence Nightingale, Amelia Edwards*, 1995

Rees, Joan, *Amelia Edwards: Traveller, Novelist and Egyptologist*, 1998

Reeves, P. D. (ed.), *Sleeman in Oudh: An Abridgement of W.H. Sleeman's A Journey through the Kingdom of Oude in 1849–50*, 1971

Roberts, Emma, *Oriental Scenes, Dramatic Sketches and Tales with Other Poems*, 1830

Roberts, Emma, *Scenes and Characteristics of Hindoostan, with Sketches of Anglo-Indian Society*, 1835

Roberts, Emma, *The East India Voyager or Ten Minutes Advice to the Outward Bound*, 1839

Roberts, Emma, *The Zenana and Minor Poems of L.E.L. with a memoir by Emma Roberts*, c.1839

Roberts, Emma, *Notes of an Overland Journey through France and Egypt to Bombay by the Late Miss Emma Roberts with a Memoir*, 1841

Robinson, G., *David Urquhart*, 1920

Robinson, Jane, *Wayward Women: A Guide to Women Travellers*, 2001

Ross, James Clark, *A Voyage of Discovery and Research in the Southern and Antarctic Regions during the Years 1839–43*, 1847

Royal Geographical Society, *Hints to Travellers*, 4th edn., 1878

Scott-Stevenson, Mrs, *Our Ride through Asia Minor*, 1881

Seymour, M. C. (ed.), *Mandeville's Travels*, 1968

Silver, S. W. & Co. (pub.), *Handbook for South Africa: including the Cape Colony, Natal, the Diamond Fields, and the Trans-Orange Republics*, 1875

Sleeman, Sir William, *A Journey through the Kingdom of Oude, in 1849–50 by Direction of the Right Hon. The Earl of Dalhousie, Governor-General*, 1858

Speke, John Hanning, *Journal of the Discovery of the Source of the Nile*, 1863

Stafford, R. A., *Scientist of Empire: Sir Roderick Murchison, Scientific Exploration and Victorian Imperialism*, 1989

Stanley, Henry Morton, *How I Found Livingstone. Travels, Adventures, and Discoveries in Central Africa; including Four Months Residence with Dr Livingstone*, 1872

Stanley, Henry Morton, *In Darkest Africa*, 1890

Stevenson, Catherine Barnes, *Victorian Women Travel Writers in Africa*, 1982

Sturt, Charles, *Narrative of an Expedition into Central Australia Performed under the Authority of Her Majesty's Government during the Years 1844, 5, and 6, Together with a Notice of the Province of South Australia in 1847*, 1849

Taylor, Andrew, *God's Fugitive: The Life of C.M. Doughty*, 1999

Taylor, Anne, *Laurence Oliphant, 1829–1888*, 1982

Thesiger, Wilfred, *Arabian Sands*, 1959

Thomas, Nicholas (ed.), *Nineteenth-Century Travels, Explorations and Empires: Writings from the Era of Imperial Consolidation 1835–1910. Volume 6: South Seas and Australasia*, 2004

Thurin, Susan Schoenbauer, *Victorian Travelers and the Opening of China, 1842–1907*, 1999

Thurin, Susan Schoenbauer (ed.), *Nineteenth-Century Travels, Explorations and Empires: Writings from the Era of Imperial Consolidation 1835–1910. Volume 4: The Far East*, 2003

Tidrick, K., *Heart-beguiling Araby*, 1981

Trench, R., *Arabian Travellers*, 1986

Tristram, H. B., *The Land of Israel; A Journal of Travels in Palestine Undertaken with Special Reference to its Physical Character*, 1865

Turner, Lois, and Ash, John, *The Golden Hordes: International Tourism and the Pleasure Periphery*, 1975

Urquhart, David, *The Lebanon (Mount Souria): A History and a Diary*, 1860

Ward, Herbert, *Five Years with the Congo Cannibals*, 1890

Whitehead, Neil (ed.), *Nineteenth-Century Travels, Explorations and Empires: Writings from the Era of Imperial Consolidation 1835–1910. Volume 8: South America*, 2004

Williams, John, *A Narrative of Missionary Enterprises in the South Sea Islands; with Remarks upon the Natural History of the Islands, Origin, Languages, Traditions, and Usages of the Inhabitants*, 1838

Wingfield, Lewis, *Wanderings of a Globe-Trotter in the Far East*, 2 vols., 1889

Withey, Lynne, *Grand Tours and Cook's Tours: A History of Leisure Travel 1750 to 1915*, 1997

Young, G. M., *Victorian England: Portrait of an Age*, 1936

Youngs, Tim, *Travellers in Africa: British Travelogues, 1850–1900*, 1994

Youngs, Tim (ed.), *Nineteenth-Century Travels, Explorations and Empires: Writings from the Era of Imperial Consolidation 1835–1910. Volume 7: Africa*, 2004

# INDEX

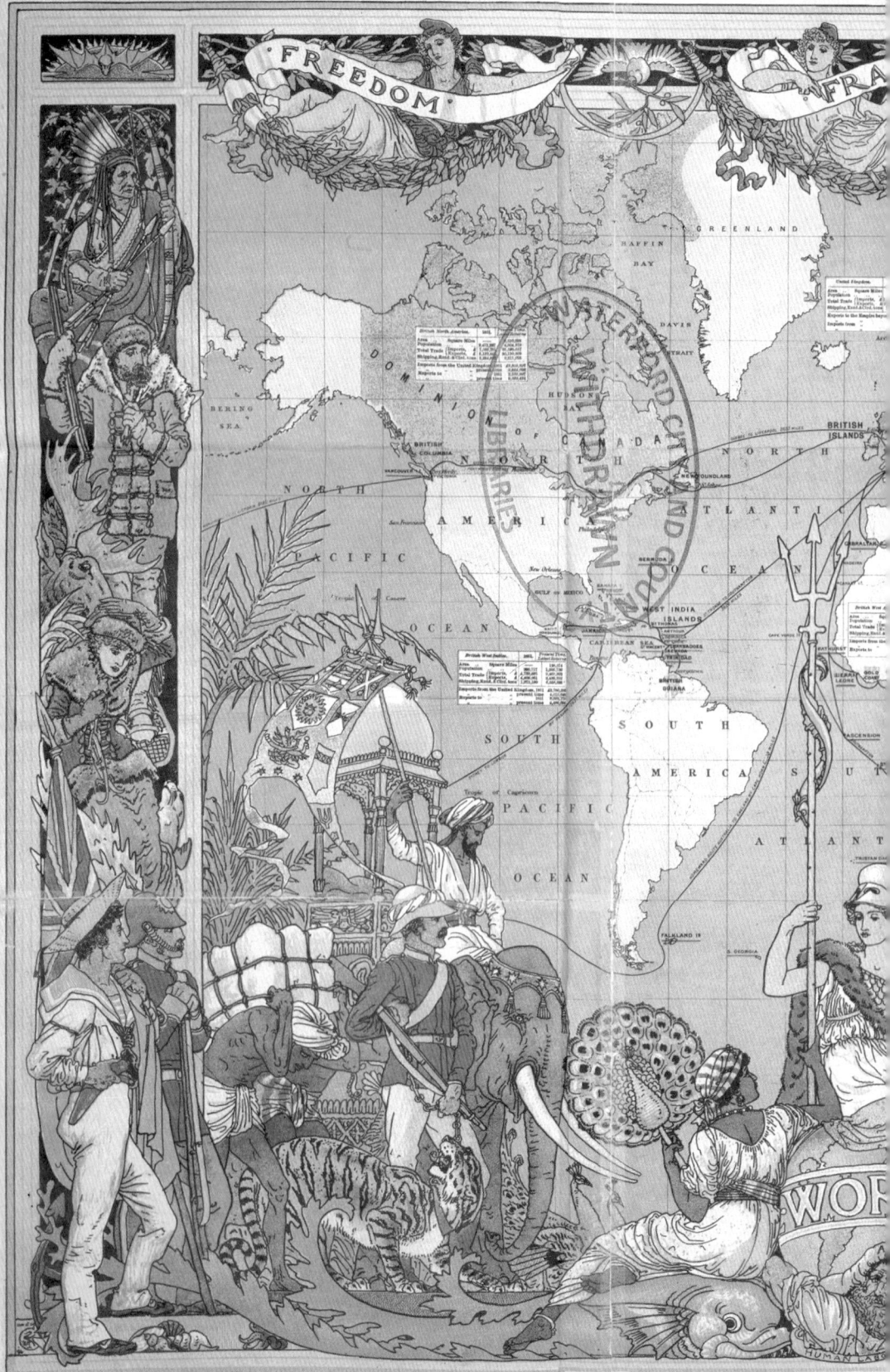

IMPERIAL FEDERATION,—MAP OF THE WORLD